Embedding *Mahr* (Islamic dower) in the European Legal System

Rubya Mehdi and Jørgen S. Nielsen (Eds.)

Embedding *Mahr* (Islamic dower) in the European Legal System

DJØF Publishing
2011

Rubya Mehdi and Jørgen S. Nielsen (Eds.)
Embedding *Mahr* (Islamic dower) in the European Legal System
First Edition

DJØF Publishing is a company of the
Association of Danish Lawyers and Economists

Print & Binding: Scandinavian Book, Aarhus
Printed in Denmark 2011
ISBN 978-87-574-2476-8

Cover design by Fatima and Rasheed Seck
Multan College of Arts, 2010
Chamak Patti artwork created by Faiza Rouf and Ustaad Nadeem *Pakistan* font
by Syed Mashad Ali Jafri

Published with Support from
The Migration Initiative

Sold and distributed in North America by
International Specialized Book Services (ISBS)
Portland, OR 97213, USA
www.isbs.com

Sold in Scandinavia by
DJØF Publishing
Copenhagen, Denmark
www.djoef-forlag.dk

Sold in all other countries by
The Oxford Publicity Partnership Ltd
Towcester NN12 6BT, UK
www.oppuk.co.uk

Table of Contents

Acknowledgements

We are grateful to "The Migration Initiative" and "Centre for European Islamic Thought," University of Copenhagen, for their generous financial support for the arrangement of the *Mahr* workshop, which became an opportunity for the junior and senior scholars from the law and a range of disciplines to exchange experiences and ideas on the topic of *Mahr*.

We are grateful to "The Migration Initiative" for financing the publication of this book and to the Department of Cross-Cultural and Regional Studies, University of Copenhagen, for their full and active support for this project.

We are thankful to the authors of this volume. Without their cooperation this volume would not have been possible.

We are also thankful to Pernille Kaervad Jacobsen for making the index.

Last but not the least we are grateful to the editor in chief of DJØF Publishing, Vivi Antonsen, for her support during the process of publication.

The Editors

Biographical Notes

Matilda Arvidsson is a Doctoral Candidate in Legal History and Public International Law, and a lecturer at the Faculty of Law and at the Centre for Middle Eastern Studies at Lund University. Her academic writing is oriented towards Critical Studies of International Humanitarian Law, Judicial Culture, and the encounter between Islamic law and the Swedish Judiciary. Current publications are "How Long is 'Now'? The Christian Eschatological Concept of Time within International Laws of, in, and after War: A Critique of Law and our Nordic Societies", in Christoffersen et al (eds) *Law & Religion in the 21st Century – Nordic Perspectives*, DJØF Publishing Copenhagen, 2010. "Shari'ah from Behind the Bench: A Judge-made Discourse on Shari'ah at a Swedish District Court", in Nielsen & Christoffersen (eds.) *Shari'ah as discourse: Legal traditions and the encounter with Europe*, Surrey: Ashgate.

Samia Bano is a lecturer in Family Law, Research Methods in Law and Gender and Law at the University of Reading law school. She obtained her PhD at the University of Warwick, Department of Law where her doctoral thesis explored the relationship between 'Muslim Family Law and South Asian Muslim Women in Britain' (2006). Her research interests include the practice of Islamic family law in the UK and Europe, Islamic jurisprudence and human rights and issues concerning the rights of Muslim women. Her current work explores the relationship between Muslim communities, informal systems of dispute resolution and gender relations in the UK and is due to be published as a book in early 2011 (Palgrave MacMillan).

Camilla Christensen is student at the Faculty of Law University of Copenhagen. She is writing her master thesis on Islamic law and the concept of *Mahr*. She is working as Legal adviser at the municipality of Copenhagen. She is also an external legal adviser at the department of equality for the Ministry of Equality.

Susanne Dahlgren is PhD in 2004 in Anthropology, dissertation "Contesting Realities. Morality, Propriety and the Public Sphere in Aden, Yemen", PhD studies in Univ. of Helsinki, the Univ. of Edinburgh and the London School of Economics. Post-doctoral fellow at the Helsinki Collegium for Advanced

Studies (2005-2008) with research project Spatial Moralities, Islam and the Public Sphere in the Middle East which formed a part of the Academy of Finland research project "Making a Good Muslim: Contested Fields of Religious Normativity in the Age of Global Islam". Since 2008 Academy of Finland Research Fellow at the Helsinki Collegium for Advanced Studies with the project "Rights in Law and at Home: Islamic Shari'a as Formal and Informal Legal Practice", which takes her back to Southern Yemen and the city of Aden where she carries out ethnographic field studies in a family court. She has published among other issues on Islamic and colonial law, segregation, sexuality, the family and the public sphere.

Inger Dübeck Senior lecturer in legal history 1977-91, Doctor juris 1978 at the Faculty of Law, University of Copenhagen, and professor in Family Law 1991-99 at the Faculty of Social Sciences of Aarhus University. Literature: *Købekoner og konkurrence*,1978 (dissertation), *Personers rettigheder,* 1997, *Kvinder, familie og Formue: Studier i dansk og europæisk retshistorie*, 2003. Den kirkelige retshistorie. Confessio Augustana og prærogativanordninger", i: *Bekendelse og kirkeordninger. Kirkeretsantologi* 2010, (ed. Zacharias Balslev- Clausen et alia) (København og Århus 2010), pp.17-44.

Katja Jansen Fredriksen, drs., holds a masterdegree in Arabic Language and Culture from the University of Leiden, the Netherlands, and is currently working on a PhD at the Faculty of Law, University of Bergen, Norway about "Muslims in Norwegian Family Law Litigation: Conflicts of Laws, Possible Solutions and the Threshold for Tolerance." She has written several articles and chronicles on Islamic law, legal pluralism and conflicts of law. Her published articles include

"Sharia in Norwegian Courtrooms?", in: *ISIM review 20*, autumn 2007, "Kunnskap om Sharia viktig for norske domstoler", in: *Rett på sak,* nr. 1, 2009.

Lene Løvdal is a Norwegian lawyer, specialised in private international law, women's law and human rights, and equality and anti-discrimination law, with a background in Arabic and Middle Eastern studies in addition to her law degree. The article is based on her master's thesis *Private international law, Muslim laws and gender equality. The adjudication of Mahr in Scandinavian, English and French courts*, published in *Kvinnerettslig skriftserie* nr. 78/2009. The thesis was written as part of the research programme From formal to real rights: Minority women's protection against discrimination in a culturally complex and transnational Norwegian context led by Professor

Anne Hellum, and funded by the Norwegian Research Council. She now works as a legal advisor in the Norwegian LGBT Organisation.

Rubya Mehdi holds a Ph.D. in Law from the University of Copenhagen and is a senior researcher attached to the Department of Cross-Cultural and Regional Studies, University of Copenhagen. She has written on the issue of Islamic law, gender, and legal pluralism. Her publications include *Islamization of the Law in Pakistan*, Curzon, London & Vanguard, Lahore (1994); *Women Law in Legal Education and Practice in Pakistan: North South Cooperation* (edited with Farida Shaheed) New Social Science Monograph, 1997; *Gender and Property Law in Pakistan*, DJØF Publishing, Copenhagen & Vanguard, Lahore 2001, *Integration and Retsudvikling* DJØF, 2007 and *Law and Religion in Multicultural Societies* (with Hanne. P, Erik.R.S & Gordon R.W), DJØF Publishing, 2008. She is chief editor of "The Journal of Law and Social Research" anchored by Bahauddin Zakariya University, Multan, Pakistan.

Annelies Moors is an anthropologist and professor of contemporary Muslim societies at the University of Amsterdam. She directs a research programme on Muslim Cultural Politics, is the primary investigator of a NWO Cultural Dynamics programme on 'Islamic cultural practices and performances: New youth cultures in Europe'. She has published widely on gender, nation and religion. Her publications include *Women, property and Islam.Palestinian experiences 1920-1990* (Cambridge 1995), Public Debates on Family Law Reform. Participants, Positions, and Styles of Argumentation in the 1990s, guest editor of a special issue of *Islamic Law and Society* 10 (2003), 1, and *Narratives of Truth in Islamic Law* (London, 2008; edited with Baudouin Dupret and Barbara Drieskens)".

Jørgen S. Nielsen is Danish National Research Foundation Professor of Islamic Studies and director of the Centre for European Islamic Thought, Faculty of Theology, University of Copenhagen. With degrees in Arabic, Middle East Studies and Arab History he has since 1978 focused his research on Muslims in Europe, based at the University of Birmingham till 2005. His publications include *Muslims in Western Europe* (3rd ed., Edinburgh University Press, 2004) and he is chief editor of *Yearbook of Muslims in Europe* (Leiden: Brill, annual from 2009).

Susan Rutten is employed as a lecturer on Private Law, especially Private International Law and Family Law at the Law Faculty of the Maastricht University. She also works as a substitute family law judge at the Court of Appeal in 's Hertogenbosch. She is specialised in multicultural legal issues on family law, more specific family law issues of Muslims residing in the Netherlands and elsewhere in Europe.

Nadjma Yassari is a senior fellow at the Max-Planck-Institute for Comparative and International Private Law in Hamburg, where she heads the Department for the Civil Laws of Islamic countries. Her main fields of research are private national and private international law of Islamic countries, in particular the Arabic Middle East, Iran and Afghanistan with a special focus on family and successions law. Since October 2008 she is leading a Max-Planck Research Group investigating the contemporary Family laws of Islamic countries. Her publications include the edited volumes *The Sharīa in the Constitutions of Afghanistan, Iran and Egypt – Implications for Private Law*, Mohr Siebeck: Tübingen 2005, in English und Dari and *Iranian Family and Succession Laws and their Application in German Courts*, Mohr Siebeck: Tübingen 2004 (co-edited with Jürgen Basedow).

Introduction

Rubya Mehdi and Jørgen S. Nielsen

Globalization and migration have served to make European societies multicultural to an unprecedented extent since 1945, but they have also increasingly brought multicultural life into the court rooms and administrative institutions. Not many years ago the topic of parallel legal systems was restricted in use to social anthropologists working on legal systems in Africa and Asia. The multicultural experience, especially with reference to communities of immigrant origin, has brought questions of parallel legal processes and legal pluralism into current socio-legal discussions. However, there remains a lack of in-depth research investigating particular issues of Muslim family laws and how these interact with society on an unofficial level as well as in relation to the official legal processes. It is especially this latter aspect, i.e. how alternative norms play out in the formal courts, which is the focus of this book, with *Mahr* as the main reference point.

Mahr, usually translated as dower (to distinguish it from dowry as the contribution which a bride brings to a marriage), is an amount of money or property which in a Muslim marriage is an obligation of the husband to the wife. It is regarded as an essential part of an Islamic marriage contract. However, the husband is not obliged to transfer the whole of the *Mahr* to the wife at the time of marriage, and there is a common distinction between the prompt and the deferred *Mahr*. The deferred part may be paid at a later time, which can be specified in the contract, but in all circumstances it falls due at the point when a marriage is dissolved, whether by divorce or death.

The concept of *Mahr* has generally been more sympathetically treated by European courts than any other aspect of Islamic family law. This could be due to the assessment that it has not been regarded as conflicting with 'public policy' (*l'ordre public*), in the way that, for example, polygamy has. *Mahr* understood as a bride price clearly would conflict with public policy, but repeated case arguments have made it clear that *Mahr* cannot be understood as such, even though the argument does occasionally reappear in the form of a 'consideration for marital sexual intercourse' (see Rutten and Yassari in this volume).

Although its foundation is religiously sanctioned *Mahr* has developed to serve a number of different purposes in Muslim societies and in particular in fulfilling social and economic needs of women around marriage. Among the economic roles are maintenance, supplementing inheritance rights, security against – and in – divorce and widowhood. Among social functions are those of a gift from husband to wife, confirming of social prestige, pressure against the husband taking a second wife, or simply a statement of religious piety.

It is also worth recalling that *Mahr* in Muslim societies is practised in various forms, appears with different terms, and that the original concept of *Mahr* is linked also to a variety of customs and traditions (Mehdi 2003). The application of *Mahr* can become further complicated in a European context, in that an application for payment of *Mahr* can depend on a variety of conditions including various forms of dissolution of marriage, in some of which only part payment or even non-payment of the *Mahr* applies. Also the question of whether a marriage has been consummated or not can affect the application of any agreed *Mahr*.

The special characteristics of *Mahr* have not lessened as it has been transferred to the European environment. Does it any longer serve a purpose and, if it does, are such purposes similar to those served in Muslim societies, or are they different?

In European courts there is no single mechanism of law by which *Mahr* contracts can be enforced. European courts have had to assess and interpret *Mahr* from different perspectives. *Mahr* in European courts can be compared to a multi-facetted diamond: it provides changing reflections depending on which side and from which angle the diamond is viewed. The courts have approached *Mahr* with reference to different aspects of the law: maintenance after divorce, matrimonial property regimes, prenuptial agreements, etc. So *Mahr* engages various branches of the law such as gender equality, status of religion, contract, family including inheritance, and private international law.

It has become clear that the courts find it extremely difficult to engage with the multifunctional character of *Mahr*. They tend to prefer to fit it into one or other existing legal category: should *Mahr* be dealt with under rules of international private law or the national law; is it an aspect of the matrimonial property regime, a matter of post-marital maintenance arrangements, or is it purely contract? Placing *Mahr* into one or other category is not simply a legal exercise; it has practical consequences with the decision leading to sometimes markedly different results. It is as though *Mahr* gets entrapped in a web of rules and divided legal areas once it comes before European courts.

One of the central tensions raised by *Mahr* is the one of the principles of gender equality, simply because it is a gift from husband to wife. In developing Muslim countries a bridal gift such as *Mahr* clearly contributes to a woman's financial security. But what is the situation then in European countries where the financial situation of a woman is relatively better secured? Do women in Europe require, and can they justify a requirement for the extra financial security which *Mahr* in principle provides? Some would respond in the affirmative, arguing that law is also culture and that Muslims with a family heritage in the Muslim world remain closely linked to the family patterns of the countries of origin. Even if it is argued that rules which appear to be Islamic are, in fact, more expressions of local customs than of religion, from the argument culture still applies. At the same time, Muslim 'feminists' particularly will argue that the younger Muslim generation in Europe is often doing well, especially the young women, and it is therefore not necessary for them to have this privilege.

It can be argued that European courts have taken on an impossible task in seeking to fit *Mahr* somehow into its existing legal frameworks. What is true about *Mahr* would then appear to be the case about Islamic family law generally. The papers in this book illustrate this tension very clearly as they analyse the process of embedding *Mahr* within the European legal environment. This question of how to fit *Mahr* into European legal contexts has therefore necessarily become one of the main focuses of most of the papers in this volume.

Central is the challenge it raises to the discussions about legal pluralism and the coexistence of legal systems. Should – can – systems mix, entangle, or should they maintain their separate existences? How far do and can different systems affect each other? We are here talking about a normative recognition relying on a narrow, technical and institutional understanding of law. But if we adopt a broader definition, such as has John Griffiths (1986), the answer is that we have no choice: legal pluralism is a fact of life. Building on this, Gordon Woodman (2008) suggests that there are four options for dealing with such tensions: unification, continuing conflict, agglomeration, and integration. A broader discussion of the issues of both cultural and religious pluralism and the implications for legal pluralism within the Nordic countries takes place in the papers collected by Christoffersen *et al* (2010).

A further dimension of tension which arises in this connection is the question of the relationship between the secular courts and religious matters. This threatens to become an aspect of the centuries old complex of problems and rivalries between state law and religion in the European context – a tension which is not unknown also in the history of many Muslim regions, despite the ideological insistence of certain contemporary Muslim movements. Currently this problem is especially acute given the insistence in the public political discourse on the ideal of the secular state. This leaves religion to function within certain, often quite restricted spheres, while excluding as far as possible all trace of religion within the sphere of state activity, if not even from the public sphere generally. Even when both law and religion have, together or separately, provided the foundations of certain social institutions, marriage in particular, clashes have been avoided by admitting access to one or the other or, more commonly, to both simultaneously behind the fiction that one has legal validity and the other is a socio-religious custom. An example of this compromise is the insistence of the French state that only the civil wedding has legal validity, and that it is illegal to conduct a church ceremony beforehand.

The papers in this book have been brought together to throw some light on this subject. The first section makes it clear that both in the Muslim world and in Europe there is a wider context and history. Annelies Moors and Susanne Dahlgren each show how *Mahr* has been a core dimension of the processes of modernization and reform in the Middle East, exemplified respectively with reference to Palestine and South Yemen. Both papers show how, each in their own way, *Mahr* both in law and application reflects social, economic and political developments as well as how attempts to regulate its application have been an element in political programmes of family law reform aimed at improving the position of women. That *Mahr* is not alien to Europe is illustrated by Inger Dübeck's survey of the *longue durée* of dowry and dower customs and law in Europe with a special focus on Denmark.

In the second part we bring together three papers looking at the subject comparatively across Europe. While Løvdal focuses on the variations, and what they imply in the legal practice of *Mahr*, of private international law regimes in four European countries, Rutten analyses more generally the challenges that *Mahr* raises to European laws, especially the problem of placing it in a known legal category. Fredriksen looks at how parties in *Mahr* cases can and do use the absence of clarity in the courts to achieve desired results.

The papers in the third and final part look much more closely at the situation in individual countries. They analyse a number of specific cases in each of these countries in such a way as to illustrate the issues faced in a domestic jurisdiction while at the same time providing raw data for the reader's own further comparative thinking.

The background of this book is a workshop held in Copenhagen in October 2009 with the intention of combining the perspectives of lawyers and social scientists, especially anthropologists. On the face of it, *Mahr* seems a quite narrow technical focus, but the experience of the workshop, which we trust is reflected in the contents of this book, showed clearly that it is a topic which functions as a prism through which much broader issues of cultural, religious and legal pluralism can be brought together for an analysis with implications beyond the apparently narrow focus of the immediate subject.

But the workshop also highlighted aspects which were missing, above all the matter of what Muslim women in Europe think of *Mahr*. This gap is due to the fact that research in this area is virtually non-existent. Some work has been done on how Muslim women negotiate their interests in official and unofficial contexts, in relation to power processes within their own communities and in relation to the state, as well as more broadly on the intersection of gender with culture, human rights and official and unofficial law, but much more needs to be done. The papers in this volume suggest that *Mahr* can be a fruitful theme through which to focus such larger research questions.

References

Christoffersen, Lisbet, Kjell Å. Modéer and Svend Andersen (eds) (2010), *Law and Religion in the 21st Century – Nordic Perspectives,* Copenhagen: DJØF Publishing.

Griffiths, John (1986), 'What is legal pluralism?', *Journal of Legal Pluralism and Unofficial Law*, 24, pp.1-55.

Mehdi, Rubya and Jørgen S. Nielsen (2010) 'Islam and Law in the Nordic Countries in the 21st Century. Challenges and New Perspectives', In: Lisbet Christoffersen, Svend Andersen and Niels Valdemar Vinding, (red.), *Law and Religion in the 21st Century – Nordic Perspectives,* Copenhagen: DJØF.

Mehdi, Rubya (2003), 'Ægteskab, formue og medgift – ret og sædvane i fire pakistanske landsbyer', In: Sten Schaumburg-Muller and Bodil Selmer (eds), *Retlig mangfoldighed, en fælles udfordring for retsvidenskab og antropologi*, Copenhagen: DJØF, pp. 215-228.

Woodman, Gordon R (2008), 'The possibilities of co-existence of religious laws with other laws' in Rubya Mehdi *et al* (eds), *Law and religion in multicultural societies*, Copenhagen: DJØF, pp. 23-42.

PART I

Contexts Trans-National and Historical

CHAPTER 1

Mahr Meanings – Dower Dealings: Reflections from Palestine

Annelies Moors

> "If one directly questions the fellahîn women about this and says: 'Is it not the custom among you for a man to buy his wife?' or if one suggests that a father sells his daughter as a bride to a man – which is the same thing – they deny it with as much indignation as the educated Arabs in the town. The bride money does not appear to them to be payment for a purchase; it is only Westerns who unhesitatingly called the giving of a bride price in Palestine a purchase (...)" (Granqvist 1931: 143).

1. Introduction

Writing in 1931, Hilma Granqvist, a Finnish anthropologist who did extensive fieldwork in a village near Bethlehem in the 1920s, strongly argued against Western misconceptions of the dower as equating to the sale and purchase of women. Islamic legal thought also rejects such a point of view. Husbands are indeed to pay a dower at the time of marriage, but with marriage not entailing community of goods between husband and wife, the dower is the property of the wife only; neither her husband nor her father can legally exert control over it.

Misunderstandings about the meanings of the dower are particularly problematic when dower cases arise in settings such as Europe where the dower is not part of national legislation. Whereas the dower is a central feature in the Islamic marriage contract, amongst those working in the legal field in Europe the dower is a rather unfamiliar institution. Confronted with dower cases, legal practitioners face the question according to which law settlements should be reached. This then raises the issue how to qualify the dower. As others in this volume argue, attempts to answer such questions require an investigation into the function and meanings of the dower (Yassari) and/or the intentions of the parties involved (Rutten) at the moment of marriage.

If in Europe the dower has drawn little public attention, it has been the topic of considerable debate in the Middle East, where the dower is an integral part of family law. Complaints about the high demands of brides and their families, leading to a rapid increase in the sums registered as dower, have been a major issue. A common line of argumentation is that because of high dowers it has become increasingly difficult for men of modest means to marry, resulting in the postponement of marriage, women remaining single, men marrying foreign wives, and young people running the risk of engaging in extramarital sexual relations. Although people often see such rising dowers as a new development, similar complaints have emerged previously during times of economic insecurity or as part of a national crisis. At various moments, attempts have been made to set an upper limit to the dower, but these have largely been unsuccessful.[1] Also other aspects of the dower have been the focus of debate. Religious scholars have deliberated about the decreasing real value of that part of the dower of which payment has been deferred; in some cases this has led to the indexation of the deferred dower.[2] Women activists and modernists have raised the issue whether the dower can indeed be considered as a financial resource for women or whether it should be considered as a mechanism for or a sign of women's subordination.

Rather than presenting an overview of dower trends in the Middle East, in this contribution I focus on developments in Jabal Nablus, the northern region of the Palestinian West Bank, where I started my research on the dower in the 1980s.[3] Concentrating on a smaller, sub-national region enables a closer look into diachronic trends and synchronic differentations, without losing sight of

1. See Badran (1995: 139) for debates in Egypt in the 1930s, Lazreg (1994: 181) for unsuccessful attempts during the Algerian war of liberation, and Dahlgren (2005 and this volume) for a discussion about dower regulations in former South Yemen. During the first intifada attempts of communities to set an upper limit to the dower were also short-lived. Moreover, it is often not the dower itself, but rather the costs of marriage celebrations or the costs of housing that is a major impediment. In order to lower the costs of marriage, associations in Gaza and the West Bank have supported collective weddings (Jad 2008) while the various emirates of the UAE have institutionalized a marriage fund to provide aid to husbands with insufficient means.
2. Welchman (2007: 91) mentions a 1999 decree in Iraq which stated that in the case of divorce the deferred dower stands at its gold value at the date of the marriage contract. A strong case is Iran, where a law was passed in 1997 requiring the dower to be reevaluated in line with inflation (Mir-Hosseini 2000: x).
3. This contribution builds on Moors 1995 and 2008.

the relevant contexts. I will start with a brief description of how the dower is conceptualized in codified law. In the following I will then discuss trends in dower registrations, with an emphasis on the second half of the twentieth century. These registration practices will then be compared and connected to the ways in which the dower works in everyday life, especially for the women concerned. Such an in-depth investigation allows for a more detailed discussion of the multiple meanings of the dower, and raises issues that may also be relevant within the European context.

2. Dower Details in the Text of the Law

Family law legislation in Palestine, formerly part of the Ottoman Empire, has been largely based on the Hanafi school of law, although opinions of the other schools of law have been taken up to introduce certain reforms. The first codified law to be applied was the Ottoman Law of Family Rights (OLFR) of 1917. After the West Bank was annexed to Jordan in 1950, the Jordanian Law of Family Rights (JLFR), which was proclaimed one year later, was also applied to the population of the West Bank. This situation continued after Israel occupied the West Bank in 1967; when in 1976 a new code of family law, the Jordanian Law of Personal Status (JLPS), was promulgated in Jordan, this code was similarly enacted on the West Bank. Although attempts have been made to draft a new Palestinian personal status law, the latter has not yet been ratified.

Women's dower rights have sound legal foundation in the various Islamic law schools as well is in the later codifications. The JLPS also deals extensively with the dower in no less than twenty-two articles. Under the heading 'the dower is the entitlement of the wife' it not only states explicitly that 'the dower is the property of the wife', but adds to this that 'she cannot be pressured to use it for her jihaz' (art. 61).The next article further elaboratesthat 'neither the wife's father nor any of her relatives may take money or anything else from the husband in return for marrying or delivering her, and the husband may claim back anything taken from him in goods if existent or in value if perishable' (art. 62). As will be discussed later, the inclusion of such explicit exhortations already hints at the prevailence of such social practices.

The JLPS – following the Hanafi school of law – clearly considers the dower as an effect of the contract, rather than as a condition for its validity. Distinguishing between a specified dower and a proper dower (*mahr al-mithl*), the code states that the wife is entitled to a proper dower if no dower is specified in the contract, if the contract states that she is not entitled to a dower, or if the dower is specified in an irregular manner (art. 54). Such a proper dower is to be similar to that of her peers amongst her paternal relatives, or, if there are no paternal peers, then to that of those in her place of residence (art 44). The code also indicates that consummation of the marriage is another source of the right to dower. This becomes visible both in the case of an irregular (*fasid*) marriage and in the case of divorce before consummation. First, if an irregular marriage has not been consummated, it has no legal effects (i.e. no dower needs to be paid). However, if the marriage has been consummated, then the wife is entitled to a dower (art.42).[4] Secondly, in the case of divorce (*talaq*) before consummation, the wife is only entitled to half the dower (art 48).

The JLPS explicitly refers to the possibility of deferral of payment of the dower. 'The specified dower may be prompt, or all or some of it may be deferred, provided that this is supported by a written document. If deferral is not explicitly stated, then the dower shall be considered as prompt' (art 45), and 'if the period of deferral is not specified then it is assumpted to be due at divorce or death' (art. 46). The latter article builds on common practice in the area, and has been institutionalized in the marriage contracts forms. Beginning in the 1920s, marriage contracts were recorded on printed forms and kept in separate registers in the shari'a court. Such forms had entries for the amount and nature of the dower, which included a standard differentation between a prompt and a deferred dower. In the early 1950s the Jordanian authorities introduced a new registration form which included an additional separate entry for "addenda" (*tawabi`*) to the prompt dower. This format was continued in the marriage contract forms issued from 1995 by the Palestinian Authority.

Marriage contracts are carried out by a marriage registrar (*ma'dhun*) on behalf of the qadi, either at the home of one of the parties, usually the wife, or at the shari'a court. According to the JLPS the contract is concluded by the parties themselves or by their representatives (art. 14), with the wife's representative receiving the dower on her behalf.[5] As the ways in which the dower is to be registered are clearly laid out in the marriage contract forms used, issues about non-registration of the dower have not occurred. The issue of the

4. In that case she also needs to follow the rules of *idda* (waiting period before remarriage), and paternity and affinity are established, but she is not entitled to inheritance or maintenance of any kind.
5. In fact, according to the JLPS the dower of a woman not previously married (*bikr*) needs to be paid to her *wali* , that is her marriage guardian (art 64).

payment of the dower has, however, occasionally arisen, as the wife's representative may habitually acknowledge having received the dower without this being the case in practice.[6]

3. The Prompt Dower in the Marriage Contracts

How have dower registrations changed in the course of the twentieth century in Jabal Nablus? There is a major divide between prompt dower registrations where the sum noted down bears at least some resemblance to what is given or where it amounts to a 'token dower', that is when a very small sum, such as 1 JD (Jordanian Dinar) is recorded.[7] The latter needs to be distinguished from contracts where no dower is recorded and where the wife is entitled to a proper dower. For if a prompt dower is registered, even if it only amounts to 1 JD, this is considered as a specified dower.

Analysing trends in the sums registered as prompt dower, there has been a gradual increase, generally following economic trends with a certain time lag. In periods of economic growth and inflation the amounts registered have rapidly increased, while during periods of economic downturn, the rise of the dower has stagnated.[8] Whereas in the 1960s and especially the 1970s the direct and indirect effects of the oil boom in the Gulf states (e.g. through remittances of migrants), engendered rapid economic growth, from the mid-1980s economic stagnation set in, which deepened with the first intifada. This is visible in the table below, which shows that the dower increased more than tenfold between 1964 and 1984, while from 1984 to 1996 it did not even double.[9]

6. See also Welchman (2000: 152)
7. This section is based on a 10% sample of marriage contracts in the Shari'a court of Nablus in 1964, 1984, and 1996. More details about methods used and the trends presented here can be found in Moors (1995: 92ff).
8. Also political crises, such as the 1948 *nakba* (the flight and expulsion of the large majority of Palestinian population from the area where the state of Israel was established) and the 1967 war, had a strong, but temporary effect on dower payments.
9. Actually the increase was even less during this period, if the devaluation of the JD in 1989 is taken into account.

Table: Average prompt dower in JD (Jordanian Dinar)

	town	villages	Camps
1964	210	170	140
1984	1400	1170	1210
1996	2380	1980	1690

Trends in dower registrations also indicate that the differences between particular kinds of locations – town, villages and camps – have remained limited. And whereas it is true that social differention in dower payments, especially in the towns, was larger than geographical ones, they were far more limited than the great inequalities in income and wealth amongst urban households. In other words, prompt dower payments seem to be far more important for the poor (both in terms of costs for husbands and benefits for wives) than for the wealthy.[10]

The 1960s indicate the beginnings of a major break in dower registrations: the emergence of the token dower. In a few contracts a very small amount, such as one, five or ten JD was registered. The first to write down such a dower were highly educated professionals; in the early 1960s the most commonly mentioned occupation of these grooms was engineer. When, from the 1970s on, women also began to register their occupations in the marriage contracts, an even stronger correlation became visible as a token dower was most often recorded for women registering their occupation as professionals. In fact, the large majority (86%) of women professionals registering their employment as doctor, dentist, pharmacist, university lecturer or engineer in the 1980s registered a token dower.[11]

In the course of the 1970s the percentage of contracts with a token dower increased rapidly and by the mid-1980s, a token dower was registered in almost half the urban contracts; by then also men with more common occupations did so. Moreover, from the mid-1970s villagers also started to record a token dower and by the mid-1980s such a dower was registered in about one-third of the village contracts, mainly by husbands who worked as trader, em-

10. Tucker (1988) who worked with marriage contracts from the eighteenth century and the first half of the nineteenth in this region, reached similar conclusions. A middle- and upper-class dower was about two to three times the dower of a lower-class woman.
11. A more detailed search in the marriage contract registers indicates that the very few women who already registered a token dower in the late 1940s and the 1950s were women teachers, the top female professionals in those years.

ployee, teacher, or skilled labourer; those registering their occupation as farmer or worker rarely did so. In the camps the token dower only became more common from the early 1980s on. In less than one-third of all camp contracts such a dower was registered, a percentage that was similar to that of lower class urbanites.

If this trend towards registering a token dower surged during periods of economic growth, the economic realities of the later 1980s and the far greater insecurity during the first intifada reversed this trend. Especially in the urban context the token dower lost a great deal of its popularity. Whereas in the rural areas the proportion of token dower registrations did not change much (hovering around one-third of the contracts), by 1996 it had declined to less than one quarter of the contracts in the town.

As previously mentioned, the marriage contracts introduced by the Jordanians, included also a special space to note down 'addenda' (*tawabi'*) to the prompt dower. Whereas previously household goods were occasionally recorded in urban contracts as marriage stipulation, after this new form was introduced registering household goods as addenda rapidly became more widespread. By the mid-1950s more than half of the urban contracts already included such addenda. In the 1970s household goods were registered even more frequently and by the 1980s this was the case for about three-quarters of the urban contracts and those in the camps; in the latter it further increased to almost 90% of the contracts in the 1990s.

If the token dower was introduced by the elite, the urban lower middle classes took the lead in the registration of household goods. During Jordanian rule, men with a high-status profession, such as doctors, pharmacists and engineers, never recorded household goods, while labourers did so relatively often. Gradually, the registration of household goods moved up the social hierarchy, although the elite has refrained from doing so. In the villages, in contrast, registering 'addenda' remained always far less common. Even in the 1980s it never reached more than 40% of the contracts.

Through time the ways in which household goods were registered also changed. In the early years in some cases only the value of a set of household goods (*taqm bayt*) was recorded, while in other cases the nature of the items was mentioned in greater detail. By the later 1980s, however, for the first time, 'in cash' (*naqdan*) was added to the registration of a set of household goods (*taqm bayt naqdan*), indicating that a sum of money would be paid for the bride to buy certain items. Moreover, a small but increasing number of contracts – especially in the rural areas, but also sometimes in the towns – started to include not only household items but also gold jewellery (with the exact weight mentioned) under the heading of 'addenda'. In such cases, the prompt dower was usually a token one.

What can be deduced from these trends in prompt dower registrations? It is obvious that political and economic realities have an impact on the dower, while the fact that differences amongst various sections of the population remained relatively limited indicates the relatively greater importance of dower payments amongst the poor than amongst the wealthy. Other trends, in particular the simultaneous increase in registrations of a token dower and of addenda, point to ambiguous or even contradictory developments. Whereas registering a token dower entails a loss of financial entitlements for the wife, the registration of addenda extends these. It is true that the token dower and addenda were initially registered by different sections of the population, the former by the elite and the latter by the lower middle classes, the increase of both styles of registration has also engendered a larger number of contracts including both. Although generally contracts in various locations have become more similar, in some respects there are still considerable differences between the town and the rural areas. In the town the decline in registering a token dower has been much sharper than in the villages, while in the latter a far smaller proportion of the contracts includes addenda to the prompt dower.

4. The Prompt Dower: Divergent Social Practices

The question to what extent and how dower registrations materialize in practice is not only important for the parties concerned, but is also helpful to better understand the meanings of the trends deducted from the marriage contracts.[12] Rather than providing a detailed analysis of the many particularities of dower payments in Jabal Nablus, in this contribution I will highlight the main divergencies between registrations and payments. On the one hand there are contracts that mention a considerable sum of money which is either not paid or received in part or in full. On the other hand, there are contracts that mention a token dower, yet considerable sums of money or valuables are defacto given and received.

What then were the structural impediments for women not to receive what was registered for them? During the 1920s and 1930s it was common for

12. This section is based on extensive fieldwork in Jabal Nablus amounting to about 18 months in the 1980s and early 1990s, and to shorter periods thereafter. A major part of fieldwork consisted of informal conversations with women and the collection of dower stories (see Moors 1995).

women in the rural areas to only receive about one third of the amount registered. This did not happen because their husbands were unable or unwilling to pay, but because in those days in large part of rural Jabal Nablus the wife's father would reserve a substantial part of the registered sum for himself, as part of a marriage system in which the older generation exerted strong control over the younger generation. Gradually, with the further incorporation of villages into the market economy, a move away from agriculture, and the concomitant lesser dependence of sons on their fathers, the part taken by fathers diminished and by the 1970s most village brides received their dower in full.[13] This then also means that in the rural areas the amounts the women received at marriage have increased considerably faster than what trends deducted from the amounts registered in the contracts indicate.

Another reason why women did not receive their full prompt dower was that husbands would not be able to pay the amount registered because they simply were too poor to do so. There were also other, more specific circumstances that induced such a discrepancy between written contracts and social practices. In the case of kin marriages, dower registrations in Jabal Nablus do not indicate lower than average registered dowers. However, relations of trust between kin made it both less pressing, and possibly also less acceptable, to hold husbands to the full payment of the dower at marriage. In a similar vein, when husband and wife had been actively involved in the arrangement of the marriage, the financial side of the marriage was also sometimes downplayed; women may well attempt to lower dower demands when they were strongly in favour of a particular suitor. In the opposite case, that is when women were to marry someone they were hesitant about, or when it concerned a less attractive party, such as a man who was considerably older, or who had been married previously, relatively high amounts would be registered and paid as a dower in an attempt to strike a balance between emotional and material benefits.

If similar patterns are visible with respect to the payment or provision of the addenda, in this case there are two additional particularities. First, whereas the contracts show that addenda were often registered in the marriage contract, especially the middle classes would express their strong dislike for doing so, as they would consider this an indication of distrust. In other words, in this case addenda were registered more often than people would indicate in their dower stories. Secondly, it is necessary to differentiate between

13. If in 1952 76% of rural men still registered their occupation as farmer, by 1964 this had decreased to 48%, in 1976 to 21%, in the early 1980s to 15%, and by the mid 1990s 5%.

trends in town and in the rural areas. Whereas for urbanites the registration of household goods was simply the confirmation of an existing practice – urban men were expected to provide household goods in addition to the dower, in the villages it was common practice for women to buy these from their dower, something they are not obliged to do according to the text of the law. This then explains why a substantially smaller number of rural contracts includes addenda and why this often went hand in hand with registrations of a token dower. In the villages registering addenda was an indication of trust rather than of distrust.

Turning to the circumstances under which the dower mentioned in the contracts was much smaller than what the bride actually received, the token dower needs to be analysed.[14] As the dower stories indicate, the emergence of registering a token dower is often not the dramatic change it might appear to be. In urban settings it was already quite common amongst the better off that the wife's father would add to the dower of his daughter, and sometimes substantially so, while also the husband and his family would present valuable gifts in addition to the dower. The move towards a token dower in those circles, then, can be considered as the next step in a system where both the husband's side and the wife's side attempted to outdo each other in providing the bride with everything she could possibly need. However, when also those lower in the social hierarchy started to register a token dower, tensions became visible. For a token dower implies first and foremost trust in the husband's ability and willingness to provide his wife with gifts similar to what her peers would receive. Under conditions of scarcity, the token dower may easily turn into a bone of contention, with the wife's side expecting far more than the husband's side is able or willing to provide.

If wives for whom a token dower was registered would often receive large gifts similar to what they would have bought from their dower, what then was the reason to register a token dower? Doing so has a strong symbolic function. It not only indicates that the wife can afford to forego legal guarantees, something far easier for those with ample financial means or in cases, such as kin marriages, where trust has already been established, but it was also a strong marker of modernity. This symbolic function is particularly salient amongst professionally employed women, who would consider registering a

14. For a more elaborate discussion see Moors 2008, which more in detail discusses the relation between the material and symbolic meanings of registering a token dower and shifts in the evaluation of women's work. Shifts in the rural areas are not, or not only, an attempt to emulate urban practices, but rather are engendered by structural changes in the rural economy.

high prompt dower as an out-dated practice, at most helpful for those who do not have the means to acquire an income of their own. Registering a token dower also fits with new ideals about marriage. Whereas high prompt dowers were associated with strict family control over marriages, the token dower was considered particularly suitable to modern, companionate marriages. At the same time, however, in its material effects registering a token dower made a woman more dependent on the good will of her husband, as the wife had no legal grounds to claim more than the trivial amount registered in the marriage contract. Hence, it is no surprise that token dower registrations were mainly popular at times when incomes and expectations were rising, such as in the 1970s and early 1980s. During economic downturns, in contrast, the risks involved may well become too much to bear.

5. The Deferred Dower: Contracts and Everyday Life

Returning to marriage contracts, one of the most striking changes in dower registrations is the increased prominence of the deferred dower. Moreover, in this case there were major differences between the town and the rural areas. In Nablus in the 1930s a deferred dower was almost always registered and in half the cases the amount written down was larger than that of the prompt. In the rural areas in contrast, in those days a deferred dower was registered in only about one-third of the contracts, and when this was the case, it was much smaller than the prompt dower, amounting often only to one-third of it. During the 1960s there were still considerable differences. In Nablus the deferred dower was usually higher than the prompt dower, averaging 210 JD prompt and 340 JD deferred in 1964. Whereas it is true that in the rural areas registering a deferred dower was becoming more widespread, still in 32% of the contracts no deferred dower was registered at all, and the average rural deferred dower was considerably lower than the prompt, 110 JD deferred versus 170 JD prompt. There were also considerable differences between the villages, with a deferred dower more commonly registered in larger villages where agriculture was no longer the only source of livelihood. In the camps the deferred dower has become increasingly similar to that of the poorer urbanites. Although a deferred dower was always registered, it was on average less central in the total dower than in the town.[15] By the 1970s, in contrast, a deferred

15. In the first years after the *nakba*, deferred dower registration sometimes reflected the particular background of the refugees, that is, those from a more 'urbanized'

dower was registered in all marriage contracts, and from then on the average sums registered rapidly increased with differences between town, villages and camps decreasing further; also in the villages and the camps the deferred dower was higher than the prompt dower.

Table: Average deferred dower in JD (Jordanian Dinar)

	town	villages	Camps
1964	340	110	80
1984	2710	1980	1530
1996	4360	3539	3034

In short, the most striking change in dower registration is the increased prominence of the deferred dower. Rather than being recorded only in a minority of the marriage contracts, registration of the deferred dower has become universal and the proportion of the deferred dower in the total dower has increased considerably. In its most extreme form this is visible in contracts that combine a token prompt dower with a very high deferred dower. If the dower is considered as a means for women to gain access to property, recording a sum of money for a woman at marriage has given way to doing so in case of divorce or widowhood.

This then begs the question whether women actually receive their deferred dower. It is important to note that by far the largest number of separations in the region (around 90%) does not take place through unilateral repudiation (*talaq*) or a court case (*tafriq*), but rather on the basis of mutual agreement (*muqabil al-ibra'*), in which case the wife gives up her entitlement to the deferred dower. Moreover, court registrations also indicate that when a divorced woman is entitled to her deferred dower, she often needs to go to the court to claim it. Also after the judge has ruled in her favour, which is often the case, it still may be diffcult for her to actually lay hands on it.[16] In other words, the material effect of registering a deferred dower has remained limited. At the same time, however, and similar to what happens in the case of the token

background had such a dower written down, whereas those from peasant or bedouin background did not.

16. In case of widowhood, women with sons often refrain from claiming their deferred dower, in a similar vein as they give up their share in the inheritance for the sake of their sons. Only if there are more inheriting wives and/or children from other wives, will she claim it (see Moors 1996).

dower, the rapid rise of the deferred dower also has a strong symbolic effect. It underlines the centrality of the conjugal tie, indicating that women do not need their own financial means when they marry but rather when they are divorced or widowed. It both reflects and contributes to the notion that husbands are more dependable providers for their wives than father and brothers are for their female kin when they are repudiated.

Conclusion

The above points to the complexities of discussing the meanings of the dower and the intentions of the parties concerned even in one small region in the Middle East. It is true that the dower is always a financial settlement to be paid by the groom for the benefit of the wife. Yet, social practice is often different from what is registered, and such divergences can go in different directions. This in itself complicates a discussion about the intentions of the parties. In a similar vein, particular forms of registration can have multiple meanings, be it material or symbolical. But perhaps the most difficult question for legal practitioners in Europe is whether it is possible to deal with dower cases outside the wider context in which the dower is embedded. In the case of the deferred dower, for instance, this would be the question whether the nature of the divorce in itself would determine whether a woman is or is not entitled to her deferred dower.

Bibliography

Badran, Magrot, (1995) *Feminists, Islam and Nation: Gender and the Making of Modern Egypt*. Princeton: Princeton University Press.

Dahlgren, Susanne, (2005) 'Women's adah versus "women's law": The Contesting Issue of *Mahr* in Aden, Yemen', in Baudouin Dupret and Francois Burget, eds., *Le shaykh et le procurer*, pp.125-144.

Granqvist, Hilma, (1931) *Marriage Conditions in a Palestinian Village I.* Helsingfors: Akademische Buchhandlung.

Lazreg, Marnia, (1994) *The eloquence of silence: Algerian women in question*. New York and London: Routledge.

Kandiyoti, Deniz, (1998) 'Some awkward questions on women and modernity in Turkey', In: Lila Abu-Lughod, (eds.), *Remaking women Feminism and Modernity in the Middle East*. Princeton, NJ: Princeton University Press, pp. 270-89.

Mir-Hosseini, Ziba, (2000) *Marriage on trial: Islamic family law in Iran and Morocco*. London: IB Tauris.

Moors, Annelies, (1995) *Women, property and Islam. Palestinian experiences 1920-1990*. Cambridge: Cambridge University Press.

Moors, Annelies, (1996) 'Gender Relations and Inheritance. Person, Power and Property', In: Deniz Kandiyoti, (eds)., *Gendering the Middle East. Emerging Perspectives*, London and New York: IB Taurus Publishers, pp.69-84.

Moors, Annelies, (2008) 'Registering a token dower: The multiple meanings of a legal practice', in Baudouin Dupret, Barbara Drieskens and Annelies Moors, eds., *Narratives of Truth in Islamic Law*. London: IB Taurus, pp.85-104.

Tucker, Judith, (1988) 'Marriage and family in Nablus, 1720-1856: towards a history of Arab marriage', *Journal of Family History*, 13, 2, pp.165-79.

Welchman, Lynn, (2007) *Women and Muslim Family Laws in Arab States. A Comparative Overview of Textual Development and Advocacy*. Amsterdam: Amsterdam University Press.

Welchman, Lynn, (2000) *Beyond the Code. Muslim Family Law and the Shari'a Judiciary in the Palestinian West Bank.* The Hague, London, Boston: Kluwer Law International.

Welchman, Lynn, (1999) *Islamic Family Law. Text and Practice in Palestine*. Jerusalem: Women's Centre for Legal Aid and Counseling.

CHAPTER 2

Expensive Marriage or Women's Security: *Mahr* Debates from Aden, South Yemen[1]

Susanne Dahlgren

Mahr or dower forms an elemental part of marriage arrangements among Muslims throughout the world. This payment is a guarantee for the wife's security after the legitimate maintenance of a marriage finishes. In this chapter I will take a look at the purposes *mahr* fulfils in a Muslim majority community where it forms part of both marriage legislation and the traditional practices of contracting and dissolving marriages.[2] I will discuss the social, economic and psychological aspects that people link to *mahr* and ask if *mahr* is meant to act as a security, what are the insecurities that it is meant to deter? I will look at marriage payment practices from a historical perspective in the Yemeni town of Aden and attempt to map the socio-economic circumstances that affect the practices surrounding this financial institution with roots in the classical Islamic jurisprudence (*fiqh*).

1. An earlier version of this article appeared in "Women's Adah vs. 'Women's Law': The Contesting Issue of *Mahr* in Aden, Yemen." In *Le shaykh et le procureur: Systèmes coutumiers et pratiques juridiques au Yémen et en Égypte.* Égypte/Monde arabe, no. 1, 3rd series, edited by Baudouin Dupret and François Burgat, 2005, pp. 125-44. Paris: Le Centre d'études et de documentation économiques, juridiques et socials (Cedej).
2. Fieldwork in Aden in early 2001 was facilitated by the Centre français d'archeologie et de sciences sociales de Sanaa and its director, Dr François Burgat. My sincere thanks go also to Salem Banafa, who assisted me in reading handwritten materials I collected in Aden. Other material has been collected during various field trips between the years 1988 and 2009.

Mahr is one of the aspects of Islamic law that is established in the Qur'an and Sunnah and upon which there is a consensus among Muslims. There are two kinds of dower: *Mahr al-musamma* (the agreed upon amount) and *mahr al-mithl* (unspecified *mahr*, also called proper dower; usually an average amount that is determined by legal authorities to tally with the customary level). Among the four Sunni schools there are minor differences in interpreting the obligations linked to *mahr*. According to Hanafi, Hanbali, Jaʿfari and Shafiʿi jurists, it is not obligatory to name the amount of *mahr* while signing the marriage contract. Accordingly, it is not an essential ingredient (*rukn*) of the marriage contract in the way that price is in a contract of sale. Thus it is one of the effects of a marriage contract, and even without its stipulation the contract is valid (Bakhtiar 1996: 441). According to the Shafiʿi school, the major school of Yemeni Muslims, in the Islamic marriage (*nikah*) *mahr* is obligatory only as an expression of the sanctity of the subject-matter (Al-Marghinani 2006: 507). Traditionally, *mahr* has been specified in terms of currency, jewellery (silver or gold), cattle, farm land, property, profit or trade commodities. It is the wife's property and she is not obliged to use it for the support and maintenance of the family. All schools agree that the *mahr* can be divided into immediate and deferred dower. The immediate dower has to be paid prior to consummation of the marriage in sexual intercourse, which makes the marriage a legally proper union. The deferred part is due to be paid upon death of the husband or once he divorces her.

In earlier studies on *mahr*, this financial transaction has been viewed either from the perspective of women's property (Moors 1995) or as an expression of marriage regulation between social formations from kin groups to tribes (Mundy 1995: 131-138; Meneley 1996: 128-129; Dorsky 1986: 107). In this chapter I will approach *mahr* as a symbol of gender bargaining and a point at which individual, family and social interests meet and often collide. As part of that, I will take a look at *mahr* as a social security by analysing security both as an individual and a social necessity.

In Yemeni public discussions, *mahr* is talked about within the framework of divergent representations for gender roles and rights of the spouses in marriage thus reflecting the contested nature of the question. Different interpretations of Islam and notions of gender roles become manifest in these debates. In concrete negotiations between families over *mahr* payments, different interests collide: the need of a young man to get married, the expectations of a woman for a bright future, the financial concerns of the two families and, finally, considerations of social norms and idealized rules for social bonding. Discussions over *mahr* bring to the fore arguments that have to do with morality, propriety and normative order. These are debates where customary norms, interpretations of Islamic law and the enactments of statutory law clash.

In these discussions excessive spending in weddings might be contrasted to Muslim values of modesty, spirituality and abhorrence of greed. Another line of argument suggests that in *mahr*, women are inspected like camels in a market, where their "value" is measured and they are treated as commodities. According to this thinking, the father of the bride "sells" his daughter to the highest bidder. These critical views on *mahr* are contrasted to perceptions of it as a customary right of the woman (which Islam guarantees) and a symbol of her desirability, characteristics that a woman can be proud of. From the man's perspective, the ability to pay a high dower manifests his potential and strength. It also shows that he is able to call for kinship assistance to raise the required amount among his lineage.

In these different lines of argument, the *mahr* is discussed in terms of rights, morality and propriety. This debate echoes the contested nature of Adeni social dynamics, where different concepts of normativity collide. As I have argued elsewhere, in this debate three main lines of argument come up (Dahlgren 2007: 327-345; Dahlgren 2010). The local expressions for these three moral frameworks are "our customs and traditions", "our religion" and "our revolution". As the above brief characterization of different discourses on *mahr* shows, the last line of argument is typical of the "customary" framework; the idea of excessive *mahr* as un-Islamic spending belongs to the second one; while the women-as-commodity theme is familiar to the "revolutionary" framework.

Muhur in Aden

Customs linked to marriage payments vary in different parts of Yemen. In the Southern Yemeni port town Aden, *muhur* (*mahr* in plural, as it is colloquially called) is a woman's right and remains her property. Customarily *mahr* belongs to her in full, and it is both unusual and socially condemned if a father or another relative attempts to pocket it. In Aden, a groom and his family do not pay the bride's family any special share upon marriage, as it is the custom in some other parts of Yemen. Ideally the duty to support the family lies entirely with the husband, and the wife is under no obligation to use her dower or any other property for the benefit of the family but poverty and deteriorating economic circumstances have made women breadwinners, too. According to the 19th century local Islamic scholar Shaykh Abd al-Qadir al-Makkawi, *mahr* is a separate payment from *daf'a*, a present that the husband might give to his fiancée prior to signing the marriage contract. Either of these two can be withheld by the father or the husband (Al-Makkawi 1959: 269-272 and 281-288). If the woman instigates a *khul'* divorce she will have to pay the *mahr* back to the husband; otherwise the property remains her "security" for the bad times.

In different periods of time the issue of security has manifested itself, also in how the *mahr* is paid – whether the full amount is paid promptly upon signing the marriage contract (*'aqd al-nikah*), or a portion is deferred for payment in case of divorce or widowhood. In the last fifty years, the share paid immediately, called colloquially *mahr muqaddam*, and in official documents such as in marriage certificates and marriage records known as *mahr mu'ajjal*, has tended to be more popular than dividing the amount into two portions, immediate and deferred, or agreeing only on the deferred amount (officially, *mahr mu'ajjal*).[3] The amounts paid have varied according to the wealth of the families, but also with regard to other factors such as economic prospects, both from family income and national economic policy perspectives including chances for labour migration. Important to the choice made are the particular views on marriage and larger ideological considerations that the family endorses, as outlined above. Also, the desirability of the bride, especially her beauty, might increase the amount demanded.

In choosing a bride, three factors are usually taken into consideration. These include her educational level, beauty and her family's level of wealth. In close kin (*aqarib*) marriages, such as between first cousins (*bint 'amm, bint khal*), the amounts tend to be less. In Aden, people also consider such factors as the groom's income, the kind of housing he can arrange for the couple and his family's reputation as contributing factors in the negotiations over the *mahr*. It is deemed that if the bride is married with a man from the same roots her economic safety is better guaranteed than if she marries outside from her kin.

People with roots in the surrounding countryside or in North Yemen often require higher payments than Aden-born people, thereby following the cus-

3. While carrying out the fieldwork for this chapter I read through the Adeni marriage and divorce registers for the period of 1951-2001. Aden is divided into three districts, each with an official *qadhi* (judge) acting as the marriage registrar (*ma'dhun*). Sira district comprises the areas of Crater and Khormaksar, and Mina district those of Ma'alla and Tawahi. Shaykh Uthman district covers the northern suburbs on the mainland. Since the unification the number of *qadhi*s went up to 35, making administration of records more difficult. The records are stored in the Ministry of Justice and *Waqf*, Aden Branch.

tom of their place of origin. Marriage payments have always tended to be higher in the countryside than in Aden. During the previous regime in the South, the People's Democratic Republic of Yemen (PDRY, 1967-1990), the limitation in law of the amounts paid as *mahr* into 100 Yemeni dinars (Family Law 1974, § 4) contributed to equalising social differences.[4] After the unification with North Yemen, marriage payments sky-rocketed and started to follow amounts paid in some northern towns, such as Ta'izz and Sana'a.

In Aden, *muhur* is not the only marriage expense that the groom is responsible for. In the past, it was customary that the new husband gave a gift, a small amount of money, for the *subhiyya*, the tea party given by his mother after the wedding to female relatives and friends to introduce the new daughter-in-law. It has also been customary that upon agreement about the coming wedding, referred as an "engagement" (*khutba*), the groom has to bring presents and an agreed amount of money known as *daf'a*. This sum is often used for buying the bride furnishings and clothes (*kiswa*) that she will take with her into the marital home. The groom's duties also include the wedding party expenses, that is, two to three days of celebrating with a large number of guests, first in the two homes and with the last night in a public wedding club in the town. These expenses might include food and drink for the guests, a qat party (*makhdara qat*) for the male relatives and friends,[5] and the fees for the music group that entertains the guests for an evening either in the home or in a *makhdara*, a tent-like shelter erected in the street outside the home, and also on the last evening in a club. The rent of a wedding club for an evening varies according to the club's popularity and its furnishings. In 2001, Alf layla wa layla, a club in Shaykh Uthman, a northern district of Aden, charged 60,000 riyals, while at the time the most popular club, Laylati in downtown Ma'alla, charged 160,000 riyals. More recently wedding clubs with a raked auditorium have become old-fashioned while new clubs in Khormaksar with a catwalk have become popular and thus more expensive. These amounts can be compared to *mahr* payments at the same period. It was quite usual in the early 2000s that a young man who wanted to marry a virgin who was not from his

4. When South and North Yemen united in 1990, the northern riyal was adopted as the national currency. One southern dinar was fixed at a value of 26 riyals.
5. A mildly narcotic shrub chewed in societal gatherings, a habit practised by about 90 per cent of men and a much smaller percentage of women, often on a daily basis. Men's qat parties are frequently organized so that guests can contribute to the expenses the groom has to bear. Among wealthy people no contributions are expected and the guests might instead be provided with expensive *qat*, drinks and *shishas* (water pipes).

kin (*aqarib*) had to raise some 200,000-300,000 riyals (7,692-11,538 dinars) in order to get married. Currently the *mahr* can reach half a million riyals. The bridal family's share of all the wedding expenses – the furnishings for a bedroom – represents a modest amount in contrast to the groom's duties. Before independence even this was the groom's burden.

Adenis look resentfully at the payments to the bride's family that the groom and his family have to provide, which are known as *shart*, *nuqud* and *sadaq* in other parts of present-day Yemen. As Mundy describes the custom in Wadi Dhahr, north of Sana'a, the groom is obligated to pay three kinds of expenses: the costs of the festivities, a transfer of money to the wife's guardian (*shart*) and the endowment of the bride at marriage (*mahr*, *haqq al-fitsha*). Of these, the *shart* is a major transfer that performs the role of mediating the relationship between the two houses whose children have got married. The greater the risks and alienation apparent in the bride's moving to a new household, the bigger the *shart* tends to be. The bridal endowments comprise not only the direct payment, often in the form of jewellery from the groom, but also the furnishings that she receives from her own family, which are purchased with money from the *shart*. Part of *shart* acts the same way as the Adeni *daf'a*.

Haqq al-fitsha is a small amount and refers to the right that the groom purchases from the bride to be able to see her unveiled (Mundy 1995: 131-132). Such a practice exists also in some parts of the southern rural areas both north and east of Aden. In Aden this practice emerged by the 2000s, as wearing of the face veil that leaves eyes only open (*niqab*) spread here, too. Earlier the couple used to know each other and meet during the engagement period. Outside Aden, particularly in some areas in the governorates of Abyan, Shabwa and Mahra, the bride and her mother demand a separate compensation from the groom for the *laylat al-dukhla*, that is, for the first sexual intercourse. This custom is called *haqq al-sabah* ("the morning right") in some places. Such customs are generally viewed in Aden as "backward" (*takhalluf*) and manifest the lesser culture of the *badu* in the minds of the townspeople.[6]

6. Adenis have a tendency to call people in the countryside *badu*, even though they know that they are not Bedouins but settled folk. This name indicates the distinction that Adenis like to keep between themselves and these "uncivilized" or "backward" people who have "customs that degrade", as the difference is often characterized.

Too Expensive Marriage

After independence, the leftist government wanted to introduce reforms in family relations. One of the biggest changes had to do with marriage payments. The new government's rhetoric in limiting the *mahr* by law was not based on earlier arguments that claimed the marriage too expensive for young men, even though there are similarities, in particular that the government wanted to make it easier to establish a family. A new law was drafted in 1971 and subjected to popular discussion. The process of amending the draft lasted three years, and during the public debate – as recalled later by some of the notaries in the drafting committee – women were more in favour of radical reform than men (Molyneux 1982: 9 ff, 14).

The idea that through the *mahr* the father "sells" his daughter to the "highest bidder" is presented in the preamble of the law:

"(...) whereas the family ties, in all their forms, were not subject to a unified system except the feudal relations which made of the noblest human ties a business practice and placed the fate of the Yemeni woman in the hand of the highest bidder".

At the same period, the government initiated the call to women to join the labour market, and thus the mere possibility of getting a job and earning own income contributed to making the woman equal with the man in terms of choosing how to support herself. However, attitudes towards unmarried women did not change at the same pace. Even today, marriage is considered an obligation for every woman. Although the law limited the payment of *mahr*, inheritance legislation was not modified accordingly, but followed the classical *fiqh* (Islamic jurisprudence). This is in conflict with the stipulation in the family law that "expenses in respect of marriage and the conjugal home requirements shall be borne by both husband and wife according to their means" (Chapter IV, §17). Alongside this, the law laid down the duty of both the adult son and daughter to support their parents (Chapter IV, § 24).[7]

7. Family Law, official English translation, issued by the Information Department of the Ministry of Information in 1976.

Women's Law and Women's Custom

While the law set an explicit limit to the *mahr* (Chapter IV, § 19), payment of the *daf'a* was left rather vague: "*There may be exchanged during the period of engagement token gifts which shall neither form part of the 'mahr' (payment in consideration of marriage) nor be returned in case the engagement is revoked by either the betrothed or the fiancée.*" In regard to observance of the law, the same paragraph stated: "*The authority concerned with the administration of this Law may determine such maximum value for such token gifts in accordance with the prevailing standard of living and may also determine anything which is not to be deemed as a token gift*" (Chapter I, § 4).[8]

Not surprisingly, after the enactment of the law in early 1974 the practice of paying more than 100 dinars in *mahr* continued. The usual method was to sign for 100 dinars in the marriage contract in front of the *qadhi* and to agree between the two families about payments that exceeded it. These payments were either money paid as immediate dower, or gold and other financial assets, or a considerable amount of *daf'a*.

To start with, such negotiations between two families dealt with the value and number of gold items (*badla dahab*) the groom was to give to the bride. These usually comprised a wedding ring (*khatim*) and four bangles (*shawaliyya*). It is customary that if a woman gets more gold, it might be some bracelets (*asawir*), a ring attached with a golden net to a bracelet (*shabka*), a set of ear rings (*wazagh*), a necklace (*'iqd*), or a chain-like necklace (*silsil*). If the groom is very wealthy a woman might bargain for a golden belt (*hizam).* In such rare cases the marriage deal becomes the talk of the town. Women in particular are conscious of the value of gold items and often visit the numerous goldsmiths' shops in the main market in Crater to compare prices and become familiar with new items.[9] This custom, together with that of displaying the gold in women's gatherings such as wedding parties, contributes to making a distinction between people with different assets.

Other expenses that the two families negotiate between themselves and agree to verbally include expenses for the wedding party, furnishings for the bridal home and new cloths (*malabis*) to the bride. All these costs, if paid by the groom and his family upon the engagement are called *daf'a* (payment). Let us see some practical examples of marriages contracted in Aden in differ-

8. Family Law, official English translation.
9. These days the gold comes from Saudi Arabia. Only a few decades ago, gold replaced silver that was made up locally by numerous silversmiths, a profession traditional to Adeni Jewish families.

masc./fem.) but if the person was born in the "northern part of the homeland", as North Yemen was officially called during that era, it was written *fi'l-shimal* – in the North. Brides were no more classified as *bikr* or *thayyiba* (virgin and non-virgin) but as *'aziba* (single), *mutallaqa* (divorced), or *armala* (widow). The same classifications were used in recording the civil status of the groom.

By the late 1980s, a *mahr* of 100 dinars had also become the norm for marriages where the bride was no longer a virgin, a factor that had previously decreased the *mahr* considerably. On 20 June 1982, a young Aden-born man of 20 years of age and with his own business entered his first marriage with a 22-year-old divorced woman, who was recorded as illiterate and a housewife. No kinship relationship existed between them. As in most marriages at the time, the *mahr* was recorded as 50 dinars in immediate payment and 50 dinars deferred.

During the 1980s, the last decade of the PDRY, poorer sectors of society had caught up with the affluent strata in *mahr* payments. It was evident that this fact made it difficult to manifest social superiority with the means of *mahr*. Among affluent families who wanted to display their wealth upon marriage, the amount and quality of jewellery and other furnishings that the bride received, together with luxurious and pompous wedding celebrations, became ways of making a visible distinction between themselves and lower social categories. The new practice of leaving for a honeymoon after the wedding also reflected the "modern" customs introduced by the elite to Aden.

During the period of the 1974 Family Law (1974-1992) agreements between the groom's and the bride's families about exceeding the legitimate *mahr* were based on oral agreement, as is customary all around Yemen. Nobody I asked among law practitioners or lay people acknowledged the existence of secret written documents alongside the official marriage contract. After the 1974 law was replaced by new legislation for the unified country – the Personal Status Law No. 20 of 1992 – no woman brought before the Aden Divisional Court a case against her ex-husband for failing to pay the verbally agreed portion of a marriage payment that exceeded the limit set in the former law. The limitation of *mahr* was among the best-known stipulations of the 1974 law.[11] Reactions to the 1974 law varied, especially in regard to this limi-

11. The 1974 law is otherwise known, particularly among women, as the law that allowed the woman to choose her husband, "free-choice marriage", as I discuss in Dahlgren, 2010. However, the law makes no direct stipulation in regard to choice of spouse. The only requirement that hints at this is that both spouses should consent to

tation. While the law otherwise was rather well received, and those who considered that it gave women too many rights were in the minority, the issue of *mahr* aroused mixed feelings. Nevertheless, it was not a question of women opposing the limitation and men being in favour of it. As mentioned earlier, high dowers tended to be typical of people who had moved to Aden from the countryside. Such families might have properties that could be mobilized when a wedding took place. By contrast, Adenis traditionally seldom have properties.

Another salient factor seems to be the age of the respondent. As a result of the dramatic changes in Adeni history during the last 50 years, the circumstances in which people have contracted marriages have varied considerably. Based on the idea that people of the same generation do not necessarily share reactions to the circumstances where they live, but do share a common recognition of those circumstances, I have suggested that there are three markedly different generations in Aden (Dahlgren 1998/1999: 77-86).

- First, those who are now elderly contracted their marriages during the late colonial period and the early years of independence. At that time, women seldom had education or were engaged in income-generating activities, and were thus economically dependent on their husbands.
- Second, in families of the middle generation, women joined the labour market, often chose their own husbands and attempted to establish marriages based on partnership and sharing. Men of this generation usually supported the changes that improved the position of women, but not uncommonly changed their minds after unification, when women's "too many rights" were eliminated in legislation and men were once again allowed customary privileges in marriage.[12]
- Third, in contrast to this group, the younger generation tends to view marital relations in the same way as their grandparents, that is, in terms of a clear patriarchal hierarchy within the family, perceiving women's princi-

the marriage (Chapter II, § 5). Women interpreted the absence of any mention of parental or guardian consent to marriage to mean free choice marriage.

12. Women consider these privileges to be the right to repudiation (talaq), the possibility of taking a co-wife and the fact that men's right to children after divorce was facilitated, all of which were guaranteed in the 1992 Personal Status Law (as amended in 1998 and 1999) and were explained as originating in the Sharia.

pal role to be as mothers irrespective of education or profession. The young people I met called these values "Islamic" role models.[13]

When I enquired about the ways in which the law was circumvented, I also asked what women in particular thought about the *mahr* issue. Most respondents were in favour of the law.[14] As a woman whose marriage was contracted in 1979 explained: "We accepted the law and the limitation. At that period the amount was sufficient, as circumstances were such and prices were low." In her marriage contract no *mahr* was recorded. Instead she received gold, and her husband, an engineer, provided housing separate from his family, in a spacious flat with three rooms. This marriage is a typical Adeni union of the older generation, with both spouses having roots in the town and with the woman not working outside the home but managing the domestic economy.

Another older woman, married in 1966, explained: "The law has made it possible for many people to get married in the first place. Prices were low at that time and the dinar had a good value." In her marriage, which was contracted just before the independence, she received no immediate dower, only gold and equipment. Instead, the groom paid her mother 1,500 shillings (75 dinars) and an extensive *mahr mu'ajjal* (deferred dower) of 10,000 shillings (500 dinars or 13,000 rials) was recorded by the qadhi. Seven days after the wedding, on her *subhiyya* celebrations, she received a gift from her husband that he himself had initiated. She explained that before independence it was customary to demand bigger amounts in deferred *mahr* than in immediate dower, simply because the woman needed security for a possible divorce or widowhood.

Not only older women supported the limitation of *mahr*. A young woman, who graduated from the Medical Faculty and married in 2000, received a huge immediate dower of 300,000 riyals (11,538 dinars). She put it this way: "Yes, we accepted the law. Circumstances are now different. Then money was enough, today nothing suffices." Another young woman, married in 1993

13. For a detailed discussion on the generations theme see Dahlgren, 1998/1999: 77-86 and 2010, chapter 6.
14. The data I collected for this purpose does not represent a sample (fewer than thirty men and women were interviewed) and on the basis of it I cannot draw any general conclusions about sentiments towards the law. The law has been challenged from other points as well, such as allowing women too many rights in marriage or representing a deviation from Islamic law. These aspects are discussed in Dahlgren, 2010.

to a worker, told me: "The little I know about the law, yes, the amount was enough. The families agreed between them about all the other payments. If the groom was wealthy, he was expected to provide the bride with all she needs for a fine wedding, so that she is well equipped." One woman who married a government official in 1980 suggested that in actual terms the *mahr* paid during the jurisdiction of the former law became on average 10,000 shillings (5,000 dinars). That comprised the legitimate *mahr* (100 dinars) paid upon signing the contract, together with gold items and a *daf'a* for all other equipment and clothing.

Those women who did not approve of the limitation of the dower tended to be negative to the law in general. A secretary who married an electrician in 1992 explained to me: "Women had no say when the law was enacted." She seemed to be very dissatisfied with her own marriage deal, too, as she explained that her father, an engineer born in Aden, concluded the negotiations with her husband's father without informing her how much he had demanded and how much the other party had offered. She said that there should be mutual understanding in marriage and between fathers and daughters. Another woman explained her criticism this way: "Those in power watched that the set amount was not broken. The amount was not enough. We were forced to accept the law. To some extent it was sufficient anyhow." She married an aircraft engineer in 1983 in al-Mansura, a northern suburb of Aden. He was her relative and paid her father 5,000 shillings (250 dinars) in immediate *mahr*. However, part of this amount was used to feed the guests at the wedding party, and she was given only what was left over. However, all the gold items, a wedding ring and bracelets remained her property.

Beyond the generally negative attitude towards the law, economic factors were another main reason for opposing the limitation among those I interviewed. A woman married in 1989 to a broadcasting technician told me: "I could not be satisfied with so small an amount and did not support the law". She received 600 dinars as immediate dower. According to her, no separate *daf'a* was paid, and all equipment and furnishings were included in the *mahr*. Naturally, she received the customary gold items. She herself, her mother and husband were born in Aden but her father was "from a village", as she put it.

I also asked people what kind of problems arose when the law was broken. Was it difficult to break the law in the first place? Some said that since it is customary in Aden to make verbal agreements and because the payments were due to be paid before the wedding anyway, there were no risks. The marriage simply did not take place if the agreed amounts due were not produced. Some people recalled that at times the Local Defence Committee had to resolve quarrels that involved unmet promises.[15] An elderly woman recalled: "Occasionally there arose problems and the parties quarrelled. If the argument came to the knowledge of the Committee both parties might have ended in prison".

Jurists with whom I discussed the matter did not remember that many people had been sent to prison. It was anyway the practice to pay a *daf'a* in connection with an engagement where one could hide part of the payment and buy expensive gold outside the legitimate *mahr*. And since verbal agreement is the custom, few people expected or encountered problems from the authorities. More often, instead of criminal consequences, a marriage that floundered in disagreement was terminated in court.[16]

Economic Insecurities Arise

After Yemeni unification in May 1990, the 1974 law remained in force until it was replaced with the Personal Status Law that came into effect in summer of 1992. In perusing the Adeni marriage records at that time, three interesting trends emerge. The first is that marriage payments sky-rocketed and started to follow the practice in Taʿizz and Sanaa. Currently it is not uncommon to agree upon a million riyals (about 38 461 South Yemeni dinars) as the *mahr*. The second is that *mahr mu'ajjal*, the deferred dower, comes back into the picture. During the period of the 1974 law it was usually recorded, if at all, together with an immediate *mahr*. Now, several marriages are contracted with only the deferred amount documented. For instance, in a marriage contracted in summer 1992 and recorded in Sira district, a 29-year-old divorced housewife from Radfan became the fourth wife of a 57-year-old entrepreneur from Abyan. It was the bride's second marriage and the groom's fifth. The only payment recorded in the marriage contract was a deferred dower of 100 dinars. The third trend that emerged with the change in the law is that some people insisted on the previous law. In a wedding contracted in December 1992, a 20 year-old Aden-born woman whose profession is recorded as

15. A semi-governmental organization charged with tasks of local administration including providing reconciliation (*tahkim*) in marital disputes. Every couple who sought divorce had to submit their case to arbitration either by this committee or by the Women's Union's marriage counsellor. In the court decisions, the judge consulted the recommendations of the two bodies.
16. During the period of the 1974 Family Law, all divorces had to be taken to court.

"housewife", entered into a first marriage to a 35-year-old worker born in Hadramawt. The *mahr* was only 100 dinars.

Reflecting on why a working woman with a good income of her own needed a high *mahr* when marrying, I asked a women's rights activist about her opinion. She explained:

> Middle class people these days [January 2001] demand about 200,000 riyals. Two of my sisters married last year. Both chose their husbands themselves and work, but still demanded this amount. They want to have the respect of the man. They wanted to see that he is ready to pay such a high amount. They also wanted their weddings to be special; it is after all a once in a lifetime event. Both celebrations were organised in Laylati club, 160,000 riyals for the night." To emphasise her sentiments, she continued: "During the PDRY, I was brought up with different ideas. We explained that you give your life and love to your husband, [so that] there is no need to pay high dowers. Now, after the unification, backward customs are returning.

Conclusions

At different periods during the past decades discussed in this chapter, *mahr* has been debated in the public arena in terms of control and limitation, while the practice among people contracting marriages has shown two tendencies: leniency and excess. The public discourses, whether argued from an "Islamic" point of view or according to the "women's emancipation" politics, have collided with customary practices that argue in a variety of ways in favour of high dowers. Nevertheless, these public discourses have been widely supported.

While the 1974 Family Law has been commonly called the Women's Law (*qanun al-mar'a*), with the idea that its provisions favoured women in particular, in light of the *mahr* question such an interpretation is highly controversial. This finding puts the arguments of those who criticize the law, who say that it uniformly favoured women and gave them "too many rights", in a new light. Even though it would be easy to think that the contested *mahr* issue divides people according to gender, with women favouring excessive amounts and men opposing them, in this chapter I have showed that this is not the case. In discussions with people of different age categories and representing various social ranks, and of both sexes, it became evident that people link their positive or negative attitude to high dowers to wider aspirations about society and to their expectations as to what kind of security for the woman a period calls upon.

In Aden, the *mahr* is rarely discussed in reference to property; this probably has to do with the fact that Adeni families seldom have had properties that they could sell or move when contracting marriages. Instead, bridal payments are mulled over in terms of security, respect and dignity. People talk about how much *mahr* is sufficient, recommended or decent. Criticism is expressed in terms of greed, commoditization, or as offensive to Islam. All this debate is inevitably discussion on propriety (*adab*) and public moralities. On the issue of *mahr*, people argue moral values and social ideals. In legal discussions, *mahr* is addressed in terms of regulation, sufficiency and decency, values on which different societies construct their ideals for the family, too, as a basic tenet of society. In these colliding discourses, the *mahr* is argued in reference to larger visions for a desired future for society.

In this chapter, I have suggested that alongside the usual and still accurate perspective of looking at *mahr* as property or as a tool in social bonding, assessing the practice as a discourse on security and propriety might bring refreshing new viewpoints to this centuries-old controversy. In reviewing how marriage settlements (as expressions of customary practices) have historically collided with marriage regulation (in statutory or other types of laws) the *mahr* question has proved fruitful: in Aden these two forms of normativities have seldom been in peaceful coexistence.

Bibliography

Al-Marghinani, Burhan al-Din al-Farghani, (2006) *al-Hidayah* (Bristol: Amal Press).

Bakhtiar, Laleh, (1996) *Encyclopedia of Islamic Law. A Compendium of the Major Schools* (Chicago: ABC International Group, Inc.).

Constitution of the People's Democratic Republic of Yemen, 1971, enacted in 1970 (Aden, Republic Press).

Dahlgren, Susanne, (2010) *Contesting Realities. The Public Sphere and Morality in Southern Yemen* (Syracuse: Syracuse University Press).

Dahlgren, Susanne, (2007) 'Islam, Custom and Revolution in Aden: Reconsidering the Background of the Changes of the Early 1990s', in Kamil A. Mahdi, Anna Wuerth and Helen Lackner (eds.), *Yemen into the Twenty-First Century, Continuity and Change* (Reading: Ithaca Press, 2007), pp. 327-345.

Dahlgren, Susanne, (1998/1999) "The chaste woman takes her chastity wherever she goes". Discourses on Gender, Marriage and Work in Pre-and Post-Unification Aden, *Chroniques yéménites*, 1998/1999, pp. 77-86.

Doe, D. B., (1965) *Aden in History* (Aden: Government Printer).

Dorsky, S., (1986) *Women of Amran: A Middle Eastern Ethnographic Survey* (Salt Lake City: University of Utah Press).

Family Law, Law No.1 of (1974) official English translation, issued by the Information Department of the Ministry of Information (1976), (Aden: 14th October Corporation).

Fatat al-Gazira, issue no.1568, February 1961.

Ghanem, I., (1976) "A note on Law No.1 of 1974 concerning the family, People's Democratic Republic of Yemen", in R. B. Serjeant and R. Bidwell (eds), *Arabian Studies III*: (London: Hurst).

Halliday, F., (1974) *Arabia Without Sultans* (Harmondsworth: Penguin).

al-Makkawi, Shaykh Abd al-Qadir, (1959) *Al-nahr al-fa'idh fi 'ilm al-fara'idh wa'l-idhah fi huquq al-nisa' wa-ahkam al-nikah* (A Treatise on the Muhammedan Law, entitled "The Overflowing River of the Science of Inheritance and Patrimony" together with an exposition of "The Rights of Women, and the Laws of Matrimony"), third edition (Cairo: Moustapha El Baby El Halaby & Sons, 1959, originally printed in Syria in 1886).

Meneley, A., (1996) *Tournaments of Value. Sociability and Hierarchy in a Yemeni Town* (Toronto: University of Toronto Press).

The Middle East, February 1983.

Molyneux, M., (1982) "State Politics and the Position of Women Workers in the People's Democratic Republic of Yemen 1967-1977", *Women, Work and Development*, vol. 3 (Geneva: International Labour Office).

Moors, A., (1995) *Women, Property and Islam: Palestinian Experiences 1920-1990* (Cambridge: Cambridge University Press).

Mundy, M., (1995) *Domestic Government. Kinship, Community and Polity in North Yemen* (London: I. B. Tauris).

Nagi, S.A., n.d., "Historical glimpse of Yemen", in Luqman, F.M. (ed.), *Democratic Yemen Today* (Bombay: No printing place).

Al-qarar al-jumhuriyyat bi-l-qanun raqm (20) li-sanat 1992m (Personal Status Law, Law No. 20 of 1992), Wizarat al-shu'un al-qanuniyya (Aden: 14th October Corporation).

CHAPTER 3

Morning Gifts in the Legal History of Europe and Denmark

Inger Dübeck

Migration and the Clash of Legal Cultures

The populations of the Northern European countries were since the late bronze age mixed with different tribes migrated from the Asian, Indian and Persian cultures, of which some were warriors and nomads or merchants, while others were agriculturers. The warriors took the leadership as chiefs, lawmakers and kings. Their religion reflected their own social differences with gods like Odin, Tor and Tyr as the warrior gods on one side, and on the other side gods that were to secure peace, richness and fertility, like Nerthus, Njord and Freja. In the third century before Christ and during the following 700 years a more or less constant migration took place from Asian and east European territories to west Europe of tribes speaking Indo-European languages and bringing their cultures and habits to their new dwelling places (Bæksted 1963: 11-19).

1. Roman Law and Legal Culture

The classical Roman legal culture was a culture of written laws such as the *Edictum perpetuum* from the *praetor urbanus* and different constitutions. *Jus civile* was law for people with citizenship in the city of Rome. Aliens were outlawed and without legal rights, *peregrini*. But in practical life the citizens of Rome wanted to be friends with strangers who settled down. Private and public guest friendship often developed through commercial connections or marriages. Gradually all people in Italy gained Roman citizenship. But they had no rights in procedural connections. To solve this problem, a special *jus gentium* developed through the praetorian practice by the *praetor perigrinus*. His decisions were codified in special praetorian edicts, which constituted the *jus gentium*. Most of the rules concerning strangers, the law of *perigrini*, were made by the *perigrini-praetor* on the basic of other peoples' law and customs.

Such legal loans were used also in *jus civile* among Roman citizens, and in this way *jus gentium* became the law for both Roman citizens and strangers. *Jus gentium* was influenced by Greek legal thinking, when it was understood as a sort of Natural law, given with the human nature, a *jus natural* as the opposite of *jus positivum* (Iuul 1944: 34-40).

The influence from Greek legal culture was obvious in many relations such as the use of written law and legislation, but also the concept of *aequitas* (equity) as complement to the concept of strict rule of law, which was to be used in the post classical time. After the promotion of Christianity to the state religion of the Roman Empire, the church became a state in the state with its own jurisdiction and legislation. This so called "canon law" of the Church came to have great influence upon secular law on marital relations (Iuul 1944: 157).

A very early Latin source from the year 98A.C. was written by the Roman writer, Tacitus, who in his work, *Germania*, title18, told of marriages among the Germans who lived east of the river Rhine, who took marriage seriously, and probably was the only people, where the men had only one wife, except a few nobles ones, who got many marriage offers. The wife did not give the husband a gift, but the man gave a gift to her. Parents and family were present to accept the gift, which consisted of oxen, tamed horses, shield, spear and sword. The gifts should remind her of her duty to share his life in war as in peace (Tacitus 1974: 52-53). In German legal history it has been the opinion, that the gift mentioned by Tacitus in title 18 in a way was identical with the West Gothic morning gifts from the 7th century for the nobility, the *Morgingiba*, which consisted of soldiers, horses and weapon, and later was changed into ornaments or money. Many marriage settlements with the same conditions over and over again made a general legal principle or practice, which were used if no written settlement existed in the concrete case (Schröder 1919: 340-50). The Roman *dos* was a contribution by the bride or by persons on her behalf for the upkeep of the shared household.

The Roman Empire was always under a certain cultural influence from the peoples in the conquered areas. When the empire was divided in an Eastern and a Western Roman Empire, the eastern part, the Byzantine Empire, came under a stronger Greek and oriental legal and cultural influence through the close commercial and also cultural connections with oriental and Arab regions, which had developed a special practice of morning gifts for the benefit of widows or divorced wives. The ordinary classical Roman *dos* was to be transferred before the marriage as normal donations, because exchange of gifts between husband and wife during their marriage was illegal. But from around the 6th century a promise to give in the future was sufficient to bind the property while it remained in the husband's domain. Technically this sort of morning gift was called donation *propter nuptias* (Prichard 1961: 107). It was probably a result of an oriental or Arab inspiration, where such gifts were meant to honour the wife and to secure the maintenance of the widow or divorced wife. The specific "donation *propter nuptias*" came from the Greek-Egyptian family law and was adopted in the Code of Justinian, under the title of *graeci parapherna*, Codex, 5.14.8. (Sohm 1920: 680). I have chosen to mention this interesting connection between oriental and western culture and practice, but I dare not state that this connection alone caused that the medieval Europe also got a morning gift system, although the great law books of the emperor Justinian I from the 6th century were not only valid in the Eastern Roman Empire with the close connections to Arab tribes but also in certain parts of the Western Europe, especially in parts of Italy, and it came in different ways to influence those parts, which after the Great Migration from the northern German and Slavic areas was formed by the new barbarian societies between 400 and 1100 A.D.

2. Early Medieval Customary Law among the New Tribal Societies in the Former Western Roman Provinces

The new societies under different dukes or kings such as the Lombard, the Burgundy, the Frankish, the Saxon and the Anglo-Saxon, were cultures without written laws, but with unwritten, oral customary law. It was understandable that the new rulers in their consolidating period in the former Roman provinces such as the Gallic and the German parts, engaged former Roman civil servants and political members of the senatorial class to help establishing a relevant new administration and legislation. But in the long run more help was given by bishops and other learned persons from the Christian Church. Perhaps this fact was one of the reasons why nearly all of the new rulers in Europe got written laws as soon as they converted to Christianity, for instance king Rothari and Charlemagne. The bishops got a strong political role, not because the church was strong, but because the late Western Roman Empire was weak. The last Western Roman emperors ceased to make new laws, and soon the laws of the church were the only written sources of law. The position of the Church had been established by the help of the written Roman law, with which the new rulers were unacquainted.

During roman antiquity between 300 and 600 AD the Roman law had been the only legal system, but the barbarian tribes, which settled down in the Western Roman provinces between 500 and 1000 AD were unfamiliar with the Hellenistic-Roman legal culture. In the classical Roman law family and inheritance law had been looked upon as part of the personality principle concerning the lawyer, Gajus (I.1.1.2.) and (D.1.1.9.): each people had two legal systems: Its own *jus civile* and the common *jus gentium* for all human beings. When all citizens of the Roman Empire with Caracalla´s edict from 212 were made Roman citizens, it was no longer necessary to implement a personality principle in legal questions concerning family law and inheritance law. But the new barbarian tribal societies from the Great Migrations became new *peregrini*, and the personality principle was revived between the different tribes and their different customary laws (Gihl 1951: 26-37).

The Church employed the categories of Roman law, as they were understood in the early middle Ages, for there was no other law at hand. The new rulers had to face a lot of problems in their new surroundings, and the Church helped them to formulate and to write down rules concerning problems alien to their tradition (Lupoi 2007: 1-20).

The Frankish territories were soon Christianized and the Roman courts disappeared in favour of local courts under the kings. But in Italy among Roman people, Lombard, Frankish and Alamans, it became tradition in the courts to ask by which law the persons lived, because the new inhabitant had to follow the law of the people among whom he was born. A conflict about a morning gift given by the husband should be judged by the law of the husband. If a woman of a Roman family married a man of another nation, the gift should be judged on the basis of Roman law. Around the year 800 AD the royal and imperial legislation had altered this situation both in Italy and in the North-Western Frankish and German territories, because the new rulers began to make legislation for the whole realm or kingdom. But in medieval France, people in the North in many questions followed the old customary laws, while people in the South followed late Roman law.

In the Spanish parts of Europe we find a particular history. Tribes coming from Eastern Europe, called the Visigoths (western Goths), settled down in the former Roman Spain. They adopted some of the existing Roman legal culture, which was written in king Alaric´s codebook, *Breviarium Alaricianum*, from 506 AD. It was a law book for the Roman people in Spain and the Southern France. The western Goths later got their own customary laws written down in the *Lex Visigotorum* from 654 AD, but it was also to be the law for the Roman people, because the *Breviarium* was replaced by the *Lex Visigotorum* (Tamm 2005: 42-53).

In 711 AD most of Spain was conquered by North African Arabs, or Moors, but they were soon forced to withdraw to the southern areas of Spain and Portugal. They called the new land – al-Andalus, and they stayed there until 1492, when Granada as the final stage of the *Reconquista* was conquered by Queen Isabella and King Ferdinand 2. Not only the new Islamic law, but probably also the secular customary Arabian practices concerning morning gifts may in a way be said to have been part of the European medieval legal systems, although the Islamic law is not known to have inspired the law of their Christian next-door neighbours or vice versa, but the conquered populations were allowed to live on the basis of their own laws, unless they should break Islamic law, then they were brought before Islamic courts (Iuul 1970: 7-8).

A German-Jewish Lawyer, Johan David Michaëlis, wrote in his work on Mosaic Law from 1780 about morning gifts, that among Arabs he finds that the men give their brides a gift called *Mahr*, about which Muhammad gives a lot of rules in case of divorce. The Hebrew have the same word, pronounced as *mohar*, but the Hebrew *mohar* is given to the father and the brothers and not to the bride and that is the reason why Moses does not say a word concerning morning gifts (Michaëlis 1780: 424-26). *Mohar* was a sort of bride price, while *Mahr* was and is a sort of morning gift.

The legal concept of a morning gift and the claims to the gift transaction itself are to be found in most of the Western Gothic and Frankish sources of which more have been written before the Arab capture of Andalusia, a fact which speaks against a presumption that such gifts and promises of gifts were inspired by the Arab gift, *Mahr* (Surah IV, 4, 20). On the other side it should be remembered, that the *Mahr* was a result of a social practice concerning which a man legally might have more wives and in an easy and informal way might divorce a wife. The gift should compensate for this risk as well as for the risk of the man´s early death. The Christianized tribes in Western Europe no longer had a legal right to divorce a wife and no longer a right to have more wives, though this last problem was often solved through concubines among rulers and knights.

Among the early medieval legal systems developed in the new western European societies, most of them originally had rules on a sort of "bride price", a payment for the taking over the protection of the bride from her father and brothers. A "rape marriage" was illegal, and the Danish-English king Canute the Great is remembered prohibiting that a woman in England should be sold to a man whom she disliked. The bridegroom had to ask her personally before the making of a covenant with her kinsmen about her morning gift. Both in England and in the Frankish and German countries the original bride price and the younger morning gift so to say became fused over time, so that widows obtained a right to enjoy for her life time some share of the husband´s property, a fourth, a third or a half, so that this right often became a right to a charge on her husband`s land as a right of use (Pollock & Maitland vol. 2, 1968: 364-65 and 415-26).

As to the question, if there might have been some one-way or mutual influence between the Arabs and Jews on one side and the West-Gothic Christians on the other side as to the special practice with payment in relation to marriage covenants between the bride groom and the family of the woman, I am tempted to conclude, that both the Arab *Mahr* and the Jewish *mohar* may have inspired their Christian neighbours in the forming of their own rules concerning marriage gifts and covenants on gifts to the benefit of the widows, because the main marital property system was separate property among all three groups. If this holds true, we cannot totally refute this presumption, which needs to be explored more thoroughly.

Examples of Early Medieval Rules on Morning Gifts:

<u>*The Burgundian Code (c. 501A.D.): Titl. XLII:*</u> *On the inheritance of those, who die without a child.*

"Num. 2: Let that remain in effect, which has been stated previously concerning the morning gift. For if she wishes to marry within a year from the time of the death of her first husband, let her have full right to do so, but let her give up that third part of the property, which she had been permitted to possess. However, if she wishes to take a husband after a year or two have passed, let her give up all as has been stated above, which she received from her first husband, and let the heirs in whose portion the inheritance of her former husband belongs receive the price which must be paid for her (second) marriage" (Peters 1949/ 1972: 50-51).

<u>*The Lombard Laws: Rothair's Edict (643 A.D.) , Title 182*</u>*: On the rights of the widow and the disposition of her guardianship after the death of her husband.*

"The second husband who wishes to marry her should give, from his own property, for her marriage portion to him, who is the nearest heir of the first husband half of that amount, which was offered, when the first husband betrothed her. If the heir does not wish to accept this amount, then the woman shall have it together with (her first husband´s) morning gift…" (Peters 1973: 85-86).

<u>*The Laws of King Liutprand (717 A.D.):*</u>

"Title 7: If a Lombard wishes to give his wife a morning gift at the time he marries her, we decree that before the marriage in the presence of friends and relatives he announces the gift by means of a written instrument confirmed by witnesses which states "Observe that which I give as a morning gift to my wife", so that in the future she may not lose the gift by any perjury. The morning gift may not be more than a fourth part of the property of him who makes the gift. If a man prefers to give his wife less than the fourth part, he may give whatever amount, pleases him; but more than a fourth part he may not give" (Peters 1973: 147).

The Alamannic Laws (600-700 A.D.):
Title LIV: If anyone dies without heirs;

§ 3: "If however that woman says "My husband gave a morning gift to me", let her estimate its worth, either in gold, silver, slaves or horses, estimating the property at twelve *solidi.* Let it be permitted to that woman to swear on her heart and say "My husband gave this property to me under my own jurisdiction, and I should possess it" (Rivers, 1977: 84-85).

The Bavarian Laws (c. 740 A.D.):
Title VIII § 14:" If any free man (noble) dismisses his wife, a freewoman, without any fault, except his dislike, let him compensate with forty eight *solidi* to her relatives. However, let him pay the woman her lawful morning gift according to her status, and whatever she brings with her from her relatives´ property, let all those things be returned to the woman".

Title XV § 8: "But if a mother contracts another marriage, on that day let the sons, who are born of the earlier marriage take over her portion of the usufruct from her husband's property, whatever remains of the paternal inheritance. However, let a mother depart if she has her own property (with) her morning gift, which she possesses legally. And if she has borne neither sons nor daughters (from her former marriage), let everything she took away from the late husband's children (that is those, of a former marriage) be returned to them after his death." (Rivers 1977: 84 – 85).

A common trait of the new Germanic or Gothic laws, which were inspired by Roman law, was their being written in Latin language. The oldest German laws written in the mother tongue were the laws by the Anglo Saxon king Aethelbert of Kent and his so called "dooms" from c. 600 AD. Concerning these dooms, marriage should be a costly matter, and it was necessary for the groom to give a morning gift (*morgengifu*) either in form of money or in land. This was not a bride price, but a way of endowing her. The gift gave the security to the woman, if the husband died. The morning gift among the Anglo Saxons was a widows` rent and it claimed that the husband died from a childless marriage (Leyser 1999: 41-42). If there were children, the widow would not get the morning gift, only her part of the property, because the children were the heirs of the deceased father. Probably the Anglo Saxons had brought the idea of morning gifts from the continent to England, when they settled down.

A special trait concerning the early tribes in Denmark before the 12th-13th centuries was, they did not produce written law or legal thinking, at least for the homeland, although the king, Canute the Great, gave rules for all his people in England. We do not know if he gave his Danish people corresponding rules, and we do not know if the Danes in Denmark followed some customs, which had any sort of resemblance with the early German or Gothic legal sources, concepts or ideas.

This fact is so much more surprising looking to the fact, that the Danes and the Swedes from the 8th to the 11th century under the name of Vikings travelled all over Europe with their ships, the Danish normally along the western coasts of the continent and along the coasts of England, and further came into the coasts of the Mediterranean countries from the Atlantic Sea, while the Swedish Vikings normally followed the Russian and Central-european rivers from the Baltic Sea to the Black Sea and Constantinople. Sometimes they settled down and stayed for a shorter or longer time. In some places they plundered, took slaves and whatever they wanted, and then returned to Denmark. But some of the Danish Vikings became ordinary merchants and settled down in the Frisian and Frankish territories, others became soldiers in the armies of the new rulers on the continent. Where they settled down they soon formed an integral part of the society.

The Vikings in England were known to have their own legal thinking or customs. In England the territory, where the Danish Vikings settled down, was called *Danelagen*, which meant the land where Danish customs made the law of the territory, and whose customs also became law for the following English kings. It contained rules concerning administration, jurisdiction, criminal law, and rules about land tax (*danegeld*) and a few rules concerning buying and selling in market places, but not concerning family, marriage or inheritance (Steenstrup 1882/1972: 9, 34; Pollock & Maitland vol. 1, 1968: 142).

But even those Danes, who did not travel in Europe, but stayed at home as merchants or farmers or as chiefs or headmen (housecarls) defending the country, might have had friendly relations with foreign headmen or chiefs in other neighbor countries. So even if we today do not know, if they had rules concerning gifts in order to make alliances or in relation to marriages, the archeologists have during the last many years found many examples of rich gifts consisting of gold, silver, bronze, glass, weapon and ornaments made in Europe, from the Roman empire or from Frankish or Gothic realms.

4. Medieval Law in Northern Europe and the Influence of the Church

The English marital donation system developed after 1066 followed partly the Roman principles, concerning which only nuptial gifts were legal, that is the dower from the husband which was given to the bride during the marriage ceremony with the priest as witness. But the gift was not to become effective until the death of the husband. The dower was the share of the wife in the husband`s property, which she might claim, when he died. The dowry could have the same purpose as the marriage portion to the wife. The dowry, which was a gift from the groom to the bridegroom (*propter nuptias*) was also called a morning gift. To secure the gift for the woman´s widowhood, it was necessary to make a will, in order to escape lawsuits from the heirs of the husband. There was another possibility to safeguard the wife in her widowhood, which became more common, the contractual arrangements, which gave the wife a right to use (a part of) the land and other property rights for her lifetime, instead of the dower, when the husband died. But such arrangements might cause troubles with the family of the deceased husband. Common law courts did not accept a prenuptial contract as a lawful marriage settlement, because the following marriage made the woman "under cover" and consequently made the agreement void.

In the Court of Chancery suits concerning marriage settlements were accepted, because Equity law should protect widows as well as orphans and other miserable persons according to the teachings of the church. Such agreements or jointures became common in the late Middle Ages and early modern time. They secured the widow a right to use the land of the husband, because the jointure meant a joint tenancy during the marriage (Dübeck 2003: 71-74). The making of a jointure usually involved a trust and as such it could be enforced in Equity courts.

In Germany the *Sachsenspiegel*, or the Saxon provincial law from c.1215-1275, Book I, Title 20, regulated the rules concerning morning gifts for knights. The knight could give a servant or a maid room (a house) and cattle as morning gift, while a common, not noble, man could give the best horse or cattle.

In Denmark, Norway and Sweden any knowledge or use of morning gifts is not known before the 12th or 13th century, with one exception: the isle of Gotland in the Baltic Sea along the eastern coast of the southern part of Sweden. In the so called *Gutalag* (1100 – 1300), chapter 20, concerning inheritance, we find a rule about morning gifts in title 10 which declares, that a woman should inherit *hogsel* and *Id* (a special widows gift). If she married another man after the death of the first husband, and left her children alive, she should have only *hogsel* and *Id* and no more. If she stayed with her sons and they died before the age of eight, then she should have the right to one mark money for each year the sons lived.

An explanation of this difference between Denmark, Sweden and Gotland might be that Gotland from the early Viking age around 800 AD was a commercial centre for all the countries around the Baltic Sea. Many different foreign coins have been found by archeologists in modern time, among many others 70,000 Arab coins from 800-900 AD stamped in Tashkent and Samarkand. Gotland was in this period under the reign of local chiefs and later under the Hanseatic Merchants. In 1361 to 1645 it came under the Danish kings. Until then the *Gutalag* was in force. Under the following Swedish regime new legislation put an end to the use of the *Gutalag*.

On the mainland of Sweden all provincial laws and the special land laws and municipal laws from the late Middle Ages had rules about the amount of morning gifts to widows, the size of which depended on the social social status of their respective husbands, that is: morning gifts for the nobility and for common people: Knights might leave their widows a gift of 40 mark, their men a gift of 20 mark, common lords of a manor a gift of 10 mark, a farmer a gift of 3 mark, and a servant a gift of one mark.

2. Morning Gifts in Denmark: Danish History, Law and Practice

1. The Viking age: 800 to 1100 AD

The Vikings seemingly did not have rules about morning gifts or about inheritance for women. The learned Bishop Adam of Bremen (c.1041-1081), who in his famous *Chronica* wrote the history of the diocese of Hamburg in which he told the history of the Nordic countries, claimed that the men in Denmark, especially the mighty leaders, had as many wives or concubines they wanted, but that they would be punished by death if they took another man´s wife (Lund 2000: 216). We know for sure, that the Viking kings, the Danish kings in the 11th century, had concubines and that some of the sons of the concubines became kings after their fathers , if the legitimate son was dead, this holds true for five sons of king Svend Estridssen (1047-1074), born by concubines.

It is difficult to believe, that the Vikings did not know that nearly all the German tribes and states in the Western Europe had accepted the practice of giving morning gifts in connection with marriages. During centuries these states were visited by Vikings in different ways, such as plundering intruders, peaceful merchants or new inhabitants settling down as farmers, craftsmen or merchants. We have no written Danish sources telling us if morning gifts were given in practice or not. If not, the reason might be that the Vikings followed other cultural and legal customs than those of German and Gothic tribes and people.

A Danish study on rune inscriptions tells us, that more than 20 rune stones, and rather big ones, have been erected by women of great influence. The inscriptions also show, that a woman could claim divorce from her husband, which was an amazing experience for an Arab visitor in the market town Hedeby in the year 960. The study confirms the impression, that these women might have been well off and capable of paying for the inscription and the erection of the rune stone (Moltke 1976: 252-56) The question comes forward: Did a sort of deathbed gift exist in practice during the Viking age? A rune inscription tells us that the father gave his possessions to the son, who gratefully set up the stone.

The change of burial practice is generally by archeologists supposed to have taken place after 1000 AD, where a new habit of giving away such belongings to the heirs is supposed to have started. Perhaps this view may have to be altered, if more Christian graves from 800 and 900 are to be found in the future. The archeologists have until now proved that such valuables and ornaments no longer are to be found in the younger graves from the 11th-12th centuries (Jensen 2006: 336-37). The supposed change in burial practice corresponds in a way to the legend told by Saxo Grammaticus in his great epos: *Gesta Danorum*, X, 187, (Horn 1898/1975: 396-97) according to which all Danish women got a right to inheritance, because they had given all their golden ornaments as ransom payment for the Danish and English king Sweyn Forkbear (d. 1014). It is a good, but not very credible story. A change in property and inheritance practice, would probably develop over a much longer period, and perhaps especially as a consequence of the growing influence of the Roman Church, which had a great interest in the protection of widows. In England under the reign of his son Canute the Great (c. (995) 1014-1035) it was normal that a dying man on his deathbed could declare his "last word" called a *cwithe* about the distribution of his movables between wife, children (*bairn*) and his own part, the so-called "dead´s part", which often concerned close friends. In the late medieval England and especially in York and Scotland a man's chattel might be divided in three: the wife´s part, the *bairn*´s part and " dead´s part" The word *cwithe* is an Old-Danish word meaning sorrow and fear. It is tempting to presume, that this deathbed *cwithe*-declaration, might have consisted of horses, weapon, cloth and other movable items, also became a practice in Denmark from around the 11th century. The mentioned rune inscription may lead to the assumption, that Canute instead might have brought this practice to England from Denmark.

In my opinion the documented changes of the burial culture as to valuables might indicate a change in direction of acceptance of inheritance for wife and children, rather than a change into a practice of morning gifts, that is, that it became a general practice, that a man on his deathbed, could declare as his will, that his own part, "the dead´s part", should be given to one or more persons according to his own wishes (Dübeck 2003: 59-67).

The question of mutual influences between England, Normandy, Flanders, Friesland and Denmark in relation to rules about marital property problems during the medieval period, especially concerning questions about community property among the spouses, and the question of inheritance for the widow versus a marriage system with separate property for the spouses and morning gifts for the widows, is not easy to answer. The reality seems to have been community property in municipal practice in the greater commercial towns. For merchants and craftsmen the joint or community property was preferable to separate property, which on the contrary was preferable for the landed gentry. A practice of community property regarding property acquired during the 11th and 12th centuries was spreading among merchants and other traders in the towns along the coasts of the North Sea and the English Channel, in the French-speaking cities in northern France, and in nearby German- and Dutch-speaking areas and in Northern England. Inherited property in land normally was separate property. This community practice existed for a long time as an unwritten custom, but in many towns in England a new practice with written contracts suppressed the community property and introduced a sort of "dotal" marriage with separate ownership and morning gifts (Howell 2007: 425-29).

2. Morning Gifts for Queens, for Ladies of the Higher Nobility and for Common Women

Settlements with the special purpose of securing morning gifts, as widows` pension are known in Danish sources from the 13th century, though most of the older contracts concerning morning gifts were gifts between royal persons. Such gifts were not part of the existing Danish common family law which is to be found in the medieval Landscape or Municipal laws. The morning gift from a king to his queen might be characterized as a sort of public law, being a matter of state, and the King´s Council would accept the size and content of the gift. When Queen Margarete I as "Principal Lady of the Realm" in 1412 was followed by her adopted son, Erik, on the throne, she was allowed as widow to keep her morning gift of Norway from her late husband, King Håkon VI. When Dorothea married Christoffer of Bavaria in 1445 she was given Jämtland as her morning gift. The gifts to queens should be of such value that the queen in her widowhood could go on living under the same social and economic conditions as during the marriage.

Several letters of morning gifts are preserved from the Danish Middle Ages in Scania, which was a prosperous part of Denmark until 1658, when it was conquered by Sweden. Such gifts had the legal form of private contracts between ordinary burgers. This practice probably was influenced by the Swedish practice. Except for the Scanian practice and the royal morning gifts and a few morning gift contracts from the southern part of Jutland, which probably were under influence from Northern Germany, morning gifts were not used in the Danish realm as such. Between common people, *Fæstensgaver* (betrothal gifts) were common practice. During the Kalmar Union 1389-1521, when Norway, Denmark and Sweden had common kings, the connections between the higher nobility in the three countries grew closer, and the Swedish practice with morning gifts among noble person was adopted by the Danish and Norwegian nobility, but not by the commons.

An Act, The Copenhagen Recess from 1547 given by the King and his council took away the possibility for noble widows to inherit manor farms and land of the nobility, if such gifts should interfere with the interests of male heirs. Settlements of morning gifts became a new possibility as compensation for this obvious discrimination of noble wives, and a possibility in marriages with no children to favour the widow to the detriment of more distantly related families or the husband´s children of a former marriage. A decision by the King´s Court in 1562 allowed morning gifts to be paid from the estate, when the husband died and before the division of the estate, which made widows with morning gifts attractive on the matrimonial market, but to the detriment of the heirs, who might be left behind heavily indebted. The amount of morning gifts consequently grew to as much as 10,000 and 15,000 Daler, with the consequence that a royal act of 18 October 1577 reduced the maximum amount to 2,000 Daler, unless the heirs accepted a higher amount of money for the morning gifts. The King, Frederik II (1559-88), and his Council had to admit, that their court decision was wrong and had caused economic tragedies (Secher 1889/90: 71-74).

The consequence of this reduction was that morning gifts no longer could fulfill the intended purpose of securing the noble lady her pension. Another possibility, mutual wills, was hereafter preferred. Such wills might be made during the marriage in practice, though they were normally made as prenuptial wills just before marriage. The mutual wills would, though, not be valid if the spouses had children who lived at the time of the death of the husband. According to the Danish Code from 1683, 5th Book, fourth chapter, §20, the mutual will should be registered in court together with an affirmation concerning all economical transactions in relation to the other heirs. But it was still possible to contract the smaller morning gifts among childless married couples of the nobility under the provision of the Danish Code according to the 5th book, second chapter § 25, and this right was still being upheld by the Act on Heredity from 1845.

Two very special general privileges were in 1672 given by the absolute king, Christian V, the so called "Privileges for the Counts" and "Privileges for the Barons". These counts and barons formed new high nobility, which was created by the absolute kings in order to favour distinguished and loyal persons in the kings′ military and civil service. The privileges stated that the count or baron, who would wish to claim *jus majoratus* for the oldest son, was obliged to secure his wife "an honourable and decent *livgeding*" (a sort of morning gift or pension).The privileges were rather special and astonishing seen in a historical perspective, because they introduced some rules which represented a medieval feudal legal thinking, which as such was disappearing in greater parts of Europe.

The first democratic Constitution of Denmark in1849 abolished all privileges for the whole nobility, not only for the new Counts and Barons, but for the old born nobility too, and the possibility of making morning gifts for the nobility. But the rules about morning gifts in the Danish Code from 1683 were not formally repealed, therefore the legal principle of morning gifts may be said to disappear by not being used.

3. The Danish Property System: Before the Danish Code of 1683 – and After

We have very little knowledge about the existence of a formal marital property system from the time before the 11th century. The change in the burial practice around 1000 AD, or perhaps earlier, from a practice with valuable and personal belongings such as weapon in the graves of men, and golden ornaments in the graves of women to a burial practice without such valuables, had brought the archeologists to presume, that from that time the valuable items were inherited by the family. This would indirectly tell us, that between 800 and 1000 AD a system without inheritance to movables may have been changed into a system of inheritance for the family members as to movables. The earlier mentioned English practice with the so-called *cwithe*, a sort of legal deathbed declaration or will, might as also earlier mentioned have been followed in Denmark during the Viking age according to which the dead husbands movables were to be divided with one third to the children, one third to the wife, while the last part was given according to his own free will.

During the 11th and 12th century a system of community property as to movables acquired during the marriage probably was inspired from western European municipal practice among merchants. Rules concerning ownership of landed property cannot be traced in the same way, but such property may well have been separate property for the owner. The Danish Landscape Laws from the 12th and 13th centuries show us different variations of family community to movables for both parents and children and to acquired land too, but inherited land was separate property for the spouses, and this practice might well have continued from the Viking age.

The Danish property system for married couples was according to the Landscape Laws a family community as to movables and acquired land for parents as well as for children, but after 1547 the community system was changed into a joint ownership of community property for the spouses alone with equal division in case of dissolution of the marriage. It was still possible for both spouses beside the community property to have other categories of separate property than inherited land, for instance the morning gift or mutual wills among the landed gentry.

The Danish Code of 1683, though, made the community property absolute in the sense, that it was no longer possible for the spouses to arrange separate property before or during the marriage. On the other hand, the widow in addition to her half of the estate acquired a right to inherit a portion of the husband's half of the common property. The widow was in fact given a choice between this heredity part of the husband´s community part or an eventual morning gift. The problem for the wife after 1683 was not so much that the husband legally could dispose as he wished over the whole community property during the marriage, a much greater problem was, that she had no autonomy either to her own person or to the community property. She could not dispose over even small everyday economical transactions for the household without the acceptance of husband. She was of course not a minor, but she was legally treated as if she were a minor, and the husband was her guardian in all decisions concerning children, household and property. Unmarried women were not given full autonomy until 1857, when they were given this right with the age of 25 like men. Once married, however, wives were looked upon as minors until 1899, when married women formally got full autonomy. Wives were in practice still not yet given a right to dispose of the community property, although a right for self-supporting wives to dispose over their own income was given in 1880.

The Marriage Act of 1925 was the first act to declare man and wife equal in all matrimonial affairs. As a consequence, each spouse had the right to dispose over his or her part of the common estate. And if the wife did not have a special income, the husband had a duty to let her have as much of his income and means that was necessary for her own needs, for the children´s needs and for the household (Dübeck 2003: 74-90, 210ff. and 318ff.).

4. Death and Divorce

1. Division of the Community Estate: After the Death of the Husband
According to early medieval Danish family law the widow had no legal claims against any part of the husband´s separate property, which was his landed property from his parent or special gifts, but the husband had the right to dispose over her separate property, the inherited land or the dowry from her parents. On the other hand she had a right to a double part, a "brother´s part", of the community property together with their sons, while daughters only had right to one single part, when the estate was to be divided after the husband`s death. If the daughters were the only children, they would get the brother´s part together with the widow. Concerning late medieval Danish practice, the surviving spouse could claim a "brother´s part" of the deceased spouse´s landed, separate property, but no part of the husband´s community property, when the estate was divided with the heirs. A court decision from the King's Court in 1515 declared that a claim for part of the husband´s part of the community property from the widow presupposed special legislation concerning the rights of the children and the widow. Such legislation was not given before the Recess of 1547 § 28, according to which children no longer could have rights in connection with the division of the community property, which on the other hand should be divided between the spouses in equal parts (Dübeck 2003: 74-90).

The Danish Code from 1683 made common property the legal property system in marriages, whether it consisted of inherited land or moveable property. Separate property could no longer be arranged between the spouses. But their parents or other persons could by Will ensure that a gift or an inheritance would be separate property for the husband or for the wife. Such dispositions became more frequent during the 18th and the beginning of the 19th century in relation to married women, often because the women´s parents and family did not believe her husband to be a good and fair administrator.

The Danish Code gave the widow a choice between a share of inheritance from the husband`s part, called the "brother´s part", or her betrothal gift or her morning gift. It might have been a difficult choice, because the brother`s part might be of greater value to her than his gift. If she remarried, the "brother´s part" should be repaid to the children or the heirs, but the two sorts of gifts, the betrothal and the morning gift, were not to be repaid, because they were looked upon as separate property. The Inheritance Ordinance of 1845 decided that the surviving widow or widower after a childless marriage should inherit one third of the deceased´s part. If no other heirs were left, the survivor would take the whole share of the deceased. If there were common children the survivor got a right to one quarter of the deceased`s part. The 1925 Marriage Act no longer prevented the making of prenuptial marriage settlements, but gave clear rules concerning the conditions, which should be kept in order to make the settlement valid.

2. Division of the Community Estate: in Case of Divorce

Before the Lutheran reformation of the Danish Church the question of divorce was one of only minor practical relevance. The Roman Catholic Church did not accept divorce, only separation and annulment, because matrimony was looked upon as for lifetime and as a holy sacrament. Annulment of marriages though was accepted as a possibility to dissolve a marriage, which had been formalized despite one of the serious marriage impediments, e.g. coercion or close affinity. Shortly after 1536 the opposite situation concerning dissolution of marriages appeared, because Luther and the new Lutheran ideas found, that divorce was the only human solution for the innocent spouse in the case of adultery or desertion or impotence from the side of the guilty spouse. As a consequence separation was no longer a legal possibility. Divorce was granted by a court decision. Separation, though, again became a possibility during the 18th century, but now as a condition for a later divorce and granted through a special royal concession given through the royal chancellery as an act of grace. It was also made possible for the spouses to make an agreement about separation and later after some years about a divorce, which agreements should be confirmed by the king through the royal chancellery, later the central administration or the decentralized authorities.

As to the division of the community property, the Code was not clear, because the rule in 5th book, 2 chapter § 19 did not relate to divorces, but only to the situation, where one of the spouses was dead. A famous court decision between a couple from the higher society concluded, that the wife, who was forced to divorce for adultery and for desertion with her lover, should have no part in the community property, but a lifelong pension from her former husband. This solution was not followed in later practise.

The distinguished lawyer A.S. Ørsted was in his learned publications concerning legal science in Denmark more specific concerning the situation of separation and divorce. In his opinion the separated or divorced wife could only claim half of the community property, and not her betrothalt or her morning gift, because these gifts were only valid for the widow, for widowhood in case of the death of the husband. (Ørsted 1825: 226-27). With the Act on Administration of Estates from 1874 special rules were introduced concerning division of community property in case of either separation or divorce. The main principle was now that the division should take place with the help of the probate court.

3. The Possibility to Retain Undivided Possession of the Common Estate at the Death of the Husband

The widow's liberty to continue the community together with the children, was abolished with the Recess of 1547 and later legislation, although a possibility of retaining the possession of the undivided estate was accepted. But King Christian IV (1588-1648) annulled this possibility in 1604, because he had discovered that some women had misused this freedom to their own benefit and to the detriment of other heirs. The size of the estate should be registered in court, before the widow could take care of the children's inheritance. The Danish Code 1683 had no rules about the possibility of retaining undivided possession of community property, but stated that a division of the estate should take place shortly after the death, which might be a catastrophe for the survivor, especially a business man.

During the period of absolutism (1660-1848) it was often possible in concrete situations to get dispensations from strict rules with unfair consequences as a sort of equity solution. An ordinance of 10 August 1697 altered the rules especially for Copenhagen, so that the survivor, under the threat of punishment, should immediately inform the probate court about the death and at once ask for division of the estate. The delegates in the council of the city tried to get exemptions for people with a documented reliable and healthy economy. After some pressure the Chancery Department in 1698 allowed the municipal authorities to let widowers retain undivided possession of the estate, but widows could under no circumstances get an exemption. Widows had to wait more than 200 years until the Inheritance Act of 20 April 1926 before such possession became a normal right for the widow. But in practice the possibility of exemption was also used for the benefit of widows to allow them to retain the possession of the undivided estate. But the Chancery administration's permission was made dependant of the widow´s staying unmarried. If she should enter a new marriage, she would have to make the division arrangement at once.

4. Widows' Pension and Life Assurance

Special widows' pension funds were established during the 18th century. One of the first was instituted for officers in the army. From 1740 it was opened for ordinary members in all sorts of government employment. The pension funds were under state control and had to have royal confirmation of their foundations.

For a very long period members of trades and craft guilds had had their own widow's pension funds. In 1775 a general widow's pension fund was established for everybody, who was able to fulfill the general conditions. In 1842 it was replaced by a so called "Annuity and Charitable Institution", in which the insurance for the widows could be paid yearly in the form of insurance rates instead of the former way, where the payment had to be paid in the form of one fixed capital.

5. Conclusion

The main purpose with this work has been to discuss the use of morning gifts in the legal history of Europe and Denmark. One trait seems to have been common: the connection between the choice or common practice of marital property and the use/non-use of morning gifts. The European societies, which were developing in the medieval period from the 7th century in the former Roman provinces, especially among the leading strata, military chiefs, kings and nobility, preferred some combinations of separate property and morning gifts. The morning gifts may originally have been intended as payment for the taking over the guardianship of the bride or it may have been to secure the woman´s widowhood. Over time the bride price fused with the morning gift to one obligation, the commitment for the husband´s heirs to let the widow use a certain part (½, $^{1}/_{3}$, ¼) of the deceased husband´s immovable property for her life time.

Poor people in the towns and villages, as well as well-off merchants in the bigger towns over time preferred different variations of community and separate property. In these municipal arrangements, morning gifts do not seem to have been very attractive, even if such gifts for instance in Sweden and in the Northern German areas were common practice. It is interesting to compare the European laws and practice with the state law and customary law of modern Pakistan, and to find the two fundamental conditions for the choice of marital property system: separate property for both spouses and morning gifts for the widow both in eastern and in western legal Culture (Mehdi 2007: 103-109).

I have not found any certain documentation for the possibility of mutual inspiration between the Muslims in Spain and Portugal and the Christian inhabitants of Andalusia. But the Greek-Egyptian legal influence upon the Justinian Roman marital law on gifts from the 6th century at least shows us, that some sort of contact between different legal cultures was possible and acceptable. So, why not on the Iberian Peninsula?

The Danish marital property system was until the Danish Code 1683 a mixed one with both separate and community property, that is, the inherited landed property was separate, while movables and acquired land was community or joint property. The landed well-off nobility normally had great inherited manors and castles with a lot of land, which is why most of their property would have been separate property, which seems to be the normal condition for the practice of morning gifts. But in Denmark this practice started as a protest action against a discriminating legislation. When a new legislation reduced the maximum of money spent for the gift, the interest in such gifts fell. Noble ladies could not get much security for their widowhood with the reduced amount of morning gifts, and the spouses had to make other arrangements, such as mutual wills. After 1683 all wives, noble as well as common women, got the right to half of the community property and a right to inherit a part of the husband´s community property. The Danish marital property system favoured morning gifts only for a short period. Since the medieval Landscape Laws the Danish marital property system was primarily a community property system with different variations, this is also the case for the marital legislation and law of wills and succession from the beginning of the 21st century.

Bibliography

Bæksted, Anders, (1963) *Guder og helte i Norden,* København: Politikens Forlag.

Dübeck, Inger, (2003) *Kvinder, Familie og Formue. Studier i Dansk og Europæisk Retshistorie,* København: Museum Tusculanum Forlag.

Gihl, Torsten, (1951) *Den internationella Privaträttens Historia och allmänna Principer,* Stockholm: Kunglika Boktryckeriet P. A. Norstedt & Söner.

Horn, Fr. Winkel, (1898/ 1975) *Danmarks Krønike"* translation, København: Vinten.

Howell, Martha C., (2007) 'Marital Property Law as Social-Cultural Text', in *To have and to hold, Marrying and its Documentation in Western Christendom 400-1600,* Philip L. Reynolds and John Witte Jr. (eds), Cambridge: Cambridge University Press.

Iuul, Stig, (1944) *Grundrids af den romerske Formueret*, København: Nyt Nordisk Forlag, Arnold Busck.

Iuul, Stig, (1970) *Forelæsninger over Hovedlinjer i Europæisk Rets Udvikling fra Romerretten til Nutiden,* København: G.E.C.Gads Forlag.

Jensen, Jørgen, (2006) *Oldtid, Yngre Jernalder og Vikingetid 400-1050,* København: Gyldendal, 2006.

Leyser, Hemnrietta, (1999) *Medieval Women. A Social History of Women in England 450-1500,* London: Phoenix Orion Books Ltd.

Lund, Allan, (ed.) (2000) *Adam af Bremen's Krønike* Århus: Wormianum.

Lupoi, Maurizio, (2007) *A European Common Law Before Bologna?* In: *Law before Gratian. Law in Western Europe c.500-1100.Procedings of the Third Carlsberg Academy Conference on medieval Legal History,* (ed.) Per Andersen et alia, Copenhagen: DJØF-Publishing

Mehdi, Rubya, (2007) *Danish Law and the Practice of Mahr among Muslim Pakistanis in Denmark,* in: (ed.) Rubya Mehdi, *Integration & Retsudvikling*, København: Jurist-og Økonomforbundets Forlag,

Michaëlis ,Johan David, (1780) *Mosaisk Ret, Første Deel*, Kjøbenhavn: Gyldendals Forlag.

Moltke, Erik, (1976) *Runerne i Danmark og deres oprindelse,* København: Forum,

Peters, Edward, (ed.), (1973) *The Lombard Laws,* Philadelphia: University of Pennsylvania Press.

Peters, Edward, (ed.), (1949/ 1972) *The Burgundian Code Book of Constitutions or Law of Gundobad,* Philadelphia: University of Pennsylvania Press Prichard, A. M. , (1961) *Leage's Roman Private Law founded on the Institutes of Gaius and Justinian, Third Edition,* London: Macmilland &Co Ltd,

Pollock & Maitland, (1968) *The History of English Law, Vol.1 and 2,* Cambridge: University Press.

Rivers, Theodore John, (ed.), (1977) *Laws of the Alamans and Bavarians,* Philadelphia: Pennsylvania Press.

Schröder, Richard, (1919) *Lehrbuch der deutschen Rechtsgeschichte, Erster Teil,* Leipzig: Verlag von Veit & Comp.

Secher, V. A. ,(ed.) (1889-90) *Corpus Constitutionum Daniae, Forordninger, Recesser og andre kongelige Breve, Danmark Lovgivning vedkommende 1558-1660, vol. II*, København: G.E.C.Gad.

Sohm, Rudolph, (1920) *Institutionen, Geschichte und System des römischen Privatrechts,*(München und Leipzig: Verlag von Duncker & Humbolt).

Steenstrup, Johannes, (1972) *Normannerne, Fjerde Bind, Danelag,* Kjøbenhavn: Rudolph Klein, 1882, Reprinted by Selskabet for udgivelse af Kilder til Dansk Historie.

Tacitus, Publius Cornelius,(1974) *Germaniens historie, geografi og befolkning,*(eds) Niels W.Bruun og Allan A. Lund, (Århus: Wormianum).

Tamm, Ditlev, (2005) *Retshistorie, Danmark – Europa – Globale Perspektiver,* København: Jurist- og Økonomforbundets Forlag.

Ørsted, A.S., (1825) *Haandbog over den danske og norske Lovkyndighed med stadigt Hensyn til Etatsraad og Professor Hurtigkarls Lærebog, Vol. 2*, Kjøbenhavn: Græbes Officin.

PART II

Contexts Comparative

CHAPTER 4

Mahr and Gender Equality in Private International Law: The Adjudication of *Mahr* in England, France, Norway and Sweden[1]

Lene Løvdal

1. Introduction

When Muslim immigrants in Europe bring with them their countries' laws and norms, these are to a large degree seen as part of their culture and religion. To be able to live in accordance with these norms is important for these people's construction of identity and belonging in a new context. Many of these norms, however, are at odds with the gender equality norms of Western Europe, e.g. the European Convention on Human Rights (ECHR) Protocol 7 Article 5 on gender equality, since family law in most Muslim countries give men and women different rights and duties in marriage. In private international law, if the result of the foreign law in question is too much at odds with what is considered to be public policy or fundamental values and norms in the

1. This article is based on my master's thesis Private international law, Muslim laws and gender equality. The adjudication of *Mahr* in Scandinavian, English and French courts, published in Kvinnerettslig skriftserie nr. 78/2009 . The thesis was written as part of the research programme *From formal to real rights: Minority women's protection against discrimination in a culturally complex and transnational Norwegian context* led by Professor Anne Hellum, and funded by the Norwegian Research Council. Anne Hellum and Tone Linn Wærstad were supervisors. My thanks go to them and the lawyers and others in France and Britain who helped me understand the judgments in their context in particular. My thanks also go to all the others who helped and supported my in writing this thesis, too many to mention here.

courts' own country, the court can refrain from applying the foreign laws through the so-called *ordre public* reservation. But if this is practiced too widely, both the individuals and countries in question tend to feel that their values, culture and even religion – when the laws in question have a clear or perceived religious basis – are not respected. How can courts best take care of the gender equality issue while at the same time respect Muslim men *and* women's sense of religious and cultural identity? My hypothesis is that in order to handle Muslim laws in private international law cases the court should apply a gender equality norm of equal worth, while it needs to apply comparative legal method in order to interpret these laws correctly.

Mahr is well suited as a focal point in order to highlight these issues, both since it is a concept that does not exist at all in Western European law and thus is particularly challenging to understand and interpret, and since it is a Muslim legal concept that gives women specific rights on the sole basis of them being women. There are few judgments concerning *Mahr* from Scandinavia; only two cases from Norway and three from Sweden, and no private international law judgments from Denmark, but one that concerns a claim for *Mahr* within Danish law. Judgments from two legal systems with a much longer history of Muslim immigration and with very different approaches, France and England, provide a wider basis for analysis. There are three Court of Cassation cases from France, and two High Court cases from England[2] have been published as case law on the matter.

Private international law cases can be seen as situations of formal or "weak" legal pluralism as described by John Griffiths: when the dominant legal system "commands different bodies of law for different groups in the population". (Griffiths 1986: 5)[3] But the line between formal and informal pluralism is a continuum rather than clear cut, and this also makes it a challenge to determine which cases concerning *Mahr* should be seen as private international law cases. In the cases I have chosen to study private international law is often not mentioned. The major variables that determine whether it's a private international law case or not, are the personal status of the spouses and where the contract containing a clause of *Mahr* was signed. Only

2. Since there are differences between different parts of the UK, I have chosen to focus on England.
3. "In general the groups concerned are defined in terms of features such as ethnicity, religion, nationality or geography, and legal pluralism is justified as a technique of governance on pragmatic grounds." (Griffiths 1986: 5) In private international law it is for the most part based on nationality or domicile – a variety of geography as basis for the choice of laws.

a case where two citizens of the same European country sign a marriage contract with a clause of *Mahr*, in the same European country, has no elements of private international law (Sayed 2008: 188-189). I have chosen primarily to look at cases where private international law was an issue, except for the Norwegian cases; there were none such. But I found two cases that dealt with *Mahr*, where private international law should have been an issue.

I will start by looking briefly at the human rights obligations these countries have today in relation to *Mahr*. In section 3 I will briefly discuss relevant aspects of comparative law methodology. In section 4 I present a summary of the relevant cases before analysing them in sections 5 to 7.

2 Human rights obligations at the interface between gender justice and legal pluralism

2.1 Introduction

Cultural norms are often seen as conflicting with a gender equality norm, to a large extent implemented in all the countries studied in this article, although to a somewhat lesser degree in the United Kingdom (Welstead 2006: 7).[4] The quest for women's rights is unlikely to be successful if we don't take the cultural context into consideration. I will thus focus on the state's obligations concerning gender justice in a context of legal pluralism. The human rights obligations of the state may be seen as either negative or positive; i.e. a negative duty to refrain from certain actions, or a positive duty to provide.[5] The cases in this study are litigations between two individuals. The main focus will therefore be on the state's duty to provide gender justice between these individuals, as stated in the Convention on the Elimination of All Kinds of Discrimination against Women (CEDAW) of 1979 articles 2 and 3, which is the most detailed human rights convention concerning women's rights. How should the convention be interpreted in order to incorporate the cultural dimension of women's lives? In order to answer this, we first need to take a brief look at various theories concerning gender justice, both in a European and a Muslim context. More specifically, we need to examine how the CEDAW may be interpreted concerning *Mahr*. It should be mentioned, although

4. Significant changes have happened since the Human Rights Act of 1998 required that family law comply with the European Convention on Human Rights.
5. This dichotomy is used less often today, to the benefit of a more nuanced and complex approach, but is useful in this specific context. (Steiner 2000 181 as quoted in Wærstad (2006): 111)

there is not enough space to discuss it, that a negative duty may arise through the question of whether the result of the application of foreign law is against *ordre public*, which may be interpreted in relation to the state's human rights obligations. Since about half of the judgments came into being before the entry into force of the CEDAW[6] I shall not go into detail, and use the CEDAW and related theory mainly as a standard of gender justice in general. The CEDAW committee also provides some views on *Mahr* in relation to gender justice that are highly relevant here.

2.2 The CEDAW and Gender Justice Norms

2.2.1 Gender Equality Theory

For a very long time, the campaign for gender justice in Western Europe mainly happened within the paradigms of Liberalism and Marxism. One of the main ideas of both of these is that all human beings are equal. A major criticism of this approach is that it may disguise inequality; that it gives women formal, but not substantial rights (See e.g. Barnett 1998). Both types of feminists have been important in ensuring that the two sexes have formally equal rights. This is the gender *equality* approach, which was the dominant feminist approach until the 1980s. MacKinnon criticises liberal feminism for not taking into consideration that "men are as different from women as women are different from men", and that men continue to set the standard for comparison (as quoted in Barnett (1998) p. 133). The Marxists were among the main critics of liberalism, but this ideology has been criticised for being too essentialist and exclusionary, "essentialist because of the centrality of economic determinism, exclusionary in its failure to examine the position of women in society." (Barnett 1998: 133)

2.2.2 Theories of Equal Worth

Both in Europe and elsewhere, several scholars have argued for a different approach, known as difference feminism or cultural feminism, in a reaction to the gender equality thinking in liberalism and Marxism. There are a variety of theories, which count among them those of Luce Irigaray and Carol Gilligan. They all strive to explain the differences between the sexes and promote women's perspectives without falling into the stereotype trap, to promote the concept of equal worth rather than strict, mechanical equality. Theories of equal worth do, however, tend to essentialise the concepts of man and woman. One of the major postcolonial feminist scholars, Gayatri Chakravorty

6. Of the ECHR protocol 7 also, of which article 5 sets forth equality between spouses.

Spivak, considers it important to use two approaches at the same time: Deconstruction as described by Jacques Derrida, while using a certain degree of gender essentialism as a *strategy* to promote gender equality (Mortensen et al. (2008) pp 93 ff), which may be seen as a strategy of equal worth as well, but not a *theory*. According to Spivak, neither approach is sufficient without the other.

One has to distinguish between gender equality in a legal sense, and in terms of feminist theory. Gender equality as a legal obligation is most often interpreted in a manner that incorporates both of these. Thus the recognition of women's work at home as a basis for their financial claims in divorce situations may be seen as a gender equality measure, although the underlying thought is obviously one of equal worth (Ncube 1989), Sverdrup (1997). The CEDAW committee explicitly recommends this approach (CEDAW General Recommendation no. 13 s2). This is even more important in situations of legal pluralism: Research on the interrelationship between human rights and legal pluralism from Africa and South Asia, some of which concern Muslim laws, shows that a mechanical gender equality approach often leads to unfair results (e.g. Hellum 2007). The equal worth approach must be used with caution, however, as one risks falling into the trap of stereotyping, which is prohibited in article 5 a).

Most feminists working within the framework of Islam are promoting women's rights on the basis of equal worth. This is mainly because the Qur'an very explicitly confers on men and women different rights and obligations, in conjunction with the fact that it is read as the words of God, as spoken directly to Muhammad. Shaheen Sardar Ali, a Pakistani legal scholar, former politician and a major proponent for the compatibility of CEDAW with Islam, interprets CEDAW in terms of the equal worth norm (Ali 2000); Hellum 2004).

2.2.3 Mahr *and CEDAW*

CEDAW article 16 obliges the state parties to "take all appropriate measures to eliminate discrimination against women in all matters relating to marriage and family relations and in particular ensure, on a basis of equality of men and women (…) The same rights and responsibilities during marriage and its dissolution" (art. 16 c)). The text indicates that *Mahr* is contrary to CEDAW, as it is a right that only women have, on their basis of being women, and it is part of a set of legal effects of marriage which are not based on gender equality. At the same time, according to CEDAW art 3, the signatory states are obliged to provide *substantial* equality, rather than just formal equality. If one goes straight to a strict gender equality norm by rejecting rights women have that are contrary to this norm then this may have the effect of making the situation worse for women, rather than better, thus not fulfilling the obligation to provide substantial equality. This is particularly relevant to the courts, which are perhaps the most important part of the state when it comes to the actual application of the law.

Initially, the CEDAW committee was very negative towards the Muslim dower, *Mahr*. During the 14th session of the committee, committee member Ms Cartwright, in the committee's comments to the Tunisian country report, "noted that the persistence of the custom of providing a dowry indicated that women were still, to some degree, regarded as a commodity".[7] In the 27th session, committee member Ms Manolo remarked, in the comments upon the Tunisian country report, "that the continuation of that practice gave the impression that the bride was bought and could be managed like a chattel".[8] However, in the 38th session of the Committee on the Elimination of Discrimination against Women it urged Syria to "review its existing laws and policies to ensure that women who go to shelters do not forgo other legal rights, such as rights to maintenance and dower".[9] Most country reports from Muslim countries from after the year 2000 mention their legislation concerning *Mahr*, but the comment just mentioned is the only response I've found from the committee. This seems to imply that the committee has changed its views on *Mahr*, from something approaching the "sale price" of the woman, to a financial right vital for the economic situation of women. Since it's a claim only women have, and thus not in line with a strict gender *equality* norm, this may indicate that the CEDAW committee is open to the equal worth standard of gender justice also concerning *Mahr*, and chooses a more culturally sensitive approach, instead of rejecting *Mahr* on the basis of a strict and rather mechanical gender equality approach – in all likelihood as a strategy, not a theory, and we do not know how situation specific this approach is. In this article we will look into whether European courts try and promote gender equality in cases concerning *Mahr*, and if so, what kind. We will also look into the courts' use of comparative law in relation to promoting gender justice.

7. http://www.un.org/womenwatch/daw/cedaw/14sess.htm#report
8. http://www.un.org/womenwatch/daw/cedaw/27sess.htm
9. http://www.un.org/womenwatch/daw/cedaw/38sess.htm

3 Using Comparative Legal Method in this Article

3.2 Introduction

An assumption underlying comparative legal method is that if "legal science" is understood as including the discovery of models for preventing or resolving social conflicts, in addition to the techniques of interpreting the texts, rules etc. of the national system, then comparative law can provide a far richer range of model solutions than a single legal system (Zweigert 1998: 15). *Mahr* has only been dealt with in a few cases in Scandinavia, and in a small number of published cases in France and Britain. The aim of this article is to engage with this assumption by looking into the techniques used by the different courts in dealing with the Muslim legal concept of *Mahr*, in a gender equality perspective. Comparative law "dissolves unconsidered national prejudices, and helps us to fathom the different societies and cultures of the world and to further international understanding." (Zweigert 1998: 16) The part of my hypothesis that concerns the use of comparative law in the courts is based on this assumption by Zweigert and Kötz, which is in line with my own views regarding how one understands foreign cultures – which the legal system is a part of.

There has been little systematic writing about the methods of comparative law. Experienced comparatists have found that a detailed method cannot be laid down in advance, and the right method must largely be discovered by gradual trial and error (Zweigert 1998: 33). I have found no literature on the comparative analysis of judgments, only on the comparison of legal rules and concepts. Since interpretation of principles and concepts are an inherent part of court reasoning, the situation is perhaps not all that different. As follows, I analyse how the various legal systems deal with the same problem. The overall question is: How do courts within these different jurisdictions handle *Mahr* in divorce settlements between spouses who have married in accordance with Muslim laws, but who live in Europe?

3.3 The Method of Comparative Law

"The basic methodological principle of all comparative law is that of functionality. From this basic principle stem all the other rules which determine the choice of laws to be compared, the scope of the undertaking, the creation of a system of comparative law, and so on. Incomparables cannot usefully be compared, and in law *the only things which are comparable are those which fulfil the same function.*" (Zweigert 1998: 34, my italics) This is indeed valid as long as one studies concepts, although slightly less so when one studies judgments. The Swedish scholar in comparative and private international law,

Michael Bogdan, maintains that "[f]or a comparison to be meaningful, the two objects of the comparison must share some common type of characteristics, which can serve as the common denominator. (…) Within comparative law, one is normally interested in comparing the substantive contents of the legal rules, or more specifically, how the various legal systems regulate a certain situation that arises in both of the countries. (…) When comparing legal rules from different countries, one should consequently strive to compare such rules which regulate the same situations in people's lives." (Bogdan 1994: 58-59) There are no rules in Scandinavian, British or French law that deal with *Mahr* directly, which is what makes it so interesting to study. There are rules of private international law, but as we will see later in this article, it is often unclear how concepts that are totally foreign should be qualified and interpreted. The main object of this study is thus how the *courts*, as the ultimate interpreter of a country's laws, handle "a certain situation". The case studies selected for the purpose of this study all concern the division of property in connection with divorce, and the interpretation of the *Mahr* clause in Muslim marriage contracts within a European context. Important human rights issues are at stake at the intersection between gender justice and minority rights. There are some minor differences. For example, the French cases never concern a direct claim to *Mahr*, only choice of property regime – of which *Mahr* is considered an indicator. However, the situational context is very much the same in all the judgments, thus providing comparable objects for my analysis; the judgments "share some common type of characteristics, which can serve as the common denominator" as mentioned above.

Kötz and Zweigert distinguish between *microcomparison*, which concerns specific legal institutions or problems and *macrocomparison*, which focuses on methods of thought, techniques of legislation and similar (Zweigert 1998: 4-6). For the purposes of this article, I take these two categories to be parallel, to a certain extent, to the situational and cultural contexts, respectively. The main focus is however on the former: How do the courts interpret the Muslim legal concept of *Mahr*? It is, however, seldom possible to carry out a good comparison without using both; macrocomparison of e.g. general policies provides a basis for the microcomparison of the adjudication of *Mahr*.

3.4 The Relationship between Comparative Law and Private International Law

Comparative law is essential for private international law, in that it provides tools for understanding the two legal systems and their concepts in relation to one another, and also in the application of the foreign law indicated by the conflict rules of the home system, when foreign terms have to be converted into the language of the court. The only way of doing this is to compare the rules and concepts of both systems. Comparative law is also essential for the proper treatment of the concept of *ordre public*: when the result of a foreign rule is considered so alien or unjust that the domestic court is unwilling to apply it, even if it should according to a conflict of laws rule (Zweigert 1998: 7). It is necessary to understand the foreign rules thoroughly before one can determine whether they will give a result contrary to *ordre public* in a particular case.

3.5 The Use of Comparative Legal Method in this Article

Comparative law is essential when dealing with legal pluralism. A basic rule in comparative law is to compare the *function* of the rules and concepts in question. The most natural choice of a method of approach in order to understand the Muslim norms in question is therefore the comparative legal method. In this article, the comparative legal method is used to understand the norms concerning *Mahr* in their Muslim contexts, but with more emphasis on the *functions* of *Mahr* than the comparison. Comparative law is also used in the comparison of the judgments and in the analysis of the courts' handling of the foreign norms. The comparative legal method is a necessity when the courts deal with legal pluralism, in order for them to understand and apply the norms in question correctly. When the courts have to deal with matters of private international law, comparative legal method seems to be the best tool also for determining the contents of the Muslim laws in question. If the choice of laws rules determine that a claim for *Mahr* is governed by the European laws in question, comparative legal method is every bit as important in order to interpret the claim and adjudicate it within that same European legal system.

The comparative legal method should provide the courts with a way to follow the approach used by the a group appointed by the Churches' Committee for Migrants in Europe in the 80s in a major effort to find ways to bridge the gap between the Muslim immigrants and the majority populations: to focus on the functions of the foreign laws, not their ideological basis (Nielsen in Foblets 1996: 41). Whether they use it, and if so, how, is looked into in the analysis of the international private law cases selected for the purpose of this study. The overall purpose of my analysis is to discuss the assumption underlying this article: that the courts must apply comparative legal method in order to provide a foundation for making a correct and fair decision; if they don't, they won't be able to achieve a fair result in terms of gender justice. When I try to determine whether the courts apply the method of comparative law, I focus on whether they try and investigate the functions of *Mahr* in a

Muslim legal context compared to the concepts and rules with similar functions in the European legal system. On the basis of information in the judgments themselves I have also paid attention to the sources the courts use as basis for their comparison.

4 The Judgments

4.1 Introduction

Having presented the framework for the analysis and given a brief overview of the most relevant rules of private international law, I shall now present the judgments that constitute the objects of analysis. In Scandinavia there has been no case concerning *Mahr* in the Supreme Courts, while the judgments from France and England are from the Court of Cassation and the High Court respectively. The cases are few, from all of the countries in question. The reason why the English judgments are so old and few, is the enactment in 1973 of the Domicile and Matrimonial Proceedings Act, now section 44(2) of the Family Law Act 1986. This act came in part as a reaction to Qureshi v. Qureshi, and severely limited the courts' opportunity to recognize foreign divorces, and thus also the number of private international law cases concerning *Mahr* (Pearl and Menski 1998: 384 ff). As to the other countries, we do not know the reason why there is only such a small number of cases.

4.2 The Norwegian Judgments

4.2.1 Mr Q. versus Mrs K: RG 1983 page 1021

The first judgment concerns the Muslim marriage contract; whether it implies a choice of laws regulating the matrimonial property, or a choice of matrimonial property regime. Mr Q. and Mrs K. married in Pakistan in 1975, with the intention of settling in Norway afterwards. The first joint domicile was therefore in Norway. The parties separated in 1979, and the husband claimed that the couple by signing a Pakistani Muslim marriage contract with a clause of "dower", i.e. *Mahr*, had agreed that Pakistani law should regulate the financial effects of the marriage, alternatively that the marriage contract was an equivalent to a marriage settlement[10] stipulating separate estates as the matrimonial property regime plus the payment of dower. The wife responded that Norwegian law was applicable to the settlement, since Norway was their first joint domicile, and that the signed marriage contract only implied the parties'

10. Norwegian: *ektepakt.*

consent to marry and the obligation of dower. She seems not to have claimed *Mahr*, as this probably would have meant that she accepted that the matrimonial property regime was that of separate estates. The court held that since the first and only joint domicile was in Norway, and the matrimonial property in its entirety had been acquired during their residence in Norway, Norwegian law was applicable and the matrimonial settlement court[11] thus had jurisdiction. The Pakistani form of marriage contract was not considered a sufficient basis for stating that the couple had chosen Pakistani law to regulate their marriage or matrimonial property regime.

4.2.2 Mrs A versus Mr B: LE-1986-447

Mrs A and Mr B married in Pakistan in 1960, and had a daughter who was born in 1962. Mr B lived in Oslo from 1975. Since 1985 he had been living on social security benefits. In 1983 he married F, who joined him in Norway in 1987. She had no income at the time of the judgment. Mrs A was assumed to be living in the house the couple lived in together in Karachi. Since 1986 she had accumulated a large debt to her brother, who had maintained her and their daughter D from then on. Mrs A claimed that there had been no rupture of the relationship; that she had not consented to the second marriage, which therefore should be pronounced invalid. She claimed that her husband had not paid her dower, but not that he should pay it. Her lawyer only claimed maintenance, with reference to the Marriage Act section 56(2),[12] which concerns the duty of maintenance, and the Norwegian Spouses' Act[13] section 3, which sets forth the enforceability of this duty. The dower is mentioned only as part of the woman's supposed financial resources. The result, "under doubt", as the court states, was that the wife got no maintenance, but this was in part due to the husband's economic situation. This judgment can be said to be of a rather poor quality, the court neither having ensured that it had the necessary facts before adjudicating nor mentioning private international law at all.

11. *Skifteretten.*
12. Lov om indgaaelse og opløsning av egteskap av 31.mai 1918 nr. 02 (Ekteskapsloven av 1918).
13. Lov om ektefellers formuesforhold av 20. mai 1927 nr. 01 (Ektefelleloven).

4.3 The Swedish Judgments

4.3.1 Mr S. versus Mrs S: T137-92 and RH 1993: 116[14]

Mr S and Mrs S. were both Palestinian citizens of Israel. They got married in Israel, and lived together there for a few months before Mr S. returned to Sweden, his country of residence. Not long after his return, in March 1988,[15] Mrs S. arrived in Sweden to join her husband. They lived together for about five months in Sweden before the marriage irretrievably broke down and she went back to Israel. Mr S. petitioned for divorce in October 1988. Mrs S. countered this by demanding that he pay *Mahr*[16] amounting to NIS [17] 11,250[18] plus maintenance during the divorce proceedings and for three months after the completion of the proceedings (the '*idda* period of three menstrual cycles). She further claimed the dispute should be solved according to the Ottoman Family Code of 1917, which is used for Muslims in Israel. Mr S. claimed it should be solved according to Swedish law, and that *Mahr* is a concept alien to Swedish law and that it in any case is in conflict with the Swedish *ordre public*. The municipal court gave the wife the right to *Mahr*, in accordance with Israeli Muslim family law, and saw this as not contrary to Swedish *ordre public*, but rather as a kind of maintenance after divorce, and did not grant her maintenance during the divorce proceedings and the ʿ*idda*. The court of appeal upheld the judgment on all major points.

4.3.2 Mrs M. versus Mr A: T952-99 and RH 2005: 66[19]

Mr A. had never been back to Iran after coming to Sweden in 1986, but had kept his Iranian citizenship in addition to his Swedish citizenship. He married his cousin, Mrs M, in July 1998 by giving her mother authority to negotiate and sign the marriage contract on his behalf. The couple spent ten days together in Cyprus in August 1998, and then went back to their respective countries. Mrs M. was granted leave to go to Sweden by the Swedish and Iranian authorities in December 1998. According to the husband, he started investigations since she postponed the departure without giving any reasons,

14. Malmö tingsrätt 1992-02-10 and Hovrätten över Skåne och Blekinge. I have not been able to obtain a copy of the entire municipal court (*tingsrätt*) judgment, so my analysis is based upon the parts that are quoted in the court of appeal judgment.
15. The remaining facts indicate that there must be a typing error, the judgment says 1989.
16. *Mahr* is in this judgment called *mohar*, which is the Hebrew term for *Mahr*. O. Spies on *Mahr* in *Encyclopaedia of Islam* online, read 17.06.2008.
17. New Israeli Shekel or ILS
18. In 1993 equivalent to approximately 4,200 USD.
19. Halmstads tingsrätt 2002-10-24 and Hovrätten för Västra Sverige 2004-11-22.

and found that she had a relationship with another man. She went to Sweden in January 1999, and stayed with Mr A.'s sister. He there announced that he wanted to divorce her, but she was the one who went to court to claim divorce with payment of *Mahr*. At the time of the court of appeal's judgment, she was still living in Sweden, illegally since her residence permit expired in June 1999. He claimed not to be bound by the *Mahr* clause in the marriage contract, or that he had already paid the equivalent in the form of *shir baha*.[20] He wanted the court to use Swedish law in solving the case; she wanted the court to use Iranian law. The dispute is whether the husband is under obligation to pay a *Mahr* amounting to 500 Bahar Azadi gold coins, the equivalent of which at the time was SEK 250,000.[21] The court sees Mr A. as bound by the actions of his chosen representative, and that he has not proven that he has already paid, and is thus seen as obliged to pay the full sum of SEK 250,000 to Mrs M.

4.3.3 Mrs G-A. versus Mr T: T2624-04 and T10083-04[22]

Mr T., residing in Sweden, married Mrs G-A. by giving her authority to act upon his behalf. The marriage contract contained a clause of *Mahr*; 800 Bahar Azadi gold coins should be payable upon demand, determined by Mrs G-A. on his authority. Mrs G-A. arrived in Sweden in September 2001 and was still in Sweden at the time of adjudication, but the couple never lived together. Mrs G-A. was at the time of adjudication residing illegally in Sweden. She wanted the clause of *Mahr* enforced by the court, while the husband pleaded that she had acted outside the authority he had given her.

The municipal court simply stated that the act concerning financial effects of marriage in private international law (Act 1990: 272 LIMF) should be applied when there is no written agreement on the choice of laws, without interpreting *Mahr* or making any kind of qualification or investigation into Iranian law. Referring to the *travaux préparatoires* the court stated that the couple

20. This is an Iranian custom where the groom gives the bride's mother money to buy furniture etc. for the couple's new residence (Mir-Hosseini 2000: 74).
21. The couple never really lived together, and the judgment does not clearly state whether the marriage was consummated, although this is likely since they spent time together in Cyprus after the marriage. The question concerning the payment of *Mahr* in marriages that have not been consummated remains, as far as I know, open in a Scandinavian context. The French judgment from the Cour d'appel de Douai, ch.7, 8 January 1976 seems to open up the possibility of a total refund, but this may depend on the situation. In Muslim laws the wife is normally entitled to half the dower in such cases.
22. Uppsala tingrätt 2nd December 2004 and Svea Hovrätt 20th December 2005.

has been residing in Sweden for two years, which is what the law puts down as required to obtain a joint domicile, and that Swedish law therefore should be applied, even though the couple had not lived together. Since only a third party can act on authority between two people, the *Mahr* clause was not considered valid, and therefore unenforceable. The decision was upheld in the court of appeal on all major points.

There is a discrepancy in the last two judgments as to what it takes to be considered as domiciled in Sweden. In both cases the women were residing illegally in Sweden after the divorce, but in one she was considered as domiciled in Sweden, in the other, not. The result was that Iranian law was applied in one case, Swedish in the other. For the purposes of this article this is only relevant in that the concept of *Mahr* and rules concerning it are neither qualified nor interpreted in any other way in T2624-04 and T10083-04, only in T952-99 and RH 2005: 66, so the discussion of which judgment is the most correct one has to be left aside for now.

4.4 The French Judgments

4.4.1 Mrs K. versus Mr T. – "the Paris case" [23]

Mrs K. and Mr T. had lived together in Paris from 1969. Mrs K. was a Polish citizen; Mr T. was Lebanese of the Greek Catholic confession.[24] Mr T. was already married to a Lebanese woman, whom he long ago had ceased to live with. According to Lebanese law, however, his personal status was governed by the Lebanese laws for his religious community,[25] which in this case meant that he could not get a divorce. The only way the couple could marry was if he converted to Islam, and they married in Lebanon according to Muslim rites. Then he could take a "second wife" without having to divorce the first one. So they did, and the marriage certificate stipulated a deferred dower of 3,000 Lebanese pounds.[26]

This case does not concern the wife claiming *Mahr*, but rather the choice of property regime. *Mahr* is in the Court of Appeal and in the Court of Cassation seen as an indicator of the choice of the regime of separate estates, in French courts assumed to be the regime of all Muslim marriages. The Municipal Court pronounced a divorce following the French *régime legal,* com-

23. Cour d'Appel de Paris, 2e ch., no.4, 14th June 1995 and Cour de Cassation, ch.civ.1, 2nd December 1997.
24. Family law matters and similar issues are in Lebanon regulated by the law of the confession you (or your ancestors) belong to.
25. This is still the case today, and no civil marriage exists.
26. 918 USD in 1970.

munity of after-acquired property, where the wife was accorded the usufruct of an apartment and a monthly alimony of 6000 FF. In the Court of Appeal the husband claimed that the marriage should be considered as void as he was married to another woman at the time when he married Mrs K, that the consequences of this should be regulated by French law, and that the property regime was the Muslim one of separate estates, as indicated by the clause on *Mahr*, and that the liquidation of property should follow Lebanese law. The wife claimed a divorce based on the fault of the husband, that the division of property should follow French law, an allowance of 720,000 FF and the ownership of their marital home. The marriage was declared void on the basis of bigamy, using Polish law, Mrs K. still retaining her Polish citizenship[27] at the time of marrying, but since both were in good faith, the economic consequences were still valid. Since Mrs K. had signed the Muslim marriage contract, and the French *régime legal* can only be assumed if the couple did not agree on a different regime, the matrimonial regime of this marriage is considered by the court to be the Muslim regime of separate estates. This case was adjudicated by the Court of Appeal of Paris, and I will use the term "the Paris case" when I refer to it later on.

4.4.2 Mr H. versus Mrs R. – "the Lyon case"[28]

Mr H. and Mrs R., a Muslim couple of Indian origin, married in Karikal, a former French colony in India, in 1969. Shortly afterwards they took up residence in France, where they divorced in 1990. The issue at stake in this case as well was how the financial settlement should be done, focusing on the choice of matrimonial regime. As in the Paris case, the wife claimed a division of property following the French *régime legal*; the husband claimed that there was a valid agreement on the adoption of the regime of separate estates: the marriage contract from India which contained a clause concerning *Mahr*. The first Court of Appeal judgment does not really address the question of *Mahr*, only states that the division of property shall happen in accordance with the French *régime legal*. The Court of Cassation says that the Court of Appeal should have investigated whether the payment of *Mahr* indicated that a Muslim marriage, *nikah*, had been contracted, as this would mean that the couple had chosen Muslim law to regulate their marriage. According to the

27. French private international law has nationality as basis for determining a person's personal status law. See chapter 4.
28. Cour d'Appel de Lyon, 1996-01-11, Cour de Cassation, ch.civ.1, 7th April 1998, Cour d'appel de Lyon, ch.civ.1, 2nd December 2002 and Cour de Cassation, ch.civ.1, 22nd November 2005.

Court of Cassation, the regime of separate estates is the only one accepted by Muslim law. When the Court of Appeal treats the matter again, *Mahr* is then seen as the sale price of the woman, but this view as well is annulled by the Court of Cassation. All judgments except for the last two were in favour of the wife; the final result was an acceptance of *Mahr* and the *nikah* as indicators of the choice of the Muslim property regime, the husband thus winning through with almost all of his claims. I have studied both of the Court of Cassation judgments, and the Court of Appeal judgment between the two. I have not been able to get a copy of that last judgment, nor the first Court of Appeal judgment, but according to the husband's lawyer, the result was in accordance with the last Court of Cassation judgment: the couple was considered to have adopted the regime of separate estates.[29]

4.5 The English Judgments

4.5.1 Shahnaz versus Rizwan [1965]

Mrs Shahnaz and Mr Rizwan married in India in 1955 in accordance with Muslim law, but were residing in England at the time of litigation, since when is not specified. The husband filed for divorce in 1959 and the wife subsequently claimed the recovery of £1,400 in deferred *Mahr*. The whole case concerns a preliminary issue: whether or not the claim on *Mahr* is within the jurisdiction of English courts. It is from the Queen's Bench division of the High Court, which in this case seems to be the court of first – and last – instance. The wife claimed *Mahr* "on the ground that the claim was a lawful contractual one enforcing a proprietary right arising out of a lawful contract of marriage." The husband claimed that "the marriage was polygamous or potentially polygamous and that the English court has no jurisdiction over, or should not extend jurisdiction to, the wife's claim, since the provision in the marriage contract relied on was in consideration of a polygamous or potentially polygamous marriage; alternatively that the claim was in the form of matrimonial relief; in the further alternative that the claim was unenforceable since the contract of marriage and the dower provision was contrary to the policy and good morals of English law." (Shahnaz v. Rizwan pp. 390-391) Moreover, according to English law at the time, any effect, whether personal or financial, of what was seen as a "polygamous marriage" – including "potentially polygamous marriages" – was beyond the jurisdiction of English courts.[30]

29. Conversation with the husband's lawyer, Maître Courjon, January 16, 2008.
30. For many years, and at the time of *Shahnaz* and *Qureshi*, English law regarded marriages contracted under a system that permits polygamy as "polygamous" – even if

The result was not that the woman received *Mahr*, as the court only adjudicates upon whether or not it has jurisdiction, it was that English courts *have* jurisdiction. The only way to reach that decision without overruling the precedence on so-called "polygamous marriages" was to qualify it as something other than an effect of marriage, i.e. an obligation based on a pre-nuptial agreement. One might say that the entire case is about the qualification of *Mahr*; although, as far as I can see, the court does interpret the concept of *Mahr* in greater depth than is strictly necessary here. Thus questions such as how *Mahr* should further be interpreted and its relation to British public policy[31] are touched upon.[32]

4.5.2 Qureshi versus Qureshi [1972]

The husband, a Pakistani citizen, and the wife, an Indian citizen, got married in Britain on 9 March 9 1966 and had lived there since. The marriage ceremony was conducted in Britain at the Kensington Register Office. "This was followed by a further ceremony in accordance with Muslim rites; but it is common ground that the register office ceremony constituted a legal marriage and that the subsequent religious ceremony had no legal significance." (Qureshi v. Qureshi p. 186.) It was probably during the religious ceremony that *Mahr* was agreed upon, but the judgment does not provide any direct information upon this matter. The marriage did not work out very well and they separated in June, the same year. The wife obtained a weekly allowance of maintenance at the Magistrates Court on the basis of "persistent cruelty and desertion" by the husband. The husband divorced her by sending a letter dated 27 April 1967 which contained the phrase "I divorce you" three times.

the marriage in fact was and had always been monogamous. The matter was further confused with the use of the sub-category "potentially polygamous" for *de facto* monogamous marriages. Duties between man and wife, arising from their being so, were considered, based on the judgment Hyde v Hyde and Woodmansee (1866), to be outside the jurisdiction of English courts. "Polygamous" marriages were thus denied matrimonial relief by the English courts, but the marriages were considered valid for tax and legitimacy purposes. Today the marriage of a person domiciled in Britain, who has married in a country where polygamy is permitted, is normally considered valid for the spouses to be able to seek matrimonial relief for example, provided the marriage is *de facto* monogamous. There are exceptions, but none that concern the matter of this article (Balchin (2006) pp. 7 and 41-46). For more information, see Balchin, Poulter (1986) p. 47 ff or the judgment Hyde v Hyde.

31. The concept in British law that is the closest to *ordre public.*
32. Whether these deliberations should be reckoned as *obiter dicta*, and the further evaluation of their value as precedent is beyond my knowledge to comment upon.

Reconciliation was sought via mediation by counsel and head of chancery at the London Office of the High Commissioner for Pakistan, Tabarak Husain, in accordance with Pakistani law, before the divorce was pronounced to be absolute 90 days after the wife was notified, on 1 August 1967.

The case cited is from the Probate Division of the High Court. The wife's principal claim is that the marriage subsists and that the husband continues to provide maintenance. Alternatively, if the marriage has been validly dissolved, she claims a dower of £788 33s 5d plus maintenance of £5 a week. The main question in the case is where the couple was domiciled and thereby which laws should govern the case in determining the validity of the divorce; although, this is also the second of the two judgments that provide the basis for case law on *Mahr*. The divorce was found to be valid, which proved rather controversial as it was a divorce by repudiation that had taken place on British soil.[33] As a result, the husband's cross-prayer that the court had no jurisdiction to adjudicate upon the claim for *Mahr* had to be considered. I shall concentrate on the parts of the judgment that concern this matter.

A significant difference between the Shahnaz and the Qureshi judgments is that, in Shahnaz, the wife was excluded from seeking ancillary relief on the basis that the marriage was considered potentially polygamous, while in the case of Qureshi the marriage was considered monogamous so the wife could seek ancillary relief. As the husband was planning to return to Pakistan, the only realistic way for the wife to get any money after the divorce, as the court saw it, was through *Mahr*, as this would be easier to enforce by English courts than any ancillary relief.

5 *Mahr* and the Comparative Legal Method in European Courts

5.1 Introduction

The focus in this article is on the courts' approaches in dealing with Muslim laws in a gender justice perspective. My hypothesis is, as mentioned earlier, that in order to handle Muslim laws in private international law cases the

33. As mentioned, this case was a major reason behind the enactment of the Domicile and Matrimonial Proceedings Act 1973, which severely limited the courts' opportunity and also their duty to recognize foreign divorces through giving a number of public policy grounds for refusing to recognize such. This was an effort to protect the wives from being left with nothing at divorce, since the English laws of maintenance were not applicable in cases where a foreign divorce was recognized (Pearl and Menski1998: 384-385)

court should apply a gender equality norm of equal worth, while it needs to apply comparative legal method in order to interpret these laws correctly. In this section, I will look at the use, or absence of use, of the comparative legal method, firstly in the qualification process, in interpreting the claim for *Mahr* in terms of domestic law when Muslim laws are not applied. In the next section I will look at the use, or absence of use, of gender justice norms; and in section 8 I will look at both together. I shall finish by saying something about the limits of what can be learned from this study, and what I believe merits further investigation.

5.2 The Qualification of *Mahr*

Muslim laws don't distinguish between personal and financial effects of marriage. *Mahr* has elements of both, plus contractual elements. This explains some of the difficulties European courts have when they qualify, interpret and apply the concept of *Mahr*. In the Norwegian judgments, *Mahr* cannot be said to be qualified at all, and in France it is the Muslim marriage contract rather than *Mahr* which is qualified. In France, the doctrine is to qualify *lex fori*; this is also the majority view in Norwegian law. Thue maintains that in cases concerning *Mahr* and other concepts that don't exist in Norwegian law, the Muslim laws in question should be applied to determine which category of conflict of laws rules the court should apply, in practice a qualification *lex causae* therefore (Thue 2002: 395). It is thus not certain what the result should be in Norwegian law. In the remainder judgments, *Mahr* is qualified *lex fori*, even though *Mahr* is a foreign concept to all the European courts studied.

The only country in this study where the qualification is very clear and discussed by the court in explicit terms is Sweden. It seems likely that this is due (at least in part) to the fact that Sweden is the only country that has an act on the matter,[34] the *travaux préparatoires* of which, Prop. 1989/90: 87, designates two options for the qualification of the payment of a lump sum between spouses. It takes the form of either a redistribution of property or maintenance, i.e. either a financial or a personal effect of marriage.

Both English and French courts rely on jurisprudence to determine the contents of the rules concerning qualification, the French ones also rely upon the Hague convention on the law applicable to matrimonial property regimes of 1978.[35] French law does not classify the financial effects of the marriage as

34. *Lag* (1990: 272) *om internationella frågor rörande makars och sambors förmögenhetsförhållanden* (LIMF).

35. The UK is also a party to this convention, but the English judgments came into being long before this convention entered into force on 1 September 1992.

part of the family law, but of the law of obligations. On the one hand, this distinguishes between the financial and personal effects of marriage, a distinction that does not exist in Muslim laws, and thus emphasises the difference between the legal systems. On the other hand, this may allow French law to pick up more of the obligation law aspects of Muslim marriage, and is perhaps closer to the notion of Muslim marriage contracts than financial effects of marriage are in Swedish law, for example.

The Swedish solution implies a qualification *lex fori* with very limited options, which may narrow the options of qualification down so much that it could lead to incorrect results and provide an erroneous basis for the further interpretation of the foreign concept and laws, particularly with respect to concepts that are very different from those in Swedish law. Therefore, while clear legislation makes the courts more aware of the qualification process, it can at the same time lead to a situation where the court finds itself barred from the best approach, e.g. the application of comparative legal method in the case of concepts that are entirely foreign to the European legal system. Although rules based upon principles and jurisprudence may be more flexible, they are more difficult to apply, demand a high degree of awareness and knowledge from the courts and lawyers, and may lead to more unpredictable results.

Sayed argues, *de lege ferenda*, for a new private international law rule in using *lex loci contractus* – the law of the country where *Mahr* was agreed upon – in cases concerning *Mahr* (Sayed 2008: 206-207). His main argument is that this is applicable as a general principle and therefore a practical solution. He further maintains that this approach will supposedly be "in line with the spouses' intention on the matter of the applicable law at the time of signing the contract", and that this would "better fulfil the objectives of *Mahr* agreement in every specific case". He admits that this solution may have weaknesses in relation to spouses who change residence and stay in Europe for a very long time. The original purpose of *Mahr*, which he considers to be "a safeguard within marriage or against divorce", "may not be enforceable (or meaningful) after a long residence in the new country". He proposes to use the *ordre public* reservation in such cases. One weakness in his reasoning is that *Mahr* has many purposes and functions, which vary with the type of *Mahr* and other circumstances in each case; a redistribution of property is only one of them. Another weakness is that it is not at all clear whether the *ordre public* reservation could be used in such cases as it takes quite a lot to refuse the enforcement of a foreign rule on this basis. His solution has some similarities with the French one, although French courts see *Mahr* rather as an indication of which property regime is chosen. As we have seen, this solution has received a great deal of criticism, the most thorough – and knowledgeable – criticism is from Marie-Claude Najm Najm, (2006). Her main point is that, when it comes to laws based upon religion, one has to be careful of assuming that there is an explicit choice of matrimonial regime that can be read out of the choice of marriage rites. She proposes that if no clearly formulated, written agreement is made, the law of the first common domicile should be applied – as was done in the last of the Swedish cases (T2624-04 and T10083-04). Another argument against Sayed's solution is that one cannot isolate one legal effect of a marriage contract, i.e. *Mahr*, thus the entire contract must be considered enforceable, with the reservations of *ordre public* only. This would create a situation similar to the one in countries that apply the nationality principle, where the couple may, after residing in Europe for decades, nevertheless find themselves bound by the laws of the Muslim country they originate from, or even only contracted the marriage in. This solution has been criticised in a study by Foblets, on the basis of interviews with a large number of Muslim women residing in Belgium. A major finding in her study is that Muslim women who know both sets of rules prefer the European solution, which in most cases is more favourable for them. Foblets, as well as Najm, is of the opinion that the law of the first common domicile should be applied if no written agreement between the spouses is provided (Foblets (2005) pp. 307-308, Najm (2006) p. 1373), which is the rule set forth in the Hague convention on the law applicable to matrimonial property regimes of 14th March 1978, article 4 and the main rule in Swedish and Norwegian law.

Both in France and England, the judgments seem to build upon each other regarding the qualification of *Mahr* or the Muslim marriage contract; there is no indication that the qualifications are inconsistent. The only exception is the French Court of Appeal in the Lyon case, which repeatedly wanted to qualify *Mahr* differently from the Paris case (and perhaps more correctly) but was overruled by the Court of Cassation. Remarkably, *Mahr* is qualified in two different ways in the Swedish judgments, even though the factual situations are fairly similar. In all three cases, the marriages were very short and the husband was resident in Sweden while the wife moved to Sweden from the couple's country of origin. This solution is interesting in that it allows for different qualifications and therefore also interpretations depending on the situation in each case. Bogdan proposes that this may be a correct way of qualifying *Mahr*: a prompt *Mahr* is seen as a redistribution of property, while a deferred *Mahr* is seen as maintenance (Bogdan 2007) pp. 184-185). I fear, though, that Bogdan's qualification based on the differences between prompt and deferred dower is based upon a misconception. Bogdan sees prompt *Mahr* as being paid either at the time of marriage or on demand, although it is a deferred *Mahr* which must be paid upon demand, at the latest at the dissolution of the marriage by death or divorce. However, this may not cause any problems in practice as a deferred *Mahr* is very rarely claimed before the dissolution of marriage, as this is seen as an indication that the marriage is not going well (WLUML 2003: 181).

Mahr can have so many functions that it may be a good solution to be open to different qualifications and interpretations. This is a way of admitting stronger elements of the comparative legal method into the process of qualification while at the same time maintaining *lex fori* as a basis for it. It creates the possibility of taking various functions of the concept into consideration, and that the concept may have different functions in different situations. The actual method of qualification is closer then to what is sometimes called the private international law method, see section 4.1. A problem that then arises is that the results are unpredictable. However, as Najm states in her thesis: While an inequitable result is most often unpredictable by the parties, since they will not have been able to adapt, the contrary is not necessarily the case; an unpredicted result is not always inequitable (Najm 2005 note 242 on pp.360-361). Potentially relevant variables for the qualification are the duration of the marriage in question, the type of *Mahr*, its size, and the financial and other circumstances of the couple concerned. The actual phrasing in the laws of the Muslim country in question is likely to play an important part, as these are bound to differ, see for example the Swedish judgments, and not only on the basis of which law school is predominant in the area.

5.3 The Use of Comparative Law in the Interpretation of *Mahr* and Muslim Laws

Surprisingly, it is in the oldest judgments that the courts are apparently the most thorough and capable in application of the comparative legal method. According to Kötz and Zweigert, the French Court of Cassation "has adopted a style of judgment which precludes any reference to considerations of sociology, legal history, policy or comparative law," while the English courts have a reputation of using a completely different approach, applying foreign law and comparative legal method to a considerable extent (Zweigert 1998: 19). My investigations confirm these views. The Norwegian courts don't seem to have really discovered the comparative legal method, while in Sweden things have noticeably improved from 1993 to 2005. In all the judgments, the degree of misinterpretation of the Muslim laws in question seems to be directly related to the lack of use of the comparative legal method.

5.4 The Various Interpretations and Functions of *Mahr*

5.4.1 Introduction

As mentioned, *Mahr* is qualified and interpreted in a variety of ways: as maintenance or a personal effect of marriage, as redistribution of property or a financial effect of marriage, and as Common Law consideration for entering into a Muslim marriage contract. In the French Court of Cassation judgments, it is viewed as an indicator of the choice of matrimonial property regime. The functions of *Mahr* and the subsequent interpretation of it in a European context depend on the circumstances of each case. Additionally, the concepts of the *lex fori* shape the interpretation of *Mahr,* particularly through the qualification process. As comparative legal method is to a small extent applied in the judgments that I have studied, these concepts have a strong influence on the courts' further interpretation of the Muslim laws in question too. However, some interpretations are more correct than others and in this section I shall present and evaluate the various interpretations of *Mahr* in the judgments studied, in relation to the courts' use of comparative legal method.

5.4.2 Mahr *as maintenance*

It is clear that *Mahr* is not a kind of maintenance in the terms of Muslim laws, but this does not mean that to interpret it as such in a European context is wrong. The actual function of *Mahr* may indeed be a kind of maintenance, when analysed through the comparative legal method. However, if the qualification of *Mahr* as maintenance is seen as a general principle, this may lead to a loss of rights for Muslim women at times, as was the case in the first Swedish judgment. In Islamic law, the woman has a right to maintenance during the *'idda,* the first three months after divorce, and in some Muslim countries the woman has a right to maintenance beyond this.[36] It is clear that the Swedish judgment is based on a misinterpretation of Muslim Israeli law and the court did not use the comparative legal method to investigate its contents.

Sayed upholds the example where the wife is a Swedish citizen and the husband domiciled in a Muslim country. According to Swedish jurisprudence, questions concerning maintenance are regulated by the personal status law of the person entitled to it. Suppose then that the woman is the one with the greatest wealth and income; is it still possible to talk of *Mahr* as a maintenance obligation? In Swedish law, maintenance is seen as aimed at meeting the recepient's needs, compensating for a low income or none at all. Should this not be the case, we cannot, according to Sayed, say that *Mahr* is mainte-

36. See e.g. the Tunisian Code du Statut Personnel.

nance in the Swedish sense (Sayed (2008) p. 202). Indeed, in Muslim laws, *Mahr* is the wife's right and property regardless of the economic circumstances of the spouse. Upon the husband's death, if it has still not been transferred to her then it is separated from the husband's estate prior to the wife's share of inheritance being calculated. If the complete rules concerning *Mahr* are to be practised in Europe, the outcome may at times actually be unfair to the husband. Nevertheless, this appears to be the exception thus far (Bano 2004: 251 ff). Even if *Mahr* can never be seen as maintenance in the sense of Swedish domestic law, this does not mean that *Mahr* may not be seen as maintenance in the private international law sense, especially if a comparative approach is used. As we saw in part 6.2, Bogdan is of the opinion that a deferred *Mahr* should be qualified in Swedish law as maintenance. Only a deferred *Mahr* should be qualified as maintenance, and then only if that is the approximate function it has in that particular case. Accordingly, a condition is that the husband is the one with the most money. Bogdan maintains that the qualification should be based on the circumstances at the time when the agreement was signed and not take later developments into account (Bogdan 2007: 184-185). Since the right to, and the amount of, maintenance can only be determined at the time of divorce, this may not be the best solution if *Mahr* is qualified as maintenance. If *Mahr* is qualified as a redistribution of property, however, it may be a different case.

5.4.3 Mahr *as a redistribution of property*

Another Swedish solution was to see *Mahr* as a redistribution of property between the spouses (RH 2005: 66). Again, the correctness of this depends (among other things) on the economic situation of the spouses in each case. In my opinion, it should be a requirement that *Mahr* is prompt. This is probably one of the objects of *Mahr* in Muslim laws, dating back to the Qur'an, and must *be* seen in relation to the absence of matrimonial property regimes in Muslim laws: there is no joint matrimonial property, but the husband is required to provide for his wife and their children. In this way, the woman has some property of her own, of which she disposes freely. Depending on the circumstances, a redistribution of property may also be a vital function of *Mahr* in a Muslim legal context, especially in situations where the woman has no paid work outside of the home. For a prompt *Mahr*, this solution often proves to be very good from a comparative legal perspective. In terms of which factors should be taken into consideration, I agree here with Bogdan, that only the circumstances at the time of signing the agreement are relevant; in any event, it is unlikely that much time has elapsed between this and the litigation.[37] Once more, it is a requirement that the husband is the wealthiest of the spouses.

5.4.4 Mahr *as consideration or sales price*

The interpretations of *Mahr* in Shahnaz and in the second Cour d'Appel de Lyon judgment have several features in common: both see Muslim marriage as very degrading for the woman, for which *Mahr* is a financial compensation. The French court goes farther in seeing *Mahr* as "the sales price a woman claims for herself when marrying" (Cour d'appel de Lyon, ch.civ.1, 2nd December 2002 p. 3), although in a comparative perspective, the function of consideration is not so different; in reality the sales price of an item will most often be the consideration for one of the parties in a sales contract. However, there is no requirement that consideration has the same value as the counter-performance (Cheshire (1996) p. 73 ff), thus the comparison has its limits. Compared to the function of *Mahr* in a Muslim legal system, the correctness of such an interpretation is uncertain. It is still debated in Muslim countries whether *Mahr* is the sales price of the woman's uterus, her virginity or something approaching this. Although the majority view is that it is not, the answer is not a given, due to the rights and duties that still follow from marriage in the majority of the Muslim countries. Nevertheless, this debate concerns the symbolic value of *Mahr* rather than its actual functions. It is therefore not an approach to be recommended from a comparative perspective. In these judgments, this interpretation seems to be based on erroneous assumptions about the nature of Muslim marriage in the English judgments and on a mistranslation of a custom certificate in the French Court of Appeal of Lyon judgment, the latter of which was actually repealed by the Court of Cassation on the basis of misinterpretation of the foreign law.

5.4.5 Mahr *as part of a pre-nuptial agreement*

When *Mahr* is qualified as part of a pre-nuptial agreement, which has many of the same functions as the French *contrat de mariage*, it is apparently considered to be within the parties' autonomy and it is the actual contract that is the main object of interpretation. An advantage of both interpretations is that

37. In Scandinavian law, a consequence of this interpretation might be that prompt *Mahr* is seen as part of the woman's own property and not part of the matrimonial property, which is divided equally upon divorce. A requirement might be that Muslim laws are applied on her right to *Mahr*, but Scandinavian law on the divorce settlement, however, the entire question merits a much more thorough discussion than space permits here.

they include some of the contractual aspects of Muslim marriage contracts, of which *Mahr* is a part. Contrary to the French concept, however, a pre-nuptial agreement is not seen as binding in English law, but as one indicator, among many, of the parties' intentions.[38] Another major difference between them is that in English law matrimonial property regimes exist mainly in private international law, while this is a major feature of French law on marriage. Najm criticises the French judgments for seeing the *Mahr* clause as an explicit choice of matrimonial property regime, i.e. that the Muslim marriage contract is an equivalent to the French *contrat de mariage,* while a better interpretation would have been to see it as one of several indicators of the spouses' implicit intentions, i.e. more in line with a pre-nuptial agreement in English law. Perhaps the most correct solution is that expressed by the Norwegian court in RG 1983 p.1021: the Muslim marriage contract with a clause of *Mahr* neither implies an explicit choice of matrimonial property regime, nor a choice of laws regulating the matter. Islam requires a marriage contract with a clause of *Mahr* for a marriage to be valid, as Najm quite rightly stated (Najm 2006: 1369 ff). In many Muslim countries, civil marriage doesn't even exist. On this matter, the comparative legal method, with its focus on the functions of a concept, and Nielsen's statement about the necessity of not taking the ideological background of the rules into consideration,[39] exclude an aspect that is vital for the understanding of the Muslim laws in question.

5.4.6 Other possible functions of Mahr *in European private international law*

There is no doubt that *Mahr* can be qualified and interpreted in other ways than those mentioned above, depending, among other things, on the specific circumstances in each case and the European legal system. One of the most interesting features of *Mahr* is that it has so many functions depending, for example, on the type of dower, the amount, and other circumstances in each case. In my opinion, one should not adopt only one qualification and interpretation of *Mahr*, as this may lead to erroneous and sometimes unfair results. In the following section, I shall further explore this, from a gender justice perspective.

38. See Blenkhorn (2002) concerning the effect of interpreting *Mahr* as a pre-nuptial agreement in US law.
39. See the introduction of this article.

6 *Mahr* and Gender Justice in European Courts

As stated in section 2, the CEDAW committee's views on *Mahr* seems to have developed from a rather mechanical gender equality approach which rejected *Mahr*, to an equal worth approach accepting *Mahr* as important for women in Muslim countries in a gender justice perspective. This may be interpreted as a move from principles to pragmatism. In the European judgments I have studied, the CEDAW is never mentioned, even in cases where the adjudication was conducted after its coming into force, nor are any other human rights obligations concerning gender equality. While the English courts have a more of an equal worth approach to the gender equality issue, the Swedish court in RH 1993: 116 is rather mechanical in its approach. This is not particularly surprising in terms of English judgments from the 1960s and 1970s, when the gender equality movement still only had limited influence on English courts, especially on issues such as these, even more so for the Swedish judgment from 1993. Of the two approaches, the equal worth approach appears to lead to a more equitable result for the woman involved. Nevertheless, the most striking discovery in this respect is that so few courts take gender justice into consideration in cases concerning *Mahr*: less than half of the cases studied. Gender justice is not an issue in any of the Norwegian and French cases, nor is it in the two most recent Swedish judgments. France has a monistic system with regard to treaties signed by the French state, this means that the CEDAW was part of French law at the time of adjudication of both the Lyon and the Paris case.

7 *Mahr*, Comparative Law and Gender Equality

7.1 Introduction

In this section, I shall look into questions concerning the interaction of the comparative legal method and gender equality approach as a final test of the hypothesis we started out with: that the courts must apply comparative legal method in order to provide a foundation for making a correct and fair decision, and that they also need to apply a gender justice norm of equal worth to obtain an equitable result when they apply Muslim laws. How do the comparative law and gender equality approaches interact? What happens if neither or only one of them is applied? What happens if both are?

7.2 When Neither a Comparative nor a Gender Justice Approach are Applied

In none of the French or Norwegian judgments did the courts use the method of comparative law or appear to make any effort to promote gender justice. In both of the French judgments, in the Swedish T10083-04 and in the Norwegian LE-1986-447, the outcome was that the women were left with either nothing or very little upon divorce, undoubtedly less than they had reason to expect. In all three cases, the Muslim laws and concepts in question must be said to have been misinterpreted by the European courts.

In RG 1983 p.1021, the issue was the same as in the French judgments: whether the Muslim marriage contract with a clause on *Mahr* expressed a choice of matrimonial property regime or a choice of laws regulating the effects of marriage. The court didn't have to interpret the Muslim laws in question, only the marriage contract, and seems to have applied common sense rather than comparative legal method. The result of this was that the marriage contract was seen as nothing more than an agreement to marry, in accordance with the wife's claims. Therefore, in this individual case, pragmatism and common sense seem to have done the job of both gender justice awareness and comparative legal method. With this exception, in addition to the Swedish case RH 2005: 66, the result in the remainder cases seems to have been rather inequitable towards the women concerned.

7.3 When a gender justice approach alone is applied

In the Swedish judgment RH 1993: 116, the court makes a particular effort to promote gender justice, to the point of reinterpreting case law. However, the method of comparative law is not used in attempts to interpret the Muslim laws in question; as a result, not only is the nature of *Mahr* misinterpreted, but the woman does not receive any maintenance during the *'idda*. In Swedish law, it takes time for a joint matrimonial estate to be established, prior to that each party takes from of the matrimonial estate only that which he or she brought into it. If the court had not made an effort to promote gender equality, the woman would probably have been left with nothing, as the marriage was so short. Nevertheless, if the court had applied comparative legal method and made a correct interpretation of the Muslim laws in question, she would have been awarded three months' maintenance in addition to *Mahr*. In this example, the result is thereby only partly favourable for the woman when a gender justice approach alone is applied, and a somewhat mechanical one at that.

7.4 When a Comparative Approach Alone is Applied

In the two other Swedish judgments, T10083-04 and RH 2005: 66, gender justice does not feature, although in the latter the court does apply comparative legal method to a certain degree. This is the only judgment where the equity of the result seems to be debatable from the point of view of the husband. He had to pay 250,000 Swedish kroner to the woman after a few months' marriage, the allegations that he was being used to obtain a residence permit in Sweden are not addressed by the courts, nor are the nature and limits of the authority he has given to his proxy. The reasons for this remain uncertain, in terms of whether the court simply wasn't thorough enough in its interpretation of Iranian law, the lack of gender justice approach in a man's favour, or other reasons. As the Canadian Professor in Sociology and Equity Studies in Education, Sherene Razack, has pointed out, there is a risk of essentialising and stereotyping too much, with the result that the Muslim woman is classified as a victim too often and the Muslim man as an offender, leaving no room for nuances and complexity (Razack 2008).[40] However, there is not enough information in this judgment to say whether this happened in this particular case.

7.5 When the Two are Applied in Combination

What happens, then, when the two approaches are applied in combination? There is only one judgment in this study where this was done in relation to *Mahr*: Shahnaz v. Rizwan. The other English judgment, Qureshi v. Qureshi, is based on this one in terms of the interpretation of *Mahr* and related rules, and cannot therefore shed any light upon the application of the two approaches together in relation to *Mahr*. Within the boundaries of the legal[41] and cultural[42] context of the judgment, the court makes a significant effort both to try to understand the Indian laws in question and to promote gender justice. Within the boundaries of its context, this undoubtedly appears to be the most equitable judgment, which is the most correct in terms of its outcome even if the reasoning behind it is less correct. However, owing to the legal reasoning and the views on Muslim marriage that it is based upon, the equity – and quality – of the case law derived from it remains questionable. It is surprising that no further case law on the matter has been published.

40. See also Phillips (2007), esp. chapter 3.
41. I.e. Hyde v. Hyde and other case law at the time.
42. I.e. the 1960s when orientalism was still a major feature of the world view in Western Europe, see e.g. Said (2004).

8 Conclusion

What can we learn from these judgments? Since there are so few, one must be cautious not to generalise too much from the discoveries,[43] although they may give some indication of how the courts could proceed to promote gender equality when they apply Muslim laws. As we saw in chapter 6, there seems to be a direct connection between the use of comparative legal method and the correctness of the interpretation of the foreign law. The Swedish examples showed that narrow options concerning the qualification of *Mahr* may lead to incorrect interpretations of the Muslim laws concerned, but also that it may be a good solution to allow for different qualifications and interpretations of *Mahr* depending on the type of *Mahr*, the Muslim laws in question and the circumstances in each case. This solution also enables a wider use of the comparative legal method and, since *Mahr* may have such a variety of functions, it may yield more correct results in each case. However, as seen with the French judgments and Najm's criticism of them, the religious aspect is vital for the full understanding of a Muslim marriage contract, and the comparative legal method with its focus on functionality does not take this into consideration.[44]

In terms of gender equality, it seems that the courts are not or to a very small degree aware of their positive duty to provide gender equality, and that gender equality is most frequently not an issue. It also seems that the most correct and equitable results are obtained when the courts use both a comparative approach and also try to actively promote gender equality in a wide sense, with a view to accommodating gender difference. This points to the potential of an equal worth standard that is sensitive to the social and cultural aspects of the laws in question, without going too far. As we saw in chapter 2, the CEDAW committee's views on *Mahr* seem to have developed from a rather me-

43. Pearl suggests that the lack of further case law on *Mahr* from Britain may be "to some extent due to pressure being placed on Muslim wives, or ex-wives as the case may be, not to approach English courts for relief of this kind." (Pearl 1998: 233) See also Schmied (1999), Foblets (1994) and Bano (2004). In Norwegian conflict of laws, it is the couple's *domicile* that determines which laws govern the legal effects of the marriage. This probably limits the number of cases where Muslim laws concerning *Mahr* should be applied, perhaps unless we see it as part of the wife's property in terms of the Norwegian Marriage Act of 1991 s66, but this needs further discussion.

44. See also Fournier (2007:. 303-304) where she states that the courts in trying not to get involved in religious matters, as a result "fail (...) to appreciate the richness and heterogeneity of both legal systems".

chanical gender equality approach that rejected *Mahr* to an equal worth approach or strategy accepting *Mahr* as important for women in Muslim countries, at least in some cases, and there is no doubt that this strategy is essential for promoting substantial gender equality in a whole range of situations.

It is noteworthy that in the few cases we have looked at, the tendency was that the Muslim women who had been in Europe for a while would rather have a settlement following European law. This is confirmed by the study by Marie-Claire Foblets mentioned in section 4.3, and should be taken into consideration when making rules of private international law. The trend now appears to be a move away from the nationality principle to the domicile principle in such matters, which has much to recommend to it, but this remains to be seen. This kind of policy is not, however, contradictory to the application of the gender equality norm of equal worth as a strategy when faced with real life situations in the courtroom; such a norm may be easier to use as a strategy for substantial equality in individual cases than when making laws that are applicable to everybody domiciled in the European country in question.

Still, to follow the recommendation of Spivak as described in section 2.2.2, there is a continuous need for deconstruction and critical analysis as well, which courts are perhaps not best positioned to do. Thus continuous research on gender issues in laws and judgments, which also takes ethnicity into consideration, is required, alongside a number of other issues. First, more knowledge is needed concerning the relationship between *talaq*, *Mahr* and other effects of Muslim marriage in relation to European human rights obligations and private international law; second, on the implementation of CEDAW in each state in relation to dealing with both strong and weak legal pluralism among minority groups, formally and substantially; third, on how to deal with the religious aspects of the norms in question, also in relation to human rights obligations in the intersection of freedom of religion and gender equality.

Bibliography

Ali, Shaheen Sardar, (2000) *Gender and human rights in Islam and international law*. The Hague: Kluwer Law International.

Annoussamy, David, (1998) 'Cour de Cassation (1ere Ch.civ.) – 7 avril 1998', in *Revue critique du droit international privé* 87 pp.644-651.

Balchin, Cassandra and Souhail Akbar Warraich, (2006) *Recognizing the Un-Recognized: Inter-Country Cases and Muslim Marriages & Divorces in Britain*. London: WLUML

Bano, Samia, (2004) *Complexity, difference and 'Muslim personal law': rethinking the relationship between Shariah Councils and South Asian Muslim women in Britain*, unpublished PhD thesis, University of Warwick.

Barnett, Hilaire, (1998) *Introduction to feminist jurisprudence*. London: Cavendish.

Bell, John... [*et al.*] (1998) *Principles of French law*. Oxford: Oxford University Press.

Blenkhorn, Lindsey E., (2002) 'Islamic marriage contracts in American courts: Interpreting *Mahr* agreements as prenuptials and their effect on Muslim women', in: *Southern California Law Review* November pp.189-234.

Bogdan, Michael, (1993) 'Islamisk brudpenning (*Mahr*) inför svensk domstol', in: Svensk juristtidning 7 pp.597-599.

Bogdan, Michael, (1994) *Comparative law*. Oslo: Tano.

Bogdan, Michael, (2004) *Svensk internationell privat- och processrätt*. 6. uppl. ed. Stockholm: Norstedts juridik.

Bogdan, Michael, (2007) 'Något om den kollitionsrättsliga behandlingen av islamisk morgongåva (*MAHR*)', in: *Rett og toleranse: festskrift til Helge Johan Thue: 70 år*. Oslo: Gyldendal akademisk.

Cheshire, G. C., M. P. Furmston and C. H. S. Fifoot, (1996) *Cheshire, Fifoot and Furmston's law of contract*. Oxford: Oxford University.

Foblets, Marie-Claire, (1994) 'Community Justice among immigrant family members in France and Belgium' in: *Law & Anthropology* VII, p.371 ff.

Foblets, Marie-Claire, (2005) 'Mobility versus Law, Mobility in the Law? Judges in Europe are Confronted with the Thorny Question "Which Law Applies to Litigants of Migrant Origin?"', in *Mobile people, mobile law: expanding legal relations in a contracting world.* Aldershot: Ashgate.

Fournier, Pascale, (2007) *Islamic Marriage in Western Liberal Courts: Beyond "Recognition", "Equality" and "Fairness"*. Unpublished PhD thesis, Harvard.

Frantzen, Torstein, (2002) *Arveoppgjør ved internasjonale ekteskap: studier i norsk internasjonal privatrett med særlig vekt på gjenlevende ektefelles rettsstilling*. Bergen: Fagbokforlaget

Griffiths, John, (1986) 'What is Legal Pluralism?', in *Journal of Legal Pluralism* 24, pp. 1-55.

Hellum, Anne, (2004) 'Se for dere et sammenfiltret kratt: omtale av to bøker om islams samspill med internasjonal og lokal rett, belyst gjennom kvinners stilling i Pakistan', in: *Retfærd* 107 p.46-56.

Hellum, Anne, (2007) *Human rights, plural legalities and gendered realities: paths are made by walking*. Harare, Zimbabwe: Weaver Press.

Mayer, Pierre, (1994) *Droit international privé*. Paris: Montchrestien.

Mehdi, Rubya, (2007) 'Danish law and the practice of *Mahr* among Muslim Pakistanis in Denmark', in: *Integration & retsudvikling*. København: Jurist- og Økonomforbundets Forlag.

Mir-Hosseini, Ziba, (2000) *Marriage on trial: Islamic family law in Iran and Morocco.* London: I.B. Tauris.

Mortensen, Ellen et al., (2008) *Kjønnsteori.* Oslo: Gyldendal akademisk.

Moss, Giuditta Cordero, (2007) 'Lovvalgsregler for internasjonale kontrakter: Tilsynelatende likheter og reelle forskjeller mellom europeiske og norske regler' In: Tidsskrift for Rettsvitenskap 5, pp.679-717.

Najm, Marie-Claude, (2005) *Principes directeurs du droit international privé et conflit de civilisations: Relations entre systèmes laïques et systèmes religieux*. Paris: Dalloz.

Najm, Marie-Claude, (2006) 'Conflit de lois.', in: *Journal du droit international* 4 (2006) pp.1365-1377.

Ncube, Welshman, (1989) *Comparative matrimonial property systems: the search for an equitable system of re-allocation of matrimonial property*. University of Oslo, Department of private law, stensilserie: Oslo.

Nielsen, Jørgen, (1996) 'Aux sources des revendications des musulmans en matière de droit de la famille en Europe', in: *Familles-Islam-Europe: Le droit confronté au changement – Musulmans d'Europe*. L'Harmattan: Paris.

Pearl, David S. and Werner Menski, (1998) *Muslim family law*. London: Sweet & Maxwell.

Phillips, Anne (2007) *Multiculturalism without culture*. Princeton, N.J.: Princeton University Press.

Poulter, Sebastian and Desmond de Silva, (1986) *English law and ethnic minority customs*. London: Butterworths.

Razack, Sherene H., (2008) *Casting out: the eviction of muslims from western law and politics*. Toronto: University of Toronto Press.

Said, Edward W., (2004) *Orientalismen: vestlige oppfatninger av Orienten*. Oslo: Cappelen.

Sayed, Mosa, (2008) 'The Muslim dower (*Mahr*) in Europe – with special reference to Sweden,' in: *European challenges in contemporary family law*. Antwerp: Intersentia.

Schmidt, Torben Svenné, (1954) *Kvalifikationsproblemet i den internationale privatret*. København: Gads Forlag.

Schmied, Martina, (1999) *Familienkonflikte zwischen Scharia und Bürgerlichem Recht: Konfliktlösungsmodell im Vorfeld der Justiz am Beispiel Österreichs*. Frankfurt am Main: P. Lang.

Steiner, Henry J. and Philip Alston, (2000) *International human rights in context: law, politics and morals: text and materials*. Oxford: Oxford University Press.

Stone, Peter, (1995) *The conflict of laws*. London: Longman.

Sverdrup, Tone, (1997) *Stiftelse av sameie i ekteskap og ugift samliv*. Oslo: Universitetetsforlaget

Thue, Helge J., (2002) *Internasjonal privatrett: personrett, familierett og arverett: alminnelige prinsipper og de enkelte reguleringer*. Oslo: Gyldendal akademisk.

Vandenhole, Wouter, (2005) *Non-discrimination and equality in the view of the UN human rights treaty bodies*. Antwepen: Intersentia.

Welstead, Mary and Susan Edwards, (2006) *Family law*. Oxford: Oxford University Press.

WLUML (2003) *Knowing our rights. Women, family, laws and customs in the Muslim World* London: WLUML.

Wærstad, Tone Linn, (2006) 'Retten til ikke å bli diskriminert ved skilsmisse: En rettsantropologisk studie av skilte muslimske innvandrerkvinner i Norge', in: Kvinnerettslig skriftserie 64.

Zweigert, Konrad and Hein Kötz, (1998) *Introduction to comparative law*. 3rd rev. ed. Oxford: Clarendon Press.

Interviews etc.

Interview with Maître Courjon, French lawyer at the Court of Cassation, 16 January 2008.

Conversation with Ezekiel Ward, 3 March 2008.

Conversation with Dr. Taj Hargey, Islamic scholar and head of the Muslim Educational Centre in Oxford, 6 March 2008.

List of Judgments/Decisions

England

Shahnaz v. Rizwan [1965] The High Court, Queens Bench division, Weekly Law Reports 390

Qureshi v. Qureshi [1971] The High Court, Probate Division, Weekly Law Reports 173

White v. White [2000] House of Lords, [2001] 1 A.C. 596

France

Cour de Cassation, ch.civ.1, 6 juillet 1988
Cour d'Appel de Paris, 2e chambre, no 4, 14 juin 1995
Cour d'Appel de Lyon, 11 janvier 1996
Cour de Cassation, ch.civ.1, 2 décembre 1997
Cour de Cassation, ch.civ.1, 7 avril 1998
Cour d'appel de Lyon, ch.civ.1, 2 décembre 2002
Cour de Cassation, ch.civ.1, 22 novembre 2005

Norway

RG 1983 p.1021
LE-1986-447

Sweden

NJA 1986: 615
T137-92, Malmö tingsrätt 1992-02-10
RH 1993: 116 1993 Hovrätten över Skåne og Blekinge,
RH 2005: 66 2005 Hovrätten för Västra Sverige
T2624-04, Halmstads tingsrätt 2002-10-24
T952-99, Uppsala tingsrätt 2004-12-02
T10083-04, Svea hovrätt 2005-12-20

Treaties and related documents

The Convention on the Elimination of All Forms of Discrimination against Women of 1979

CEDAW General Recommendation no.13

The European Covenant on Human Rights (ECHR)

The Hague Convention on the Law Applicable to Maintenance Obligations of 2 October 1973

The Hague convention on the Law Applicable to Matrimonial Property Regimes of 14 March 1978

The Rome convention of 1980

Statutes and travaux préparatoires

England

The Civil Evidence Act of 1972
The Domicile and Matrimonial Proceedings Act 1973

France

Le Code Civil

Iran

Iranian Civil Code at http://www.alaviandassociates.com/documents/civilcode.pdf, read 18.06.2008.

Israel

The Ottoman Family Code of 1917

Norway

The Marriage Act of 1918, Lov om indgaaelse og opløsning av egteskap av 31. mai 1918 nr. 2

The Matrimonial Property Act, Lov om ektefellers formuesforhold av 20. mai 1927 nr. 1

The Marriage Act of 1991, Lov om ekteskap av 4.juli 1991 nr.47

The Civil Litigations Act, Lov om mekling og rettergang i sivile tvister av 17. juni 2005 nr.90

Pakistan

The Muslim Family Law Ordinance (MFLO)

Sweden

The International Matrimonial Property Relations and Guardianship Act of 1904, Lagen (1904: 26) om vissa internationella rättsförhållanden rörande äktenskap och förmynderskap (IÄL)

The International Matrimonial Property Relations Act of 1990, Lag 1990: 272 om internationella frågor rörande makars och sambors förmögenhetsförhållanden (LIMF)

The Marriage Act, Äktenskapsbalken

Prop. 1973: 158 med förslag till lag om ändring i lagen (1904: 26 s. 1) om vissa internationella rättsförhållanden rörande äktenskap och förmynderskap, m. m. 1973

Regeringens proposition om vissa internationella frågor rörande makars förmögenhetsförhållanden 1989/90: 87.

Tunisia

Le Code du Statut Personnel

Internet literature and websites

The CEDAW committee's comments to the Tunisian country report the 14th session at http://daccessdds.un.org/doc/UNDOC/GEN/N95/801/12/PDF/N9580112.pdf?OpenElement read 10.09.08. The report can now be downloaded from this web page: http://www.un.org/womenwatch/daw/cedaw/14sess.htm#report

The CEDAW committee's comments to the Tunisian country report the 27th session at http://daccessdds.un.org/doc/UNDOC/GEN/N02/426/33/PDF/N0242633.pdf?OpenElement read 10.09.08. The report can now be downloaded at http://www.un.org/womenwatch/daw/cedaw/27sess.htm

The CEDAW committee's comments on the Syrian country report at the 38th session at http://daccessdds.un.org/doc/UNDOC/GEN/N07/375/96/PDF/N0737596.pdf?OpenElement read 10.09.08. The report can now be downloaded at http://www.un.org/womenwatch/daw/cedaw/38sess.htm

The 2007 report to the CEDAW committee made by the Lebanese Committee for the Follow-Up on Women's Issues, at http://www2.ohchr.org/english/bodies/cedaw/docs/ngos/CommitteeFollow-uponWomen.pdf

Encyclopaedia of Islam online at http://www.brillonline.nl/subscriber/uid=3220/title_home?title_id=islam_islam

Exchange rates in space and time: https://www.highbeam.com/reg/reg1.aspx?origurl=http%3a%2f%2fwww.highbeam%2fdoc%2f1G1-14676058.html&refid=lsfa_gorp&docid=1G1%3a14676058 read 30.06.2008.

CHAPTER 5

The Struggle of Embedding the Islamic *Mahr* in a Western Legal System*

Susan Rutten

1. Introduction

In Islam acts are divided into five categories, ranging from "mandatory", "recommended", "neutral", "condemnable" to "prohibited". Respecting these qualifications determines the position one holds in the hereafter. The dower, as part of an Islamic marriage, falls within the "mandatory" category. This means that at the formation of an Islamic marriage, whether this occurs in the country of origin or that of residence, a dower is agreed upon. The dower, *Mahr* or *sadaq* in Arabic, is paid to the wife by the husband, and can consist of a sum of money or of goods, for example gold jewellery, copies of the Qur'an, real estate, usufruct or the like. The *Mahr* knows no maximum amount and it is not rare for a *Mahr* to comprise large sums of money or substantial assets. The *Mahr* is prescribed by Islamic law and is stipulated as such in several verses of the Quran, confirmed in the *Sunna* and *Ijma*. (Linant de Bellefonds, Y, 1965: 199). There exists a range of different ways in which the *Mahr* is arranged within the different schools of law. Contemporary codifications in Islamic countries generally remain faithful to the Islamic rules concerning the dower. Also, in practice, the tradition of the *Mahr* is maintained.

This means that in many marriages between Muslims who reside in Europe the obligation to arrange a *Mahr* exists. It is permitted that only a part of the *Mahr* is paid at the formalization of the marriage, while the remainder is deferred to a possible divorce or death of one of the spouses. In practice it appears that often the remainder is considerably larger in terms of value than

* I would like to thank Anna Berlee for her assistance in writing this article.

the part paid at the nuptials.[1] It is even allowed to defer the entire *Mahr*. This does not hold true for the Maliki School of law where the *Mahr* is perceived to be a prerequisite to the formation of a marriage rather than a consequence thereof, it follows that it does not permit unlimited deferral (Linant de Bellefonds 1965: 219). In any event it is permissible within this school of law to agree to postpone the payment of the *Mahr* until the consummation of the marriage. This is the moment spouses have sexual contact with each other. Nevertheless, some modern codifications based on the Maliki School follow other schools of law regarding the *Mahr* and often do accept a deferral of payment of the *Mahr* until the dissolution of the marriage.[2] The *Mahr* becomes the property of the wife at the conclusion of the marriage; (Linant de Bellefonds, 1965: 233). She is the only one who has the power to dispose of this.

The prospective bride and groom can expressly agree upon the content of the *Mahr* (the *Mahr musamma*). If there no such express agreement, then an appropriate *Mahr* will be set. The content of the *Mahr* is then determined by looking at the *Mahr* given to "similar women". These are women of the same family (on the male side) with similar physical and moral condition, etc. (the *Mahr al-mithl)* (Linant de Bellefonds 1965: 212-215; Nasir 1986: 82). [3]

While the *Mahr* is not a typical Islamic feature, and was also present in Catholic and Jewish religious practice, many contemporary West-European legal systems no longer know the *Mahr*, and therefore do not regulate it.[4] Because of this, in the event that the *Mahr* leads to legal questions in Europe, the codified law does not provide fitting answers. These questions are partly in nature questions of principle, such as: Can a secular judge give a ruling on a religious marriage institution? Or: Is the *Mahr* reconcilable with the gender equality principle? The other part of the questions relate to integration of the *Mahr* in western legal systems and the way in which to achieve concrete solutions. A marriage generally has specific property law related consequences

1. Though this is not true everywhere. From research conducted by Wynn it appears that in Saudi Arabia the deferred dower as such does not exist and the dower is transferred in full at the nuptials. (Wynn, 2008: 205).
2. Examples: Algeria (art. 20 Law 1984, as amended in 2005) and Morocco (art. 30 Law 2004), on which Jordens-Cotran, 2007: 133-135.
3. In practice also the financial means of the man play a part; see for Egypt: Fawzy, 2004: 50-51.
4. Mohamed Jindani pleaded for statutory recognition in English law (Jindani, 1995: 219-227).

for the spouses, but are these also applicable to property received as a *Mahr*? Can a woman claim the remainder at the end of the marriage?

In short, this contribution will take note of some of the legal questions that a judge has to answer when confronted with a claim concerning a *Mahr*. In particular the following questions:

- Is there a place for the *Mahr* as such in western European legal systems, or does the nature and character of the *Mahr* resist recognition thereof?
- How are the legal questions pertaining to the *Mahr* qualified?
- Often the spouses, or one of them, hold a non-European nationality, and first the applicable law has to be determined. Private international law (PIL) distinguishes various categories under which a legal question can be brought. As there is no "*Mahr*" category a different category has to be found for this type of question. Which category should this then be? This is a question about qualifying the *Mahr*. Both the pros and cons of the several qualifications will be examined.
- Which questions arise within the applicable law in the course of the substantive review of the *Mahr*?
- Does the mixture of multiple legal systems require a certain degree of alignment?

The countries examined for this contribution are: Germany, the Netherlands and the United States. Examples from other legal practice in other countries will be featured incidentally.

2. The *Mahr* and Public Policy

2.1 Character, Purpose and Functioning of the *Mahr*

The dower was originally seen as a price for the bride (Linant-de Bellefonds 1965: 201; Motahari 2000: 131); by way of the *Mahr* the husband bought his wife. That was, and still is, emphasised by the size of the *Mahr* which still depends on matters such as the beauty of the woman, her social status, and her virginity. This no longer applies in current Islamic matrimonial law (Mir-Hosseini 2000: 32-22). The character of the buying price is no longer seen as essential to the *Mahr*. Marriage is, however, still perceived as a sort of exchange agreement; an agreement whereby on the one hand the husband takes on a number of financial obligations towards his wife, one being the *Mahr*, and whereby the wife in turn assumes certain obligations towards her husband, such as obedience, arranging the household, sexual availability and care of the children (Linant-de Bellefonds 1965: 287-295; Pearl and Menski 1998: 178). The *Mahr* is significantly linked to consummation of the marriage; as soon as the marriage is consummated, the husband owes the wife the full amount of the *Mahr* (Linant-de Bellefonds 1965: 223). An underlying thought that plays a part in this reasoning is that before there is sexual intercourse the wife is still believed to be a virgin, and her value on "the marriage market" has not decreased. This makes the *Mahr* by nature an institution based on a subordinate position of the woman (Welchman 2007: 92). In an attempt to take away this unfriendly-towards-women character of the *Mahr*, the Moroccan legislature chose to give the *Mahr* a completely symbolic meaning when redrafting the family law in 2004 (Welchman 2007: 92). According to article 26 of the Moroccan family law the *Mahr* which the husband hands over to his wife is a token of his wish to enter into a marriage contract and the formation of a stable family in conjunction with laying the foundations of affection and togetherness between spouses. The legal basis of this is its symbolic and immaterial value, and not its material value. This meaning of the *Mahr* is reflected in a great deal of contemporary literature on the topic of Islamic matrimonial law (Blenkhorn 2002: 6; Pearl and Menski 1998: 178-179; Nasir 1986: 83; Fournier 2006: 649). It is not uncommon for the part that is paid at the nuptials only to have a symbolic meaning.[5]

In the literature of late, the function of the *Mahr* seems to attract more attention than its character, in particular that the women have financial means for their own, especially if the marriage ends. (Fawzy 2004: 50-51; Sayed 2008: 190 & 194; Moors 1995: 82; Wynn 2008: 206; Wurmnest 1879; Yassari 2003: 199). This function is realised by deferring a part of the *Mahr* and making it payable at dissolution of the marriage.

In addition, it becomes clear that the obligation to *Mahr* for the husband and the entitlement of the wife to the *Mahr*, can be a means for the woman to improve her position. Firstly, she could use the obligation to arrange a *Mahr* as an instrument at the nuptials-negotiations, for example with the aim of attaining certain conditions that she wishes to be reflected in the marriage contract. Secondly, the wife can use her *Mahr* in order to effectuate a divorce, specifically the *khul'* divorce. She could offer her husband, in return for repudiation, to waive her entitlement to the *Mahr*, and possibly also repay the previously received part (Jacobson 2003: 7 & 10; Moors *1995*: 142; Sayed 2008: 197-198). If her husband initiates the divorce, the *Mahr* can be used by

5. In countries where there is a tendency for Islamisation you can see in contrast that the price of the dower rises, for example in Iran, see Yassari, 2003: 200.

the woman as an instrument in the negotiations to enforce her position in relation to the children (Mir-Hosseini 2000: 154; Yassari 2003: 201). Moreover, the *Mahr* seeks to prevent the husband from initiating repudiation impulsively; for there is still the obligation to pay the remainder, and in a new marriage also provide for a *Mahr* (Blenkhorn 2002: 5; Coulson 1994: 207-208; Jacobson 2003: 8; Mir-Hosseini 2000: (73 *et sec.*); Jacobson 2003: 9; Sayed 2008: 194-195; Welchman 2007: 92; Wynn 2008: 206-207; Zulficar 2008: 235). The *Mahr* also dissuades the man against polygamy for the reason that the obligation to arrange for a *Mahr* stands for all wives.

2.2 Review of the *Mahr* in light of public policy considerations

The compatibility of the *Mahr* with public policy has been questioned on several occasions in the case law. The reason for this can be traced back to the idea that the *Mahr* could possibly be considered as a type of price for the acquisition of the woman. In general, this question is nowadays answered in the negative. In France the *Cour Supreme* expressly stated that the *Mahr* clause cannot be considered as a type of buying price, and that the *Mahr* agreement is not contrary to public policy.[6] Neither in Germany is the *Mahr* agreement as such held to be contrary to public policy.[7] More often the courts not only look at the original character of the *Mahr*, but rather at the current purpose it serves. Since the *Mahr* still is an essential part of an Islamic marriage, and currently has as its primary goal to offer the woman a certain degree of financial security after a divorce, such is not contrary to German public policy. In New Jersey the judge formulated it as follows: "the *Mahr* Agreement continues a custom and tradition that is unique to a certain segment of our current society and is not at war with any public morals."[8]

6. Cour de cassation (1re Ch.civ) 22 November 2005; with note Najm, 2006: 1365-1377).
7. See for example OLG Stuttgart 3 November 2008, *NJW-RR* 2009, 585 and the therein referenced case law and literature; OLG Köln 23 March 2006, *NJW-RR* 2007, 154, p. 4 with reference to BGH NJW-RR 2005, 81/ *FamRZ* 2004, 1952; (Rohe, *European Yearbook of Minority Issues* 3, 2003/2004, Koninklijke Brill NV the Netherlands 2005: 190).
8. 355 New Jersey Trial Court Super. 305. 810 A.2d 93 (Ch.Div. 2002)(*Odatalla* v *Odatalla*).

3 Claims of the Woman to the Payment of the *Mahr*

3.1 Ability to Claim of the *Mahr*

We have already seen that husbands can defer the payment of the whole of the *Mahr*, or a part thereof, to a later moment in the marriage or until the moment of the dissolution of the marriage. Although the husband already owes the obligation at an earlier moment, the claim is only payable on this later date. It is *this* issue which has kept the judges busy: the wife claiming fulfilment of the deferred part of the *Mahr*, the remainder. In most cases this was in the context of divorce proceedings.

The *Mahr* is due in full as soon as the marriage is consummated (or deemed to have been consummated[9]) and at the death of one of the spouses prior to consummation (Linant-de Bellefonds 1965: 223; Nasir 1986: 84-87). In case the marriage is dissolved before consummation has taken place, the wife is entitled to half of the *Mahr*, provided that the reason for the dissolution of the marriage is through no fault of hers.[10] However, if the woman can be blamed and the marriage is not yet consummated, then she receives no *Mahr* whatsoever (Linant-de Bellefonds 1965: 223). The contemporary codifications have remained faithful to these rules from Islamic law.

The *Mahr* is essential for the marriage and concerns an Islamic obligation to which adherence is given high priority. Rejection of a claim to the payment of the remainder is in principle not up for discussion.

3.2 Qualification in the Netherlands, Germany and the United States

In the event the woman during the marriage, or more often at some point during the divorce proceedings, with reference to the matrimonial contract, claims payment of the remainder, then the most difficult question to answer is how such a claim should be qualified. Can payment of the deferred *Mahr* be considered a provision in the sustenance? Does the entitlement to the *Mahr* fall within the matrimonial property regime of the spouses? Is it another obligation ensuing from the marriage? Or is it simply an obligation arising out of contract? The correct qualification is of more than mere academic importance. The manner in which the claim will be qualified has far reaching implications for the subsequent substantial judging of the *Mahr*. This contribu-

9. This last variety is not true for the Shafi'i school.
10. Linant de Bellefonds, 1965:. 223 & 228. Is the dower not explicitly agreed on, then the wife is entitled to either half of the *Mahr al-mitl* (Malikis) or exclusively entitled to a gift as compensation, the *mut'a* (Hanafi, Hanbali, and Shafi), Linant de Bellefonds, 1965: 215-216.

tion will, without intending to be exhaustive, examine the viewpoints defended in both jurisprudence and the literature.

3.2.1 The Netherlands

In the first cases in which the Dutch judges had to give a ruling on claims of the wife to the payment of the remainder, virtually no consideration was given to the qualification of the claim other than the fact that PIL might be relevant to the case. There was an agreement to a *Mahr* at the nuptials which the husband would have to pay to the wife; he has yet to pay a part or the full *Mahr*; the claim was now due, accordingly it could be granted.[11] Granting a claim for payment of a *Mahr* was no more than granting a claim for performance of the contract. The first real qualification is given by the Appellate Court of The Hague on 23 December 1994[12] In the context of the divorce proceedings the wife claimed payment of the outstanding part of the *Mahr*. The Court considered that the claim had to be qualified as a subsequent claim to the main action to divorce and that this claim follows the same regime which governs the main action. However, in recent years the claim to payment of the *Mahr* in divorces is qualified by the judges as alimony. Three things are striking in this practice: First that the judges do not easily come to this qualification but often extensively motivate their decision.[13] Regularly experts are called upon for advice.[14] Second, it is striking that the judges do not give a general qualification to the *Mahr*, but that circumstances of the concrete case at hand determine the qualification. In a case before the Court of First Instance in Utrecht on 10 December 2008[15] the Court was confronted with an Iranian marriage in which a *Mahr* of 250 *Bahar Azadi* pure 18 carat

11. In this sense Rb.'s-Gravenhage 10 July 1989, *NIPR* 1989, 399, and Ktr. Beetsterswaag 7 August 1990, *NIPR* 1990, 446. We see this approach returning in, among others, Rb. Rotterdam 20 July 2000, *NIPR* 2001, 10, and in Hof's-Gravenhage 5 November 2003, in: HR 10 February 2006, *NIPR* 2006, 94/ *LJN*: AU5275. In this last case the Court treats the claim as a contract, to be judged by Book 6 CC.
12. Hof's Gravenhage 23 December 1994, followed by Hof 's Gravenhage 29 September 1995, can be found indirectly in HR 21 February 1997, *NJ* 1998, 416.
13. See in particular Rb. Utrecht 10 December 2008, *LJN*: BH3018 and Hof's-Gravenhage 17 December 2008, *LJN*: BG9476 / *JPF* 2009, 50.
14. The International Legal Institute (IJI) reported in cases that have lead to: Hof's-Gravenhage 17 December 2008, *LJN*: BG9476/ *JPF* 2009, 50; but also in the later to be discussed, and also extensively motivated decision of the Rb.'s-Gravenhage 29 October 1997, *NIPR* 1999, 142.
15. *LJN*: BH3018.

gold coins were agreed upon, to be paid by the husband to the wife upon her request, and jewellery worth 4 million *riaal* which is somewhere in the region of €38,575. The Court qualified the claim to the payment of the *Mahr* of the wife brought before the judge by the wife as maintenance. The two reasons given for this were firstly that the marriage contract in no way provided for the maintenance of the woman, and secondly the Court was of the opinion that the *Mahr in these proceedings* in its nature looked more like a lump-sum contribution to the maintenance of the woman after divorce than a type of division of capital. In a case before the Appellate Court in The Hague of 17 December 2008[16], the court was confronted with a situation in which a *Mahr* of 255,000 Egyptian pounds was agreed upon. The Court considered it reasonable and fair *in the given circumstances, in this particular case* to qualify the *Mahr* as a form of maintenance of which entitlement is obtained after divorce.

Finally, it is striking that the focus of the judiciary is not so much on the *Mahr* or the *Mahr* -agreement itself, but of much more importance is the character of the *Mahr* and which functions it has, in particular which function the *Mahr* fulfils in the given circumstances.[17] While the *Mahr* in Islamic law is something with which the (prospective) spouses *step into* the marriage (no marriage without a *Mahr*!), the qualification is determined mainly by the function of the *Mahr* at the time of the payment thereof.[18]

The Court of First Instance considered in a judgment of 30 January 2008[19] that the *Mahr* (in this case a *Mahr* pursuant to Iraqi law) in principle is meant as a (deferred) payment for maintenance by the husband for and to his wife, and is to be qualified as a latent alimony obligation. Also in the previously discussed judgment of the same Court of 10 December 2008 the character of the *Mahr* was decisive.

Against this background, it appears that in the case law there is a preference to qualify the *Mahr* as alimony. In a few judgments the Dutch judges reasoned why they considered some alternative qualification inappropriate. Here, too, it holds true that these are not general rejections, but rather that the qualifications considered did not suit the particulars of the case. Thus, the Court of First Instance of Utrecht dismissed the qualification “marital law” because the dower apparently had a real financial meaning and was not a

16. *LJN*: BG9476/ *JPF* 2009, 50.
17. In that respect also Groot, 1979: 364.
18. Wurmnest, 2007: 549 states that for this reason it is illogical to come to the alimony qualification.
19. Rb. Utrecht 30 januari 2008, *LJN*: BC2923.

mere formal requirement at the nuptials. The qualification "matrimonial property" was also dismissed since the marriage contract contained a separate clause which entitled the woman to half the husband's property in the event of a divorce.[20] The Court of the Hague discarded the qualification as "matrimonial property" or "gift" on the basis that the parties married with marital conditions, to the exclusion of any community of goods and declared Dutch law to be applicable, and there were no arrangements as to the *Mahr* in the marital conditions.[21]

3.2.2 Germany

Also in Germany the question on how to qualify a claim to the payment of the *Mahr* has not been without controversy.[22] The German judge has on a regular basis qualified the *Mahr* as an alimony claim.[23] Similar to Dutch practice the German judges consider of importance that the payment of the *Mahr* in the particulars of the case fulfilled the same function as alimony.[24] More than once it was reasoned that the *Mahr* was subject to the rules governing the marriage[25] and if the question arose in the context of a divorce, from the rules governing divorce.[26] In some cases the *Mahr*-agreement was labelled as an agreement concerning the matrimonial property between parties.[27] Various Higher Regional Courts (*Oberlandesgericht*) have also con-

20. Rb. Utrecht 10 December 2008, *LJN*: BH3018.
21. Hof 's-Gravenhage 17 December 2008, *LJN*: BG9476/ *JPF* 2009, 50.
22. Bettina Beck'scher Online Kommentar zu Art. 17 EGBGB; (Wurmnest, 2005: 1878); (Wurmnest, 2007: 548); Müncher Kommentar, Art. 15 EGBGB, d) Morgen- und Brautgabe, und Einleitung 1) Doppelqualifikation; for an overview of the developments in the German jurisprudence see: (Jones-Pauly, 2008:. 303-321).
23. Staudinger, Art. 14, no. 275; Wurmnest, *o.c.* 2005, p. 1880, with reference to (in note 31): AmtsG. Memmingen, *IPRax* 1985, 230; AmtsG. Fürth, *FPR* 2002, 450; Wurmnest, 2007: 548; OLG Düsseldorf *FamRZ* 1998, 623; OLG Saarbrücken 9 March 2005, *NJW-RR* 2005, 1306.
24. In that respect for example OLG Saarbrücken 9 March 2005, *NJW-RR* 2005, 1306; (Jones-Pauly, 2008: 306 & 312).
25. Müncher Kommentar, Art. 13 EGBGB, k) Fehlende Braut- oder Morgengabe, with reference to case law; *idem* Staudinger, Art. 13 EGBGB, no. 386 en Art. 14 EGBGB, no. 273.
26. See for example: OLG Stuttgart 29 January 2008, *NJW-RR* 2008, 742, and OLG Köln 23 March 2006, *NJW-RR* 2007, 154; Staudinger, Art. 14 EGBGB, no. 273.
27. Jones-Pauly, 2008: 303-321, concretely on for example p. 308; Staudinger, Art. 14 EGBGB, no. 274; (Wurmnest 2005: 1880).

sidered the *Mahr* obligation as an obligatory contract[28], or as a consequence of marriage *sui generis*[29]. Other judges were pragmatic when they decided to avoid qualifying the *Mahr*, because whatever qualification was given, in all cases would have lead to the same applicable law.[30]

3.2.3 The United States of America

In the United States, as well as in Canada, the question whether the claims stemming from "religious marriage contracts" can be brought before a secular judge has been an issue for quite some time. Is this compatible with the concept of separation of Church and State? Within both Jewish and Islamic communities it is common that prior to a wedding a marriage contract is drafted. Concerning the Islamic marriage it is also questionable if this persistently should be considered as a religious marriage. On the one hand the marriage is based in Islam and the Islamic law, on the other there is no religious sacrament involved, nor is there always an imam present. The tone was set in the case of *Avitzur* v *Avitzur*, in which the judge of New York had to give a ruling on a claim by a woman arising out of a Jewish marriage contract (*ketubah*).[31] Despite the religious character in the case, the judge did not deny jurisdiction, and considered the action as a claim arising out of contract. The first case, in which this was raised in respect to a claim of a woman to the payment of the deferred *Mahr*, is the case of *Aziz* v *Aziz* from 1985.[32] In the context of the divorce the woman claimed payment of the deferred *Mahr*, worth $5,000. The husband argued in his defence that the *Mahr* agreement concerned a religious document which could not, in contrast to a regular contract, be enforced. With reference to the judgment in *Avitzur v Avitzur,* and holding for the wife, the Court was of the opinion that the religious character of the contract did not stand in the way of enforcing the secular provisions as normal contractual obligations. In later jurisprudence the American judges

28. Wurmnest, 2007: 550, with reference to: OLG Düsseldorf 12 August 1992 and OLG Köln 21 April 1993.
29. BettinaBeck'scher Online-Kommentar, Art. 17 EGBGB bb) Unselbständige Scheidungsfolgen. No. 37, with reference to OLG Köln 23 March 2006, *NJW-RR* 2007, 154.
30. BGH 14 October 1998, NJW 1999, p. 574-575 (German law); OLG Hamburg 21 May 2003, *FamRZ* 2004, p. 459-461 (German law); OLG Köln 23 March 2006, *NJW-RR* 2007, 154 (Iranian law).
31. *Avitzur v Avitzur* , 58 N.Y. 2d 108, 459 N.Y.S. 2d 572, 446 N.E.2d 136, 1983.
32. *Aziz* v *Aziz*, 127 Misc. 2d 1013, 488 *N.Y.Sup.Ct* 2d 123, 1985.

remained faithful to this position.[33] This is different from Canada where in a dispute regarding payment of the *Mahr*, a judge in 1998 considered this to be a purely religious affair. The judge should not set out "into the 'religious thicket', a place that the courts cannot safely and should not go".[34]

While the American literature also suggests numerous other qualifications, the American judges often choose to qualify a *Mahr*-agreement as an antenuptial or prenuptial agreement.[35] Occasionally the agreement is considered to be a regular contract.[36] The qualification "alimony", as requested by the man so that he would be rid of his alimony duty with a single payment was denied by the Court in appeal in *Chaudary* v *Ali.*[37] Nor was it accepted that the agreement was governed by Islamic law because this was intended by the parties (*Shaban* case[38]). The Californian Court considered the reference to "Islamic law" to be too vague and unsure.

3.3 Qualification as Alimony; Analysis and Consequences

The German and Dutch judges most often opted for the alimony qualification. The accuracy of this qualification, however, is frequently contested in the literature. An important objection is that the claim to the payment of the *Mahr* when qualified as alimony is measured against a bar which applies very different standards from those set by Islamic law. This in turn can lead to a result which would harm the institution of the *Mahr*. Another objection is that the qualification of alimony is not appropriate to be applicable to all cases.

33. *Akileh* v *Elchahal*, 666 So. 2d 246, Florida 2d Dist. Court App., 1996 and *Odatalla* v *Odatalla*, 355 New Jersey Trial Court Super. 305. 810 A.2d 93, 2002.
34. *Khaddoura* v *Hammoud*, 168 D.L.R. 4th 503,511 Ontario Ct. Justice, Gen. Div., 1998 (r.o. 30). For a more detailed description see also: Cotter, 2003: 6.
35. In this sense also, among others: *Chaudry* v *Chaudry*, 388 A 2d 1000, 1006, N.J. Super Ct 5 App Div 1978, *Aziz* v *Aziz*, 127 Misc. 2d 1013, 488 N.Y.Sup.Ct 2d 123, 1985, *Re Marriage of Dajani (Dajani* v *Dajani*), 204 Cal. App. 3d 1387, 251 Cal Rptr. 871, 1988, *Chaudhary* v. *Ali* , No. 0956-94-4, Va. Ct.App., 1995, *Habibi-Fahnrich* v *Fahnrich*, 1995 WL 507388, N.Y. Sup.Ct, 1995, *Akileh* v *Elchahal*, 666 So. 2d 246, Florida 2d Dist. Court App., 1996; *Shaban v Shaban*, 88 Cal. App 4th 398, 105 Cal Rptr. 2d 863, 2001; *Ahmad v Ahmad*, No L-00-1391, 2001 L 1518116, Ohio Ct App., 2001.
36. *Solati* v *Solati*, 2000 WL 38876 Conn. Super. Ct. 2000, en *Odatalla* v *Odatalla*, 355 New Jersey Trial Court Super. 305. 810 A.2d 93 Ch.Div., 2002.
37. See note 35.
38. See note 35.

3.3.1 Qualification "alimony" harms the institute of the dower, is unintended by the parties, and can have harmful and unjust consequences for the woman

When a qualification as alimony leads to the applicability of the own substantive law of the court, the *lex fori*, the judge will apply his own law on maintenance with its own standards set therein. Occasionally, this has lead the judge to consider that the *Mahr*-agreement should be labelled as an alimony-agreement; that the agreed upon sum had to be paid, as a lump sum, and that this in turn meant that there was no more room left to grant any alimony.[39] More often, however, the judge looked at the financial means of the man and the needs of the woman. In that case, the *Mahr* virtually looses its meaning. In a case before the Court of First Instance in Utrecht where the judge, in the context of the alimony request, already ruled that no contribution had to be paid, this had as its consequence that the request for the *Mahr* was also denied. In that case it concerned a hefty *Mahr* of several gold coins and up to €38,575 in jewellery.[40]

Where the result of the calculation of the alimony is higher in value than the *Mahr*, then the payment of the *Mahr* was deducted from the final amount to be payable in spousal-alimony.[41]

Where the husband in the meantime is without the means, then the request by the woman to the payment of the agreed upon *Mahr* was denied on account of a lack of financial capacity. For that reason the woman could whistle for the 20,000 Egyptian pounds that the husband owed her as a remainder.[42] In other cases the woman did not receive her money because she had sufficient earnings or capital to provide for her own maintenance. In a case that was brought before the Court of The Hague on 17 December 2008 the claim of the woman to the payment of the agreed upon 250,000 Egyptian pounds was denied for that reason; this while the husband had plenty of capital and was very much able to pay the *Mahr*. The Court held it could not be required of him to eat into his own capital for the payment of the *Mahr*.[43]

39. In this sense Rb. Rotterdam 20 July 2000, *NIPR* 2001, 10. This conclusion also seems to have been drawn from OLG Saarbrücken in a ruling of 9 March 2005, *NJW-RR* 2005, 1306 in which the man already had paid alimony for quite some time. This amount paid was deducted from the dower he was due. Therefore, only a part of the dower was granted. The woman in this case soon remarried another man after the divorce.
40. Rb. Utrecht 10 December 2008, *LJN*: BH3018.
41. In that respect also: (Wurmnest, 2005: 1880).
42. Rb. 's-Gravenhage 24 January 1996, *NIPR* 1996, 69.
43. Hof 's-Gravenhage 17 December 2008, *LJN*: BG9476/ *JPF* 2009, 50.

What is so unsatisfactory with these results is that the spouses, upon agreeing to a *Mahr*, do not intend payment thereof in the event of a possible divorce to be dependent upon their financial capacity and needs at the time of divorce.[44] Consequently, a qualification as alimony is not concurrent with the parties' intentions (Wurmnest 2005: 1880). After all, the amount of the *Mahr* is determined by the situation at the time of the nuptials; that is completely different from a alimony claim because the amount by definition varies depending upon the particulars of the case at the time of the divorce.[45] In Islamic law the maintenance duty of the husband towards his wife ends on divorce. Formally, the maintenance duty to provide for the woman falls back to her father. Agreeing to alimony in case of a divorce is therefore incompatible with this idea. Thus, the *Mahr* in Islamic law exists irrespective of the needs of the woman and so fulfils another function.[46]

The claim to a *Mahr* does not lapse for women who can tend to their own needs and livelihood.[47] For that reason the *Mahr* should be considered alongside, not instead of, alimony. At most the *Mahr* can be taken into account when assessing the extent of the alimony.

3.3.2 Qualifying the dower as alimony is inappropriate in different circumstances

In at least two situations the qualification of the *Mahr* as "alimony" is unsuitable; first when the *Mahr* is claimed *during* the marriage and second in the event one of the spouses dies and the *Mahr* is claimed. Parties can agree that the dower can be claimed in full during the marriage. As for the Netherlands, I am only aware of one case where the *Mahr* was claimed in full by the woman during the marriage. The parties agreed that the remainder of the *Mahr*, fl. 3,000[48] would be paid six months after the nuptials. The claim of the wife was granted without any further qualification and without any additional PIL-considerations.[49] Concerning the *Mahr* obligation in the event of death, the literature seems to be in unison that a qualification as the law of succession is fitting (de Groot 1979: 364). It is apparent that the existence of

44. In that respect also OLG Köln 23 March 2006, *NJW-RR* 2007, 154; (Rutten, 2007: 101).
45. In that respect also Wurmnest, 2005: 1880.
46. Staudinger, Art. 14 EGBGB, no. 275; (Wurmnest, 2007: 55).
47. Compare also in this respect: OLG Nürnberg 25 January 2001, *NJWE-FER* 2001, 116.
48. The equivalent of some € 1,361.
49. Ktr. Beetsterswaag 7 August 1990, *NIPR* 1990, 446.

a *Mahr* obligation or alternatively entitlement in the context of the law of succession is simply assumed, as respectively a debt or a claim of the estate. That means that the question of the entitlement of the wife to the *Mahr* is wholly dependent upon the circumstances in which the claim becomes demandable. This is odd, given the fact that we are dealing with an agreement between two parties as regards a commitment between them.

Circumstances in which the qualification of "alimony" can also be problematic, are those in which the agreed upon *Mahr* is of very little or only symbolic value, and in the cases in which the marriage is dissolved after a very short period of time or where the wife soon after the divorce, remarries.

With a very low or symbolic *Mahr*, it is not only that the parties did not intend to replace alimony in case of a divorce, but that maintaining and limiting the alimony to such a low amount would on top of that also possibly be very unreasonable.

Furthermore, a qualification as alimony would lead to surprising results if according to the applicable law the length of the marriage is a determining factor in assessing the alimony, particularly when the marriage ends after a short period of time. In the Netherlands this could mean that in a childless marriage of short duration the obligation to pay alimony would be for as long as the time the marriage lasted (article 1: 157 sub 6 CC). Parties can deviate from this default rule by agreement. How then should the claim to payment of an agreed upon dower worth €30,000 be assessed if the woman requests a divorce after only six months of 'marital bliss'? A similar question can be asked when the *Mahr* is claimed by a woman who shortly after the divorce remarries. Some judges ponder whether in such a case there is a reason to mitigate the claim.[50] Paragraph 4.3 will look further into this particular question.

3.4 Qualification as Matrimonial Property; Analysis and Consequences

In the examples where the claims to the payment of the *Mahr* are concerned, we can ascertain that the judges hardly consider this question to be a matter of matrimonial property. This is remarkable. The claim to the *Mahr* is irrefutably of a property law nature, and comes into existence through and with the nuptials. The most obvious qualification therefore would appear to be a matrimonial property qualification. In the literature there is regular support for such a qualification (Blenkhorn 2002: 18; Sayed 2008: 205-206). Arguments

50. For the woman who remarried shortly after the divorce, see: OLG Saarbrücken 9 March 2005, *NJW-RR* 2005, 1306.

against such a qualification from a German perspective are that the *Mahr* is calculated at the time of the nuptials and hence not completely independent of potential acquired property during the marriage (*Zugewinn*)[51] and that the *Mahr* in principle is not connected to the state of the matrimonial property regime.[52]

We have seen that the judges often turned to the function the deferred *Mahr* fulfilled. If the function of the *Mahr* is to grant the woman the power over a certain amount of capital in the event she has to continue her life as a single person, why then would the only possible qualification be that of alimony, why not also a qualification as matrimonial property? Also by shifting capital between (former) spouses one could fulfil this function. As to the question whether payment of a lump sum or transfer of goods after divorce should be regarded under matrimonial property law or as alimony, this has been decided by the Court of Justice in 1997 as follows: in the event that the goal is to ensure the maintenance of the other spouse it should be alimony.[53] Whether this is the case when it comes to the *Mahr*; I have my doubts. I consider the position that the *Mahr* serves as a sort of nest egg to have more standing. Wurmnest also declares that the *Mahr*, when paying heed to her purpose, offering financial security to the woman in the event of a divorce, comes close to the *Zugewinnausgleich* (Wurmnest 2005: 1879).

What the consequences of a matrimonial property law qualification are would be determined by the applicable matrimonial property regime. In the Netherlands, where in a marriage everything in principle falls within the community of goods, the entitlement to the *Mahr* would also in principle fall within the community. During the divorce proceedings this would have to be divided. In the German system of the *Zugewinngemeinschaft* the size of the *Zugewinnausgleich*, the claim is calculated in a divorce at the moment of petition for divorce by reference to the property present at the beginning of the marriage (Wurmnest wonders in this instance whether the *Mahr* should exist next to the *Zugewinnausgleich*, which leads to a double entitlement of the wife, or that the *Mahr* should mitigate the *Zugewinnausgleich* (Wurmnest 2005: 1882).

In both the Dutch and the German system the spouses are free to deviate from the legal regime by agreement. This can raise the question whether spouses deviate from the marital property regime regarding the *Mahr* when they put their agreement to a *Mahr* in the marriage contract. You can find ar-

51. OLG Köln 23 March 2006, 21, *NJW-RR* 2007, 154.
52. Staudinger, Art. 14, no. 274.
53. HvJ EG 27 February 1997, *NJ* 1999, 112.

guments supporting this view in the literature.[54] The formal requirements under Dutch law would be marital agreements[55]; such agreements will have to be observed and parties must have had the intention to deviate from the legal regime.

If such a preclusion can be supposed then the woman makes the entitlement to the *Mahr* completely independent of her other entitlements arising from the marital property law.[56]

Usually parties only have the arranging of the dower itself in mind when they record a *Mahr* agreement, and not the rest of the property.[57] Sometimes this follows from the wording of the marriage contract itself. So it is possible that a *Mahr* has been agreed and in addition parties have specified that the woman is entitled to the assets built up during the marriage.[58]

3.5 Qualification as Prenuptial Agreement; Analysis and Consequences

The American judge has frequently opted to qualify the *Mahr* as a prenuptial agreement.[59] Such an agreement has to satisfy the criteria of a normal contract. In that respect we are dealing with a contract and the qualification as contract would also be suitable. This kind of qualification means that the agreed *Mahr* would be tested against the regular law of obligations. An investigation would turn to whether the *Mahr*-agreement was valid, for instance

54. Rutten, 2007: 101; Wurmnest, 2007: 556: The agreement can following §1408 BGB be considered as an *Ehevertrag.*
55. See for the applicable law question regarding the form: Article 12 Hague Convention on the Law Applicable to Matrimonial Property Regimes 1978.
56. In this respect also Wurmnest, 2005: 1881, with reference to BGH *FamRZ* 1987, 463/465.
57. In this respect also Marie-Claude Najm, note with Cour de cassation (1[re] Ch.civ) 22 November 2005, *Journal de droit international* 2006, p. 1371; Similar reasoning in OLG Frankfurt/M. 29 February 1996, *FamRZ* 1996, p. 1478-1479.
58. Example: OLG Hamburg 21 May 2003, *FamRZ* 2004, p. 459: in the Iran concluded marriage contract a dower was agreed upon encompassing a Qur'an worth 10.000 Riaal, 1 mirror, 1 set of candlesticks worth 200.000 Riaal and 500 Bahar Azadi gold coins, to be paid to the woman upon her request. In addition it was agreed that in the event of a divorce the woman would receive half of the built up assets during the marriage.
59. Case law can be found via Westlaw. The case law is frequently featured in also accessible via Westlaw and via HeinOnline sources, such as: . Blenkhorn, 2002: 189; Cotter, 2003: 45; Estin, 2004-2005: 501-527; Freeland, 2000-2001: 2; Jacobson, 2003: 143; Siddiqui, 2007: 639; . Thompson en F. Soniya Yunus, 2007:, 361. *See further*: Qaisi , 2001: 67-81; Quraishi and Najeeba Syeed-Miller, 2004: 200-208.

Mahr clauses deemed too vague were held to be invalid.[60] Also invalid was a *Mahr* agreement which was sprung on the husband just before the marriage ceremony (*in casu* two hours prior) and which he, without having had the opportunity to seek legal advice, signed. The judge ruled in this instance that the *Mahr* agreement came about as a result of overreaching and coercion.[61] Likewise, investigations into the legality of a *Mahr* agreement as such were conducted. With that in mind, it is important to note that a prenuptial agreement, different from a regular obligatory contract, cannot be enforced if it encourages a divorce by stipulating a provision only accessible in the event of a divorce (Freeland 2000-2001; Estin 2005: 420). Such a clause would be against morality and public policy. Judges within the United States do not agree on whether this also holds true for the *Mahr*. While judges in New York[62], Florida[63], and New Jersey[64] consider the *Mahr* agreement enforceable and granted a claim by the woman to compliance thereof, a Californian judge held on several occasions the *Mahr* agreement to be against public policy for this reason.[65] Paragraph 4.2 will go into more detail on this topic.

Against a qualification as a prenuptial agreement the scholars advance that parties when entering into a *Mahr* agreement did not take such a qualification into account (Blenkhorn 2002: 6; Freeland, 2000-2001: 3) Certainly none of the parties had in mind that with the *Mahr* the entire matrimonial property law relations (after divorce) would be arranged (Siddiqui, 2007: 4.). Also, a qualification as agreement would be bestowing too much "credit" upon the *Mahr* agreement, because a contract implies freedom to contract for both parties, and women often lack such freedom (Blenkhorn 2002: 11).

60. *Habibi-Fahnrich* v *Fahnrich*, 1995 WL 507388, N.Y. Sup.Ct, 1995 (clause: Half of the husband's possession ...) and *Re Marriage of Shaban (Shaban* v *Shaban*), 88 Cal. App.4th 398, 105 Cal. Rptr. 2d 863, 2001.
61. *Zawahiri v Alwattar*, 07AP-925, Ohio Ct Apop., 2008
62. *In re Aziz.* 127 Misc. 2d 1013, 488 N.Y.Sup.Ct 2d 123, 1985.
63. *Akileh* v *Elchahal*, 666 So. 2d 246, Florida 2d Dist. Court App. 1996.
64. *Chaudry* v *Chaudry*, 388 A 2d 1000, 1006, N.J. Super Ct 5 App Div 1978, and *Odatalla* v *Odatalla*, 355 New Jersey Trial Court Super. 305. 810 A.2d 93 Ch.Div., 2002.
65. *Re Marriage of Noghrey*, 215 Calif. Rptr. Ct App. 1985, and *Re Marriage of Dajani* (*Dajani* v *Dajani*), 204 Cal. App. 3d 1387, 251 Cal Rptr. 871 (1988).

3.6 Other Qualifications; Analysis and Consequences

Other qualifications presented in the literature include: ancillary provisions with divorce, following the applicable law of the divorce[66], join in with the nuptials and the applicable law of the wedding, consequences of marriage, gift, obligatory contract; and qualification *sui generis*. All these qualifications will now be considered briefly.

The qualification "ancillary provisions" is not completely illogical. It is less apparent to subject this to the *lex causae* of the divorce. After all, the ancillary provisions have their own conflict rule determining the applicable law.

I consider following the law that governed the nuptials a more defendable alternative in that the obligation to a *Mahr* comes into existence at the very moment that parties wed in accordance with that law and arrange a *Mahr* pursuant to the same law.[67] The claims and duties that flow from the *Mahr*-agreement are then no longer determined by the nationality of the parties and are also valid for Muslims who have been naturalised. A disadvantage of this qualification is visible when the parties have concluded two marriages: a civil marriage without a *Mahr* and a marriage under an Islamic system in which a *Mahr* is agreed. Usually, the civil marriage will be the legally valid marriage. The law applicable after the marriage has been concluded does not know of the *Mahr*, and, as a result, a second qualification is necessary.

A qualification as a consequence of the marriage can be advanced so that the obligation to payment of the *Mahr* on the agreed upon time flows from the marriage. In most schools of law the *Mahr* is seen as corollary to the marriage.[68] A contrasting opinion is that, considering the property law consequence, the matrimonial property law qualification is a more understandable option (Wurmnest 2007: 552). Another argument that is put forth is that the duty to payment does not flow from the marriage but from the dissolution of the marriage, where so provided, when payment can be demanded and claimed.[69]

A frequently heard argument against qualifying the *Mahr* as a gift is that such a qualification is incorrect because in Islamic law the dower is not a gift but an obligation for the husband. (Wurmnest 2007: 550; Siddiqui 1995: 21 ; Siddiqui 2007: 5)

66. Example: Hof 's Gravenhage 23 December 1994, followed by Hof 's Gravenhage 29 September 1995, can be found indirectly in HR 21 February 1997, *NJ* 1998, 416.
67. In this light also Jordens-Cotran, 2000: 392; Rutten, 2007: 101.
68. Proponant of such a qualification: Henrich, 2004: 393 *et sec.*
69. See in the same light Rb. 's-Gravenhage 29 October 1997, *NIPR* 1999, 142 ; Rutten, 2007: 104.

An obligatory contract as a qualification also has not been readily accepted by the literature where it is stated that the *Mahr* is a family law contract which should assessed differently from a property law agreement.[70] The difference between the two, however, is flimsy, which is also apparent from the jurisprudence of the United States. While the *Mahr* agreement might be held to be a prenuptial agreement by the judges, a prenuptial agreement is also subject to the rules of a regular contract. At the most some additional special rules will govern the prenuptial agreement on account of its specific character.

4 Entitlement to the *Mahr*

4.1 Entitlement to the *Mahr* in Relation to the Different Types of Divorce

In a divorce, ordinarily the woman can claim the remainder of the dower, for in most cases the marriage will have been consummated. If the marriage is not consummated, then, in principle, only half of the *Mahr* is owed (see par. 3.1 for a more extensive review).

That does not alter the fact that there are ways of divorcing in which the woman has no possibility to lay a claim on the remainder. In a so-called *khul'* divorce it is customary for the woman, as compensation for the divorce she wishes, to renounce her claim to the remainder. As part of the compensation scheme it can also be that she has to pay back the already received part of the *Mahr*. Also in a *mubarat* divorce, i.e. a divorce with mutual consent, the spouses can agree on whether or not payment of the remainder should take place.[71] Traditionally, this boiled down to the situation in which the woman wanted a divorce, but not on account of a fault of the husband's, which meant she only had the *khul'* and *mubarat* divorce at her disposal which in turn had as its consequence that she had to relinquish her rights to the *Mahr*. This however, is something different from the case in which the woman, if she is the one initiating a divorce, has no entitlement to the payment of the deferred part of the *Mahr*. As soon as the *Mahr* is due in full there is a claim and payment will have to take place, except in those cases in which the woman renounces her claim (Siddiqui 1995: 17).

70. Jones-Pauly, 2008: 320; Staudinger, Art. 14 EGBGB, no. 276; Wurmnest, 2007, 550, who points out that the family law agreement also falls outside of the scope of the EVO.
71. In this respect also OLG Stuttgart, 3 November 2008, *NJW-RR* 2009, 585.

Thus, the indebtedness of the *Mahr* is not so much related to the divorce, but is primarily linked to the consummation of the marriage. The link of the indebtedness of the *Mahr* to whether or not one is to blame or initiates the divorce proceedings is therefore sometimes wrongly made. In court cases in front of uninformed judges it is not uncommon for the husband to try and defend against a claim for the payment of the *Mahr* by stating that it is the wife who is seeking the divorce, or that the cause of the dissolution of the marriage lies with the woman.[72] Such a defence should in my opinion not stand and from an Islamic perspective in principle should only be of help if the marriage had not been consummated. Nevertheless, judges in Islamic countries seem to want the woman to renounce the *Mahr* when she initiates a divorce on the grounds of a discord, where the cause of the breakdown of the marriage lies with her.[73]

4.2 Contrary to Good Morals or Public Policy, and Abuse of Power

The *Mahr* is an obligation under Islamic law embedded in the Islamic family law system. The *Mahr* will, other than in Islamic countries, be placed in a different context in Europe and thus be disconnected from other parts of the Islamic matrimonial law. It is so that in PIL, legal relationships are cut into little pieces, and for each subject matter it is decided which law is applicable. It is therefore conceivable that the *Mahr* is recognised without the other rights and duties flowing from Islamic matrimonial law being accepted. Also, generally it is possible for the Islamic married woman to opt for a secular way of dissolving the marriage with the European judge, even if her marriage was concluded in Islamic law. This means that in a way she is able to forum shop between the two legal systems for the best option. The woman could have the marriage dissolved pursuant to the law of the land where she now resides, in

72. For example in *Akileh* v *Elchahal* en in *Dajani* v *Dajani,* and for the German Federal High Court: Jones; Pauly, 2008: 318.

73. Compare Quraishi and Syeed-Miller, 2004: 190. This was, according to Moors, 1999: 142, also legal practice in Palestine, but afterwards the legal possibility for women to ask for a divorce without losing their right to the remainder, was enlarged (Moors, 1999: 147). In Morocco the woman retains her right, in accordance to the law, to the dower with the introduction of the *shiqaq*. Nevertheless in article 97 it is stated that the judge pronouncing the divorce on the grounds of *shiqaq*, in determining what caused the permanent breakdown of the marriage can take into consideration the contribution of each of the estranged partners. Also, parties could have agreed among themselves that the remainder is only due in the event that the husband was responsible for the divorce, see for *Ahmad* v *Ahmad*, No L-00-1391, 2001 WL 1518116, Ohio Ct App. 30 November 2001.

circumstances which according to her national "Islamic" law would not, or not without further conditions, lead to a dissolution of the marriage, while at the same time she *could* claim the agreed upon *Mahr* from her husband. Indeed, in principle she could request a divorce for no other reason than to collect the *Mahr*. The question has been raised, in particular when the marriage was a short one, if this would constitute a so-called abuse of power and that the public policy exception ought to be invoked.[74]

As mentioned above, the Californian judge has turned down previously the claim of a woman to the payment of a deferred *Mahr* in several cases on the grounds that the *Mahr* agreement facilitated a divorce.[75] The case of *Dajani v Dajani* (1988)[76] concerned a Jordanian marriage contract. A deferred *Mahr* was agreed upon with a value of 5,000 Jordanian dinars (equivalent to about 1,700 American dollars), to be paid at the moment of divorce or the death of one of the spouses (Estin 2004: 219). It was the wife who after three years of marriage, commenced divorce proceedings. The Californian Court argued that the *Mahr* agreement facilitated divorce by providing for a settlement only in event of such an occurrence. The Court therefore refused to enforce the *Mahr* agreement based upon public policy. In the case of *In re the Marriage of Noghrey* (1985)[77] the spouses agreed that in the event of a divorce, the wife would be entitled to a house and 500,000 dollar or one-half of the assets of the husband, whichever was greater. After seven and a half months of marriage the wife filed for divorce. Enforcement of the *Mahr* agreement was refused since the agreement violated public policy by encouraging divorce (Estin 2004: 218-219).

That the Californian judge did not turn this line of reasoning into a general rule, can be deduced form the *Bellio* case.[78] In this case the claim of the woman was granted. The case concerned a woman who was considerably younger than her husband. At the time of the agreement the wife was receiving spousal support from her first marriage upon which she depended for financial stability and which would terminate if she remarried. The couple therefore agreed to add a term to the prenuptial agreement giving the wife $ 100,000 upon divorce, which would allow her to marry the second husband

74. Next to the following analysis of the case law, see also Wurmnest (Wurmnest 2005: 1885).
75. *Re Marriage of Noghrey*, 215 Calif. Rptr. Ct App., 1985 and *Re Marriage of Dajani* (*Dajani* v *Dajani*), 204 Cal. App. 3d 1387, 251 Cal Rptr. 871, 1988.
76. 204 Cal. App. 3d 1387.
77. 215 Calif.Rptr.Ct App., 1985.
78. *Re Marriage of Bellio*, 129 Calif. Rptr. 2d 556, 560 Ct App., 2003.

without the risk upon divorce she would be destitute. In these circumstances the judge considered the *Mahr* permissible.

We are dealing here with an exceptional example where the Islamic legal order and a secular European legal order come together. On the one hand parties agree to an Islamic legal institution, being an Islamic marriage with a *Mahr* therein, but on the other hand live in Europe where they make use of European divorce law. From the Islamic perspective there is on the one hand always a payable *Mahr* as soon as the marriage is consummated. On the other hand the woman would not so easily be able to realize a divorce if there was no fault on the side of the husband or without his consent. Abuse of divorce law in Islamic law is a lot less feasible than in systems where the question of guilt in divorce does not play a part and in those where equality between husband and wife is assumed. In contrast, however, in the event parties reside in Europe, they can take into account the usage of a very generous divorce law.[79] Parties then take in principle, by nevertheless agreeing on a *Mahr*, the risk(s) for granted. The situation is comparable with a marriage in a community of goods, as known in the Dutch system, where one spouse, by the mere nuptials, can become entitled to large property law claims on the other spouse.

4.3 Mitigation of the Claim on Grounds of Reasonableness and Fairness

Instead of opting for a far-reaching conclusion of denying a claim to the payment of the *Mahr*, a judge can, when the circumstances give reason for it, also contemplate a less far-reaching variety, being a mitigation of the *Mahr* on the grounds of reasonableness and fairness. In Dutch jurisprudence there are no examples in which this was honoured. In a case in which the spouses separated after several weeks (according to the woman she was sent away by her husband) the Court of First Instance in the Hague did not consider this a reason not to order the husband to pay the remainder worth fl. 1,000.[80] Incidentally, the woman was already pregnant.[81] Also, in a judgment of 1997 the Court did not ascertain that the short duration of the marriage was a hindrance to ordering the woman to repay the already received part of the *Mahr*.[82] The German jurisprudence does offer some cases in which the *Mahr* was mitigated. The OLG Hamburg held that even though the marriage had been con-

79. Interesting is also to note that Morocco, with adopting the *shiqaq* in 2004, maintained the permanent breakdown of a marriage as a ground for a divorce.
80. The equivalent of some €450.
81. Rb. 's-Gravenhage 10 July 1989, *NIPR* 1989, 399.
82. Rb. 's-Gravenhage 29 October 1997, *NIPR* 1999, 142.

summated, it was of a short duration while the spouses raised severe accusations against each other, that this was consideration enough to mitigate the *Mahr*.[83] Also for the OLG Köln reasonableness induced the court to award only half of the *Mahr*. The judge when reaching his conclusion took into account in the judgment the fact that the spouses only lived together for three years, the woman was a long time resident of Germany, was financially secure in her subsistence, and she could, as an independent woman in Germany, but not in Iran, hold a position.[84] The judge also referred to Iranian law where there was also a possibility to award only half of the *Mahr* in certain circumstances. This reference is somewhat unfortunate because the circumstances referred to in the Iranian law are only those in which there has been no sexual intercourse between the spouses.

5 Indexation and Inflation

When a sum of money is part of the agreed upon *Mahr*, and claiming thereof takes place sometime after the agreement, several substantial questions arise regarding the precise amount to be paid. For example, should the amount be index-linked? This question was the subject of OLG Köln of 23 March 2006.[85] The judge had to rule on the *Mahr* under Iranian law. Because the Iranian code had an indexation adjustment[86], the judge applied this, and followed the indexation of the Iranian central bank. Also the gold coins were calculated after their current value. In most court cases for that matter indexation is not applicable, and the judge simply copies the agreed upon amount.

If the currency has strongly devalued after the nuptials, and in the meantime payments are due in another currency unit, should the determination of the value of the *Mahr* then be calculated at the time of the nuptials or of the

83. OLG Hamburg 21 May 2003, *FamRZ* 2004, p. 459-461 in detail Wurmnest, . 2005: 1883.
Also: BGH FamRZ 1987, 463/466. Illustrative is also a ruling of the English Court in A v T, (2004) EWHC 471 Fam, in: *Family Law Reports* 2004, 1, p. 977-987 concerning an Iranian marriage in which the wife leaves her husband after only seven weeks. The Court mitigates the dower from £ 60,000 to £ 35,000 only if the husband is willing to facilitate the repudiation in Iran.
84. OLG Köln 23 March 2006, *NJW-RR* 2007, 154.
85. 21 UF 144/05, *NJW-RR* 2007, 154.
86. More on this: Yassari, 2003: 201.

payment? This question was under discussion at the Hague Court.[87] In an Iranian marriage contract an amount of one million rial was laid down as a remainder, to be payable on the request of the woman. At the time of the wedding this amounted to fl. 33,000.[88] During the marriage, in 1994, the woman claims the remainder of the *Mahr*. At that moment one million rial is the equivalent of only fl. 1,236 (about € 500). The Court sentenced the man to paying the fl. 33,000. The judgement endured the scrutiny of the Supreme Court ('Hoge Raad') in 1997. The man does not pay, and when it comes to a divorce between the parties, the woman again claims the payment of the fl. 33,000. The Supreme Court finally considered that the Court followed the explanation of the woman, being that in conformity with Iranian custom and Iranian law, the intention of the parties was that the sum would be calculated as requested, the value that the amount represented at the conclusion of the marriage. The Supreme Court followed the judgment of the Court.[89]

6 Scope of the *Mahr* Agreement and Concurrence with Other Property Claims

6.1 Concurrence as a Consequence of Qualification

From an Islamic perspective the *Mahr* could be an important financial security for the woman after a divorce. The obligation of the partner to maintain the other will cease and there will be no division of marital property. For women who do not have their own property and have no income of their own, the *Mahr* could be of essential importance. Usually she will be able to obtain some form of indemnity for the maintenance of the children (the so-called *hadana* compensation). In the western countries researched, the maintenance obligation for the spouses against their former spouse does not end on divorce. There is also, in divorce proceedings, a division of the marital property. An aspect that receives considerable attention in the literature is the scope of the *Mahr* agreement in relation to the other property law ancillary provisions. Is the claim to the *Mahr* an autonomous claim independent from and thus beside other claims, or does this particular claim replace another? If the latter is true, for what, and especially how far, does it replace another claim? If the *Mahr* is marked as alimony, does this mean that, for example,

87. Hof 's-Gravenhage 5 November 2003, can be found in: HR 10 February 2006, *NIPR* 2006, 94/ *LJN*: AU5275.
88. The equivalent of some €15,000.
89. HR 10 February 2006, *NIPR* 2006, 94 / *LJN*: AU5275.

the size of the alimony is completely dependent upon the quantum of the agreed upon *Mahr*? Here too, it holds true that the answer to these questions is in many respects determined by the qualification given to the *Mahr*-agreement. With that, the qualification has immediate consequences for the ancillary provisions that can (or cannot, as the case may be) still be requested.

In the case where the *Mahr*-agreement is qualified as an ancillary provision *sui generis* during the divorce proceedings, this should have the dogmatic consequence that it must be considered next to other ancillary provisions. In conjunction with the *Mahr* there could be other provisions claimed, in particular alimony and division of the community of goods. The Court of the Hague came to this conclusion in a ruling of 23 December 1994.[90] The claim to performance of the *Mahr*-agreement worth fl. 33,000 which would be qualified as an ancillary provision was granted. Subsequently, alimony was also granted.

If the claim for the payment of the *Mahr* is judged independently as a claim from contract, then likewise it is evident that the claim to a *Mahr* is separate from other ancillary provisions, and thus would come in addition to other provisions.[91] In the United States, where the *Mahr* agreement is qualified as a prenuptial agreement, and a claim to a *Mahr* must comply with the conditions of a contract, scholars at times concluded that by granting the *Mahr* there would be no entitlement to other financial provisions (Blenkhorn 2002; Siddiqui 2007: 639). Both the law of alimony and that of the marital property would be superfluous. The *Mahr* agreement will then be, one could argue, seen as an agreement which attempts to arrange all property law consequences prior and after the divorce. In the case of *Odatalla* v *Odatalla* however, the Superior Trial Court in New Jersey also granted a part of the community of goods besides the *Mahr* and alimony.[92] This judgment has been very well received.[93] Also, in the case of *Shaban* it was not accepted that the *Mahr* agreement which only mentioned the amount but no mention of the community of goods, would attempt to arrange the marital property according to Islamic law. The *Mahr* clause had no substantive terms addressing

90. *NJ* 1998, 416.
91. In the same light: Rb. 's-Gravenhage 10 July 1989, *NIPR* 1989, 399. This approach we see return in among others Rb. Rotterdam 20 July 2000, *NIPR* 2001, 10. HR 10 februari 2006, *NIPR* 2006, 94 (subjecting the Iranian dower to book 6 Dutch CC). For this reason Siddiqui, 2007: 10 supports the view to qualify the *Mahr*-agreement as a secular contract.
92. 355 New Jersey Trial Court Superior 305. 810 A.2d 93 Ch.Div., 2002.
93. See Siddiqui, 2007: 6 with references in footnote 72.

other remedies or community property rights.[94] So, it appears that there is also in the United States room to meet other ancillary provisions next to the *Mahr* claim.

Should judges come to qualify the claim to a *Mahr* as an ancillary provision, for example (partner) alimony or matrimonial property law, then two things become clear. Firstly, the *Mahr* will be treated as the appointed ancillary provision from that moment onwards. Secondly, the qualification maintains the other ancillary provisions. For example, if the claim is qualified as alimony, then this does not counter the application of marital property law, and thus does not go against the possible division of the marital property. If the claim is considered as belonging to the marital property law, then this does not prevent a possible alimony claim.

6.2 Concurrence as a Consequence of the Applicable Law

In addition to concurrence issues of ancillary provisions that can occur as a consequence of differing qualifications, several other concurrence issues might occur. I shall only examine three other issues of concurrence.

Because PIL knows different conflict rules for different provisions, it could be that different legal systems are applicable. Accordingly, it could be an extra "privilege" or extra "disadvantage" for one of the parties. If the claim to a *Mahr* is qualified as alimony and subsequently by applying the *lex fori* is denied the *Mahr* (for example because the man has no means) or if the matrimonial property law is subject to the foreign law, on grounds of which the woman, if this concerns an Islamic system, does not share in any form of marital property, the result could be that the woman is left empty handed.

Also within the applicable law certain alignment and concurrence issues can arise. We have seen that the judges were not in harmony in their judgments: a *Mahr* agreement can replace the entire alimony or marital property law system, or can be explained as being an agreement which is only applicable to the *Mahr* itself but does not regulate the rest of the alimony or martial property law.

In applying a foreign Islamic law, there can also arise some alignment and concurrence issues. Imagine for a moment that the judge qualifies the *Mahr* as alimony and a foreign Islamic law which has to be applied does not know any partner alimony after divorce should he then turn down the claim? Or should he, which is the more obvious answer, judge that the *Mahr* was validly agreed upon in accordance with the foreign law leading to performance

94. *Shaban v Shaban*, 88 Cal.App.4th 398, 105 Cal.Rptr. 2d 863, 2001.

of the obligation? And what is to be done about any other possible financial provisions from the foreign law which might also fall within the partner-alimony? I am thinking here of the continued payment of the maintenance during the waiting-period (*'idda*), the compensation (*mut'a*) and the compensation arranged for the care of the children. If the judge can, considering the request brought by the woman, rule then I believe that these provisions together with the claim to a *Mahr* should remain.[95]

6.3 Solutions?

So far we have seen that there are considerable differences between the results of the judges in the assessment of a claim to payment of the *Mahr*. The way in which a qualification is reached is a determining factor and is very important for what is and is not granted to the woman after a divorce. Where at one time she receives the entire *Mahr* as alimony as a division of the martial property, and another time she is granted the *Mahr* next to alimony or a division of the martial property. It can also be that the dower is denied, there is no right to alimony, and the woman for example only has a share of the martial property; such differences are undesirable.

In order to resolve issues of concurrence, PIL has at its disposal the technique of adaptation. In adaptation the substantive result of the differing attributions can be adapted, or all the different subjects fall under the same attributive rule or the same applicable law. The first solution, adaptation to the substantive attributive result, is not as easy as it looks. Because, what would this result be? Undoubtedly, reasonability and fairness will have to be come into play. Classifying the subjects in one attributive category would be completely random and with that unsatisfactory. With the choice for a single attributive rule or one applicable law, a similar discussion takes place which so far has lead to diverging answers.

A finishing solution, which I prefer, is to qualify the *Mahr*-agreement and the resulting claim as a *droit acquis*. The dower is part of an Islamic marriage and is established according to the rules of Islamic law or the law of an "Islamic state". The obligation to *Mahr* is not contrary to western public policy. The existence thereof as *droit acquis* implies that it is an independent claim, which is therefore detachable from other possible claims, and is decided upon in accordance with the rules that also governed its creation. Perhaps a woman

95. In a different light Rb. Utrecht 30 January 2008, *LJN*: BC2923. The Court had qualified the claim to payment of the dower worth €45,000 as alimony, and granted it. Subsequently the Court ruled that this left no room for granting any maintenance during the '*iddah* of three months and ten days.

would then be better off, as her own law (the law of the nuptials of the *Mahr*) would consider the claim in conjunction with other claims fair. That, however, is not at odds with the advantages of such an approach. It serves comprehensibility and legal certainty; this approach does more justice to the institute of the *Mahr*, and usually also to the parties' intentions. Parties that conclude an Islamic marriage will generally have intended to subject the *Mahr* to the law of the land of the nuptials. There is not a single category under which the *Mahr* can be classified without any problems (Kegel and K. Schurig 2000: 283). The *Mahr* falls outside the existing categories and can best be considered a *sui generis*[96] legal conception and recognised as such, with all the rights and obligations flowing there from. Furthermore, the approach is appropriate for all cases: it can be used for a claim to the payment during the marriage or in case of death of one of the spouses.[97] If there should be some restraints these should be on account of reasonableness or fairness, which in particular circumstances could mitigate the outcome.

7 Claims of the Husband to Return the *Mahr*

7.1 Qualification

Certain claims are not of the wife but of the husband who, in the divorce proceedings, claims the repayment of the already paid part of the *Mahr* from his estranged wife.[98] The bases for this are not always clear. It is possible that this indistinctness has contributed to the fact that judges initially do not concern themselves with PIL aspects and the question of qualification. In instances where there has been a qualification, the Court opted for the qualification "ancillary provisions"[99] or linked up with the marriage and the applicable law was the law of the country where the wedding took place.[100] The Court of First Instance in the Hague denied a qualification as "alimony" because the *Mahr* was paid in full; did not opt for a qualification as marital effects because this did not concern the effects of the marriage but of the divorce; qualifying the dower as "marital property law" was also turned down now

96. In a similar fashion Mosa Sayed, 2008: 207. and Jones-Pauly, 2008: 321: "that *Mahr* claims should be handled completely separately from divorce proceedings".
97. For all the foregoing reasons Siddiqui, 2007: 10 opts to qualify the *Mahr*-agreement as a regular contract.
98. At times it is also the father of the husband who initiates these types of claims.
99. Rb. Roermond 6 July 1989, *NIPR* 1989, 407.
100. Rb. 's-Gravenhage 29 October 1997, *NIPR* 1999, 142.

that the Moroccan law is unfamiliar with marital property law; nor was this a case of a special property law contract. In Germany a claim by the husband to recover or re-claim the *Mahr* in a divorce is considered an effect of the divorce, and thus follows the divorce statute, which can be either marital property or alimony.[101]

7.2 Evaluation

From an Islamic law perspective there are only a few instances in which the man has no obligation to provide for a *Mahr* or only a part thereof, and which he can therefore claim back. No *Mahr* is owed when there is a divorce prior to sexual intercourse of the spouses and the reason for the divorce lies, in terms of blame, with the woman (this was submitted before the Court of First Instance of the Hague, the husband claiming that his wife had fallen ill and he learned she could not conceive. The submission was negated by the factual circumstances[102]). Additionally, the husband can only claim repayment if the wife has agreed to this so she would get a divorce (*khul'* divorce) or if both parties agreed to a divorce (*mubarat* divorce) and came to such an agreement regarding the *Mahr*.[103] Attempts have been made to recover the paid *Mahr* by placing the blame for the divorce on the woman.[104] If Islamic law is applicable, there is no indebted payment and this is not a ground for an action for recovery. From the case law we can also deduce that people, especially in the past, turned to consular authorities for a solution. In the aforementioned case before the Court of First Instance of the Hague the Moroccan consulate apparently told the husband of the woman that the paid part of the dower had to be returned because the woman fell ill.[105] In the case before the Court of First Instance of Amsterdam, decided on 27 January 1988, it was agreed at the consulate that due to the ending of the marriage a part of the dower would be repaid. The Court considered such an agreement to be in line with Dutch public policy.[106]

101. Staudinger, Art. 14, no. 273, with reference to AG Kerpen, *FamRZ* 1998, 1429.
102. Rb. 's-Gravenhage 10 July 1989, *NIPR* 1989, 399.
103. For an example of this see: OLG Hamburg 21 May 2003, *FamRZ* 2004, 459-461.
104. In Rb. 's-Gravenhage 29 October 1997, *NIPR* 1999, 142 the husband reclaims the at the time of the nuptials paid part of the dower worth fl. 7.000 because he was not to blame for the divorce. The Court considers in respect of the blame that, whether or not it is of importance, it has been insufficiently proven.
105. Rb. 's-Gravenhage 10 July 1989, *NIPR* 1989, 399.
106. *NIPR* 1989, 203.

In numerous cases the claim of the husband is denied by the Court for lack of a legal basis for granting the claim.[107]

8 Ownership of the *Mahr*

During the divorce proceedings, who is entitled to what property and capital will require determination. Also regarding the part of the *Mahr* previously paid to the woman by the man and the part still due, the question concerning ownership will have to be answered. This question is unanimously answered under the marital property law by the Courts in the Netherlands. If applying the conflict rule concerning the maritial property law leads to applicability of the foreign Islamic orientated law, then this in turn leads to the woman being the owner of the *Mahr*.

However, if the maritial property regime is governed by Dutch law and the parties married in a community of goods, then the question arises if the dower also falls within the community of goods; the possibilities for this are limited. Most of the Dutch judges assume that the *Mahr* falls within the community.[108] In an article published in the NIPR magazine I have already argued that the marriage contract can be considered as marital conditions. In a divorce settlement spouses can agree that certain property law elements stay out of a community. The *Mahr* clause leads to (or could lead to) the *Mahr* being outside of the community and thus also remain under the Dutch right of private ownership of the woman. The *Mahr* also stays outside of the community if the *Mahr* clause in the marriage contract can be regarded as containing an exclusion clause, in that sense the parties have declared with this that the woman becomes the owner of the *Mahr* (Rutten 2007: 103).

107. Rb. 's-Gravenhage 14 November 2005, *NIPR* 2007, 9 considers that the payment of the dower cannot be considered as a due payment. HR 11 July 2008, *LJN*: BC 8979/ *NIPR* 2008, 163: the Court had ruled that the goods had become the private property of the woman.

108. Rb. Haarlem 10 February 2004, *NIPR* 2004, 126 (gold jewels); Hof 's-Hertogenbosch 17 January 2006, *LJN*: AV5175 / *NIPR* 2006, 105; Hof 's-Gravenhage 19 April 2006, *LJN*: AY5780; Hof in HR 8 February 2008, *LJN*: BC3841 / *NIPR* 2008, 78 (jewels); Rb. Alkmaar 16 October 2008, *LJN*: BG4548 / *NIPR* 2009, 99; Rb. Haarlem 16 June 2009, *LJN*: BJ1034 (jewels). Contrary to these: Hof in HR 11 July 2008, *LJN*:BC 8979 / *NIPR* 2008, 163 (the buckle and jewels were connected to the woman, and thus her private property).

The German judge appears to have chosen a property law qualification where he rules that the question of ownership as a result of the making of a gift is subject to the *lex rei sitae*.[109]

It could be considered obvious that a result in which the *Mahr* would fall in any community of goods or whereby the man can have any claim on the *Mahr*, would be completely irreconcilable with the idea of the *Mahr* in an Islamic marriage, where the *Mahr* is the exclusive property of the woman, is meant to give the woman a possibility to have her own property, and whereby she also has the exclusive power of disposal regarding the *Mahr*.

9 Conclusion

The struggle concerning the correct way of embedding *Mahr* in western legal systems is by no means settled neither in the Netherlands nor the other countries subject to this research. As judges have more frequently been confronted with *Mahr*, the idea of a strange and reprehensible legal institution has faded into the background. The *Mahr* agreement is generally no longer considered against public policy. Because the problems surrounding the *Mahr* usually play a part within PIL, and within PIL we work with divided legal areas and legal rules, and not so much with general principles, the *Mahr* will also have to be placed in an existing category. The legal question concerning the *Mahr* will, in other words, have to be qualified. Because there is not a single perfect qualification, judges in different countries, but also within one country, maintain a plurality of qualifications. The *Mahr* is subsequently subject to legal rules and judged by criteria which are unfamiliar to the institute. Moreover, these rules can be completely different from country to country, which in turn can lead to very different results. Finally, it became apparent that there is a lack of clarity and disagreement regarding the question of the *Mahr* in relation to other provisions arranged after a divorce.

The cause of these problems lies in the collision of different legal cultures, whose coming together is the corollary of migration and a result of a multicultural society. Western legal systems are confronted with a legal concept unknown to them; on top of that, the legal concept is part of another bigger legal system in which it is interconnected. The legal concept is then singled out and transported into another legal system, in which another legal culture

109. In this respect OLG Köln 21 April 1993, *FamRZ* 1994, 899 / *NJW-RR* 1994, 200.

reigns and is another interconnected legal system. Within this different system one endeavours to fit the concept.

This leads to, as mentioned above, inconsistent judgments, and with that to legal uncertainty, but also to unsatisfactory results. This is so because in many cases this result damages the true nature of *Mahr* and often does not coincide with the intentions of the parties. The legitimacy of the judgments is therefore in danger.

That in turn leads to the question whether we should continue to use the rigid instrument from PIL, the qualification. On the one hand we are prepared to tolerate the *Mahr* within a legal order, but, on the other, it is subjected to obligatory rules and regulations unknown to the concept, which lead to a distortion of the legal concept. This can be prevented by recognising the *Mahr* as such, with all its peculiarities as a so-called acquired right.

Bibliography

Blenkhorn, Lindsey l., (2002) 'Islamic marriage contracts in American courts: interpreting *Mahr* agreements as prenuptials and their effects on Muslim women', *Southern California Law Review* vol. 76, vol. 1, (via Westlaw; pp. 1-34)

Cour de cassation, (1[re] Ch.civ) 22 November 2005 ; with note Marie-Claude Najm, *Journal de droit international* 2006, pp. 1365-1377.

Cotter, David M., (2003) 'Constitutional questions concerning the enforcement of Islamic antenuptial agreements', *Divorce Litigation*, (online; page references not available).

Coulson, N.J., (1994) *A History of Islamic Law*, Edinburgh, Edinburgh University Press.

Estin, Ann Laquer, (2004-2005) 'Towards a Multicultural Family Law', 38 *Family Law Quarterly* 501, pp. 501-527;

Fawzy, Essam, (2004) 'Muslim personal status law in Egypt: the current situation and possibilities of reform through internal initiatives', in: Lynn Welchman (ed.), *Women's Rights & Islamic Family Law. Perspectives on Reform*, London: Zed Books Ltd.

Fournier, Pascale, (2006) 'In the (Canadian) Shadow of Islamic Law: Translating *Mahr* as a Bargaining Endowment', 44 *Osgoode Hall Law Journal*, 649, (via Westlaw; pp. 1-21).

Freeland, Richard, (2000-2001) 'The Islamic Institution of *Mahr* and American Law', 4 *Gonzaga Journal of International Law*, 2; (via Westlaw; pp. 1-5).

Groot, G.R. de, (1979) 'Enkele opmerkingen over het islamitische recht, in het bijzonder over islamitische huwelijkscontracten', *WPNR* 5482, pp. 341-343 & 5483, pp. 361-367.

Henrich, (2004) 'Die Morgengabe und das Internationale Privatrecht', in: Privatrecht in Europa – Vielfalt, Kollisions, Kooperation, Festschrift Hans Jürgen Sonnenberger .

Jacobson, Heather, (2003) 'The Marriage Dower: Essential Guarantor of Women's Rights in The West Bank and Gaza Strip', *Michigan Journal of Gender and Law*, pp. 7 & 10.

Jindani, Mohamed, (1995) 'The Concept of *Mahr* (Dower) in Islamic Law: The Need of Statutory Recognition by English Law', in: *Yearbook of Islamic and Middle Eastern Law*, pp. 219-227.

Jones-Pauly, Christina, (2008) 'Marriage Contracts of Muslims in the Diaspora: Problems in the Recognition of *Mahr* Contracts in German Law', in: Asifa Quraishi and Frank E. Vogel (eds.), *The Islamic Marriage Contract*, Harvard University Press Cambridge, pp. 299-330.

Jordens-Cotran, L., (2007) *Nieuw Marokkaans familierecht en Nederlands IPR*, Sdu uitgevers's-Gravenhage.

Jordens-Cotran, L., (2000) 'De kwalificatie van de bruidsgave', *NIPR*, pp. 391-395.

Kegel, G. and K. Schurig, (2000) *Internationales Privatrecht:Ein Studienbuch*, C.H. Beck München

Linant de Bellefonds, Y., (1965) *Traité de droit musulman comparé. Livre II: Le mariage*, La Haye: Mouton&Co. Paris.

Mir-Hosseini, Ziba, 2000, Marriage on Trial. A Study of Islamic Family Law, I.B. Tauris London/New York pp. 32-22.

Moors, Annelies, (1995) *Women, Property and Islam*, Cambridge [etc.]: Cambridge University Press.

Motahari, Mortada, (2000) *Les droits de la femme en Islam*, Editions Al Bouraq Paris, p. 131.

Najm, Marie-Claude, (2006) Note with Cour de cassation (1re Ch.civ) 22 November 2005, *Journal de droit international*, pp. 1365-1377.

Nasir, J.J., (1986) *The Islamic Law of Personal Status*, Kluwer Law International The Hague.

Pearl, David and Werner Menski, (1998) *Muslim Family Law*, Sweet & Maxwell.

Qaisi , Ghada G., (2001) 'Religious Marriage Contracts: Judicial Enforcement of *Mahr* Agreements in American Courts', *Journal of Law and Religion* pp. 67-81.

Quraishi, Asifa and N. Syeed-Miller, (2004) 'No Altars: a Survey of Islamic Family Law in the United States', in: L. Welchman (ed.), *Women's Rights & Islamic Family Law. Perspectives on Reform,* Zed books Ltd London/New York.

Rohe, Mathias, (2005) 'On the Applicability of Islamic Rules in Germany and Europe', *European Yearbook of Minority Issues* 3, 2003/2004, Koninklijke Brill NV the Netherlands, pp.181-197.

Rutten, S., (2007) 'De bruidsgave: op zoek naar goud', *NIPR*, pp.101-115.

Sayed, Mosa, (2008) 'The Muslim Dower (*Mahr*) in Europe – With Special Reference to Sweden', in: K. Boele Woelki, T. Sverdrup (eds.), *European challenges in contemporary family law*, Antwerpen [etc.]: Intersentia pp. 187-208.

Siddiqui, Mona, (1995) '*Mahr*: Legal Obligation or Rightful Demand?' , 6 *Journal of Islamic Studies* 1, pp. 14-24 .

Siddiqui, Tracie Rogalin, (2007) 'Interpretation of Islamic Marriage Contracts by American Courts', 41 *Family Law Quarterly.*

Thompson, Emily L. en F. Soniya Yunus, (2007) 'Choice of Laws or Choice of Culture: How Western Nations Treat the Islamic Marriage Contract in Domestic Courts', 25 *Wisconsin International Law Journal*, 361. (via Westlaw; pp. 1-27).

Yassari, Nadja, (2003) 'Die Brautgabe nach iranischem Recht', 7 *Das Standesamtsgesetz*.

Wynn, L., (2008) 'Marriage Contracts and Women's rights in Saudi Arabia', In: A. Quraishi and F.E. Vogel (eds.), *The Islamic marriage contract: case studies in Islamic family law*, Cambridge: Harvard Law School, Islamic Legal Studies Program, pp. 200-214.

Welchman, Lynn, (2007) Women and Muslim Family Laws in Arab States. A Comparative Overview of Textual Development and Advocacy, Amsterdam University Press.

Welchman, Lynn, (ed.), (2004) *Women's Rights & Islamic Family Law. Perspectives on Reform*, London [etc.]: Zed Books Ltd.

Wurmnest, Wolfgang, (2007) 'Die Mär von der *Mahr* – Zur Qualifikation von Ansprüchen aus Brautgabevereinbarungen', *RabelsZ*, pp. 527-558.

Wurmnest, Wolfgang, (2005) 'Die Brautgabe im Bürgerlichen Recht', *FamRZ*, pp. 1878-1885.

Zulficar, M., (2008) 'The Islamic Marriage Contract in Egypt', in: A. Quraishi and F.E. Vogel (eds.), *The Islamic Marriage Contract*, Harvard University Press Cambridge, pp. 231-274.

CHAPTER 6

Mahr (dower) as a Bargaining Tool in a European Context: a Comparison of Dutch and Norwegian Judicial Decisions[1]

Katja Jansen Fredriksen

Abstract

Immigration and other aspects of globalization have brought a wealth of new ideas, norms and values into Norwegian society and into its domestic court-rooms as well. *Mahr* or the dower[2] is one such legal institution, a phenome-

1. I am grateful to several people who have contributed to this article. First of all I would like to thank Rubya Mehdi who encouraged me to continue my focus on *Mahr* and who initiated this publication. I also would like to thank Michael Bogdan and Mosa Sayed for valuable contributions concerning legal practice in Sweden. I am also much obliged to the participants of the conference 'Religion in the Public Sphere', held i Århus in 2008, in particular Mathias Rohe and the participants of the CULCOM conference 'Islam i Norge' which was held in Oslo that same year, in particular Anne Sofie Roald, Lena Larsen, Nora S. Eggen and Lene Løvdal. I am also much obliged to Susan Rutten and Roberta Aluffi for commenting earlier versions of this article. Finally. I am most grateful to my two supervisors Helge J. Thue and Knut S. Vikør for inspiring conversations and contributions during the process of writing this article. Any possible mistakes are – of course – my responsibility.
2. The dower is most frequently referred to as *Mahr* (for example in Asian Muslim countries, including India and Pakistan), *ṣadāq* (North-African countries), or *mehr* (Turkey), but in the *Qur'ān* we may also find the following terms used: *naḥla*, *ajr* or *farida* (lawful share, statutory portion). In Norwegian the 'dower' has been translated with '*brudegave*', '*brudepris*', '*morgengave*' and '*medgift*'. Personally I prefer to use '*brudegave*' because of the neutrality of the term and the fact that it does not have any historical associations to other legal contexts. In this article I, however,

non that is unknown in most European legal orders. The *Mahr* is an essential element of a Muslim marriage contract, irrespective of whether this contract is entered into in a Muslim state or in a secular state in Europe. If the *Mahr* is not specified in the marriage contract the marriage may not always be recognized in the country of origin. This mainly concerns Muslim states that base their legislation on the *Mālikī* school of jurisprudence, according to which the *Mahr* is a condition (Arabic: *rukn*) for contracting a valid marriage. The other jurisprudential schools consider the *Mahr* a legal effect (Arabic: *ḥukm*) of the marriage contract. According to, for instance, Moroccan law, which is founded on the *Mālikī* jurisprudential school, the stipulation of *Mahr* in the marriage contract is *a condition* for contracting a *valid* marriage.[3] In the new Moroccan *Mudawwana al-usra* of 2004 this condition is still upheld (Article 13 sub 2). This article is, however, moderated by Article 27, which sets no other restrictions to the *Mahr* than that the spouses may not waive their *Mahr* agreement in the marriage contract.[4] This amendment clearly was an accommodation in Moroccan law to meet the needs of the large community of Moroccan citizens that were living abroad. The *Mudawwana al-usra* of 2004

choose to use the term in its original form, as the legal institution of *Mahr* and its religious, legal and social implications can only be fully understood in an Islamic context.

3. The function of the *Mahr* is defined in Articles 26 and 27 of the Moroccan *Mudawwana al-usra* of 2004. Article 26 states that: "the *ṣadāq [Mahr]* is [that] what the husband offers his wife as a token of his wish to [enter] a marriage contract and to establish a stable family and to establish the fundaments of affection (*mawadda*) and company (*ʿishra*) between the two spouses. The legal basis is its symbolic and immaterial value and not its material value". Article 27 states that: "[t]he *ṣadāq* is decided upon the moment of entering the [marriage] contract. If the *ṣadāq* is not specified, the agreement is considered to be a *zawāj al-tafwīd*, marriage by authorisation [my translation].
4. Article 27 states that: "[t]he *ṣadāq [Mahr]* is determined at the moment the marriage contract is entered. If the parties conceal its designation, the contract is perceived as a *zawāj al-tafwīd* (marriage by authorisation): a marriage in which either spouse is supposed to have authorised the other spouse or a third part *(tafwīd)* silently to determine the *ṣadāq* after the marriage contract is being signed, as long as there is a mutual understanding between the parties and both the minimum and maximum of the *ṣadāq* is stipulated. If the spouses disagree with regard to the monetary value of the *ṣadāq* a proper dower can be determined before consummation of the marriage or the husband can repudiate his wife without being obliged to pay the *ṣadāq*. After consummation a proper *ṣadāq* is determined [my translation]. Note that a 'marriage by authorisation' is different from a 'marriage by proxy' (*tawkīl ʿa-al-zawāj*) (Berger, 2004: 17).

opens thus for and even urges to set the *Mahr* to a small, symbolic amount, but will not allow the female spouse to completely waive the *Mahr.*[5]

The other jurisprudential schools consider a marriage contract without a *Mahr* still valid, but this does not mean that the husband is released from his duty to pay *Mahr.* In such situation the *Mahr al-mithl* ('proper' or customary *Mahr*)[6] becomes due (Ali 1976: 397; Pearl & Menski 1998: 179-180; Nasir 2002: 83). Non-recognition may have comprehensive legal and social consequences for the parties involved.

This article takes as a starting point that Norwegian courts have not formally decided any *Mahr* claims yet, while other European courts have been dealing with *Mahr* claims for several decades already. According to Nadjma Yassari, Research Director at the Max Planck Institute in Hamburg, German courts have decided about 40 cases so far. Dutch practice seems to show similar developments. This article investigates what may be the reason for this discrepancy, asking whether *Mahr* claims actually have been raised before Norwegian courts without the judiciary recognizing the legal question that the dispute represented. Furthermore the question is raised whether the socio-economic problems resulting from high *Mahr* settlements in Muslim countries[7] have been transplanted into Europe and whether the 'concept of *Mahr* as a bargaining tool' which we know from Muslim legal practice has been adopted into European legal practice as well. By comparing Dutch and Norwegian litigation this article aims to show the relevance of *Mahr* in family disputes between Muslim spouses.

5. A similar provision can be found in the Tunisian *Code du Statut Personell (CStP) of 13 August 1956* which came into force on 1 January 1957. Tunisian Personal Status Law is also based on the *Mālikī* school of jurisprudence. In the Tunisian CStP the *Mālikī* doctrine has been taken over. Article 21 I CStP. which contains the conditions for the validity of marriage does not mention *Mahr.* However, according to Article 13 I CStP the wife can refuse consumation (in Arabic: *dukhūl*) of the marriage until the *Mahr* is paid. Only when the spouses explicitly agree in the marriage contract that no *Mahr* will be paid, the marriage contract is deemed invalid.
6. Proper *Mahr* is set according to what is locally appropriate for a woman of equal social status. See for a further explanation subsection 6.1 "A definition of *Mahr* and its different functions" later in this chapter.
7. Concerns have been raised over the *Mahr* and marriage costs being so high that young men are unable to marry, leading to considerable age differences between spouses and young people to the temptation of extra-marital sexual activity or *'urfi*-marriages (customary marriages). Due to these developments Muslim men may have to save for years before being able to marry and leaving them quite often in debt to other family relatives that contribute to the *Mahr* in order to enable them to marry (Welchman, 2007: 91).

6.1 A Definition of *Mahr* and its Different Functions

Before we can continue to analyse the Norwegian and Dutch judicial decisions in which *Mahr* has played a role we first need to define what *Mahr* is. The *Mahr* is an essential element of a Muslim marriage contract and is negotiated by the bride's legal guardian (*walī*), normally her father, before marriage is agreed upon. As already explained above, is the stipulation of the *Mahr* according to the *Mālikī* jurisprudential school, a precondition for contracting a valid marriage. The other *Sunni* and *Shīʿa* schools of jurisprudence perceive the *Mahr* as an effect of marriage.

Islamic law distinguishes between 'specified *Mahr*' (*Mahr musamma*) and 'proper *Mahr*' (*Mahr al-mithl*). Specified *Mahr* is the amount of *Mahr* that the contracting parties agreed upon when signing the marriage contract and is specified in the marriage agreement. If the *Mahr* is not specified in a marriage contract a *qāḍī* (judge) may determine the value of the *Mahr*. Proper *Mahr* is set according to what is locally appropriate for a woman of equal social status. A woman's social status may be determined by her social class, her legal status (being a *bikr,*[8] a divorcee or a widow), her education or other skills, age, beauty, manners, etc. Normally, the monetary value of the *Mahr* is set to what another female family member or close relative has received prior and what is commonly accepted as appropriate for a woman of similar social status.

As Islam sees spouses as separate legal objects, the *Mahr* becomes the unilateral property of the bride over which she normally may dispose freely. This thus contradicts the widely held misconception that the *Mahr* is equal to the 'brideprice', a discussion which still can be found in academic literature and daily conversation (Nasir, 2002: 83; Jordens-Cotran, 2007: 121; Buskens, 1999: 97).

The *Mahr* can be claimed in its entirety upon consummation of the marriage (prompt *Mahr* or *Mahr mu'ajjal)* or payment may be partly postponed until the marriage is dissolved either through divorce or by one spouse's death (deferred *Mahr*, *Mahr mu'ajjal* or *mu'akhkhar*). The *Mahr* is not only an important legal institution in classical Islamic legal science, *fiqh,* it also still forms an integral element in modern Muslim legislation. Although some Muslim states have tried to set an upper limit to *Mahr* through amendments in legislation or by precluding courts from hearing cases that involve excessive *Mahr* claims and in some cases even providing for the confiscation and

8. Virgin, not previously married.

redistribution to charitable causes or national development projects of the amounts paid in excess,[9] none have gone as far as to abolish *Mahr* completely due to its important religious and economic function in Muslim society.

Mahr may have different functions in different settings. These functions can be divided into material and immaterial functions. In the legal sense, only the material functions can be regulated by European law. Yet, this does not mean that the immaterial functions are not of interest to European legal practitioners too in order to understand the importance of this legal institution for the parties involved. These immaterial functions can be divided into religious, prestigious, social and protective functions, while the material functions mainly are economic, depending on the contents of the claim.

The prime function of the *Mahr* is its religious and moral function. As the practice of *Mahr* is prescribed by the *Qur'ān,*[10] it has far-reaching religious and legal consequences, independently of whether Muslim parties are living in countries with a Muslim legal order or in secular states in the West. Furthermore, the *Mahr* is stipulated to underline the importance and prestige of the marriage and may reassure the wife of the serious intentions of her husband.[11] This explanation is repeatedly given by my informants, irrespective of gender, nationality, ethnicity or the judicial school to which they adhere to. *Mahr* also has a social function as its value reflects and confirms the social status of the contracting parties and their families.[12]

9. For example in Sudan in 1975; in the UAE in 1973; in the PDRY in 1974 as well as in the YAR in 1976. In Tunisia the Tunisian Decree of 1941 aimed to set a maximum limit to the *Mahr* (Welchman, 2007: 91, 207).
10. See, for instance, verse 4:4 which states that: "[a]nd give the women their dower, an obligation…." *Mahr* is also mentioned in verses 4:24, 4:25, 4:3 and 5:5.
11. See for example Article 16 of the *Mudawwana al-usra*, the Moroccan Personal Status Law of 2004 which defines the *Mahr* or the *ṣadāq* as "the property given by the husband to indicate his willingness to contract marriage, to establish a family and to lay the foundations for affection and companionship [my translation]."
12. Ron Shaham described in his study of Egyptian *Sharī'a* court records from 1900 until 1955 the practice of the *Mahr al-sum'a*, 'the *Mahr* of reputation', or the *Mahr al-ʿalāniyya*, 'the public *Mahr*'. This practice inplied that the parties agreed to register a much higher amount of *Mahr* in the official marriage contract than what was actually paid to the bride. The actual *Mahr*, the *Mahr al-sirr or* 'the secret *Mahr*', was considerably lower. Egyptian court records reveal that the male spouse in divorce disputes sometimes argued that the '*Mahr* of publicity' was not binding on him. Annelies Moors describes an opposite trend in her article about 'the token *Mahr*' among Palestinian women in Jabal Nablus (Shaham, 1997: 29-30; Moors, 2008: 89-91).

Beside these immaterial functions, the *Mahr* also has an economic and thus a protective function as it reassures the wife of an income in case of repudiation or widowhood. In case of divorce the husband is no longer responsible for maintaining his wife. The whole *Mahr* (including the deferred *Mahr)* becomes due usually once the husband has pronounced a *ṭalāq*[13] or passes away. The deferred *Mahr* is therefore often set to an amount that is beyond the immediate means of the husband. Deferring a larger part of the *Mahr* aims to deter the husband from rashly divorcing his wife. In this way the *Mahr* functions as a way of supplying the wife with economic security in case of divorce. The deferred *Mahr* may also financially secure the woman upon the death of her husband.

As succession rights for women are limited in Islam the spouses can by contracting a high deferred *Mahr* guarantee the wife a similar life style upon her husband's death as she was used to during marriage. As the deferred *Mahr* is payable before all other debts, it will not pass to the other heirs of the deceased as a part of the inheritance.

I therefore personally prefer to see *Mahr* as a part of an Islamic economic arrangement based on different rights and duties for the spouses and founded on a form of gender justice that focuses on 'equal worth' rather than on 'gender equality'. In Islam men and women have different tasks and consequently different duties in marital life. The husband is obliged to financially maintain his family, while the wife is responsible for the matrimonial home and the daily care of the children. In addition she is supposed to subject herself to the obedience of her husband. On the other hand, any potential income from labour or inheritance is strictly hers.

The idea of 'equal worth' has often been contested from a gender equality perspective, but not all modern Muslim laws are discriminatory towards women, not even the most patriarchal ones, as is also pointed out in Lene Løvdal's article. Although Islamic law and Sharīʿa-based Muslim law[14] generally are perceived as 'barbaric' and static, recent developments in national legislation, human rights obligations, court practice and academic literature show the opposite (Abiad, 2008; An-Na′im, ed., 2002; Nasir, 2002; Welchman, 2007). Although it cannot be denied that many Muslim legal sys-

13. Unilateral repudiation of the wife without resort to legal proceedings.
14. Muslim law here refers to Muslim Personal Status Law (*al-aḥwāl al-shakhsiyya*), which is a collective term for the modern state legislation of Muslim States which contains that part of the *Sharīʿa* that applies to family relations (such as marriage, divorce, paternity, custody of children and succession). In European legal cultures 'Personal Status Law' is comparable with 'family law' (Nasir, 2002: 34).

tems still have many challenges to overcome in order to meet the universal standards of human rights, there are weaknesses within almost every legal system. Yet, this biased vision towards Islamic legal cultures may prevent the Norwegian judiciary from applying Muslim rules of law. In doing so they may miss the opportunity to come to well-balanced results. Islamic rules of law are often closely connected, building on each other like small building stones, leading to a result that is balanced if correctly applied. *Mahr* is – in my opinion – such a building stone for the economic arrangements between two spouses, both in life and upon death. As parties in principle freely can negotiate the terms of the *Mahr* agreement, based on the idea of *kafā'a* (equality of the husband to his wife) between the spouses which guarantees the wife at least the *Mahr al-mithl,* the *Mahr* may compensate for any potential gender inequalities in terms of unequal property rights and succession rights for women. By removing one single building stone, like the *Mahr*, the whole construction may fall apart.

6.2 How can *Mahr* become applicable in Norwegian Courts?

The idea of Sharīʿa rules being applied by domestic courts gives rise to strong feelings among the majority of the Norwegian population. Yet, few are aware that Islamic provisions *can* be applied by Norwegian, as well as by other European courts. However, in order to do so, two main conditions need to be fulfilled, in two successive phases. First of all Sharīʿa provisions can only be applied within the framework of Norwegian law and within limits defined by the Norwegian legislator, based on democratic values and on Norway's international human rights obligations due to the principle of state sovereignty. Secondly, the Norwegian judiciary operates in such situations as a neutral controlling actor in clarifying the limits of the public policy and the Norwegian Constitution, in order to prevent the application of provisions that contravene the Norwegian legal standards of human rights. If and only when these two conditions have been fulfilled can Sharīʿa provisions can be applied.

Each state may thus choose a different legal and political approach to these issues. Mathias Rohe, a German legal scholar and a specialist on Sharīʿa in Europe, suggests three possible legal levels on which Islamic legal provisions can be applied in legal orders in Europe (Rohe 2004: 161-184). Although this subsection only elaborates on how these three levels are applied in the Norwegian legal-political context, they are transferable to other European legal orders as well.

6.2.1 Private International Law (PIL)

Private international law (PIL) is one such possible level that may lead to the application of Islamic legal provisions. Private international law is also called conflict of laws or choice of law and can be seen as a situation of formal or 'weak legal pluralism'.[15] Each country has its own set of national private international law rules. Private international law is based on the idea that a person's personal status law should regulate all his or her private matters. The concept of a person's personal status law in PIL is a collective term for the law of the country that regulates all issues concerning that person's personal, family and succession law. The idea behind this concept is that some things are considered to be so close to one's identity, such as marital status and parental obligations, that the laws of the country to which one has *the strongest ties* to should regulate them (Thue 2002: 9). If an individual has organized his or her life in accordance with a certain legal order, these arrangements deserve protection even if that person changes his or her place of residence. This means that individuals still may be subjected to the law of the state of origin even if that person no longer is living there.

Within private international law nationality, domicile and habitual residence are the most relevant factors in determining which law is the party's personal status law.[16] While most countries in Europe, such as the Netherlands base their private international law on nationality in the field of family law, have Norway, Denmark, Switzerland and Great Britain taken a different position. The latter base their private international law on domicile.[17] As Norwegian immigration law grants aliens residence in Norway after a relatively short period of three years, this *de facto* means that immigrants obtain

15. Legal pluralism is practised in the former European colonies in Africa and Asia. In many Muslim countries imported Western law operates side by side with religious law and customary law and is practised by different ethnic communities within the framework of a formal system of law. This formal form of pluralism was called 'weak legal pluralism' by the legal anthropologist John Griffith (Griffith, 1986: 1-55).
16. Other determining factors are 'the choice of law of the better solution' and 'party autonomy', but these factors will not be discussed here.
17. Domicile in Norwegian private international law (PIL) is more or less perceived the same in Denmark, Iceland, Swiss and USA. In Great Britain domicile can be achieved in two ways. Domicile of origin is obtained upon birth. Children born into wedlock receive their father's domicile, while children born out-of wedlock receive their mother's domicile. Domicile of choice is obtained by residing freely in a country with the intention to stay their permanently. Domicile of choice shows in this sense similarities with domicile in Norwegian PIL.

domicile after a relatively short period of three years.[18] This implies that Muslim family law rules seldom become applicable in PIL cases in Norway. Although it generally is seen as an advantage to apply domestic law (*lex fori*) as it may reassure the predictability and the quality of the judicial decisions, as well as the efficiency of the courts, it may – however – in cases with one or more Muslim parties lead to the fact that conflicts remain unsolved or even deteriorate. Given the meaning that Sharīʿa has in the daily life of many citizens of Muslim background in secular states in Europe, the option to choose the law of one's country of origin, meaning Muslim personal status law, may therefore serve many good purposes. First of all, the application of Muslim family law provisions may make it easier for Muslim states to recognize European administrative and judicial decisions in family law issues. In this way 'limping situations'[19] and 'forum-shopping' could – in certain cases – be prevented, as I will show later. Secondly, if PIL provisions were applied in a way that Muslim personal status laws more often became applicable and if facts and underlying issues were better clarified by Norwegian judges and lawyers, disputes may be tempered and cases may in fact be solved.

6.2.2 Specific Legal Provisions for Defined Groups

The second possibility of applying Sharīʿa norms is when the legislator makes specific legal provisions for defined groups (here: Norwegian Muslims). The establishment of Sharīʿa councils as practised in Great Britain since the 1980s in order to enable Muslims to receive a divorce based on religious terms or to help Muslim women with their *Mahr* claims could be such an option. The Muslim Council of Norway (*Islamsk Råd Norge*) has on several occasions proposed the establishment of such an institution (Vogt 2008: 140; Ferrari de Carli 2008: 65-71),[20] but this proposal has not been followed

18. According to Article 12 of the Immigration Act (Norwegian: *Utlendingsloven av 24. juni Nr. 64 1988*).
19. 'Limping situations' are defined as situations where a change in personal status is recognized in the country of origin, but not in the receiving state. In Dutch: "*hinkende situaties*"; in French: "*des situations boîteuses*".
20. See also comments of Secretary of State, Kristin Ørmen Johnsen in the Norwegain tabloid *Verdens Gang* (VG) 27.5.2003 about public plans to establish a *Sharīʿa* cancil in Norway; furthermore similar suggestions by Sv politician Reza Rezaee i VG 5.1.2007 in response to articles in *Hubro* and *Klassekampen* about the author's PhD research. The amendment in the Marriage Act which grants both spouses the right to divorce obviously is an attempt to solve this issue.

up by the Norwegian government.[21] The scope of this article will not allow me to further elaborate on it, but also Norwegian Muslims turn to Sharīʿa councils in Great Britain in order to receive a religious divorce that is recognized in their country of origin. To what extent *Mahr* claims are taken up during these arbitration sessions is unknown to me, but would be an interesting topic for further research.

6.2.3 Optional Civil Law

The third level of application is by means of optional civil law. This could be realized for certain economical transactions that regulate matrimonial property arrangements between Muslim parties, like for example the possibility to include *Mahr* in a prenuptial agreement. Court litigation seems to illustrate that some Norwegian Muslims are aware of this option, although not always to the benefit of women, as I will return to later when analysing litigation.

6.3 The Comparative Legal Approach

In this article the legal questions rising from *Mahr* claims are addressed in two possible ways: by means of private international law, as discussed earlier and by means of *comparative legal method.* These approaches each have a different function. Private international law aims to solve cases with a stronger connection to another country by means of deciding which country's law should be applied. This choice is being made by choosing which *set* of conflict rules regulates the legal question at hand. This process is called 'classification'. Different rules may apply to different fields of law, depending on whether the legal question is formulated as family law, personal law, succession law or, for example, contract law. If the process of classification points out Muslim law as the applicable law, the court needs to further interpret the provisions concerned. European litigation shows that different classifications are possible.

The *comparative legal method* is usually used to find inspiration from other legal orders in order to find solutions within one's own domestic legal system. This means for example that a Norwegian judge can study *Mahr* de-

21. The scope of this article will not allow me to further elaborate this, but research on *Sharīʿa*-councils in Great Britain also shows that some Muslim women felt obliged to accept divorce conditions which were based on Islamic Law provisions, that were less favourable than English law. See for more on this subject the studies performed by *Samio Bano* on English *Sharīʿa* councils.

cisions from other European countries, preferably from legal orders similar to the Norwegian one, in order to accommodate the institution of *Mahr* into Norwegian law. This article mainly focuses on Dutch and Norwegian decisions on *Mahr*. This choice is based on the following considerations. Firstly the demographics of the Muslim immigration population in the Netherlands are quite similar to the immigration population in Norway.[22] Secondly, the Netherlands bases its PIL on nationality. This implies that Muslim law, as the law of the nationality of (one of) the parties, more often becomes applicable. In addition the Netherlands has ratified all the Conventions of the *Hague Conference on Private International Law (HccH)*, of which also Norway is a Member State, and which allows parties a large extent of party autonomy in particular in family law matters. As family law harmonization processes in Europe seem to lead in the direction of granting spouses in transnational marriages[23] more freedom to choose which set of laws should regulate their marital relations, I have chosen for the scope of this article to compare Norwegian and Dutch practice on *Mahr*.

6.4 Marriage Patterns and the Practice of *Mahr* in Europe

Statistics Norway recently reported that the immigration population in Norway in the period from 1996 to 2007 had increased mainly due to transnational marriages (Daugstad 2008 (1): 2; Daugstad 2008 (2): 162-172). Statistics also show that many Norwegian Muslims (both first and second generation immigrants) still rely on their family to arrange a marriage with a suitable spouse with the same national, ethnical, religious and cultural back-

22. The largest Muslim immigrant groups in the Netherlands consist of Turkish and Moroccan nationals that arrived as 'guest workers' in the sixties, later followed by refugees from Iran, Iraq, Bosnia-Herzegovina and Somalia. In Norway the Muslim population consists of immigrants with the same national background as the Muslim population in the Netherlands, in addition to Pakistani immigrants, which represent the largest muslim immigrant group in Norway. The Netherlands also houses larger groups of Indonesians who are hardly represented in Norway.
23. Transnational marriages are here defined as marriages between a person with residence in Norway, and a person without Norwegian residence. The term describes marriages where the parties formally hold residence in different countries when the marriage is entered, and includes both marriages with Norwegian immigrants (with Norwegian residence) and Norwegian citizens. Registration of a transnational marriage may form the basis for residence in Norway, based on establishment of family (Daugstad 2008 (1): 2; Daugstad, 2008 (2): 162-172).

ground and preferably from the same geographical region as their parents (Daugstad 2008 (1): 2). It seems therefore natural to assume that Muslims in the diaspora also have brought their marriage traditions, including local practices and customs concerning *Mahr*, to Europe.

In Denmark the legal anthropologist Rubya Mehdi has performed qualitative interviews amongst the Pakistani community in Denmark about their practice of *Mahr*. As Pakistanis represent the largest Muslim immigrant group in Norway her empirical material is also of comparative interest to the Norwegian context. Rubya Mehdi's research shows that Pakistani immigrants in Denmark, coming from different provinces of Pakistan, may practice *Mahr* differently. Both the payment conditions and the monetary values of the *Mahr* varied from symbolic values of about € 50 to € 6,000. Yet, all interviewees – with the exception of those from the North-Western Frontier Province (NWFP) and Balochistan[24] – had designated *Mahr* in their marriage contracts. The largest *Mahr* stipulations were contracted between spouses that both originated from the Punjab and Sindh provinces and between young Pakistani that had grown up in Denmark and who by contracting high *Mahr* agreements wished to confirm the seriousness of their commitment.

In Sweden, the legal scholar Mosa Sayed has performed a similar survey on the value of *Mahr* as specified in 46 Muslim marriage contracts celebrated at the Uppsala mosque in Sweden (Sayed 2008: 191-192). His survey also confirms that many Muslims in Sweden despite their strong connection to Sweden (either through citizenship or residence) agreed upon a *Mahr* when contracting marriages in Sweden. Also here practice varied, both with regard to the monetary values of the *Mahr,* as well as the payment conditions. In marriage contracts in which one of the parties was of ethnic Swedish origin and had converted to Islam, *Mahr* was mainly symbolic.[25] Also in the other cases the prompt *Mahr* was mainly stipulated as a symbolic sum of money, ranging from € 0 to € 9,000.[26] The deferred *Mahr*, on the other hand, consisted more often of a considerable sum of money. In one case the couple had agreed upon € 25,000 as deferred *Mahr*, in addition to a prompt *Mahr* of € 25,000.[27] Another couple had agreed upon € 10,000 as deferred *Mahr*. In two

24. Where it is custom to pay *vulvar* to the family of the bride, instead of *Mahr* (Mehdi, 2003: 122-124).
25. Only 1 out of 46 contracts had stipulated *Mahr* to an amount of 0 Swedish *kroner*.
26. A monetary value of € 0 actually contravenes Quranic provisions.
27. T952-99 and RH 2005: 66; *Hälmstads tingsrätt* 2002-10-24 and *Hovrätten för Västra Sverige* 2004-11-22. See also Michael Bogdan, 2007: 178-180.

cases the deferred part consisted of a house.[28] The highest *Mahr* agreements were contracted between spouses who both originated from a country with a Muslim legal order.

The Danish and Swedish surveys show that Muslim immigrants may stipulate considerable amounts of *Mahr* in their marriage contracts. This raises questions to what extent Norwegian Muslims practice similar *Mahr* agreements. Faith communities in Norway may – under certain conditions – be granted the right to solemnize marriages.[29] This practice is the result of the strong position of the Lutheran State Church in Norwegian society and Norway's international human rights obligations to grant all citizens equal rights in relation to the freedom of religion.[30] These marriage ceremonies include an official Norwegian part in which the parties express their wish to enter a marriage in front of the imam. This official part is then followed by an optional religious ceremony, which includes the traditional elements of 'offer and acceptance' by the two parties and the contracting of a Muslim marriage contract.

Muslims in Norway thus have the possibility to enter Islamic marriage contracts in accordance with their own ethnic customs and traditions in Norwegian mosques. Although practices may differ from one community to another, all communities require the presence of at least two witnesses and the specification of *Mahr* in the marriage contract. In order to indicate that the Muslim marriage contract has no formal legal status as a marriage certificate in Norway from which no legal consequences can be derived, some mosques stamp the contract stating that the document is 'not valid in Norway'. This may partly explain why Norwegian courts so far have not been confronted with *Mahr* claims resulting from marriages which were contracted in Norway.

As mentioned earlier marriage customs differ from one Muslim community to another and this also includes the practice of the *Mahr*. Bosnian communities in Norway normally designate a symbolic *Mahr*, e.g. one dollar, Quran-lessons or a pilgrimage to Mecca. Among Turkish, Iraqi and Moroc-

28. One situated in Algeria and one in Sweden.
29. The right of solemnization is limited to faith communities that receive an official grant by the Norwegian state. In order to be granted this right the wedding procedures must first be approved by the Norwegian Crown, according to *Act No. 64 of 12 June 1981.*
30. According to Article 9 of the *European Convention of Human Rights (ECHR*), incorporated as Norwegian law through the Human Rights Act (*Menneskerettsloven, MRL*).

can communities money, jewellery or gold up to a value of € 6.000 to € 12,000 is not unusual.[31] Court practice seems to confirm these amounts, although the small number of cases may not necessarily be representative. Amongst Pakistani communities the dowry seems to be of more importance than the *Mahr*, but due to the sensitivity of the subject my informants do not seem willing to give me an indication of the actual values involved. Yet, some have pointed out that symbolic *Mahr* settlements may become problematic in the dissolution of marriages between close family relatives. Stories of Norwegian marriage contracts containing stipulations of *Mahr* up to a value of up to € 100,000 have also been reported by the Norwegian press and where even up for political discussion in 2005, without this leading to any form of follow-up by means of further research or regulation.[32]

We can therefore conclude that research from the Scandinavian countries shows that the monetary value of *Mahr* varies, but may involve considerable values taking into consideration the moderate incomes of the parties involved. *Mahr* agreements seem to be highest when both spouses come from Muslim legal orders where local practice and economic infrastructures with high inflation dictate high *Mahr* settlements. Further research about *Mahr* practice in other European countries could provide more insight in the practice of *Mahr* agreements.

6.5 How can *Mahr* be used as a Bargaining Tool in a European Context?

The fact that many Muslims in Europe have dual citizenship is an additional complicating factor. As the nationality laws of Muslim countries normally will not allow citizens that are domiciled abroad to surrender their citizenship,

31. According to my informants it is common amongst Moroccan communities to give jewellery, such as a golden belt, to a value of 50,000 Norwegian *kroner* (€ 6,250).
32. Political questions were raised concerning an article in the Norwegian tabloid paper *Verdens Gang (VG)* on 7 December 2005 about a contract entered by a mother of a 16 year old girl and a 67 year old man about the solemnization of a marriage between them when the girl became 18 years old against a compensation of 800.000 Norwegian *kroner* (€ 100,000). A parliament member questioned the Minister of Justice about Norwegian legislation on this point. See for documentation of the whole procedure http://epos.stortinget.no/SpmDetalj.aspx?id=33309, *Skriftelige spørsmål til skriftelig besvarelse. Dokument nr. 15 (2005-2006). Spørsmål nr. 257, datert 09.12.2005 fra Olav Gunnar Ballo (SV) til justisministeren Knut Storberget (A),* last accessed 10.10.2008.

they need to relate to two legal cultures that may be quite different from each other in family law issues. This may lead to conflict of laws. Due to this dual citizenship individuals are obliged to register all changes in their personal status both in their country of residence and in their country of origin. Second and third generations face these problems as well, as they obtain their citizenship (or ID-card) through the patriarchal line.

When European judicial or administrative decisions in the field of family law are not recognized in other legal orders 'limping' situations may arise. Norwegian Muslims have experienced such problems with 'limping marriages', meaning that citizens are considered to be divorced in one state, while married in another (Fredriksen 2006, 10-11; Vogt 2000/2008: 123; Wærstad 2006; Salimi 2001: 59-60).

The necessity to relate to two legal cultures may also have another side effect. It may increase the possibility of forum shopping. Court practice seems to indicate that both men and women, deliberately or not, make use of this option in a way that suits their interests best. Family law is a field of law in which many values, both economically and emotionally, are at stake. This may invite parties to exploit legal *lacunae* and taking advantage of the possibilities that each legal system offers. Parties may thus be tempted to use these possibilities strategically against another, as also Norwegian practice and other European judicial practice seems to show signs of.

6.5.1 Different Bargaining Strategies

In the following subsection we will elaborate how *Mahr* can become a bargaining tool between two or more Muslim parties in Norway in relation to marriage dissolution. Although this analysis mainly is based on Norwegian court decisions and interviews,[33] these arbitration processes are not exclusive for Norway, but take also place in other European states.

6.5.1.1 Mahr with regard to divorce (ṭalāq and khulʿ)

The first strategy is that of the 'recalcitrant spouse'. This strategy implies that even if spouses in principle may agree upon a divorce, the male spouse may still refuse to pronounce the *ṭalāq* in the hope to force his wife to agree upon waiving her claim for *Mahr* and other economical support in return for a

33. Based on my dissertation "Mahr as Cross-Border Conflict in Norwegian Family Law Disputes: Conflict of Laws, Possible Solutions and the Threshold for Tolerance".

khul' divorce.[34] One possible male strategy is to expose the wife to verbal or physical violence. The wife may respond by disobedient behaviour in order to provoke her husband to grant her a *ṭalāq*. If such a situation occurs the wife is normally left with the following options. She may settle for solely seeking a Norwegian civil divorce with the risk that the civil divorce is not recognised in her country of origin. This implies – among other consequences – that she can not remarry. Furthermore, she may ask relatives, an imam or another (religious) authority to mediate in order to convince the male spouse to release her from the religious tie by granting her a *ṭalāq*. Alternatively, she may engage the services of a Sharī'a council in Great Britain, in which case she often ends up with a *khul'* divorce. Finally, she may engage a lawyer in her country of origin in order to help her to seek a judicial divorce (*faskh*) or a divorce on mutual agreement (*khul'*), or she may travel herself and seek divorce in her country of origin. These last two options can be expensive and time-consuming and women may risk that their husbands or their family-in-law deprives them from their travel documents, which may cause obstacles in returning to Norway (Salimi 2001).

6.5.1.2 Mahr with regard to polygyny

As *Mahr* becomes due in case of *ṭalāq* another strategy is possible. The male spouse legally divorces his wife in Norway, but does not register the Norwegian divorce in his country of origin. The deferred *Mahr* is then not due upon him. He can remarry according to polygamy provisions in his country of origin and his new wife can apply for family reunification in Norway. The first wife receives social benefits from the Norwegian State in order to support herself and her children upon the divorce. Nevertheless, she still is formally married according to Sharī'a-based Muslim law and a divorce may be hard to acquire without her husband's permission.

If such a situation occurs the first wife may respond in two possible ways. She may accept the second marriage rather than to opt for divorce, as divorcees often have a low social status in Muslim communities. In this situation the two families continue to live separately, but still closely together as an extended family. Alternatively she does not accept the second marriage and moves out with the children. Both situations are problematic, not only for the parties involved, but also on a state level.

34. *Khul'* is a divorce at the instance of the wife in return for a compensation, for example prompt and/or deferred *Mahr*, *nafaqa* (maintenance for minor children) and/or *ḥaḍana* (custody of minor children).

The first situation is problematic for several reasons. Seen from the point of view of the Norwegian State which prohibits polygamy[35] by law and which has a legal obligation and responsibility to protect Muslim female citizens against discrimination, these 'polygamous' family constructions are 'a needle in the eye'. Also seen from the point of view of the country of origin, which by means of amendments in state legislation and administrative regulations attempts to limit the practice of polygamy, these individual strategies undermine state efforts.[36] Finally, these male strategies undermine the legal protection of Muslim women in Norway, as they are caught between two legal systems.

The second situation is problematic as well, as women despite the Norwegian divorce are still exposed to expectations from their (former) husband with regard to their 'marital obligations'. This had lead to reports about violence and rape of divorced women by their ex-husbands, often in relation to custody cases.[37] According to my informants both situations are not uncommon among certain minority groups in Norway.

6.5.1.3 Mahr with regard to the matrimonial property

Most disputes concern the division of the matrimonial property after divorce. As we may recall, Muslim legal orders do not recognize joint matrimonial property regimes. According to classic Islamic law the wife's contribution in the form of care and domestic tasks is not financially appreciated in the sense that she obtains an equal share of the matrimonial property. On the other hand, she is not expected to contribute economically to the joint household and any possible income from labour is therefore hers. Most legal orders in Europe are based on different matrimonial regimes. Both spouses are supposed to contribute to the family, either by means of labour, care for the house and the children or a combination of both. This discrepancy may lead to conflict of laws.

35. According to Article 4 of the Marriage Act. NOU 2003: 19 confirms that polygamy is contradictive to Norway's human rights obligations.
36. The Pakistani *Muslim Family Ordinance of 2nd March 1961 (VIII of 1961)* states for example in Section 6. (1) "No man, during the subsistence of an existing marriage, shall, except with the previous permission in writing of the Arbitration Council, contract another marriage, nor shall any such marriage contracted without such permission be registered under this Ordinance."
37. See, for example, *LB-2003-11758*, p. 5, by the *Borgating lagmannsrett* of 29 November 2004. Most Norwegian cases in this article are published on www.lovdata.no.

According to Norwegian law joint matrimonial property regimes are the rule. Nevertheless, Norwegian law treats both spouses as separate economic actors. This implies that each of the spouses during marriage maintains ownerships over his or her own means, while the other spouse enjoys the *usufruct* over the other spouse's property. As income from labour or other means thus in principle belongs to each individual spouse, this implies that each spouse also is responsible for his or her personal debts. Only in case of divorce, the matrimonial property will be divided equally. If spouses prefer a separate matrimonial regime, this needs to be formalized prior to marriage in a prenuptial agreement.[38] Marriage settlements may also be entered during marriage.

Norwegian litigation shows examples of Muslims couples that had arranged their matrimonial property regime on Islamic provisions.[39] In these cases women were forced to sign marriage settlement that left them with only a small amount of money or values (on a personal saving account or a second-hand car), while the male spouses were left with values and estate up to several million Norwegian *kroner*. These personal bank accounts or other values could very well be *Mahr* arrangements. In all cases the wives had been exposed to violence by their former husbands. In all cases the wives contested the marriage settlements during the divorce proceedings which were set aside by the Norwegian judge due to their unreasonableness.

6.6 The Enforcement of *Mahr* in a Transnational Legal Context

As other European countries have longer experience with the integration of Muslim immigrants European courts also seem to have more experience in deciding *Mahr* claims. *Mahr* can be translated and enforced into European legal cultures by private international law provisions and by means of substantive law. By transferring this typical Islamic legal institution from a Muslim legal order into a European one, case law attempts to recreate *Mahr* as a legal transplant.[40] These translation processes reveal that *Mahr* can be treated

38. According to Article 42 of the Marriage Act.
39. See, for instance, *LB-2003-2237* and *RG-2000-566*.
40. See, for example, Fournier, 2007: 158. The notion of legal transplants has been a central issue for the last three decades. This is also due to contributions by the legal historian Alan Watson and in particular his widely known and successful book *Legal Transplants: an Approach to Comparative Law* (Watson 1974). While the success of Watson's study emerged from the recognition that borrowing normally is the

in different ways: as an integral and essential part of the Islamic marriage contract; as a substitute for post-divorce maintenance; as the division of the surplus of marital profits; as succession; as contract law, as a gift or even as *Mahr al-mithl.*[41] As *Mahr* claims normally come up in relation to divorce petitions, European courts have mainly dealt with *Mahr* claims as a form of maintenance or as a part of the matrimonial property.

6.6.1 The Practice of *Mahr* by Dutch Courts

The following selection of Dutch private international law cases represents the different bargaining strategies as practiced by both parties. In Dutch litigation *Mahr* claims mainly come up as a result of a petition for divorce, which in the Netherlands is granted by a judge. Dutch *Mahr* claims have therefore mainly been treated as a part of the matrimonial property regime of the spouses, as maintenance or as a gift. Most cases involve Turkish, Tunisian, Moroccan and Iranian parties[42] and the choice of law therefore stands between Dutch law on the one hand and foreign law on the other hand.

6.6.1.1 A selection of Turkish cases

The following three cases concerned *Mahr* claims dated from 1999 until 2008 in which at least one party was Turkish. The application of PIL provisions either resulted in the choice of Dutch or Turkish law. As Turkish law is secular, Islamic provisions on *Mahr* are not applicable under Turkish state law. However, this did not prevent Turkish parties residing in the Netherlands from claiming *Mahr* before Dutch courts. In case Dutch law was applied *Mahr* could either be classified as a part of the matrimonial property or as a gift.

driving factor for legal change, his idea's have also been contested by others, such as the legal scholar Pierre Legrand, who was of the opinion that it is impossible to transfer rules and laws from one legal order to another (See for example Legrand, 1996: 2-19). The Italian legal scholar Gianmaria Ajani argues, on the other hand, that "law is a dynamic and transnational phenomenon" and that "legal borrowings simply occur, though they can be more or less effective, more or less persistent" (p. 1). The embedding of the legal transplant of *Mahr* in European courts seems to illustrate his point very well (Ajani 2007: 1-8).

41. As for example granted in Germany by the Hamburg Court to an Iranian wife, see *IPRax 1983*, pp. 64-65, 74-77, as well as Fournier, 2007: 162.
42. Moroccan and Turkish communities are the largest Muslim communities in the Netherlands.

The first case[43] involved two spouses of Turkish and Dutch nationality, in which the husband claimed the reimbursement of the *Mahr* as a part of his petition for divorce. The dispute concerned the legal question whether the *Mahr* was a part of their common matrimonial property regime[44] or should be granted the wife.[45] As the couple married in community of goods in the Hague on 17 September 2004 their matrimonial property regime was regulated by Dutch rules. A little more than half a year later the husband petitioned the Hague Municipal Court for divorce and asked the Court to determine the matrimonial property regime of the couple. The wife did not contest the request for divorce, but claimed that the *Mahr* fell outside the joint matrimonial property, as was claimed by the man. The Court granted the couple a divorce and decided that the *Mahr*, consisting of jewellery, was a part of the joint matrimonial property. Yet, the jewellery was granted the wife on the condition that she would return half of their value to her former husband. The Court did not allow her to return half of the jewellery.

The wife appealed to the Court of Appeal which confirmed the earlier decision on the following grounds: "*the jewellery was not given to the wife during the marriage celebration on the condition that it would be withheld from the joint matrimonial property of the spouses.* "The Court furthermore held that "*[t]he fact that* ***only the wife can wear the jewellery*** *does* ***not imply*** *that the jewellery is* ***attached*** *[my emphasis] to the wife.*" The jewellery was therefore seen as a part of the matrimonial property of the couple *"**if it [the jewellery] still exists at the moment of marriage dissolution** [my emphasis and translation]".*[46]

The dispute furthermore concerned the value of the jewellery. The man claimed that the jewellery had a value of € 13,184.00. The wife contested this, but as the jewellery had disappeared and the parties disagreed as to where they were, their value could not be estimated. The Court therefore held that the husband's claim could not be proven, but that the husband still was entitled to half of their value, leaving the question of the monetary value of the *Mahr de facto* unanswered.

The wife appealed to the Supreme Court emphasizing the religious function of the *Mahr* to which only the wife was entitled. According to her the

43. Hoge Raad, 8 February 2008, LJN: BC3841, R07/027HR, see www.rechtspraak.nl – zoeken.rechtspraak.nl, last accessed 7.11.2008.
44. According to Article 1: 94 of the Dutch Civil Code.
45. According to 81 RO.
46. See 10 sub 7 of the decision, page 3.

Mahr[47] *"was a part of by Islam inspired family law and in fact a gift by the husband to his wife – without quid pro quo [service in return]."* She held the *Mahr* translated into Dutch property law *"should be seen* ***as a religious/culturally determined gift*** *given by the man to the wife with the obvious intention that it is not a part of the community of goods"* [my emphasis].

However, the Supreme Court waived away this argument, as it had not been raised in earlier instances, which seemed to be a missed opportunity of the wife's lawyer. The appeal was denied and the husband was granted half of the value of the jewellery. In my opinion this was not unreasonable given the shortness of the marriage and the couple's choice for a joint matrimonial regime. According to Turkish (secular) law the wife would not have been granted *Mahr* either. Yet, from a Sharīʿa point of view, this decision seemed unjust, as *Mahr* is a consequence of a marriage in which the reality of the marriage, not its length is decisive. It is obvious that the marriage was a fact after half a year, a fact that was not contested by any of the parties. As we already mentioned in the beginning of this article once the marriage is consummated, the wife is entitled to the whole *Mahr*.

In 2006 the 's-Gravenhage Court of Appeal[48] came to a similar result. Dutch law was applicable concerning the joint matrimonial property regime. None of the parties contested this decision. However, as to the division of the joint matrimonial property the parties disagreed. Again considerable values were involved. The dispute concerned the matrimonial house and the *Mahr*, consisting of € 13,344.76, golden jewellery and 34 pieces of gold, as well as some closed envelopes which contained a total of € 220. Also in this case the jewellery had disappeared from the matrimonial house. The wife was of the opinion that all the wedding presents belonged to her on the basis of *"Turkish and Islamic customs and rituals"* due to which it is *"common that the wife receives a Mahr which contains money, golden jewellery and other valuable things"*. Furthermore, she argued that *"according to Turkish customs, but also to Islam, the wife is granted a Mahr when she marries as a virgin"*. Yet, the Court decided that the wife had to repay half of the total value of the wedding presents (i.e. € 15,163.90) to her former husband.

47. As incorrectly transcribed *sadag* in the court decision, referring to Moroccan practice instead of Turkish practice concering *Mahr*. It is impossible to read from the case whether it was the female party or the Supreme Court who used this terminology, or both.
48. LJN: AY5780, Gerechtshof 's-Gravenhage, 1279-H-05 NIPR 2007, p. 99.

In an earlier Supreme Court case from 2001[49] the claim concerned the return of the gifts, or the reimbursement of their values, as offered to a Turkish couple[50] after their engagement was broken off. Each of the parties claimed ownership over the gifts. The claim was sustained as the gifts were given under the presumption that the marriage would take place. In this case the male party received all of the jewellery in return (Rutten 2001: 83).

Summarising, we can say that these three Turkish cases involved disputes concerning considerable amounts of *Mahr* which were claimed after relatively short marriages. In all the cases Dutch law was applied with the result that the wife either had to return half of the value of the *Mahr* to her husband or even all of it. These results are completely irreconcilable with the idea of the *Mahr* in an Islamic marriage and the intentions of the parties.

6.6.1.2 A Tunisian case

Another interesting case involved a marriage between a Dutch woman and a Tunisian man. The couple had married in 1981 in Tunisia.[51] In 1983 the man moved to the Netherlands in 1983. In 1985 the wife petitioned for a divorce on the basis of Dutch law, which she was granted. Yet, the matrimonial property settlement was decided by Tunisian law, the first common domicile of the spouses. According to Tunisian law the spouses have common matrimonial property unless something else is agreed. In the case at stake the spouses only had an agreement concerning the *Mahr*. The couple was granted a divorce, according to Dutch law. In addition the wife was granted *Mahr*, based on the Tunisian *Mahr* agreement (Rutten 1988: 84). We may therefore conclude here that the Dutch wife, deliberately or not, managed to benefit from both legal orders.

6.6.1.3 A selection of Moroccan cases

The following two lower instance court cases both involved the claim for payment of deferred *Mahr* as strategically played out by two Moroccan spouses in case of a divorce. In the first case of 2 June 2003[52] the couple had petitioned the Court for divorce based on a mutual agreement, which they were granted. In their divorce agreement the couple had specified in relation

49. Hoge Raad, 13 July 2001, *RvdW 2001, 138.*
50. Although the normal procedure is that the gifts are offered the wife, the decision here mentions the 'couple', meaning both the male and the female party, as the recipients of the gifts.
51. Rechtbank Arnhem, November 7, 1985, *NIPR 1986, 271.*
52. LJN: AF9352, Rechtbank Maastricht, 72204/HA ZA 02-90.

to the *Mahr* that: "*[t]he wife maintains her rights to the Mahr,*[53] *as designated in the Moroccan marriage contract. The husband agrees*". The same divorce agreement stated that "*in case of potential conflicts due to this agreement Dutch law is applicable and the Maastricht Municipal Court has sole jurisdiction*". The Moroccan marriage contract designated a *Mahr* (*ṣadāq*) of 70,000 Moroccan *dirham* (about € 6,000), of which 20,000 *dirham* already were paid as prompt *Mahr.* The dispute concerned the remaining of the *Mahr,* in addition to interest.

According to the man Moroccan law was applicable for the following reasons. Firstly, he wanted "*to reassure himself by the application of Moroccan rules that he would not be met by an additional claim for payment of deferred Mahr in Morocco*". Secondly, he claimed that according to Moroccan rules the wife had no claim towards him. The wife disagreed and held that Dutch law was applicable. The Court was of the opinion that the divorce agreement could point out that the spouses had chosen a joint matrimonial property regime. This would indicate a choice for Dutch law as to the division of their matrimonial property. However, the strict conditions of the *Hague Convention of 14 March 1978*[54] had not been followed. The Court could thus not determine with certainty whether Moroccan or Dutch law was applicable. The Court concluded that the intentions of the divorce agreement were to be followed and referred to Article 20.3 of the (old) *Mudawwana* that states that the whole of the *Mahr* is payable upon death or consummation of the marriage. As the male spouse had not contested the validity of the marriage, nor its consummation, the Court ordered the man to pay the remaining 50,000 Moroccan *dirham* in Euro, in addition to interest.

In the second case from 16 March 2006 by the 's-Hertogenbosch Court of Appeal[55] Dutch law was applicable to the matrimonial property regime of two spouses of Moroccan-Dutch origin. On 5 June 1997 the couple got married at the Moroccan Consulate in 's-Hertogenbosch according to Moroccan law. Both spouses had both Moroccan and Dutch nationality and established themselves in the Netherlands directly after their marriage. After three years of marriage, the Court of Maastricht granted the couple a divorce according to Dutch law. The Court took into consideration the fact that the couple had not been granted a divorce in Morocco yet, thus clearly indicating a form of

53. In Dutch: '*bruidsschat*' (dowry), which was interpreted by the Court as '*bruidsgave*', bridal gift.
54. *Convention of 14 March 1978 on the Law Applicable to Matrimonial Property Regimes.*
55. LJN: AV5175, Gerechtshof 's-Hertogenbosch C0400125.

strong legal pluralism, in which judicial decisions in one particular legal order may influence the outcome of decisions in another.

The marriage contract designated a *Mahr* to 5,000 Dutch guilders (about € 2,500 at the time of marriage) which the husband was obliged to pay as he married his wife according to "[t]he Book and the Traditions of the Prophet". The wife claimed *Mahr* in addition to interest as a "*compensation of the emotional and economical damage [reduction in income: my insertion] that she had been suffering due to the divorce*". The male spouse rejected the claim on the basis that the *Mahr* only implies a "*moral not a legal obligation and if this Mahr would be due according to Moroccan/Islamic law this would not be applicable in a matrimonial property situation to which Dutch law is applicable.*"

Dutch law was applicable as the Netherlands was the couple's first joint domicile.[56] Therefore the wife's claim was not sustained. The Court did not sustain the wife's subsidiary claim for fairness and reasonableness either, based on the following explanation: "according *to Moroccan law upon divorce all property is returned to the man, who does not have any maintenance obligations towards his former wife, for which the Mahr offers the Muslim woman a* ***compensation***" [my emphasis].

Here the judge referred to the interconnection of Islamic rules as explained in the beginning of this article, which can be compared with 'building stones' and which – while seen in close connection to each other – may lead to a fair and balanced result in a Muslim context. If one, however, extracts those elements that are favourable to one party (in this case by granting the wife a *Mahr* in addition to the benefits resulting from Dutch law) the result may be unfair towards the other party (here: the husband who might risk ending up with paying the deferred *Mahr* in addition to an equal division of the matrimonial property with his former wife).

The Court of Appeal did therefore not sustain the claim for *Mahr*, and both parties had to cover their own litigation costs. Whether the wife later claimed her right for *Mahr* in connection to the divorce in Morocco is unknown to me.

56. According to Article 4.1 of *the Convention of 14 March 1978 on the Law Applicable to Matrimonial Property Regimes* in accordance with Article 15.2 of the same Convention, which determines that the matrimonial property regime is governed by the internal law of the State of the common nationality of the spouses. According to Article 1.1 under b jo.2 of the *Wet Conflictenrecht Huwelijksbetrekkingen* the law of their regular habitual residence (here: Dutch law) regulates all legal effects of the marriage.

6.6.1.4 An Iranian case

The last case of this selection of Dutch *Mahr* claims is an interesting lower instance case from 2006 decided by the 's-Gravenhage Court of First Instance.[57] It involved two Iranian parties who had left Iran by the end of 1994, when the wife was 19 years old, in order to settle in France. In France the wife followed a university course which she had to break off due to her husband's transfer to the Netherlands. In the Netherlands she finished her study at a Dutch university and continued with a second course.

The legal question was which law was applicable to the dissolution of their marriage and to what extent the wife could claim maintenance from her former husband. According to the wife Dutch law was applicable. The husband held that Iranian law was applicable. He was of the opinion that his wife still maintained strong ties to Iran and rejected her petition for divorce and consequently her request for maintenance.

The Court held that – in principle – the joint national law of the parties was applicable in case of dissolution of marriage, according to *Article 1.1 sub a WCE.* This would imply that Iranian law was applicable to the case. However, in case a real tie to the country of the common nationality no longer existed, this rule was not applicable. The wife contested this tie as the rest of her family had settled in Canada and she only had returned once to Iran in 1997. Out of the 11 years that she had been living abroad, she had had habitual residence in the Netherlands the last five years. Additionally, she did not intend to return to Iran, having applied for Dutch citizenship and hoped to find employment in the Netherlands after finishing her studies. The Court agreed that the wife *de casu* no longer had a real connection to Iran and therefore concluded that Dutch law, as the law of the spouses' habitual residence, was applicable.

Against this, the male spouse claimed that his former wife acted contradictorily, making the choice for Dutch law, while simultaneously starting procedures in Iran to claim the legal effects of the marriage contract there. The marriage contract stipulated a *Mahr* of € 55,000. The man argued that as long as his wife was claiming the *Mahr* in Iran, he could not return to his home country without risking not being allowed to leave the country again.

The wife counter-argued that her claim for *Mahr* was based on the marriage contract and that "this is the only thing that she has left after 12 years of marriage". She explained that in Iran such a claim should be raised prior to a

57. Rechtbank 's Gravenhage, 23 February 2006, LJN: AV2494, 23946.

request for divorce and that she had sent in such a request on 14 December 2004.

A *Mahr* of € 55,000 seems a lot of money, but high *Mahr* agreements are not uncommon in contemporary Iran. According to the Iranian scholars Ziba Mir-Hosseini and Nadjma Yassari, these excessive *muhūr* (sing. *Mahr*) can partly be explained by inflation and amendments in family law legislation (Mir-Hosseini, 2000: 74-75; Yassari, 2003: 201). That these practices have been transferred to Europe is also illustrated by a recent case from Sweden.[58]

This Swedish case involved a marriage between a man of Swedish-Iranian nationality and his Iranian niece. The marriage was contracted in Iran by proxy, meaning that the husband had been represented by his Iranian aunt and mother-in-law, who had stipulated a *Mahr* of 500 *Bahar Azahi* coins (representing a value of € 25,000) on behalf of her daughter. Three days after the wife arrived in Sweden the husband wished to end the marriage, as he suspected her of having another relationship. Yet, it was the wife who went to court in order to claim a divorce and the payment of her *Mahr*. The Swedish Court held the husband bound by the actions of the representative of his choice and the man consequently had to pay the full sum of € 25,000 to his former wife who still was living in Sweden (Sayed 2008: 203-205).

In the Dutch case the Court noticed the dispute over the Iranian claim for *Mahr,* and chose to comment on it. It confirmed that according to Iranian law a judicial divorce (*faskh*) only can be granted on a few limited legal grounds. These legal grounds mainly concern the question whom of the spouses is to blame for the divorce, either because of personal characteristics or liable behaviour and require proof, which may not always be easy to provide. The Court also confirmed that Iranian law opts for a divorce on mutual agreement or a *khulʿ*, which would imply that the wife would lose her right to the *Mahr*. The Court therefore held that the result of the Iranian case still was very uncertain, as the husband had agreed upon the divorce and none of the abovementioned divorce grounds were mentioned earlier during the Dutch proceedings. In addressing the dispute like this, the Court showed it was well-informed about Iranian rules of law and took the effort to comment the parties' arguments, although this in itself was not necessary as to the judicial decision concerning the divorce. Finally, the Court granted the couple a Dutch divorce on grounds of the permanent disruption of the marriage. Dutch law, as the law of habitual residence was applied both to the claim for mainte-

58. *T952-99 and RH 2005: 66,* Halmstad tingsrätt 2002-10-24 and Hovrätten för Västra Sverige 2004-11-22.

nance and the divorce. The Court granted the wife € 40 in maintenance per month, a claim she later withdraw, as described in Susan Rutten's article.

6.6.2 Some Summarising Thoughts as to the Selection of the Dutch Cases

The selection of the Dutch cases in this chapter is too small to be able to generalize and draw any conclusions. Yet, the decisions can be summarised as follows. In all cases the parties had entered marriage contracts that involved *Mahr,* even if the marriage was entered in the Netherlands among spouses with Dutch citizenship. All parties seem to agree as to the *Mahr*'s religious (or moral) function. Some women saw *Mahr* as a compensation for the emotional and economical damage that they had suffered due to the divorce. In only a few cases[59] did both spouses have dual citizenship or had applied for Dutch citizenship in addition to another nationality. Even if the female spouses had a foreign nationality, they all argued that Dutch law was applicable to the divorce, the matrimonial property regime, the claim for maintenance or to the return or reimbursement of the bridal gifts. Yet, this did not imply that they gave up their claim for *Mahr.*[60] Claims for *Mahr* either come up as a part of the Dutch divorce case, as a part of foreign divorce case or both.[61] This pattern shows that both parties in the cases discussed choose strategically the legal order that they assume suits their interest best.

Yet, Dutch law does not automatically lead to the desired results. In those cases that foreign law was applied the female spouse was always granted *Mahr.* In case Dutch law was applied the deferred *ṣadāq* was not granted at all,[62] divided into two equal parts[63] or returned to the husband.[64] In only one case was the male spouse ordered to pay the deferred *ṣadāq.*[65] In at least two cases the wife admits forum shopping as the result of the fact that Dutch divorces are not recognized in the country of origin to which they still are connected due to their (dual) citizenship. In all cases both parties used Islamic arguments to support their claims, even when they argued that Dutch law was applicable to their case. All cases discussed involved relatively short mar-

59. Hoge Raad, Februari 8, 2008, LJN: BC3841, R07/027HR; Gerechtshof Amsterdam 21 September 2000, NIPR, 2002, 83; LJN: AV5175, Gerechtshof 's-Hertogenbosch C0400125 LJN: AV5175.
60. LJN: AV5175 LJN; AF9352; NIPR 1986, 271; NIPR 2000, 18; NIPR 2001, 10; LJN: BC3841, R07/027HR; NIPR, 2002, 83.
61. LJN AF9352 LJN: AV2494, 239460
62. LJN: AV5175
63. LJN: BC3841, R07/027HR
64. RvdW, 2001, 138
65. LJN: AF9352

riages (half a year to five years), with the exception of the Iranian case (12 years). The *Mahr* settlements ranged from € 5,000 (Moroccan and Turkish cases) up to € 55,000 (the Iranian case).

6.6.3 Norwegian Cases Concerning *Mahr*

Several Norwegian court cases reveal the importance of *Mahr* and the different functions it may have. This includes both private international law cases and cases that have no foreign connection at all. Even in criminal cases defendants explain money transfers,[66] or the findings of considerable amounts of money in bank boxes[67] as *Mahr*. Court practice also reveals that *Mahr* may become a nice bonus in addition to a residence permit if the female spouse can prove that she was 'forced' to marry by relatives and later annuls or dissolves her marriage in Norway according to Articles 16.3 or 23.3 of the Marriage Act.

This was clearly the case in a judgement by the Toten Municipal Court (Court of First Instance) from 2002.[68] The case was raised on the basis of Article 16.3 of the Marriage Act that states that "*each of the spouses may institute legal proceedings to have the marriage declared null and void if he or she has been forced to contract the marriage by unlawful conduct*". The legal proceedings were initiated by an Iraqi woman who wished to annul her marriage that had been contracted by means of proxy in Jordan, where she had been residing with relatives after her application for reunification with her family who lived in Norway was turned down. Due to her marriage with a Norwegian citizen she had been granted residence in Norway on the basis of family establishment with her Muslim spouse. However, the spouses never actually cohabited together. The first time the couple met was in the court. During the three years that the wife had been waiting to come to Norway her husband had transferred nearly € 13,000 to her and her family, which he could document by means of bank receipts. It is obvious that the male spouse felt humiliated by the situation, even though the Court did not support the wife's claim for annulment of the marriage.

Honour often plays a role in family disputes that concern the annulment of marriages between Muslim spouses, as was the case in Rt. 2002 p.541 (Fredriksen 2007: 44-45). The annulment of a marriage in which the male spouse had paid his wife a considerable amount of *Mahr* in return for a marriage that was never consummated and shortly afterwards dissolved may be-

66. Rt. 1995 p.1768.
67. TOSLO-2002-1863.
68. RG-2002-981(151-2002).

come a way to restore one's honour. This may be part of the explanation for some of the cases that involve the annulment of marriages by male Muslim parties.

As pointed out by Lene Løvdal in her article on "*Mahr* and gender equality" no formal claims for *Mahr* have been raised before Norwegian courts. Only indirect claims are being made, although they do not seem to be recognized as *Mahr* claims by the judiciary, or by the party's lawyers. In the following three cases *Mahr* was treated indirectly as an indicator of a Muslim couple's matrimonial property regime, as a claim for maintenance and as a gift.

6.6.3.1 Mahr as a part of the matrimonial property

An interesting case from 18 April 1983 from the Eidsivating Court of Appeal (*RG 1983 p.1021*) concerned the choice of law in relation to the matrimonial property regime of a Pakistani couple that had contracted marriage in Pakistan in 1975. In Norwegian PIL the matrimonial property regime is seen as a financial effect of the marriage. The main rule in Norwegian law concerning the division of matrimonial property is that it is governed by the law of the spouses' first joint domicile (Thue 2002: 398).

For a person to obtain domicile in Norway, Norwegian PIL requires that that person actually is living in Norway and that he or she has the intention to permanently stay there. In this particular case the husband had been living and working in Norway for a little more than one year, when he went to Pakistan with the purpose of marriage. After the wedding the husband stayed in Pakistan for one month, after which he returned to Norway. His wife soon followed after, which confirmed the intentions of the couple to settle in Norway after marriage. Their first joint domicile was therefore Norway.

In the Probate Court case the legal question was whether Pakistani or Norwegian rules of law were applicable to the matrimonial regime of the spouses when the marriage was contracted in Pakistan, and the spouses shortly afterward moved to Norway. The husband was of the opinion that Pakistani law was applicable, while the wife held that Norwegian rules of law were to be applied.

As the judge did not have sufficient knowledge about the Pakistani rules that governed the matrimonial regime he asked the parties about their understanding of the rules of law that were applicable to their particular situation. Norwegian judges can do so on the basis of the principle of party autonomy. If parties agree to a set of rules, the judge can apply these rules for the case at stake. Both parties agreed that *"[t]he Mahr is a certain amount of money, specified in the "nikah nama" that either is paid in cash when the marriage contract is entered or remains liable to the husband. In addition the wife is entitled to her dowry, which is given to the bride by her parents and which normally consists of clothing and jewellery. In case the wife wishes a divorce she looses her right to the Mahr, but is still entitled to her dowry*".

The male spouse argued that the Pakistani marriage contract formed the basis for applying Pakistani law to the division of the matrimonial property. The man obviously had a good lawyer that understood the essence of the claim and who was well prepared. He held that "*the formal basis of the marriage, as well as the marriage conditions and its property regime were based on this marriage contract, the "nikah nama", that the parties had signed upon marriage. It was supplemented by the Muslim family law of 1961 which in turn referred to the Quran.*"

The question whether the marriage contract would contravene the *ordre public* in Norway was also raised by both parties. The appellant could not see any legal grounds why the spouses could not be bound by this contract. He did not deem the contract against the *ordre public* and neither could the contract be set aside due to the fact "*that Pakistan has such a different culture than Norway*". Finally, he alleged that 'the principle of the immutability of the property regime' was applicable.[69]

The defendant argued that the 'the principle of the immutability of the property regime' was not enforceable under all conditions. She was of the opinion that this principle could be set aside on the basis of *reasonableness* based on the *ordre public* reservation. According to the defendant this concerned "*in particular family cases and especially this one as the application of foreign law would contravene our [here meant as: Norwegian] feeling of justice too strongly*". The defendant continued that according to the appellant the only thing agreed upon in relation the matrimonial property is the so-called 'dower'. She maintained that all Muslim marriage contracts in Pakistan contain "*Mahr*" as was the case here, but that this could not be compared with the Norwegian "*særeie*". As the conditions in Norwegian society were so different from Pakistan that "*it would offend the Norwegian sense of justice to apply rules of law that would entitle one party to all the matrimonial property*". Finally, the defendant argued that as she had lived in Norway since 1975 and the appellant since 1973, the male spouse had domicile in Norway when the marriage was contracted. Due to the domicile principle Norwegian rules of law were applicable. The lawyer of the defendant also seemed to be very engaged in the case.

69. Rt. 1942 p. 214.

The Probate Court interpreted the legal question as whether the spouses had their first joint domicile in Pakistan or in Norway and based its opinion upon a concrete consideration. It described in detail how the husband travelled to Pakistan, bringing only clothing and personal belongings and leaving all his other property behind in Norway in an apartment which he shared with his brother. After the marriage the couple spent one month in the parental house of the wife. The Court deemed this time too short to be considered a joint habitual residence. After a month the husband returned to Norway to be followed 6 months later by his wife. Also she brought only personal belongings, including jewellery. In the meantime the husband had rented a flat for the couple to live in. All matrimonial property was thus acquired during their conjugal life in their joint apartment. The Probate Court concluded that the matrimonial property was to be divided equally according to Norwegian rules and deemed it therefore not necessary to address the question whether the marriage contract contravened the Norwegian public order.

The husband appealed the case to the Eidsivating Court of Appeal which confirmed the decision by the Probate Court. The husband appealed again to the Supreme Court.[70] The Appeal Committee of the Supreme Court concluded that the Probate Court incorrectly had taken a prejudicial decision as to the choice of law. The Appeal Committee therefore set aside both earlier decisions and the case was returned to the Court of Appeal.

The Court of Appeal considered in its decision of 18 April 1983[71] the fact that the parties had contracted marriage in Pakistan and that they had entered "*a regular agreement in Pakistan upon marriage that regulated the wife's economic rights in case of divorce or death of the husband.*" It also confirmed that Pakistani law does not recognize joint community of goods. Yet, the Court emphasised the fact that the spouse planned to live in Norway and that they "*during their 4-year-marriage had the strongest tie to Norway, where they had lived all the time and built up a home and the values this included.*" It therefore held that the agreement which was entered in Pakistan could not be seen as "*an agreement to the application of Pakistani rule*s" as claimed by the male party nor as a "separate property settlement". The matrimonial property was to be divided equally between the spouses according to Norwegian rules.[72]

70. Rt. 1980 p.1677.
71. RG 1983 p.1021.
72. The decision was again appealed to the Supreme Court, but was denied leave by the Appeal Committee of the Supreme Court to be heard.

Although the wife held that Norwegian law was applicable to the settlement, she still maintained that the contract implied the obligation of *Mahr*, an argument that also was used by female parties in the Dutch cases. Yet, the wife did not formally claim her *Mahr*, as she most probably feared that this would weaken her case with regard to the joint matrimonial property regime. Whether she later claimed the *Mahr* in Pakistan in relation to divorce procedures there, the Norwegian case does not mention.

6.6.3.2 Mahr as post-divorce maintenance

The second case concerned a Court of Appeal case from 1986.[73] The case involved a claim by a Pakistani woman with residence in Pakistan. The appellant claimed maintenance in response to a decision by the Oslo Municipal Court of 11 June 1986 in which her former husband had petitioned for divorce. The Pakistani wife contested the divorce. Although the appellant claimed maintenance, she did not claim maintenance as a result of a divorce, but on the basis of her husband's obligation to maintain her during marriage according to Islamic and Pakistani law.[74]

According to Norwegian PIL maintenance is seen as a personal effect of the marriage. However, in this case conflict of laws rules were not considered at all. Despite the fact that the appellant was domiciled in Pakistan, conflict of laws questions were not raised and addressed by the Court. Pakistani law was only mentioned once, when the Court held that it did not take into consideration the validity of the second marriage according to Pakistani law. Besides that, no investigations were made into Pakistani legislation or Pakistani case law and no expert opinions were heard. In general the judiciary seems to have made little effort to fully understand the wife's claim or to get the relevant facts on the table. The Court ended up applying Norwegian law as *lex causae*, which is the correct choice of law in cases that involve maintenance, but still this seems to be more by "accident than by deliberate thought" (Løvdal, 2009: 59).

This case clearly shows that the Norwegian judiciary does not always perceive the complicated legal questions that arise when Muslim parties argue on the basis of Islamic arguments in a Norwegian setting. Norwegian lawyers

73. LE-1986-447.

74. *The Dissolution of Muslim Marriage Act of 17th March 1939* states in Section 2 ii that "[a] woman married under Muslim law shall be entitled to obtain a decree for the dissolution of her marriage on any one or more of the following grounds, namely: – ii that the husband has neglected or has failed to provide for her maintenance for a period of two years" (Ali, 1976: 527).

also may misinterpret their client's claim, as illustrated by the lawyer in this case that claimed post-divorce maintenance,[75] despite the fact that the Pakistani wife had contested the divorce all through the legal proceedings.

The claim was set forward to the Eidsivating Court of Appeal. The facts of the case were the following. The couple married in Pakistan in 1960. Out of marriage a daughter was born. In 1975 the husband moved to Norway in order to work there and regularly transferred money in order to support his family. In 1983 the husband married a younger wife in Pakistan who followed him to Norway. In the middle of 1986 the husband stopped sending money to his wife in Pakistan, a fact that was not contested by any of the spouses. The (first) wife continued to live in the couple's matrimonial house in Pakistan, but became financially dependant on her brother to support her and her daughter. She claimed therefore that she was in debt to him.

As the (first) wife claimed not to have given permission to the second marriage she did not deem the second marriage valid. Pakistani law does indeed attempt to limit the practice of polygamous marriages by requiring prior permission by the first wife (Ali 1976: 532, 540, 548), but does not formally prohibit polygamy. The wife's claim about the invalidity of the second marriage was thus not founded on Pakistani law. The wife also contested the fact that her husband had divorced her. She claimed that according to Pakistani law "*a polygamous marriage in itself does not automatically lead to a permanent breach between the spouses*". This is true, but contradicted her earlier argument that the second marriage was invalid. Furthermore, she claimed that the husband had not paid her deferred *Mahr.* The absence of this payment would indicate that the marriage had not yet been dissolved and could therefore support her claim for matrimonial maintenance.

The wife thus claimed maintenance from 1 July 1986. According to the wife's lawyer maintenance should be set permanently, "due to the position of women in Pakistan". It is obvious that the wife's lawyer hoped to strengthen the woman's case by referring to a discourse that perceives Muslim women as the weaker part in marriage dissolution cases.

The husband was of another opinion. He claimed that the marriage had been ended on the basis of mutual agreement during his visit to Pakistan from December 1982 to the spring 1983. He showed the Court a deed of gift ('Gift Deed') and a written consent by his wife dated 12 January 1983. In the deed of gift the wife was granted a real estate that would guarantee her a monthly

75. Article 56.2 of the Norwegian *Marriage Act of 1918*, which concerns the obligation to pay maintenance **upon divorce** [my emphasis].

income of 5.000 Rupees. The husband therefore claimed that he already had divorced his wife and that she – as a result of the divorce – could not claim maintenance in Norway. In addition he claimed to have paid her the deferred *Mahr*[76].

The (first) wife countered her husband's arguments by stating that the documents were falsified. It is common knowledge that it is no problem to acquire falsified documents in Pakistan for those that wish to do so. Yet, the wife did not provide any proof that these particular documents were false and it was therefore up to the Court to decide the value of the proof.

The Court of Appeal was of the opinion that the wife had not agreed to the second marriage and that it was not proven that the husband had paid her *Mahr*. Nor would the Court accept that the husband – according to Pakistani law – already had divorced his wife.[77] Yet, the Court would not consider whether the second marriage was valid due to Pakistani law – which it in fact was even if the wife had disagreed – or whether the 'Gift Deed' was falsified or not. The Court concluded that it had come to a breach between the couple since December 1982 as "*they had been living separately for years, except for a few visits*." The fact that the husband married a second wife the Court saw "*as a confirmation that the breach was permanent. This implied that their matrimonial cohabitation had ceased without this taking place in a legal way. The fact that the husband sent her [the first wife] money, once in a while between 1983 and 1986 did not mean that the spouses had taken up marital life again*", the Court held.

Despite the fact that the (first) Pakistani wife was domiciled in Pakistan, classification questions were not raised. Norwegian divorce law was applicable and the wife's claim for maintenance was rejected, mainly due to the low income of the husband. Yet, many facts in this case remain unclear, leaving me with the impression that both the judge and the wife's lawyer should have taken more effort to get all relevant facts on the table.

6.6.3.3 *Mahr* as a gift

In the third case from 2 September, 2003 by the Borgating Court of Appeal[78] no reference to *Mahr* or *Ṣadāq was* made either. Instead, the term '*medgift*' was used, which in Norwegian legal language is an old term for dowry. In this case *Mahr* was seen as a gift. This case involved the claim for the reas-

76. In Norwegian the term '*medgift'* (dowry) is mistakenly used.
77. In Norwegian: "*Han kan ikke høres med at han allerede er skilt fra henne, slik som han overraskende hevdet under sin partsforklaring for lagmannsretten.*"
78. LB-2003-2247

surance of a Pakistani woman's 'bridal gift'[79] after separation. The wife claimed preliminary injunction according to Chapter 15 of the Act on Enforcement of Payment as "*there was reason to fear that [her] spouse will withdraw property from the division [of the matrimonial property] or otherwise will make it difficult to fulfill the other spouse's rights according to Chapter 12 to 14.*" The woman had received the gifts in relation to her marriage in Pakistan in 2000. Immediately after marriage the parties moved to Norway with the intention to build up a life there. Their first common 'domicile' was therefore Norway, which implied that their matrimonial property regime was regulated by Norwegian rules.

The Indre Follo Municipal Court[80] granted the bridal gifts to the wife. Most probably the gifts concerned the prompt *Mahr*, but they may also have concerned dowry. During the Court of Appeal case the husband did not contest the wife's entitlement to the gifts, although he earlier had contested their ownership. Although the former husband and his family had brought the gifts from Pakistan to Norway, they now claimed that they no longer had them in their possession. The female party confirmed that she "*most probably never would receive her property back*".

The wife had been mistreated by her husband during the marriage and had been "dumped" back in Pakistan, where her personal papers and other documents were taken away from her for three and a half months. Due to this episode the wife had been granted residence in Norway. The Court ruled that the male spouse most probably no longer had the gifts in his possession and the decision of the Indre Follo Municipal Court was therefore set aside. The woman therefore did not receive any of the gifts in return.

This case clearly illustrates how Norwegian rules may favour the male spouse as to claims that involve alien legal institutions. Had the matrimonial property regime been regulated by Pakistani rules of law the Pakistani woman could have claimed her right to *Mahr* no matter whether her former husband still had the gifts in his possession or not. As both spouses had Pakistani nationality and the marriage was contracted in Pakistan, the case clearly had a strong tie to Pakistan. As the marriage only had lasted for two and a half years the wife had, according to Norwegian PIL rules, not obtained domicile in Norway yet. It can not be expected either that the wife during such a short period had obtained sufficient knowledge about Norwegian family law rules to subject and adjust her matrimonial life to Norwegian law. The

79. In Norwegian: '*brudegave*'.
80. Indre Follo tingrett Nr. 03-00273 D.

woman's claim for the return of the bridal gifts seems to support this assumption.

On the other hand the woman had obtained residence on individual grounds (abuse by her husband), meaning that she had obtained domicile in Norway, independently of her husband. This seems to indicate that she intended to continue her life in Norway. This in turn implied that she obtained domicile according to the Norwegian meaning of the term. In such a situation the *Mahr* no longer fulfils the protective and economic function as a '*safeguard*' or 'an *economic necessity*' upon divorce. In Norwegian society this economic function is being guaranteed by the Norwegian welfare system, which grants individuals that are not able to support themselves through labour social benefits. However, the case does not give any indication as to what rules the parties had agreed upon in relation to the division of their matrimonial property. According to Norwegian law the spouses have party autonomy concerning the division of their matrimonial property.

If the parties had agreed upon Pakistani rules a claim for the return of the gifts could be seen as the first stage in a process to claim the wife's entitlement to *Mahr* before a Norwegian court. Now that the claim was rejected the Pakistani woman still had the option to claim her right to the *Mahr* before a Pakistani court. Yet, in this particular case this may be difficult to achieve given the fact that she might risk once more to be kept behind in Pakistan by her husband.

Even if Norwegian rules on joint property had been applicable, the wife's claim for *Mahr* could serve both a religious and a social function in restoring the imbalance between the parties due to the marital abuse that she had been exposed for. These arguments were also put forward in some of the Dutch cases though these do not make any reference to any form of conjugal violence. This last case clearly shows similarities to some of the Dutch private international law cases that concerned 'bridal gifts'. The same legal question was treated by the Dutch Supreme Court decision about the Turkish couple[81] described earlier. Here the Supreme Court ruled that the jewellery was a part of the couple's matrimonial property and the wife had to return half of the *Mahr* to her former husband. In the Norwegian case the wife did not receive any of the jewellery, simply because they could not be found. The application of Norwegian law thus seems to be in disfavour of the woman in the case at stake.

81. Hoge Raad , 8 February 2008 (LJN: BC3841, R07/027HR.

The question can be raised why the Pakistani woman did not raise a formal claim for *Mahr* as she could have done before a Pakistani court. The reason may that she expected that her interest would be better protected by Norwegian law. Another reason may be that her lawyer was not aware of the option to – for example – raise *Mahr* as a maintenance obligation, like in the Swedish decision RH 1993: 116.

6.7 Some Summarising Thoughts

The issue of *Mahr* has increasingly been raised before European courts, but in Norway no formal cases have been published so far. Still, it seems to me that *Mahr* is one of the underlying issues and possibly even one of the most important motivations for Muslim parties to go to court in order to have their marriages dissolved by a judge, rather then applying for separation at the Norwegian *Fylkesmannen* (county governor) which is the standard divorce procedure. My research also shows that some Muslims choose to go to court to have their marriages declared void, rather than having them dissolved. The explanation for this may be found in the male parties obligation to pay (half of the) *Mahr* in case of divorce, but not in case of annulment of the marriage.

In this article we elaborated at least three types of Norwegian cases in which *Mahr* was treated indirectly, as an indicator to a Muslim couple's matrimonial property regime, as a claim for maintenance and as a gift. All types of cases involved marriage contracts that were entered abroad, involving two Muslim parties. Conflict law rules should be applied when a case has a strong tie to a foreign country. Yet, in all three cases Norwegian law was applicable, either as the law of domicile or simply because the Court did not notice the international dimension of the dispute at stake.

In a study from 2000 the Norwegian legal scholar Beate Sjåfjell-Hansen showed that the Norwegian judiciary has little knowledge about foreign law and is insecure as to how to handle it. Therefore the judiciary generally tries to avoid using it. On the other hand there exists a consensus amongst scholars that foreign law should be applied *ex officio* (Sjåfjell-Hansen 2000: 3).

Quite a few of the other Norwegian cases that I have studied show the same pattern. Little is done, neither by the judge nor by the lawyers to extract the necessary facts in order to understand the legal questions and their implications for the case at stake. Islamic (legal) arguments are mostly perceived as irrelevant by Norwegian judges. Documents that could prove a party's claim, like (a translation of) the marriage contract or a *Mahr* agreement are not verified. Neither are marriage certificates, divorce certificates, bank transfer receipts and the like. Private international law provisions are not always applied the way they should or could be. Islamic legal institutions or concepts are misunderstood or denied, legal rules and ways of communicating misinterpreted, leading to unsolved cases or cases with an unfair result, seen from a Muslim perspective.

We started this article by raising the question whether European court practice could prove that the concept of '*Mahr* as a bargaining tool' was transplanted in a European, legal context. Both the Dutch and the Norwegian cases illustrate that *Mahr* can be used strategically by one party towards the other in an attempt to gain most out of the painful and emotional process that a divorce normally is. If not for economical reasons, *Mahr* can at least serve as an emotional and moral compensation for the hurtful process the parties often have been through.

Both Dutch and Norwegian practice shows that Muslim women may fall in between two stools. Norwegian or Dutch law does not always offer them the (economic) protection that they deserve or expect. The Norwegian or Dutch divorce is often not recognized in their country of origin, leading to situations of limping marriages. Women may then be forced to settle for a divorce on mutual agreement, waiving their economic rights and sometimes even the custody over their children. Some may be forced to approve that their husband remarries in the country of origin, without giving her a *ṭalāq*. In this way the husband is not obliged to pay his wife *Mahr* as the couple still is married according to Islamic law. Others are exposed to violence by their husbands in order to force them to divorce. In the least serious cases women experience that their former husbands take away the jewellery which was given to them upon marriage and that they are entitled to on the basis of their Muslim marriage contract.

Yet, Muslim men may also end up suffering economically as well due to the fact that they need to respect two legal orders simultaneously. In this process they may not only loose money, but also face, self-respect or the family's honour. They may be met with unreasonably high claims for the payment of *Mahr*, after relatively short marriages, in addition to other financial claims, like maintenance, return of the wedding gifts and the equal division of the joint matrimonial property. In some cases they may risk being sustained to pay *Mahr* twice: once in the country of residence and once in the country of origin or nationality.

Yet, most of all Norwegian courts and thus society may loose their legitimacy among certain population groups. By not adequately solving family disputes as they are raised before Norwegian courts, the legislator and the courts may risk loosing the trust of a growing majority of the Muslim population in Norway. As Norwegian divorces are not recognized in Muslim countries and family disputes are not always solved, Muslims may be forced to find alternative solutions by means of mediation in private settings, in mosques or by *Sharī'a* councils in Great Britain.

Norway has already taken important steps by initiating co-operation with Pakistan, the country of origin of one of the largest immigrant groups in Norway, in order to discuss these issues. The Norwegian government ratified on 6 December 2005 an agreement[82] with Pakistani authorities in order to exchange information and advice in marital and family matters. This agreement became into force on 1 May 2006. The agreement provides for a steering committee from both countries that consult each other in family issues. This committee has – as far as I know – only met once. Political instability in Pakistan may have been the main reason for not following up the intentions of the agreement more regularly. Although the agreement has not had the intended effect so far, it shows a willingness to discuss these issues on a governmental level and a mutual intention to find solutions in accordance with each state's national legislation.

Another option to solve at least some of the difficulties raised by Muslim parties may be to more frequently apply Muslim Personal Status Law in private international law cases that involve *Mahr* claims by one or more Muslim parties. This should of course be based on the party's free choice. Although it cannot be denied that many Muslim legal systems still have many challenges to overcome in order to meet the universal standards of human rights, there are weaknesses within almost every legal system. Yet, this biased vision towards Islamic legal cultures may prevent the Norwegian judiciary to apply Muslim rules of law. In doing so, they may miss the opportunity to come to well-balanced results. Islamic rules of laws are often closely connected and build on one another, like small 'building stones', leading to a result that is balanced if correctly applied. *Mahr* is – in my opinion – such a building stone for the financial arrangements between the two spouses, both in life and in death. Court litigation from Norway and the Netherlands shows that if Muslim Personal Status Laws are applied correctly and consequently, the result may be better for both parties, male or female. Situations of limping marriages may be prevented, as well as forum shopping and double claims for *Mahr*.

82. *Avtale om opprettelse av et rådgivende norsk-pakistansk utvalg for spørsmål knyttet til ekteskap, familie og barn som følge av migrasjon mellom de to stater. See http://www.lovdata.no/traktater/text/tra-20051206-067.html*

Bibliography

Abiad, Nisrine, (2008) *Sharia, Muslim States and International Human Rights Treaty Obligations: A Comparative Study*, (London: British Institute of International and Comparative Law (BIICL).

Ali, Syed Ameer, (1976) *Mahommedan Law, Containing the Law Relating to Succession and Status Compiled from Authorities in the Original Arabic*, Vol. II, seventh edition by Khan, Raja Said Akbar edn. (Lahore: Law Publishing Company).

Ajani, Gianmaria, (2007) "Transplants, legal borrowings and reception", in: *Encyclopaedia of Law & Society* (New York, Sage Publications,), pp.1-8.

An-Na'im, Abdullahi A., ed., (2002) *Islamic Family Law in a changing world. A Global Resource Book*, (London: New York: Zed Books Ltd.), ISBN 1-84277-093-4.

Bano, S., (2007) "Islamic Family Arbitration, Justice and Human Rights in Britain", (1) *Law, Social Justice & Global Development Journal (JGD)*, pp.2-16. http://www.go.warwick.ac.uk/elj/lgd/2007_l/bano.,

Berger, M.S., Mr., Drs., (2004) *Mudawwana. Marokkaanse familiewet (nieuwe wet van 2004)*, (Mudawwana, Moroccan family law (new law of 2004)), (Nijmegen: Ars Aequi Libri, derde herziende druk), ISBN90-6916-516-3.

Bogdan, Michael, (2007) "Något om den kollisionsrättsliga behandlingen av islamisk morgongåva (*MAHR*)", in: *Rett og toleranse. Festskrift til Helge Johan Thue. 70 år*, Frantzen, Torstein, Giertsen, Johan, Moss, Cordero, Giuditta, ed., (Oslo: Gyldendal Akademisk), ISBN 978-82-05-37592-5, pp.175-185.

Buskens, Léon, (1999) *Islamitisch recht en familiebetrekkingen in Marokko, (Islamic law and family relations in Marokko)*, (Amsterdam: Bulaaq), ISBN 90-54060-0-209.

Daugstad, Gunnlaug, (2008) (1), *Ekteskap over landegrensene. Ekteskapsmønster og transnasjonale familieetableringar i perioden 1990-2007*, Statistics Norway, Oslo-Kongsvinger, Rapportar /41.

Daugstad, Gunnlaug, (2008) (2), "Transnasjonal kjærleik i globaliseringa si tid", in: IMDI-rapport 6, 2008 *Integreringskart 2008. Tvangsekteskap – en kunnskapsstatus*, Plan of Action against Forced Marriage, 2008-2011, pp.162-172.

(2006), *Grenseløs kjærlighet? Familieinnvandring og ekteskapsmønstre i det flerkulturelle Norge* 2006, Statistics Norway, Oslo-Kongsvinger, Rapportar, 2006/39.

Fredriksen, Katja Jansen, (2007) "Sharia in Norwegian Courtrooms?", in: *ISIM Review 20*, autumn, pp.44-45.

(2006) "Dilemma i lovens navn", in: Hubro 4/2006, pp.10-11.

Ferrari de Carli, Eli, (2008) *Religion, juss og rettigheter: Om skilsmisse, polygamy og shari'a-råd*, (Oslo: Institutt for samfunnsforskning, rapport: 5), ISBN: 978-7763-280-3.

Fournier, Pascale, (2007) *Islamic Marriage in Western Liberal Courts. Beyond "Recognition", "Equality" and "Fairness"*, (Cambridge: Harvard Law School), unpublished PhD-dissertation.

Griffiths, J., (1986) "What is Legal Pluralism?", in: *Journal of Legal Pluralism*, Griffiths, J., ed., No., 24/, Birmingham: Foundation for the Journal of Legal Pluralism, ISSN 0732, 9113, pp.1-55.

Jordens-Cotran, L., (2007) *Nieuw Marokkaans Familierecht en Nederlands IPR*, (Den Haag:Sdu uitgevers bv.), ISBN 978-90-5409-494-4.

Khatib, M. M., Dr., (1986) *The Bounteous Koran. A Translation of Meaning and Commentary*, (London: MacMillan Press, 1986), ISBN 0-333-34738-2.

Legrand, Pierre, (1996) "European Legal Systems are Not Converging", in: 45 *International and Comparative Law Quarterly* (1996), pp.2-19.

Lødrup, Peter, (2002) "N Norway", in: *Family Law in Europe*, Hamilton, Carolyn, Perry, Alison, ed., (London: Butterworths, LexisNexis, Second edition,), ISBN 0-406- 94150-5.

Lødrup, Peter, (1999) *Arverett,* (Oslo: Peter Lødrup, 4. utg., 2. opplag, 1999), ISBN 82-91724-02-4.

Lødrup, Peter, Sverdrup, Tone, (2004) *Familieretten*, (Oslo: Peter Lødrup og Tone Sverdrup, 5.utg., 2. opplag,), ISBN 9-788291-724010.

Løvdal, Lene, (2009) "Private international law, Muslim Laws And Gender Equality. The Adjudication of *Mahr* in Scandinavian, English and French courts", in: *Kvinnerettslig Skriftserie,* Nr., 78/, (Oslo: Universitetet i Oslo).

Mehdi, Rubya, ed., (2007) *Integration & Retsudvikling*, (København Ø: Jurist- og Økonomforbundets Forlag, 1., udgave, 1., oplag), ISBN 978-87-574-1769-2.

(2007) "Arrangerte/tvangsægteskaber og æredrab under sharia og under pakistansk ret og sædvaneret", in: *Integration & Retsudvikling*, Rubya Mehdi ed., (København Ø: Jurist- og Økonomforbundets Forlag, 1., udgave, 1., oplag, 2007), ISBN 978-87-574-1769-2, pp.71-84.

(2003) "Danish law and the practice of *Mahr* among Muslim Pakistanis in Denmark", in: *The International Journal of Sociology of Law, Volume 31, Issue 2, June 2003,* pp.115-129.

Mehdi, Rubya, Petersen, Hanne, Reenberg, Erik, Sand, Woodman, R., Gordon, ed.,(2008) *Law and Religion in Multicultural Societies,* (Copenhagen: DJØF Publishing, 1. edition), ISBN 978-87-574-1843-9.

Mir-Hosseini, Ziba, (2000) *Marriage on Trial. Islamic Family Law in Iran and Morocco,* (London, New York: IB., Tauris & Co, Ltd.), ISBN 1-86064-608-5.

Moors, Annelies, (2008) "Registering A Token Dower. The Multiple Meanings of a Legal Practice" in: *Narratives of Truth in Islamic Law*, Dupret, Baudouin, Drieskens, Barbara, Moors, Annelies, ed., London, New York: IB., Tauris), ISBN 978-1- 84511-187-8, pp.85-104.

Mudawwana al-usra, al-mamlaka al-maghrībī, wizara al-'adl, 2005.

Nasir, Jamal, J., (2002) *The Islamic Law of Personal Status,* Arab and Islamic Law series, (The Hague: Kluwer Law International, third revised and updated edition,), ISBN 90-411- 1661-3.

Pearl, David, S., Menski, Werner, (1998) *Muslim family law*, (London: Sweet & Maxwell, third edition), ISBN 0-421-52980-6.

Rohe, Mathias, (2004) "The Formation of a European Sari'a", in: *Malik (Hrsg.), Muslims in Europe – From the Margin to the Center*, (Erlangen-Nürenberg: Friedrich-Alexander- Universität 2004), ISBN 3825876381, pp.161-184.

(2003) "Islamic Law in German Courts" in: *Hawwa*, 1, 1, (Erlangen-Nürenberg: Friedrich-Alexander-Universität), ISSN Online 1569-2086, pp.46-59.

Rutten, Susan, Mr., (1988) *Moslims in de Nederlandse rechtspraak. Een inventaris van gepubliceerde rechterlijke beslissingen waar Islamitische rechtsnormen en waarden een rol spelen. 1973-1986*, (Kampen: Uitgeversmaatschappij J.H. Kok), ISBN 90242 3493 X.

Salimi, Fakhra, (2001) *Til døden skiller oss ad. Ekteskap og skilsmisse i islamsk rettspraksis og norsk* lovgivning, (Oslo: MiRA ressurssenter for innvandrer- og flyktningkvinner).

Sayed, Mosa, (2008) "The Muslim dower (*Mahr*) in Europe- with special reference to Sweden", in: *European Challenges in Contemporary Family Law*, Katharina Boele-Woelki, Tone Sverdrup, ed., European Family Law Series, (Antwerp, Oxford, Portland: Intersentia), pp.187-208.

Shaham, Ron, (1997) *Family and the Courts in Modern Egypt. A Study Based on Decisions by the Sharī'a Courts, 1900-1955, Studies in Islamic Law and Society*, vol. 3, (Brill, Leiden, New York, Köln: E.J. Brill), ISBN 9004107428, ib., or 9789004107427, ib.

Sjåfjell-Hansen, Beate, (2000) *På fremmed grunn: den sivilprosessuelle behandlingen av saker med utenlandsk rett ved norske domstoler*, (Oslo: Juristforbundets Forlag), ISBN 82-7833-034-4 ib.

Thue, Helge, J., (2003) "Anerkjennelse av ekteskap stiftet i utlandet", in: *Tidsskrift for familierett, arverett og barnevernrettslige spørsmål, (FAB),* Nr., 01, 2003, (Oslo: Gyldendal Akademisk), ISSN Online, 0809-9553, pp.7-8.

(2002) *Internasjonal privatrett. Personrett, familierett og arverett. Alminneligeprinsipper og de enkelte reguleringer,* (Oslo: Gyldendal akademisk), ISBN 82-05-30844-6.

Velden, van der, (2001) "Erkenning van Nederlandse huwelijken tussen Marokkanen", in: *Recht van de Islam 18*, Teksten van het op 6 juni 2000 te Leiden gehouden eenentwintigste RIMO-symposium, (Maastricht, Rimo), pp.117-129.

Vikør, K., (2005) *Between God and the Sultan. A History of Islamic Law*, (London: Hurst & Company), ISBN 1-85065-783-6.

Vogt, Kari, (2000/2008) *Islam på norsk. Moskeer og islamske organisasjoner i Norge*, (Oslo: JW., Cappelen Forlag), ISBN 82-02-18463-0/ISBN 978-82-02-29346-8.

Watson, Alan, (1974) *Legal transplants: an Approach to Comparative Law*, (Edinburgh and London: Scottish Academic Press).

Welchman, Lynn, (2007) *Women and Muslim Family Laws in Arab States. A Comparative Overview of Textual Development and Advocacy*, (Amsterdam: Amsterdam University Press), ISBN 978-90-5356-974-0.

Wærstad, Tone Linn, (2006) *Retten til ikke å bli diskriminert ved skilsmisse. En rettsantropologisk studie av skilte muslimske innvandrerkvinner i Norge*, (Oslo: Avdeling for kvinnerett, Universitet i Oslo).

Yassari, Nadjma, Dr., (2003) "Die Brautgabe nach iranischem Recht", in: StAZ Nr. 7/, pp.198-201.

Legislation and Table of Cases

Germany

Litigation

IPRax 1983, pp. 64-65, pp. 74-77

Morocco

Legislation:

Code de Statut Personel et des Successions (C.S.P.S), al-Mudawwana al-usra

The Netherlands

Legislation:

Burgerlijk Wetboek Boek 1 Personen- en familierecht.

Wet Conflictenrecht Echscheidingen (WCE)

International treaties

The Hague Convention on the Recognition and Enforcement of Decisions relating to Maintenance Obligations of 2 October 1973.

The Hague Convention on the Law Applicable to Maintenance Obligations of 2 October 1973.

The Hague Convention on the Law applicable to Matrimonial Property Regimes of 14 March 1978.

Litigation:

Hoge Raad , 8 February 2008 (*LJN: BC3841, R07/027HR*

Hoge Raad, 13 July 2001, *RvdW 2001, 138*

Gerechtshof 's Hertogenbosch 4 December 2002, *NIPR 2003, 243*

Gerechtshof Amsterdam 21 September 2000, *NIPR, 2002, 83*

Rechtbank 's Gravenhage, 23 February 2006, LJN: AV2492, 23946

Rechtbank 's Gravenhage, 9 January 2006, 23 February 2006

Rechtbank Maastricht 16 April 2003, *NIPR 2003, 185*

Rechtbank Rotterdam 20 July 2000, *NIPR 2001, 10*

Rechtbank Rotterdam 29 July 1999, *NIPR 2000, 18*

Rechtbank Rotterdam 29 July 1999, *NIPR 2000, 10*

Rechtbank Arnhem 7 November 1985*, NIPR 1986, 271*

LJN: AF9352, Rechtbank Maastricht, 72204/HA ZA 02-90

LJN: AI 1398 Rechtbank 's Gravenhage, 24 June, 2003, AWB02/6383

LJN: AV2494, 239460, Gerechtshof 's-Hertogenbosh c0400125

LJN: AY5780. Gerechtshof 's Gravenhage, 1279-H-05

LJN: AV5175, Gerechtshof 's-Hertogenbosch, Co400125 LJN: AV5175

Norway

Legislation:

Lov om utlendingers adgang til riket og deres opphold her, 24 juni. Nr. 64. 1988, (the Immigration Act).

Lov av 4. juli. Nr. 47. 1991 om ekteskap (the Marriage Act).

Tvangsfullbyrdelsesloven, (Act on Enforcement of Payment).

Lov om ektefellers formuesforhold av 20. mai 1927 nr. 01 (Ektefelleloven) (Norwegian Spouses' Act of 1927).

Travaux préparatoires

NOU 2003: 19

Agreements:

Avtale om opprettelse av et rådgivende norsk-pakistansk utvalg for spørsmål knyttet til ekteskap, familie og barn som følger av migrasjon mellom de to stater. See http://www.lovdata.no/traktater/text/tra-20051206-067.html

Litigation:
Rt. 1995 p.1768
Rt. 1980 p.1677
Rt. 1942 p.214
LB-2003-11758
LB-2003-2247
LB-2003-2237
RG-2002-981, (151-2002)
LB-2000-566
RG 1983 p.1021
LE-1986-447
TOSLO-2007-143566
TOSLO-2002-1863, TOSLO-2002-7898
Indre Follo Municipal Court, 23 April, 2003, Nr. 03-00273 D

Pakistan
Legislation
The Dissolution of Muslim Marriage Act of 17th March 1939.
The Muslim Family Ordinance of 2nd March 1961 (VIII of 1961).

Sweden
Litigation:
RH 2005: 66
RH 1993: 116
T 952-99 *Hovrätten for Västra Sverige* 2004-11-22

Turkey
Legislation:
Turkish Civil Act

Tunisia
Legislation:
Le Code du Statut Personel (CstP) of 13 August 1956, Majalla.
Order no.13/1956 on the promulgation of the Code of Personal Status, Official Gazette no.66 of 17 August 1956.

PART III

Single Country Case Studies

CHAPTER 7

The Islamic *Mahr* in German Courts: Characterization in Private International Law and Accommodation in German National Family Law

Nadjma Yassari

1. Introduction

Beside the Islamic repudiation (*talaq*), the Islamic dower (*mahr*) is the most prominently represented legal institution of Islamic family law in German courts. As far as the *talaq* is concerned, the courts have developed a suitable formula for its accommodation. Accordingly, the court will grant a *talaq* divorce under a foreign law whenever the divorce would also be possible under German law and the wife has agreed to be divorced.[1] The embedding of the *mahr*, however, still causes many problems. These problems revolve around the identification of its function, i.e. its main legal aims. This element is crucial both for its characterization in private international law and for its embedding in German national family law.

In the following, I shall explore the function of the *mahr* in Islamic countries (II) in order to be able to address the question of its characterization under German private international law (III) and to analyze how the *mahr* could be accounted for within the German family law system (IV).

1. Supreme German Federal Court (hereinafter: BGH), 18 October 1989, *FamRZ* (1990: 32-35); Court of Appeal (hereinafter: OLG) Munich, 19 September 1988, *IPRax* (1989: 238); KG (Court of Appeal in the State of Berlin) Berlin, 5 May 1993, *NJW-RR* (1994: 199-200); OLG Cologne, 9 May 1996, *FamRZ* (1996: 1147).

2. The Function of the *Mahr*

2.1 German Private International Law

In cases with connection to a foreign country or a foreign legal institution, German courts must as a first step determine the applicable law. The determination of the applicable law is drawn from the German rules on private international law, i.e. the Introductory Act to the German Civil Code (hereinafter: EGBGB). The determination of the applicable law is mandatory under German law (Art. 3 EGBGB);[2] the court has to act *ex officio*, foreign law must not be pleaded by the parties.

Since the *mahr* as an instrument of family law is not known to contemporary German law, the judge has to characterize the *mahr*. Characterization means that the foreign institution has to be put in one of the categories offered by German private international law. In doing so, the German law adopts the so-called functional approach (*funktionale Qualifikation*) (Kropholler 2006: 127).[3] Thus, first, the function that instrument plays and the aims it has in its native law (i.e. the law under which it has been contracted) must be detected and second, they have to be compared to the instruments available under German law.

2.2 Function of the *Mahr*

When analyzing the many functions and aims which have been attributed to the *mahr*, two categories can be distinguished: material and immaterial functions. Furthermore, one has to consider the *fiqh* works and the interpretation of the *mahr* by the Islamic scholars of the classical period.

2.2.1 Immaterial Functions

The *mahr* is said to be a token of respect of the husband for the wife and a sign of his commitment to marriage.[4] It furthermore touches upon the idea of prestige, as the *mahr* is seen to correspond to the level of desirability of the

2. BGH, 7 April 1993, *FamRZ* (1993: 1051-1053); BGH, 15 July 2008, *BGHZ*, vol.177 (2009: 237-248).
3. BGH, 22 March 1967, *BGHZ*, vol.47 (1967: 324-339 (336)).
4. Safa'i and Emami 2002: 166; Enayat 2004: 51; Hamidian 2004: 89; Tchouar 1996: 580: "[…] expression de la franchise, de la détermination et la preuve d'attachement de l'homme qui se lie légalement à la femme. L'homme par l'intermédiaire de la dot manifeste son intention réelle en vue de fonder un foyer solide et d'affronter un acte aussi sérieux que grave."

wife (Dahlgren 2005)[5] and the financial potential of the husband. In addition, it has been said that a high *mahr* may deter the husband from a quick and thoughtless repudiation and prevent him from polygamy, as for all consequent marriages, a new *mahr* is due (Esposito 1982: 24; Mir-Hosseini 2000: 73; Moors 1995: 147). These functions are meant to influence the behaviour of the parties to act in a specific manner or are expressions of a certain status of the wife and/or the husband.

2.2.2 Material Functions

Additionally, there are material or economic aspects to the *mahr*: it is supposed to ensure financial security through the payment of a prompt *mahr* at the time of the conclusion of the marriage to provide the wife with a certain economic independence and to enable her to build up her own property (Wynn 2008: 206). It has also been seen as a financial cushion after divorce, since in most Islamic countries, there is no substantial post-marital support for the wife (Esposito 1982: 24; Mir-Hosseini 2000: 73; Moors 1995: 147). And finally, it has also been argued that the *mahr* is conceived to counterbalance the lesser inheritance rights of the wife in case of the husband's death (Safa'i and Emami 2002: 166; Safa'i 2004: 75).[6] This last function is particularly evoked in view of potential polygamous marriages of the husband, as the inheritance portion of the wife will have to be divided between all wives. Fyzee has described the *mahr* as "a provision for a rainy day" (1993: 133).

2.2.3 The Mahr *in the Classical Works of the Fuqaha*

A look at the *fiqh* works of classical Islamic scholars, on the other hand, reveals that the material aspect of the *mahr* has not really been discussed. Instead, the *mahr* is dealt with as a contract of exchange with the rules of the contract of sale being applicable to it (Linant de Bellefonds 1965: 25). In this context, some have interpreted the *mahr* as being the countervalue for sexual submission of the wife in marriage.[7] These interpretations have been taken up by some German courts to designate the *mahr* as the "price for the sexuality of the wife".[8]

5. See http://ema.revues.org/index1045.html, accessed 1 October 2009.
6. For a critical view, see Yassari 2009a: 999.
7. With a summary of the Maliki literature: Bousquet 1966: 108; for *Shi'i* law, see Emamy 1933: 13 et seq.; Emami 2005: 442.
8. See Court of First Instance (hereinafter: LG) Cologne, 27 October 1980, *IPRspr.*, no.83 (1980: 248-249) and more recently OLG Hamburg, 21 May 2003, *FamRZ*

2.3 Evaluation of the Proposed Functions

In evaluating the aforementioned functions, it will be shown that the economic function of the *mahr* is predominant. The interpretation of the *mahr* as being the price for marital sexual intercourse is not valid, if it ever was.[9] It is true that, in certain cases, the *mahr* has a symbolic value and that, in other cases, it has deterred husbands from thoughtless repudiation. However, in Islamic countries, the *mahr* is today a significant financial instrument of family law, as shall be exposed below.

2.3.1 The Mahr *as a Countervalue for Marital Cohabitation?*

The advocates of such a theory base their view mainly on two arguments: first, the nature of the *mahr* as a contract of exchange and the application of the rules of the contract of sale on the *mahr* agreement and secondly, the fact that the *mahr* is forfeited when marriage is dissolved before its consummation. Both arguments are unsustainable.

(1) The fact that the *mahr* is considered a contract of exchange with the rules of the contract of sale being applied to it does not necessarily lead to the conclusion that the *mahr* is a "purchase price" for marital sexuality. It is true that in the literature the agreement on *mahr* is called a reciprocal exchange contract (arab. *mu'awada*), to which the rules of the sales contract are applicable.[10] This has, however, a specific background: Islamic law does not know any general theory of contract (Linant de Bellefonds 1958: 88; Chehata 1968: 81; Abdel-Gawad 1963: 105; Hamid 1969: 1) [11]. General rules are derived from the regulations of model contracts, such as the contract of sale (Rayner 1991: 87-88; El-Hassan 1985: 51; Coulson 1984: 27; Saleh 1992: 63). Thus, the link to the sales contract does not reflect the nature of the *mahr* being a sale or leasing contract of the female sexuality, but is owed to the structure of Islamic contract law. It highlights that the regulations of the sales contract can be applied as general rules to certain aspects of the *mahr* (Bousquet 1966: 109). Accordingly, anything that can be subject of a contract of sale can be chosen as subject of the *mahr*. Furthermore, the conditions of a valid pur-

(2004: 459-461), basing its views mainly on a book by anthropologist Shahla Haeri 1989.

9. See Wurmnest 2005: 1878-1885 (1879); OLG Hamburg, 29 May 2008, Az. 10 UF 83/06 (not published).
10. Emami 2005: 459; Katuziyan 1999: note 84; Linant de Bellefonds 1965: 24 with an overview of the sources of the Sunni schools of law.
11. For a deferring opinion, see Amin 1984: 11; Amin 1986: 50.

chase price must also be observed for the *mahr*: the *mahr* shall have a monetary value, be determinable and its performance has to be possible and legal.

(2) It is furthermore true that there is a link between the *mahr* and marital cohabitation, in particular where the marriage is defective (*fasid*) or void (*batil*) or dissolved before consummation. These regulations, however, do not offer a consistent picture: Whereas the wife is entitled to half of the *mahr* if her husband divorces her prior to consummation,[12] this is not the case where the spouses die before consummation. In this case, the wife keeps her right to the full *mahr*, and her right will be inherited by her heirs (Linant de Bellefonds 1965: 226). On the other hand, the wife may refuse to comply with her marital duties as long as the *mahr* has not been given to her.[13] However, this right of retention is a unilateral right of the wife; the husband who has paid the *mahr* has no legal claim to consummation: He must pay the *mahr* prior to consummation (Katuziyan 2005). Thus, there is no reciprocity in this right.

If the *mahr* was really the countervalue for marital cohabitation, its regulations would have to be much more stringent and comparable to the purchase price in a contract of sale. This is, however, not the case. The wife will still be entitled to the *mahr*, even if she has not "fulfilled her duty". As a matter of fact, many of these regulations are explicable by their historical context. So, very often, the time the marriage was contracted and the time the marriage was actually consummated would be considerably apart from each other. This was in particular the case when minors were married or in marriages by proxy where the husband-to-be was absent. If in the meantime the marriage was dissolved by the husband, half of the *mahr* was due. Some argue that this amount meant to compensate the girls for their reduced chances of remarriage. In other words, it constitutes some kind of damages awarded to the girl for the delay or the shortfall of a financial provider. Others argue that half of the *mahr* was due in order to compensate the husband for the expenses incurred in view of the marriage.[14]

Furthermore, one has to consider the marriage, its consummation and the *mahr* as a unity. It is true that the consummation of the marriage is not a condition for its validity. However, marriage is considered to be the only legal frame within which sexual activities are allowed and even a duty. Thus, some authors hold that only with the consummation of marriage, the process of

12. Based on the *Koran* sura 2, verse 237 and reflected for example in Art. 1092 of the Iranian Civil Code.
13. See also Art. 1085 Iranian CC.
14. See the hadith to this end in *al-Muwatta of Imam Malik ibn Anas* (d. 795 AD), hadith no.11, 28.3 (Malik ibn Anas 1989: 210 et seq.).

marrying is completed (Siddiqui 1995: 17; Diem 2007: 29, fn.36). Consequently, the reduction of the *mahr* in case of a repudiation before consummation is not so much linked to the concept of the *mahr* as the "price for marital sexual intercourse" but is rather connected to the not yet completed process of marrying. It is also within this context that the regulation on defective or void marriages and their effect on the *mahr* become more understandable:[15] Since the right to *mahr* originates in the conclusion of a valid marriage, no *mahr* shall be due in a legally defective or void marriage.

2.3.2 The Mahr *as an Economic Factor*

The predominance of the economic function of the *mahr* is very well illustrated by the immaterial functions attributed to it. All aforementioned immaterial functions will only materialize if the *mahr* has a substantial financial value: What kind of prestige or seriousness would be expressed by a very low *mahr*? How could a low *mahr* deter the husband from repudiating his wife or prevent him from a second marriage?

Furthermore, a look at the practice of *mahr* reveals its economic importance: In Iran, for example, 80% of the divorces are *khul'* divorces, whereby, in the absence of legal or contractual grounds for divorce, the wife can attract the consent of her husband to divorce in return for some kind of consideration.[16] This consideration is usually a part or the whole of her *mahr*: According to a survey conducted by the magazine *Zanan*, Iranian women try to negotiate a high *mahr* in order to exit an unwanted marriage more easily while at the same time keeping some parts of the *mahr* for financial security.[17]

Finally, new legislation in some Islamic countries highlight the economic importance of the *mahr*. The regulations in Iran, Iraq and the United Arab Emirates illustrate this very well.

In 1998, the Iranian legislator enacted a new law, the 'Act on the Adaptation of the Value of the *mahr* to the Inflation Rate', according to which a *mahr* contracted in Iranian currency must be adjusted by the inflation rate at the time claimed.[18] Under Iranian law, the agreement on the *mahr* figures in the standardized marriage contract as prompt *mahr*. It must thus be handed to the wife upon her request. In general, as long as the marriage is working and

15. As for example Art. 1098, 1099 and 1101 Iranian CC.
16. 80% of all divorces are petitioned by women on the basis of *khul'* (Hamidiyan 2008: 211).
17. *Shahrokni* in an interview with *Mehrangiz Kar* (Shahrokni 1998: 64).
18. *Official Gazette*, no.15278 (1997); "Executory Decree of Art. 1082 Iranian CC", *Official Gazette*, no. 15497 (1998).

the couple lives happily together, hardly any woman claims her *mahr* during the marriage. In most cases, the *mahr* is claimed, like the deferred *mahr*, upon dissolution of the marriage, whereby the time gap between these two moments can be crucial, implying a substantial deflation of the monetary value. In order to secure the stability of the *mahr* and to ensure that women are not deprived of their rights, the amount of the *mahr* must be adapted to the inflation rate.

Based on similar grounds, in 1999, a decree[19] was issued in Iraq, ordering the value of the deferred *mahr*, which is expressed in Iraqi currency, to be adapted to its gold value at the time of the conclusion of the marriage (Welchman 2007: 91).

Finally, in 1997, the United Arab Emirates enacted a law, the 'Act on the Limitation of the Amount of the *mahr* in the Marriage Contract and the Expenses Incurring for Marriage', to limit the amount of the *mahr*.[20] This law contrasts with the two previous laws in that it limits the amount of the prompt *mahr* to 30,000 Dirhams and the deferred *mahr* to 50,000 Dirhams (roughly 10,000 Euros). The explanatory memorandum[21] of the Personal Status Act[22] makes clear that this law was enacted to limit the extremely high marriage expenditure, which has lead to a substantial age gap between the spouses, Emirati men taking foreign wives and the men incurring debts to afford the expenses of marriage.[23] This also points to the economic importance of the *mahr*.

To sum up, today, the primary – though not only – function of the *mahr* is to provide economic security for the wife.[24]

19. "Decree No. 127/1999 of 24.7.1999", *Official Gazette*, no. 3785 (1999: 462).
20. "Law No. 21/1997", *Official Gazette*, no.312 (1997); see also Krüger 1999: 67.
21. *Official Gazette*, no.439 (2005: 119-478).
22. "Law No. 28/2005", *Official Gazette*, no.439 (2005: 9-118); see Krüger 2007: 121 et seqq..
23. *Official Gazette*, no.439 (2005: 179 et seq.).
24. This view has also been acknowledged by German courts, see OLG Hamm, 30 June 1981, *FamRZ* (1981: 875-877); see also Mir-Hosseini 2009: 369; Yassari 2009b: 369.

3. Characterization of the *Mahr*

3.1 General Remarks

The German jurisprudence has been dealing with the *mahr* in over 40 cases since 1979 without a dominant view having emerged.[25] Jurisprudence and literature are far from being unanimous as to which norm fits the *mahr* best. The norms chosen to characterize the *mahr* have been: a. contractual obligation (Art. 28 EGBGB); b. effect of marriage (Art. 14 EGBGB); c. maintenance (marital or post-marital) (Art. 18 EGBGB); d. effect of divorce (Art. 17 EGBGB); e. inheritance (Art. 25 EGBGB); and f. matrimonial property regime (Art. 15 EGBGB).

The relevance of the choice of law norm has been attenuated to some extent by the fact that the connecting factors of any of these norms are identical. The German legislator has chosen a gradual focus first on nationality and then on residence for all norms. Accordingly, pursuant to Art. 14 EGBGB, the applicable law on the effects of marriage is determined by the law of the common nationality of the parties and, for lack of such a common law, by the law of residence, i.e. the law of the country in which the spouses resided together. If the applicable law cannot be determined in this way, the law of the country having the closest connection with the case shall apply. According to the structure of the EGBGB, all choice of law rules abide by this scale, so that, usually, any of these norms will lead to the same result as to the applicable law. However, this is not always the case.

As an illustration of the significance of the characterization of the *mahr*, I shall refer to a case which is currently under the review of the German Federal Supreme Court.[26] The facts of the case are as follows: Two Iranian nationals married in 1990 in Iran and stipulated a *mahr* of 2,000,000 Rials. Later on, they moved to Germany, settled there and acquired the German nationality. Eventually, their marriage broke down and the woman filed for divorce, claiming her *mahr*. In order to determine the applicable law for the *mahr*, the nationalities of the parties must be examined first. As they were Iranians when they married and contracted the *mahr* and Germans at the time of the divorce, the question arises as to the point in time at which the nationalities must be considered: the time of marriage or the time of divorce? This is a crucial question, since, at variance with all other choice of law rules that

25. For an overview of the state of art, see Wurmnest 2007: 527-558; Jones-Pauly 2008: 299-330.

26. In December 2009, the Supreme Court decided the case. See "Postscriptum" at the end of this article.

regard the time at which the claim for *mahr* is made as constitutive, Art. 15 EGBGB (law applicable to matrimonial property) only considers the time at which the marriage was concluded as relevant.

Thus, if one characterized the *mahr* in the aforementioned case as an effect of marriage or divorce or as maintenance or as an inheritance claim, German law applies as the law of the parties' nationality at the time of the claim. Characterizing the *mahr* as belonging to the matrimonial property regime, however, leads to the application of Iranian law. In fact, these different characterizations led to diverting judgements: Whereas the District Court of Hamburg characterized the *mahr* as some kind of post-marital maintenance claim and came to the application of German law,[27] the Court of Appeal of Hamburg reversed the decision, characterized the *mahr* under the matrimonial property regime and came to the application of Iranian law.[28] This had substantial consequences for the case: Under German law, the court admitted that the *mahr* as a contractual obligation had to be fulfilled, and converted the amount of 2 million Rials at the rate of the Iranian currency at the time of its claim in 2007, which amounted to the sum of 1,400 €. The Court of Appeal's characterization, on the other hand, led to the application of Iranian law. The Court of Appeal acknowledged the validity of the *mahr* agreement under Iranian Law. It furthermore applied the Iranian rules of the above mentioned 'Act on the Adaptation of the Value of the *mahr* to the Inflation Rate' of 1998, according to which a *mahr* expressed in Iranian currency must be adapted to the inflation rate at the time it is claimed to counterbalance the loss of monetary value in the meantime. This is done according to a specific spread sheet, released yearly by the Central Bank of Iran.[29] Accordingly, when inflation was considered, the agreed 2 million Rials in 1990 corresponded to 14,000 Euros in 2007. In comparison with the first judgement, this meant an augmentation of ten times the initial value. Thus, the characterization is crucial to the outcome of the case. I shall now explore the options German private international law offers for the characterization of the *mahr*.

27. District Court (hereinafter: AG) Hamburg, 16 November 2006, Az 891 F 21/06 (not published).
28. OLG Hamburg, 29 May 2008, Az. 10 UF 83/06 (not published).
29. See the spread sheet until 1381 (= 2003) "Annex A", in Basedow and Yassari 2004: 171 et seq.; For the years 1382-1385 (= 2004-2007), see spread sheet of the Iranian Central Bank in Hamidiyan 2008: 222. On 22 June 2007 (month *tir* 1386), a new spread sheet was released, see Iranian Central Bank, www.cbi.ir/page/4930.aspx, accessed 1 October 2009.

3.2 Choice of Law Rules

3.2.1 Contractual Obligation (Art. 28 EGBGB)

Some courts have characterized the *mahr* as a pure contractual agreement and submitted it to Art. 28 EGBGB.[30] It is true that the *mahr* is a contractual obligation of the husband. However, in Islamic law, the *mahr* is seen as compulsory (*wajib*). Thus, even if it is not mentioned and even in cases where it has explicitly been excluded, the proper *mahr* (*mahr al-mithl*) must be given to the wife. Strictly speaking, it is only its amount and the time it becomes due which can be regulated by the parties. Secondly, the *mahr* is undoubtedly an instrument of family law. In order to understand it properly, it must be evaluated against and within any given system of family law. A purely contractual characterization will not do justice to the *mahr*.

3.2.2 Effects of Marriage (Art. 14 EGBGB)

The advocates of this characterization maintain that in Islamic countries the *mahr* is considered an effect of the marriage, *athar an-nikah,* and that the claim to *mahr* is generated by the conclusion of the marriage (Henrich 2004: 393).[31] However, under the laws of most Islamic countries, the term "effect of marriage" encompasses both the immaterial effects, such as obedience, headship of the household, as well as the material effects, such as maintenance and matrimonial property regime. The German legislator, on the other hand, has a much more specified and detailed classification. The "effects of marriage" under German law are mainly concerned with conjugal rights and duties on a personal basis. The financial effects of marriage are dealt with in specific categories and have their own norms, such as maintenance or matrimonial property regime (Wurmnest 2007: 553). As the *mahr* has a wide financial dimension, it would be short-sighted to include it in the narrow category of the effects of marriage.

3.2.3 Maintenance (Art. 18 EGBGB)

German law has conceived a choice of law rule specific to maintenance claims and some have advocated that the *mahr* should fall into this category as its main aim is to provide financial help to the wife, a task that is fulfilled

30. OLG Düsseldorf, 12 August 1992, *FamRZ* (1993: 187-189 (188)); OLG Cologne, 21 April 1993, *NJW-RR* (1994: 200-201).
31. OLG Cologne, 23 March 2006, *FamRZ* (2006: 1380-1383).

by the right to maintenance under German law.[32] In Islamic countries, however, maintenance and *mahr* always stand next to each other and are separate rights. A woman who infringes upon her marital duties may lose her right to maintenance, but this will not affect her right to *mahr*. And conversely, if a women gets her prompt *mahr*, this will not lead to a reduction of her marital maintenance because she is not needy. This does not match German law, where a right to maintenance depends on the need of the one spouse and the capability of the other spouse to provide for it. To interpret the *mahr* as maintenance claim would negate its nature.[33]

3.2.4 Effects of Divorce (Art. 17 EGBGB)

The *mahr* may be due at the time of the divorce, as regards, for example, the deferred *mahr*. But it is not a consequence of divorce in the strict sense, as its raison d'être results from the conclusion of the marriage rather than its dissolution. Furthermore, in some countries, *mahr* is always prompt and only claimed (at the latest) at the time of divorce. In this sense, the *mahr* is not necessarily a consequence of divorce either.

3.2.5 Inheritance (Art. 25 EBGBG)

When the *mahr* is claimed upon the death of the husband, some have argued that the *mahr* must be characterized as an inheritance claim (Heldrich 1983: 64-65). However, this does not correspond to the institution of the *mahr* either. The *mahr* is not part of the inheritance share of the wife. The unpaid (deferred or not claimed) *mahr* is a debt of the deceased husband which becomes (at the latest) due upon his death. It has to be settled from the estate like all other debts of the deceased before the shares of the heirs are distributed. Although it will increase the wife's portion of the estate, legally, it is a priority debt due to the wife from the estate of the deceased.[34] In this sense, the *mahr* cannot be characterized as inheritance.

32. See for example KG Berlin, 12 November 1979, *FamRZ* (1980: 470-471); AG Hamburg, 19 December 1980, *IPRax* (1983: 74-76); OLG Celle, 17 January 1997, *FamRZ* (1998: 374-375); AG Kerpen, 29 January 1999, *FamRZ* (1999: 1429-1430).
33. This view is also held by a majority of German commentators, see for example Mankowski 2003: note 275; Mörsdorf-Schulte 2008: note 20; Henrich 2003: note 6; Wurmnest 2007: 551.
34. See for example Art. 87 No. 3 Law of Personal Status of Tunisia, Art. 114 of the Afghan Civil Code, or Art. 231 of the Iranian Act of Probation of 23 June 1940.

3.2.6 Matrimonial Property Regime (Art. 15 EGBGB)

The matrimonial property regime defines the property of the assets brought into and acquired within marriage. Generally speaking, it regulates proprietary aspects of assets in marriage and defines which asset belongs to which spouse.[35] In this respect, the concept of *mahr* matches well, as it is a property whose ownership is transferred as a result of the conclusion of marriage and it is of high economic importance.

The continuity of matrimonial property issues is so important to the German legislator that the choice of law rule concerning matrimonial property regime (Art. 15 EGBGB) does not suffer any changes of status, be it nationality or domicile. In other words, the law applicable to the matrimonial property regime of a couple is determined at the moment the marriage is concluded, unless they agree otherwise by choosing the applicable law.[36] It is at this moment that they make the arrangement for separation or community of goods under a certain law and their choice deserves to be respected and preserved to ensure that the applicable law is predictable and remains applicable in the future. Even if, by change of nationality or domicile, divorce proceedings may be governed by the law of a country which, at the time of marriage, was not thought of, the law applicable to property regime will remain the law under which the marriage was concluded.

In my opinion, this continuity must also unfold for the law applicable to the *mahr*, which ought to be characterized under the matrimonial property regime.[37] The parties who marry and contract a *mahr* can rely on the applicability of the law under which they concluded the *mahr*. This serves both parties: The wife can be sure to have continuity under the law under which the *mahr* was contracted as to its validity, and the husband can be sure that the law governing matrimonial property regime will be preserved and an accumulation of claims avoided: Under the laws of most countries, the statutory matrimonial property regime will be separation of goods, so that he "only" has to pay the *mahr*.

35. See Gernhuber and Coester-Waltjen, § 31 I (2010: note 1).
36. The party's autonomy is limited to choosing the law of the country to which one of the parties belongs, or the law of the domicile of one of the spouses or, as far as real estate is concerned, the *lex rei sitae* (Art. 15 Sec. 2 EGBGB). The agreement on choice of law must be notarized to be valid (Art. 15 Sec. 3, Art. 14 Sec. 4 EGBGB).
37. OLG Bremen, 9 August 1979, *FamRZ* (1980: 606-607); OLG Cologne, 29 October 1981, *IPRax* (1983: 73-74); OLG Frankfurt, 29 February 1996, *FamRZ* (1996: 1478-1479); No. 17, *IPG* (2002: 224-237).

3.3 Result and Conclusion

The question of characterization in private international law is a very technical one on a high level of abstraction. However, confining the concept of the *mahr* to its primary economic function makes the choice more limited. In my opinion, the characterization of the *mahr* as belonging to the matrimonial property regime will lead to a uniform result regarding the applicable law and will ensure that matters of property (separation or community of goods) and the *mahr* are determined under the same law.[38] This serves legal certainty and continuity in the financial relations of the couple.

4. Accomodation of the *Mahr* in German Law

4.1 Setting

Once the *mahr* is characterized, there can be two possible results. The applicable law may be the law of a country that knows the *mahr*. In this case, the court can directly apply the regulations on the *mahr* of that country. In doing so, German courts have to observe the rule of public policy (Art. 6 EGBGB). Accordingly, a foreign legal provision shall not be applicable if the result of its application is obviously incompatible with essential principles of German law. The foreign rule shall not be applicable, especially when it is incompatible with the German constitution, the *Grundgesetz*.

Public policy thus strikes generally under two conditions: first, if the result of the application of the foreign rule is in an unbearable discordance with fundamental principles of justice or the German constitution (Blumenwitz 2003: 86; Sonnenberger 2010: note 133); and second, there must be a strong connection to Germany (*Inlandsbezug*). This can be a German domicile/residence, the German citizenship of one of the spouses, the fact that the couple lived in Germany for a long time, planned their life here, had children that were born and raised in Germany, and so on (Heldrich 2010: note 6). Furthermore, every case has to be studied on its individual merits *in concreto:* it is the concrete case that matters, not abstract considerations on the possibility of infringement of a constitutional right. And finally, all this stands under the

38. For a characterization of the *Mahr* under the matrimonial property regime, Krüger 1977: 114, 116; Schurig 1996: note 35; regarding the part due on the conclusion of marriage, see also Rauscher 1999: 194, 197; Andrae 2006: note 149; Wurmnest 2007: 527, 553; Siehr 2010: note 97; OLG Bremen, 9 August 1979, *FamRZ* (1980: 606-607); OLG Köln, 29 October 1981, *IPRax* (1983: 73-74); OLG Frankfurt, 29 February 1996, *FamRZ* (1996: 1478-1479).

principle that public policy shall be applied within narrow limits and be used very scarcely and cautiously.

As far as the *mahr* is concerned, there is only one judgement from the early 1980s on Iranian law, where a court of first instance ruled the *mahr* to be against German public policy.[39] In that case, the court had asked for an expert opinion by the University of Cologne. The expert described the *mahr* as a consideration for sexual availability of the woman in marital life and the court concluded that such a legal institution could not be enforced in Germany, as it was against the fundamental principles of German law. That decision was overruled by the Court of Appeal[40] and the *mahr* was upheld as an agreement that was usual and common in Iran and had nothing dubious to it. Since then, the issue of public policy was occasionally raised, but the courts have always rejected it.[41]

On the other hand, the law of a country which does not know the *mahr*, such as German law, may be applicable. In this case, the court must accommodate the *mahr* into German national family law. In doing so, the *mahr* has to be evaluated as a contractual agreement and needs to be interpreted by the court as to the intention of the parties. The jurisprudence of the German courts shows several directions; I shall concentrate on two interpretations: the *mahr* as an agreement on post-marital maintenance and the *mahr* as an agreement modifying the statutory matrimonial property regime. I shall explore the jurisprudence of the German courts in this respect and try to assess how the *mahr* could be accommodated within German family law.

4.2 Interpretation of the *Mahr* Agreement According to German Law

4.2.1 Principles of Contractual Interpretation

Whenever the *mahr* has to be assessed under German law, it can only be validated as a contractual agreement, as there are no legal rules on it under German law. The concept of freedom of contract eminent in German family law leaves ample room for the acknowledgement of such agreements (Hofer and Henrich 2005; Hahne 2004). When interpreting the *mahr* agreement, the court must enquire as to the real intention of the parties[42] and not stick to the literal wording of the expressions used (§ 133 German Civil Code (BGB)). The court has to assess what the parties had in mind when they concluded the

39. LG Cologne, 27 October 1980, *IPRspr.*, no.83 (1980: 248-249).
40. OLG Cologne, 29 October 1981, *IPRax* (1983: 73).
41. See for example OLG Stuttgart, 3 November 2008, *FuR* (2009: 231-232).
42. BGH, 28 January 1987, *FamRZ* (1987: 463-466); OLG Hamburg, 21 May 2003, *FamRZ* (2004: 459-461 (460)).

Islamic *mahr* and translate this perception into German law. Furthermore, the Federal Supreme Court held that the agreement on the *mahr* shall be interpreted with due consideration of the changed circumstances that have occurred in the meantime, in order to assess whether the performance of the *mahr* is still due.[43] Finally, the interpretation has to be done in accordance with the principle of good faith in the performance of contracts (§ 157 BGB). German courts have interpreted the *mahr* mainly as an agreement by which the parties modified the statutory regulations on maintenance or their matrimonial property regime.

4.2.2 Maintenance

In German law (§ 1569-1573 BGB), each divorced spouse is expected to provide for his or her own maintenance. However, there are several instances where post-marital maintenance may be claimed. These are cases of maintenance for a spouse who, because of the care for a minor child, is prevented from earning a living (§ 1570 BGB). Other cases are maintenance for an aged divorced spouse (§ 1571 BGB), sickness or infirmity (§ 1572 BGB), maintenance until appropriate employment is found (§§ 1573, 1574 BGB) and further education or retraining is completed (§ 1575 BGB). There is also a general hardship clause (§ 1576 BGB). The rule for obtaining maintenance is neediness of the spouse.

Spouses may also agree on their reciprocal maintenance duties contractually and derogate from statutory law (§ 1585 c BGB). Accordingly, some courts have interpreted the agreement on the *mahr* as a lump-sum agreement on post-marital maintenance and attributed the *mahr* as such to the wife,[44] denying her further maintenance under German law.

Interpreting the *mahr* as maintenance allows the court to make use of all adjustment instruments that German maintenance law offers: If the marriage was of short duration, the court can reduce the amount of the *mahr* on the basis of § 1579 No. 1 BGB and the theory of change of circumstances, according to which a change in the economic, legal and business realities underlying

43. BGH, 28 January 1987, *FamRZ* (1987: 463-466).
44. KG Berlin, 12 November 1979, *FamRZ* (1980: 470-471); AG Memmingen, 11 January 1984, *IPRax* (1984: 219); AG Memmingen, 12 December 1984, *IPRax* (1985: 230-231); KG Berlin, 11 September 1987, *FamRZ* (1988: 296); OLG Frankfurt, 26 May 1989, *Streit* (1989: 110-111); AG Kerpen, 29 January 1999, *FamRZ* (1999: 1429-1430); AG Aachen, 7 February 2000, *IPRspr.*, no.67 (2000: 140-142); AG Fürth, 10 April 2002, *FPR* (2002: 450-451); OLG Saarbrücken, 9 March 2005, *NJW-RR* (2005: 1306-1308).

a contractual agreement can invalidate or modify the terms of a contract (Wurmnest 2005: 1880).[45] Moreover, a very high *mahr* can be adapted to the financial capability of the husband (§ 1581 BGB), and a very low *mahr* may be raised according to the needs of the divorcee. Since 1 January 2008, the provisions of Art. 1585 c BGB have been amended insofar as agreements on post-marital maintenance are subject to formal requirements and must be certificated by a notary.[46] The validity of the *mahr* agreement would then depend on the fulfilment of this formality.

Interpreting the *mahr* as maintenance does, however, not always match the intention of the parties (Wurmnest 2005: 1880). If at the moment of the marriage and the agreement on the *mahr* the parties had the intention to move to Germany or if one of the parties was a German citizen, it is doubtful whether with the acceptance of the *mahr*, the wife intended to waive her maintenance rights awarded to her under German law. But even if both parties are of foreign origin, a waiver of maintenance cannot be presumed,[47] since – as mentioned before – the *mahr* and maintenance claims stand next to each other in Islamic countries as well. Thus, *mahr* is not the equivalent of maintenance (Wurmnest 2005: 1880; Henrich 2000; Mankowski 2003: note 275). In one case, the wife remarried soon after her divorce, with the result that the remainder of the *mahr* which was paid by instalments was forfeited.[48] The claim to the *mahr* must stand next to the claim to maintenance and be independent of it under German law. Since the *mahr* enriches the wife and reduces her need for maintenance, her maintenance claim under German law may then be reduced. This will prevent the husband from being charged twice.

4.2.3 Matrimonial Property Regime

Under statutory law, German matrimonial property regime is one of separation of property with an equalization of surplus (*Zugewinnausgleich*) after the marriage has come to an end. This regime becomes legally important mainly at the breakdown of marriage. Marriage has no impact on the property previously owned by the spouses; assets acquired after the marriage remain the sole property of the acquiring spouse. In principle, each spouse owns and

45. BGH, 28 January 1987, *FamRZ* (1987: 463-466); OLG Saarbrücken, 9 March 2005, *NJW-RR* (2005: 1306-1308).
46. Art. 1585 c BGB new version, of 21 December 2007, *Federal Official Gazette I*, p.3189.
47. See for example OLG Hamm, 30 June 1981, *FamRZ* (1981: 875-877).
48. OLG Saarbrücken, 9 March 2005, *NJW-RR* (2005: 1306-1308).

administers his or her property independently. There are no common goods. However, in order to secure the common household and the material existence of the family, a spouse can only dispose of household objects and the whole of his or her assets with the consent of the other (§§ 1365-1369 BGB). Most married couples live under the statutory matrimonial property regime.

Upon termination of marriage, the accrued gains, i.e. the additions to the assets of each of the spouses achieved during the marriage, are equalized. This means that the increase in the value of the assets during the marriage is divided equally between the two spouses. The decisive factor is the amount by which the value of the assets owned by a spouse at the end of the matrimonial regime exceeds their value at the beginning of the marriage. Some assets acquired by the spouse as a gift or by succession are exempted (§ 1374 II BGB). In principle, however, it is assumed that the surplus is due to the efforts of both spouses and it is therefore divided equally. Assets not separately listed at the beginning of the marriage (such lists occur very rarely in practice) are presumed to be assets realized in the course of the marriage. The spouse with the higher surplus has to pay the partner with the smaller increase one half of the excess (§1378 BGB). The surplus is a cash value. The statutory provisions can be modified by the partners (§ 1408 BGB) in a marriage contract that must be officially notarized (1410 BGB) and can be also registered as well (1558 BGB). If no marriage contract is concluded, the statutory matrimonial property rules apply (§§ 1363 et seq.).

In Islamic countries, on the other hand, the principle of separation of property holds supreme: each spouse remains the owner of his/her assets before, during and after marriage.

In assessing the *mahr*, in some cases, German courts have interpreted the agreement on the *mahr* as a modification or supplement to the German matrimonial property regime, whereby the parties exclude the equalization of surplus and install a regime of separation of goods with the *mahr* being a lump sum to be paid to the wife upon divorce.[49]

However, it is questionable whether this interpretation is valid in all cases and matches the intention of the parties. If both parties are Muslims living and marrying in Germany and additionally contracting a *mahr*, this agreement might rather be made out of respect for their religious background rather than be an expression of their intention to exclude the regime of sur-

49. OLG Bremen, 9 August 1979, *FamRZ* (1980: 606-607); OLG Cologne, 29 October 1981, *IPRax* (1983: 73-74); OLG Munich, 26 November 1985, *IPRspr.*, no.67 (1985: 177-183).

plus upon divorce.[50] This is even more so when one of the spouses is German and the other is of foreign origin. If, however, the parties are both foreigners who married in their country of origin, then such an interpretation could be considered if none of the parties had a close connection to Germany (Wurmnest 2005: 1881).

Finally, the formal requirements for a contract modifying the matrimonial property regime (§ 1410 BGB) must be observed. Accordingly, the contract must be certified by a notary and registered if contracted in Germany or if contracted abroad, the formal requirements of the place of conclusion must be observed. These requirements have in some cases led to the invalidation of the *mahr*.[51]

4.2.4 A Contract Sui Generis

The *mahr* does not fit any of the available categories of German family law. It cannot, however, just be disregarded, as it is a valid contractual agreement between the spouses meant to regulate some proprietary aspects of their marital relationship. I would thus argue that the agreement on the *mahr* should be considered as an independent family law contract that need not be squeezed into one of the German national family law categories. Nevertheless, the *mahr* must be contextualized within the setting of German family law and the available family law instruments to make sure none of the spouses is disadvantaged. If the award of the *mahr* would stand as a contract *sui generis* next to a valid maintenance claim and the equalization of surplus, it would have a significant effect on their respective amounts: The payment of the *mahr* to the wife will increase her assets and thus influence the amount of surplus that has to be equalized. Additionally, a substantial *mahr* will decrease the wife's need for post-marital alimony, so that here again a fair financial balance is achieved between the parties. It must after all be borne in mind that the *mahr* is conceived to provide a certain economic security for the wife in a system which hardly knows any financial (post-)marital solidarity between the spouses. It is a tool to protect the wife in a specific legal surrounding. Whenever this situation changes to the benefit of the wife, her need to be protected will diminish.[52] This is also why the *mahr* must be accounted for within the

50. In this sense also OLG Stuttgart, 29 January 2008, *FamRZ* (2008: 1756-1758).
51. For example, OLG Celle, 17 January 1997, *FamRZ* (1998: 374-375).
52. In a case in the early 1980s, the court of first instance held that an agreement on a *Mahr* was not enforceable under German law, as its function of safeguarding the wife financially was perfectly fulfilled by the instruments of German family law, LG Cologne, 27 October 1980, *IPRspr.*, no.83 (1980: 248-249).

new legal context it is being evaluated in. However, this does not change its character as an independent contract *sui generis* and the fact that the parties must honour their contractual obligation.

5 Conclusion

The characterization and appraisal of the *mahr* in German courts will remain a tricky and unforeseeable undertaking as long as the Federal Supreme Court has not taken a decision. In the meantime, I would advocate to characterize the *mahr* under Art. 15 EGBGB as part of the matrimonial property regime of the spouses. This will ensure that both the *mahr* and the financial equalization of the spouses' property upon divorce are governed by the same law. If this law is the law of their country of origin, then the wife can be sure to obtain her *mahr* and the regime of separation of property will serve the husband as no further payment will be due. If on the other side, German law governs both the matrimonial property regime and the destiny of the *mahr*, the principle that the accrued property shall be divided will lead to a fair result: The wife will have a right to her *mahr* and, at the same time, this increase in her asset will affect the equalization of the financial accrual of the spouses.

As far as the applicable law is concerned, one will always have two possibilities: If the applicable law is the law of a country that knows the *mahr*, its regulations will apply directly. As in all Islamic countries, the *mahr* is considered a contract *sui generis*, it will be awarded next to any other family law instrument available under that law.

Conversely, if the law of a country not knowing the *mahr* is applicable, then the *mahr* must be set within the framework of the available family law instruments of that country. In other words, the *mahr* must be reappraised within the context of the applicable law and the court should not be bound to its assessment for characterization if it does not fit. For German law, this means that first, the *mahr* will be validated as a contractual agreement. Secondly, as the agreement on the *mahr* does not fit any of the statutory known family law agreements existing in German law, I would argue that the *mahr* should be interpreted as an independent contract *sui generis*, as it is done in Islamic countries. The result of such an assessment would be the following: If the *mahr* is of low value, the wife will have the protection provided to her by the instruments of German law, which have no gender bias and accord financial help to the needy spouse. Conversely, if it is of high value, the *mahr* will reduce the need of the wife for maintenance, so that the husband will not have to pay twice. As far as matrimonial property regime is considered, the amount of the *mahr* will be added to the wife's accrual, so that the difference between their respective properties will decrease, too.

This will result in a fair distribution of the financial burden of the ex-spouses, respect the agreement on the *mahr* and bring legal certainty to both characterization and appraisal of the *mahr* under German law.

6 Postscriptum

This article was finalized in October 2009. On 9 December 2009, the German Federal Supreme Court issued a judgement according to which the Islamic *mahr* was to be characterized as an effect of the marriage under Art. 14 EGBGB.[53] The court dismissed all relevant norms of the German international family law as addressing inadequately the nature of the *mahr*, and subsumed the *mahr* under Art. 14 EGBGB as a kind of backup-norm (*Auffangtatbestand*). The court explicitly rejected the characterization of the *mahr* as belonging to the matrimonial property regime under Art. 15 EGBGB. It held that firstly, the *mahr* did not constitute, amend or replace a matrimonial property regime. Secondly, it was said that the *mahr* did not consider the real accrue of the husband's property for the equalization of assets as the German regime of equalization of surplus does. Finally, the court considered the unchangeable nature of the connection of the matrimonial property regime under Art. 15 EGBGB (*Unwandelbarkeit*) to be too static to accommodate the changes in the life of people who had immigrated to Germany, acquired German nationality and left behind any relation to the law of their former nationality.[54]

This judgement will lead to an increase of cases in which the *mahr* will fall under German law. Unfortunately, however, the court gives only little guidance as to the accommodation of the *mahr* in German national family law. The court limits itself to declare the agreement on the *mahr* to be valid under German law, but fails to give details on its relation to the "native" claims awarded under German law, i.e. maintenance and the equalization of the matrimonial accrue. Finally, one also misses conclusive hints on the form requirement for the validity of the *mahr* agreement contracted in Germany.

53. BGH, 9 December 2009, FamRZ (2010: 533-537).
54. For a critical assessment of this decision, see Yassari 2010.

Bibliography

Abdel-Gawad, M., (1963) "L'autonomie de la volonté en droit musulman" (The Autonomy of Will in Islamic Law), *Égypte contemporaine*, vol.54, pp.105-114.

Amin, Sayed H., (1986) *Commercial Law of Iran*, Tehran: Vahid.

Amin, Sayed H., (1984) *Remedies for Breach of Contract in Islamic and Iranian Law*, Glasgow: Royston.

Andrae, Marianne, (2006) *Internationales Familienrecht* (International Family Law), Baden-Baden: Nomos.

Basedow, J. and N. Yassari (eds.), (2004) *Iranian Family and Succession Laws and their Application in German Courts*, Tübingen: Mohr Siebeck.

Blumenwitz, Dieter, (2003) Commentary on Art. 6 EGBGB, in Julius v. Staudinger (ed.), *BGB*, Berlin: Schweitzer de Gruyter.

Bousquet, Georges-Henri, (1966) *L' Éthique sexuelle de l'Islam* (The Sexual Ethics of Islam), Paris: Maisonneuve & Larose.

Chehata, Chafik, (1968) "Le contrat en droit musulman" (The Contract in Islamic Law), *ZvglRWiss*, p.81-96.

Coulson, Noel J., (1984) *Commercial Law in the Gulf States: The Islamic Legal Tradition*, London: Graham & Trotman.

Dahlgren, Susanne, (2005) "Women's *adah* versus 'women's law: the contesting issue of *Mahr* in Aden, Yemen", *Égypte/Monde arabe*, 3rd series, vol.1, pp. 125-144.

Diem, Werner, (2007) *Ein arabisches Rechtsgutachten zum Eherecht aus dem 11.-12. Jahrhundert* (An Arabic Legal Opinion on Marriage Law from the 11th-12th Century), Wiesbaden: Harrassowitz.

El-Hassan, 'Abd El-W. A., (1985) "Freedom of Contract, the Doctrine of Frustration, and Sanctity of Contracts in Sudan Law and Islamic Law", *ALQ*, vol.1, pp.51-59.

Emami, Sayyed H., (2005) *hoquq-e madani* (Civil Law), vol.4, Tehran: Ketabforushi-ye eslamiye.

Emamy, Hassan, (1933) *L'institution juridique du Mahr (dot) en droit musulman du rite chiite* (The Legal Institution of the *Mahr* (Dower) in Shiite Islamic Law), Lausanne: Imprimerie C. Risold.

Enayat, Magid, (2004) "Länderbericht Iran" (Country Report Iran), in Bergmann, A., M. Ferid and D. Henrich (eds.), *Internationales Ehe- und Kindschaftsrecht*, as of 1 October 2002, Frankfurt on the Main: Verlag für Standesamtswesen.

Esposito, John L., (1982) *Women in Muslim Family Law*, Syracuse: Syracuse University Press.

Fyzee, Asaf A. A., (1993) *Outlines of Muhammadan Law*, Delhi *et al*: Oxford University Press.

Gernhuber, J. and D. Coester-Waltjen, (2010) *Familienrecht* (Family Law), Munich: Beck.

Haeri, Shahla, (1989) *Law of Desire: Temporary Marriage in Iran*, London: Tauris.

Hahne, Meo-Micaela, (2004) "Vertragsfreiheit im Familienrecht" (Freedom of Contract in Family Law), in Schwab, D. and M.-M. Hahne (eds.), *Familienrecht im Brennpunkt*, Bielefeld: Gieseking.

Hamid, M. E., (1969) "Islamic Law of Contract or Contracts?", *JICL*, vol.3, p.1.

Hamidian, Hassan, (2004) "Jurisdiction of Family Courts in Iran", in Basedow, J. and N. Yassari (eds.), *Iranian Family and Succession Laws and their Application in German Courts*, Tübingen: Mohr Siebeck.

Hamidiyan, Hasan, (2008) "mehriye be nerkh-e ruz" (The *Mahr* Calculated at the Current Rate), in Hasan Hamidiyan (ed.), *majmu'e-ye maqalat-e hoquq-e khanevade*, Tehran: Entesharat-e hamun.

Heldrich, Andreas, (2010) Commentary on Art. 6 EGBGB, in Otto Palandt (ed.), *Bürgerliches Gesetzbuch*, Munich: Beck.

Heldrich, Andreas, (1983) "Das juristische Kuckucksei aus dem Morgenland" (The Legal Cuckoo's Egg from the *Orient), IPrax*, pp.64-65.

Henrich, Dieter, (2004) "Die Morgengabe und das Internationale Privatrecht" (The Dower and Private International Law), in Coester, M., D. Martiny and K. A. von Sachsen Gessaphe (eds.), *Privatrecht in Europa: Vielfalt, Kollision, Kooperation, FS Hans Jürgen Sonnenberger*, Munich: Beck.

Henrich, Dieter, (2003) Commentary on Art. 14 EGBGB, in Johannsen, K. and D. Henrich (eds.), *Eherecht: Trennung, Scheidung, Folgen*, Munich: Beck.

Henrich, Dieter, (2000) *Internationales Familienrecht* (International Family Law), Frankfurt on the Main *et al*: Verlag für Standesamtswesen.

Hofer, S., D. Schwab and D. Henrich (eds.), (2005) *From Status to Contract? Die Bedeutung des Vertrages im europäischen Familienrecht* (The Significance of Contracts in European Family Law), Bielefeld: Gieseking.

Jones-Pauly, Christina, (2008) "Marriage Contracts of Muslims in the Diaspora: Problems in the Recognition of *Mahr* Contracts in German Law", in Quraishi, A. and F. E. Vogel (eds.), *The Islamic Marriage Contract*, Cambridge: Harvard University Press.

Katuziyan, Naser, (2005) *hoquq-e madani, khanevade* (Civil Law: Family Law), Tehran: Bahman Borna.

Katuziyan, Naser, (1999) *hoquq-e madani: khanevade* (Civil Law: Family Law), vol.1, Tehran: Entesharat-e bahman borna.

Kropholler, Jan, (2006) *Internationales Privatrecht* (Private International Law), Tübingen: Mohr Siebeck.

Krüger, Hilmar, (2007) "Grundzüge des Privatrechts der VAE" (Main Features of the Private Law of the UAE), in Ebert, H.-G. and Th. Hanstein (eds*.), Beiträge zum islamischen Recht VI*, Frankfurt on the Main: Lang.

Krüger, Hilmar, (1999) "Das Recht der Eheschließung in den Vereinigten Arabischen Emiraten" (Marriage Law in the United Arab Emirates), *StAZ*, pp.65-68.

Krüger, Hilmar, (1977) "Ehe und Brautgabe" (Marriage and Dower), *FamRZ*, pp.114-118.

Linant de Bellefonds, Yvon, (1965) *Traité de droit musulman comparé* (Comparative Treatise of Muslim Law), vol.2, Paris: Mouton.

Linant de Bellefonds, Yvon, (1958) "L'autonomie de la volonté en droit musulman" (The Autonomy of Will in Islamic Law), *Revue algérienne, tunisienne et marocaine de législation et de jurisprudence* (Revue Algérienne), pp.87-111.

Malik ibn Anas, Abu 'Abdullah, (1989) *Al-Muwatta of Imam Malik ibn Anas: The First Formulation of Islamic Law*, transl. by A. A. Bewley, London: Kegan Paul International.

Mankowski, Peter, (2003) Commentary on Art. 14 EGBGB, in Julius v. Staudinger (ed.), *BGB*, Berlin: Schweitzer de Gruyter.

Mir-Hosseini, Ziba, (2000) *Marriage on Trial: A Study of Islamic Family Law*, London: I.B. Tauris.

Moors, Annelies, (1995) *Women, Property and Islam*, Cambridge: Cambridge University Press.

Mörsdorf-Schulte, Juliana, (2008) Commentary on Art. 14 EGBGB, in Bamberger, H. G. and H. Roth (eds.), *BGB*, Munich: Beck.

Rauscher, Thomas, (1999) "Entscheidung des BGH zur Brautgabe" (Judgement by the Federal Supreme Court on Dower), *DEuFamR*, vol. 1, pp.194-198.

Rayner, Susan E., (1991) *The Theory of Contracts in Islamic Law*, London: Graham & Trotman.

"Report of the legal office of the Ministry of Justice No. 7/2989 of 15.7.2003" (2005), in The Directorate General for Codification and Compilation of Laws and Regulations (ed.), *majmu'-e qanun-e madani* (Civil Law Statutes), Commentary of Art. 1085 Iranian CC, Tehran: Mo'avenat-e pazhuhesh, tadvin va tanqih-e qavanin va moqararat.

Safa'i, Hossein, (2004) "Le Mariage et le Divorce en Droit Iranien" (Marriage and Divorce in Iranian Law), in Basedow, J. and N. Yassari (eds.), *Iranian Family and Succession Laws and their Application in German Courts*, Tübingen: Mohr Siebeck.

Safa'i, Hossein and Assadollah Emami, (2002) *hoquq-e khanevade* (Family Law), vol.1, Tehran: Entesharat-e daneshgah-e tehran.

Saleh, Nabil A., (1992) *Unlawful Gain and Legitimate Profit in Islamic Law*, London: Graham & Trotman.

Schurig, Klaus, (1996) Commentary on Art. 15 EGBGB, in Hans Theodor Soergel (ed.), *Bürgerliches Gesetzbuch*, Stuttgart: Kohlhammer.

Shahrokni, Nazanin, (1998) An interview with *Mehrangiz Kar*, *Zanan* (monthly journal), vol.33, pp.60-66.

Siddiqui, Mona, (1995) "*Mahr*: Legal Obligation or Rightful Demand?", *Journal of Islamic Studies*, vol.6, no.1, pp.14-24.

Siehr, Kurt, (2010) Commentary on Art. 15 EGBGB, in Kurt Rebmann (ed.), *Münchener Kommentar zum Bürgerlichen Gesetzbuch*, Munich: Beck.

Sonnenberger, Hans J., (2010) Commentary on Art. 6 EGBGB, in Kurt Rebmann (ed.), *Münchener Kommentar zum Bürgerlichen Gesetzbuch*, Munich: Beck.

Tchouar, Djilali, (1996) "Régime juridique de la dot en droit algérien" (The Legal Status of the Dower in Algerian Law), *Revue Algérienne*, vol.34, no.4, pp.569-596.

Welchman, Lynn, (2007) *Women and Muslim Family Laws in Arab States: A Comparative Overview of Textual Development and Advocacy*, Amsterdam: Amsterdam University Press.

Wurmnest, Wolfgang, (2007) "The Tale of the *Mahr* – Characterization of Islamic Dower Agreements", *RabelsZ*, vol.71, pp. 527-558.

Wurmnest, Wolfgang, (2005) "Die Brautgabe im Bürgerlichen Recht" (The Dower in Private Law), *FamRZ*, pp.1878-1885.

Wynn, Lisa, (2008) "Marriage Contracts and Women's Rights in Saudi Arabia: *Mahr*, Shurut and Knowledge Distribution", in Quraishi, A. and F. E. Vogel (eds.), *The Islamic Marriage Contract: Case Studies in Islamic Family Law,* Cambridge: Harvard University Press.

Yassari, Nadjma, (2010) "Die islamische Brautgabe im deutschen Kollisions- und Sachrecht" (The Islamic Dower in the German Conflict of Laws Rules and in Substantive Law), IPRax (forthcoming).

Yassari, Nadjma, (2009a) "Die iranische Reform des Ehegattenerbrechts: Ein Beispiel für die Wandelbarkeit des islamischen Rechts" (The Reform of the Spousal Share under Iranian Succession Law: an Example of the Transformability of Islamic Law), *RabelsZ*, vol.73, pp. 985-1004.

Yassari, Nadjma, (2009b) "Zwei Bemerkungen zur islamischen Brautgabe" (Two Remarks on the Islamic Dower), *StAZ*, pp.366-371.

Abbreviations

AG	Amtsgericht [District Court]
ALQ	Arab Law Quarterly (*journal*)
Art.	Article
Az.	Aktenzeichen [file number]
BGB	Bürgerliches Gesetzbuch [German Civil Code]
BGH	Bundesgerichtshof [German Federal Supreme Court]
BGHZ	Entscheidungen des Bundesgerichtshofes in Zivilsachen [Decisions of the German Federal Supreme Court in Civil Law Disputes]
CC	Iranian Civil Code
DEuFamR	Deutsches und Europäisches FamilienRecht (*journal*)
ed(s).	editor(s)
EGBGB	Einführungsgesetz zum Bürgerlichen Gesetzbuch [Introductory Act to the German Civil Code]
FamRZ	Zeitschrift für Familienrecht (*journal*)
FPR	Familie, Partnerschaft, Recht (*journal*)
FuR	Familie und Recht (*journal*)
GG	Grundgesetz [German Basic Law = Constitution]
IPG	Gutachten zum internationalen und ausländischen Privatrecht [Expertise on Foreign Private and Private International Law]
IPRax	Praxis des Internationalen Privat- und Verfahrensrechts (*journal*)
IPRspr.	Die deutsche Rechtsprechung auf dem Gebiete des internationalen Privatrechts [Collection of Cases Relating to Private International Law]
JICL	Journal of Islamic and Comparative Law
KG	Kammergericht [Court of Appeal in the State of Berlin]
LG	Landgericht [Court of First Instance]
MünchKomm	Münchener Kommentar zum Bürgerlichen Gesetzbuch [Commentary to the German Civil Code]
NJW	Neue Juristische Wochenschrift (*journal*)
NJW-RR	Neue Juristische Wochenschrift – Rechtsprechungs-Report (*journal*)

No[s].	Number[s]
OLG	Oberlandesgericht [Court of Appeal]
p(p).	page(s)
Palandt	Palandt, Bürgerliches Gesetzbuch, 62. und 63. Auflage München 2003 und 2004 [Commentary on the German Civil Code]
PC	Iranian Probate Code
RabelsZ	Rabels Zeitschrift für ausländisches und internationales Privatrecht (*journal*)
sect.	section
Staudinger	J. von Staudingers Kommentar zum Bürgerlichen Gesetzbuch mit Einführungsgesetz und Nebengesetzen [Commentary on the German Civil Code, Introductory Act and Ancillary Acts]
StAZ	Das Standesamt (*journal*)
vol.	Volume
ZvglRWiss	Zeitschrift für Vergleichende Rechtswissenschaft (*journal*)

CHAPTER 8

Mahr in Danish Law

Camilla Christensen[1]

In Denmark today there is much concern about whether external influences will affect the so-called Danish values negatively. The issue of Islamic law is of particular and, arguably, growing interest in this connection. Islamic law, *Sharia*, is a frequently discussed topic on the political scene in Denmark; discussions usually begin due to passing or anecdotal interest from the general public and are perhaps for that reason rather less nuanced than they could be. In 2003 the Danish Minister of Justice was asked to elucidate how she would ensure that Muslim women living in Denmark under *Sharia* were not deprived of their rights under Danish law. The Minister referred to a survey conducted on how often *Sharia* influences the Danish courts in family matters – the survey showed that only few cases on family matters involved foreign law, which would include *Sharia* (Danish Ministry of Justice 2004).

When *Mahr* is applied in Western legal systems, those who apply it attempt to place *Mahr* in the context of Western legal concepts, a very complex process that often leads to a questionable result. Cases involving *Mahr* raised in Western legal systems often result in *Mahr* being imposed on either the man or the woman in an unjust manner. In both cases one part is in effect punished improperly (Fournier 2010: 67-68).

The question of *Mahr* is of great interest in divorce cases and can often lead to disputes between the parties. The High Court of Copenhagen[2] addressed the issue of *Mahr* in 2005 (U.2005.2314 Ø) and concluded that *Mahr* is to be equated with a gift according to Danish law, so to be enforceable *Mahr* must meet the same legal conditions as a gift.

1. I would like to thank Rubya Mehdi for her support and guidance in writing this chapter.

2. The High Court of Copenhagen is the appeals court for the eastern region of Denmark; the equivalent court for the western region is located in the Jutland town of Viborg.

This article will look at *Mahr* according to Danish law, including case law, by looking at *Mahr* as a legal concept under Islamic law, and by relating it to the Danish *morgengave* or morning gift as well as the current treatment of gifts between husband and wife under Danish legislation.

Danish Case Law on *Mahr*

Pakistani "*Mahr*" is a gift according to the Law on Legal Effects on Marriage paragraph 30 (1) (*retsvirkningslovens § 30 stk. 1*) (U.2005.2314 Ø).

In 2005 the High Court of Copenhagen passed a verdict on the question of *Mahr* under Danish law. The High Court concluded that *Mahr* is a gift according to Danish law and hence must meet the same requirements to be valid. It is therefore interesting to examine the case closely to establish how the result was reached.

The parties W (the wife) and H (the husband) were married in 1988 in Denmark in an Islamic Culture Centre; both parties were of Pakistani origin. In the Islamic marriage contract it was stated that H had to pay W 25,000 Danish kroner (DKK) in "dowry"[3]. The parties were separated in 2001 and they disagreed whether H had already paid the DKK 25,000 according to the marriage contract. In 2001 W sued H claiming that H owed her DKK 25,000 in *Mahr*.

The marriage contract contained a section named "Details of Dowry", in which the following was written:

Total amount	D. Kr. 25,000.00
Advance	D. Kr. 00,000.00
Balance	D. Kr. 25,000.00

The parties agreed that the dowry is an amount H was obliged to pay W in connection with the marriage. The parties disagreed about whether H had already paid the amount to W.

3. *Mahr* is often mistakenly translated as "dowry". *Mahr* is an amount given to the wife from her husband, while dowry is an amount of money or property that the wife brings into the marriage. Nonetheless the two words are often confused. In the marriage contract of the above-mentioned case from 2005 the *Mahr* is referred to as "dowry", however the parties in the case agree that the provision called dowry in the marriage contract is in fact not dowry but *Mahr*.

During the District Court case W explained that her mother had agreed with defendant's family that the defendant had to pay DKK 25,000 in *Mahr* to his wife. She explained that the amount normally has to be paid before the wedding night, but that the parties often agree on a later time of payment – even as late as the time of an eventual divorce. H did not have the means to pay the amount when he arrived in Denmark and W's mother paid the expenses of H's flight ticket to Denmark as well as the wedding party. The parties had not agreed on a date of maturity of the *Mahr*, but agreed that H could defer the payment until after the wedding and that H should then pay when W demanded her *Mahr*.

H explained to the District Court that he had paid *Mahr* at his arrival in Denmark in form of 700 grams of jewellery of 24 carats gold, and that he the day before the wedding paid additionally USD 2000.

By her statement of claim W alleged that *Mahr* is a contractual agreement or a promissory note signed by the parties in Denmark. W further alleged that the *Mahr* should be paid on her request and that H had not documented that he had in fact paid the DKK 25,000. Additionally, W claimed that *Mahr* has resemblance to a §56 compensation according to the Danish Marriage Act, because *Mahr* is an amount that secures the woman in case of divorce.

By his statement of claim H alleged that the provision of *Mahr* conflicts with the provision of Danske Lov 5 – 1 – 2[4] (*Danish Law 5 – 1 – 2*), because *Mahr* is a bride price. Additionally H alleged that the claim was paid upon marriage or that the claim was obsolete. H claimed that, in any case, W forfeited her claim of *Mahr* when she initiated the divorce.

The District Court found for the defendant because neither the legal effects of the agreement of *Mahr* nor the date of maturity for the *Mahr* were clear. Additionally, the District Court found that the date of maturity was not sufficiently clear and it wasn't clear whether the demand for *Mahr* could lapse at a certain point. Further, the Court emphasized the "special character" of the demand and that the defendant at the time of the marriage did not have any financial means, and that savings thus had to be made during marriage where community property exists.

W appealed the case to the High Court of Copenhagen who affirmed the District Court's judgement, though with another argumentation.

At the High Court the parties each repeated their former claims, while W further emphasized that *Mahr* is not equivalent to a gift according to Danish

4. King Christian V's Law 5-1-2 states that agreements are binding as long as they do not go against the law or, significantly, the concept of chastity. In Danish, "*ikke er imod Loven, eller Ærbarhed*".

legislation, since *Mahr* is not given out of generosity but as an act of obligation. By her statement of claim W alleged that in this specific case the *Mahr* must be considered a promissory note incorporated into the marriage contract.

By his statement of claim H alleged that *Mahr* is in fact a gift according to Danish law, as it is granted out of generosity and therefore according to the law on legal effects of marriage, paragraph 30(1), it is only valid when the parties have signed a prenuptial agreement.

The High Court determined that *Mahr* is considered a gift according to Danish legislation, and therefore a prenuptial agreement is needed to ensure the validity of the gift, unless the gift is proportionate to the financial situation of the person giving it. The High Court of Copenhagen found that DKK 25,000 was disproportionate to the financial situation of H, whence a prenuptial agreement would have been required to ensure H's payment of the *Mahr* to W. The parties had not signed a prenuptial agreement, and so the obligation to pay the gift was declared invalid.

It is stated in the High Court judgment that the two parties had agreed that Danish law should be used to solve the case. However, it is interesting to note that H argues according to both Islamic and Danish law. H claims that the agreement of *Mahr* is invalid because the agreement is contrary to *Danske Lov* 5 – 1 – 2, as mentioned above. H furthermore states that W has forfeited her right to *Mahr* because W initiated the divorce and hence lost her right to *Mahr* – this claim is according to Islamic law, not Danish law.

A case from 1998 (TFA.1998.36OE) is relevant here insofar as it concerns treatment of Islamic marriage law in Denmark. The case involves an agreement made in Syria obliging the husband to pay his wife a compensation of approximately DKK 100,000 in case of divorce; the term *Mahr* or dower is however not mentioned. It is stated in the verdict that such an agreement is common in Syria. The High Court of Copenhagen stated in the verdict that the woman had not presented evidence that convinced the Court that she was entitled to compensation. It can be argued that the agreement from Syria concerns *Mahr* even though the Court does not go into the issue of *Mahr*, because the agreement seems to be about *Mahr*. In this case the High Court does not qualify *Mahr* as it later does in the case from 2005.

Cases regarding *Mahr* in Denmark have mainly been dealt with within the District Courts and it would be interesting to see how the District Courts deal with the issue. I have, however, not been able to locate any of these judgements in connection to this article. Danish case law is made available to the public on the UfR database (*Ugeskrift for Retsvæsen*, Weekly Journal for the Danish Legal System). This database consists mainly of judgements delivered by the Danish Supreme Court, the High Courts and the Maritime and Commercial Court. Unfortunately, the verdicts delivered by the District Courts are as a general rule not included.

Mahr as a Legal Concept according to Islamic Law

Mahr in Islamic law is defined as an amount of money or property, which the husband gives his wife in connection with their marriage (Mehdi 2007: 102). *Mahr* is a sign of the husband's respect for his wife and a sign of commitment to the marriage. The purpose is to secure the wife economically (Nørgaard 2001). It is the wife's separate property and the husband has no access to the *Mahr* once he has paid it to his wife. (Tucker 2008: 137). *Mahr* is a legal concept in Islamic law and is often written into state legislation.

Community or Separate Property

Today the wife and her husband automatically have community property when entering into marriage in Denmark, unless they actively choose differently, cf. Law on Legal Effects on Marriage, paragraph 15 (1). The spouses can choose to have separate property but this requires them to register their property agreement. In earlier times in Denmark the spouses normally had separate property (Dübeck 2003: 91). Community property implies that in case of divorce there will be a division of the matrimonial property in equal shares. During the marriage however, the spouses each own their own belongings, and is as a main rule free to do what he or she wishes with their belongings (Andersen *et al* 2008: 778). The spouses are free to make legally binding agreements with each other, as well as other people, cf. Law on Legal Effects on Marriage paragraph 29. The Law on Legal Effects on Marriage dates back to 1925 and the community property concept is from a time where the wife usually worked as a housewife and therefore depended on her husband's income. Today most women in Denmark work and the family patterns have changed. The Ministry of Justice has therefore asked some experts to look at different aspect of the Law on Legal Effects on Marriage and to give their suggestions of changes to fit the legislation to the current family pattern. One of the paragraphs that the experts are asked to look at is the one on community property. The experts are asked to finish their work within a period of three years from 2009, which means that we won't know the results for a least one more year (Danish Ministry of Justice 2009).

In Islamic law the spouses have separate property (Nørgaard 2001). This means that there is no property to be divided between the parties in case of divorce. The *Mahr* when given to the wife is her separate property over which she has complete disposal. She can choose to forgo her *Mahr* as a sign of generosity but otherwise it belongs to her (Pearl 1979: 61). In Islamic law the spouses are also free to make contractual binding agreement with each other (Quraishi 2008: 193).

The District judge in the above-mentioned case from 2005 emphasized that the concept of private savings in a marriage of community property is a bit peculiar and calls the claim, a claim of "special character". The women in marriages with community and separate property have different needs for *Mahr*, because community property entitles the woman to half of the husband's fortune. This is not the case in Islamic marriages where the wife is entitled to keep her personal property, including her *Mahr*, but not entitled to half of her husband's fortune. The different property arrangements in Islamic and Danish law makes is even more difficult to place *Mahr* within the Danish law and reach a result that is fair to both parties.

The Danish 'Morning Gift' according to Danish Law

The *morgengave* or morning gift is today primarily used as a tradition at weddings in which the husband gives a gift to the wife. In earlier times, though, the morning gift was regulated by law and was an essential part of a marriage. The husband gave his wife a morning gift that in some cases represented a significant value e.g. a farm or a large amount of money. In one particular law of the year 717 it was stated that the value of the morning gift should be one fourth of the husband's fortune (Dübeck 2003: 67). The purpose of the morning gift was to secure the wife in case of the husband's death, in which case she could withdraw her morning gift from the estate in advance of settlement of debts. In the year 1562 the king decided that a widow could withdraw her morning gift in advance – even when the estate was indebted (Tamm 1992).

In recent years legal centralism has lost ground in popularity to legal pluralism according to which customs and informal law are given a significant value (Mehdi 2003: 215). The different norms that are developed within a certain community will often be binding for the people living within the community and could be referred to as a kind of informal law. The norms are based on the morality of the community – a common unspoken agreement about what is right and what is wrong. Hereby the law and morality become integrated to a certain degree. The rise of informal law can be based on formal law, and formal law in some cases can be interpreted with reference to informal law, for instance in relation to the finding of a fair result (Petersen 1996: 37-38). Customs, traditions and social connections are of great importance to how we act in different situations and hence it is important to understand as well as recognize these relations. Immigrants bring their legal traditions with them to Denmark and practise them while living in Denmark outside of the official Danish legal systems. The *Mahr* is one of these customs. The need for regulation of these unofficial practices is rising, but the complexities of the unofficial law should not be undermined in the process (Mehdi, Petersen, Sand & Woodman 2008: 201). In current Danish legislation the practice of giving a morning gift is not regulated and the husband is thus not legally obliged to give his wife a morning gift. Nonetheless it is a tradition that the husband gives his wife a morning gift and there is a certain social pressure on the husband to do so. It is therefore safe to say that it is expected of him. Certain gifts, e.g. the morning gift, that are expected and given as a result of unwritten rules, are not codified in formal law. Some legal experts have argued that the element of generosity that defines a gift in Danish legislation is weakened when the person giving the gift is socially obliged to do so. The gift is in these cases not given as a sign of generosity but is even so defined as a gift (Andersen 1998: 359).

In 1999 the High Court of Viborg delivered a judgement (V1999.B-3065-97) concerning a gift, given in connection with the parties' marriage, referred to by the wife (W) as a morning gift. The parties married in 1994 and separated in 1996. The husband (H) had given his wife a gift of DKK 85,000 in connection with the marriage. H now claimed that the gift was invalid and should be returned to him because the parties had not signed a prenuptial agreement. The High Court of Viborg stated that because the gift was not disproportionate to H's financial situation, a prenuptial agreement was not required. Based on this argumentation, the High Court of Viborg found that the gift was valid and should not be repaid to H.

It is interesting that the concept of morning gifts arises in a judgement as recent as in 1999 (V.1999.B-3065-97). The parties did not agree on whether the gift was a morning gift or not. The gift was referred to, by the wife, as a morning gift and was given in connection with the marriage. It would be interesting to know if the outcome of the verdict was in any way influenced by the fact that the gift was referred to as a morning gift.

In most Muslim countries *Mahr* is a legally binding concept. Despite the fact that the legislation of Denmark does not regulate the concept, a large number of Danish Muslims still act according to customs that oblige the husband to pay his wife the *Mahr*. Also it is expected by both families that the husband pay his wife her *Mahr*. Customs in general are dynamic and practices change over time, according to the changing of the surrounding relations (Mehdi 2003: 221-223). The practice of the morning gift has changed from being a legal concept regulated by law in a time in which that was necessary, to now being more of a ritual or tradition. Today most morning gifts are given as part of a ritual or tradition where the purpose is not to secure the wife economically, as was the case in the above-mentioned case of 1999.

The Danish Legislation on Gifts between Spouses

The majority of Danish legislation does not regulate the concept of gifts. One of the few places where gifts are regulated directly by law is in matters concerning gifts between spouses, which are regulated in the Law on Legal Effects of Marriage, paragraph 30 (1). The provision regulates gifts within marriages with community property as well as marriages with separate property (Danielsen 1986: 247). The High Court of Copenhagen stated in the above-mentioned case from 2005 that the specific requirements of the provision were not met in this case, which makes it interesting to look closely at the provision and the requirements. The provision does not define a gift, but the legal theory has defined a gift in Danish Law as "*en vederlagsfri indrømmelse af en formuefordel på giverens bekostning som et udslag af gavmildhed og ikke til opfyldelse af en pligt, der påhviler giveren*" (Danielsen 1986: 247) ("a concession of an advantage of property, paid with no remuneration as a result of generosity and not paid to meet any duty incumbent upon the donor"). Both the case law and the legal theory seem to agree on this definition. Furthermore Nielsen states that the gift cannot be given to fulfil any legal or moral obligation and that the payment cannot have the characteristic of an alimony (Nielsen 2006: 136-137). The primary criterion regarding the qualification of a gift is whether the gift is given as a sign of generosity. The reason for the restrictions under which spouses can give each other gifts is to protect the creditors of the person giving the gift (Andersen *et al* 2008: 788). Spouses are therefore, as a main rule, obliged to sign a prenuptial agreement to secure the validity of a gift, unless the gift is an occasional gift proportionate to the economic situation of the person giving the gift, cf. Danish Marriage Act, paragraph 30 (1). Gifts for birthdays, Christmas or other occasions do not require a prenuptial agreement, as long as they are proportionate to the financial situation of the person giving the gift. Whether a gift requires a prenuptial agreement or not depends on the financial situation of the person giving the gift. A very wealthy person will be able to give a gift of a substantial value to his or her spouse without a prenuptial agreement; this might not be the case with a gift of the same value, however, given within a marriage where the giver's financial situation is different.

Is *Mahr* a Gift According to Islamic Law?

The High Court of Copenhagen stated in the above-mentioned case from 2005 that *Mahr* in Danish Law is equivalent to a gift; hence *Mahr* requires a prenuptial agreement for the parties to uphold it at a Danish Court. Considering the Danish legislation on gifts between spouses, it is interesting to assess whether *Mahr* in a gift according to Islamic law.

According to Islamic law the husband is obliged to pay his wife her *Mahr*, even when it is not specified in the marriage contract (Quraishi 2008: 302). When *Mahr* is not specified in the marriage contract, the husband is obliged to pay his wife a proper *Mahr*, the size of which depends on the wife's social and personal qualities (Mehdi 2007: 106). The wife cannot release her husband from his obligation to pay her the *Mahr* prior to the marriage; however she is free to forego her *Mahr* after entering the marriage. A provision in the marriage contract stating that no *Mahr* shall be paid is considered invalid and the husband must then pay his wife a proper *Mahr* (Nørgaard 2001 and Pearl 1979: 61). The purpose of the *Mahr* is, among other things, to provide economic security for the wife in case her social circumstances change, for instance after a divorce. The *Mahr* however also represents a social obligation (Mehdi 2003: 225).

Nørgaard concludes that *Mahr* is a gift since it is neither a bride price nor a leasehold. She further emphasizes that *Mahr* can in fact be applied under Danish law because it has the characteristics of a gift and is therefore not contrary to Danish legislation (Nørgaard 2001). The Turkish jurist Özlan states that *Mahr* in Turkish law is considered a binding agreement when this is the intention of the parties, but if the intention is that the *Mahr* is a gift then that is the case. According to Özlan the decisive element as to whether *Mahr* is considered a gift or not is therefore the intentions of the parties (Quraishi 2008: 316). Welchman however makes the argument that *Mahr* is not a gift but a kind of debt the husband owes his wife from the time of entering the marriage and until he pays her the *Mahr* (Welchman 2004: 206). Mehdi (U.2005.2314 Ø) states when asked by the parties in the above-mentioned case from 2005 from the High Court of Copenhagen that "*Den pakistanske Mahr, som oversættes til morgengave eller brudegave er ikke en gave i dansk forstand, da den gives som opfyldelse af en retspligt*" ('the Pakistani *Mahr*, which translates to morning gift or bride gift, is not a gift according to the Danish definition because it is given as a legal obligation'). Mehdi further states that *Mahr* is the wife's absolute right. Pearl & Menski define *Mahr* as a corresponding duty the husband pays his wife, in exchange for her obedience to him (Pearl & Menski 1998: 178-179). Fournier argues that *Mahr* is a romantic constellation that the husband gives his wife as a gift to express his love for her and his respect for God (Fournier 2010).

In short, there is no definitive answer to the definition of *Mahr* in Islamic Law. It is however safe to state that the husband is obliged to give to his wife her *Mahr* in connection with their marriage.

Is *Mahr* a Gift in the Danish Legal Sense?

Mahr is by some theorists defined as a sign of respect and love for the wife, as a commitment to their marriage and respect for God, which is in line with the Danish definition of a gift. The current practice of the traditional Danish morning gift is close to these concepts. Many newlyweds in Denmark exchange morning gifts as a sign of their love and respect for each other, thereby maintaining an old tradition. The Danish morning gift is no longer a legal obligation as it has been in earlier times. Today the morning gift is an expectation based on tradition, and the practice of the tradition is most likely based on a mixture of social pressure and the partner's expectations.

The fact that *Mahr* is given without a *quid pro quo* suggests that *Mahr* could qualify as a gift according to Danish law. On the other hand a gift according to Danish law should be given as a sign of generosity, which is not necessarily the case for the *Mahr* as it is an obligation on the husband as well as an absolute right of the wife. However in Danish law there is no legal concept similar to *Mahr*; the closest concept is probably the Danish morning gift, which used to be regulated by law. In earlier times when morning gifts were still regulated by law, the concept had other aims. Morning gifts were then given to fulfil a husband's obligation to secure his wife in case of his death. Nowadays, this security is no longer necessary, since other regulations have been introduced. When engaging in marriage in Denmark, the fortune of both spouses is assumed to become community property. This means that the wife by act of marriage is entitled to half of her and her husband's fortunes, whereby additional regulation of transfer of property – similar to *Mahr* – seems unnecessary.

In Islamic law the *Mahr* is a legal obligation and the spouses cannot decide not to uphold this obligation, which is contrary to the Danish morning gift, which can be omitted at any time. In Islamic marriages the wife cannot prior to the marriage release her husband from the obligation of *Mahr* (Nørgaard 2001). She can however release her husband from the obligation after the entering of the marriage because she is free to forgo her *Mahr*.

The case law in Denmark suggests that *Mahr* is a gift and therefore requires a prenuptial agreement. However the amount of *Mahr* in some cases is relatively small and therefore the parties might not find it economically defensible to pay a lawyer to draw up a prenuptial agreement. It is possible for the parties to make the agreement themselves and get this registered; they will have to pay a fee of 1400 D.kr but it is still cheaper than paying a lawyer.

Most people act according to a combination of religious laws, customary practices and state law. Beside the state law customary practice has great influence on how people act and interact, so it is of great importance that the customary law is taken into consideration. The United Kingdom has so-called Sharia councils that make decisions in family matters. The vast majority of cases brought before the MLSC (a Sharia council) concern marital disputes, especially divorce cases (Shah-Kazemi 2001: 10). The applicants can conduct their cases before the Council in writing, which makes it possible for Muslims all over Europe to have their cases heard by the Sharia Council (Shah-Kazemi 2001: 18). This makes it possible for women, the primary users of the Sharia Councils, to have their cases dealt with according to Islamic law. It can be argued that this is used because the civil courts do not provide an effective legal system for these women, where proper consideration is taken to their religious beliefs. The consequence of this practice is that cases are solved outside the Danish legal system and outside Denmark, since relevant options are not offered Muslims by the Danish legal system. In the case from the High Court of Copenhagen, the Court did not recognize the wife's claim to *Mahr*, because the Court applied the Danish legislation on gifts between spouses, which requires a prenuptial agreement. It can be presumed that a large number of people are not aware of the legal rights and obligations that derive from their marriage, both ethnic Danes and Danes with Muslim background. Muslim women will often believe that they are entitled to their *Mahr* and that they can claim it at the Danish courts. For this reason, they might unexpectedly find themselves in a very precarious financial situation if they at a later point wish to terminate their marriage.

Conclusion

In an answer to the Danish Parliament, the Danish Minister of Justice stated that the she believes that the rising internationalization will increase the number of cases concerning family matters that are affected by foreign law, especially Islamic law. She further stated that she believes that the parties are properly protected by the Danish legislation because of the extensive freedom given married couples to determine themselves the arrangements regarding their economic relations. Provisions that protect the economically weak party complement this freedom. The financially weak party will therefore not find themselves in an unreasonable situation because the party enjoys these prerogatives. The Minister suggests that the solution is to enlighten people on their legal rights and obligations according to Danish Law[5] (Minister of Justice 2003). The Department of Equality, for the Ministry of Equality, has an ongoing campaign that aims to offer lectures on Danish family law to women of ethnic minorities. The purpose of the campaign, called "*Rettighedskampagnen*" (Campaign of Rights) is to enlighten women about their legal rights including the concept of community property rights in marriage. The teaching material used in this campaign includes the decision from the High Court of Copenhagen concerning *Mahr*, to ensure that Muslim women are aware of the precarious nature of *Mahr* in Denmark.

The current Danish case law suggests that the best option for the Muslim women in order to secure their *Mahr* under Danish legislation is to make a prenuptial agreement classifying *Mahr* as a gift. In the above-mentioned case from 2005 at the High Court of Copenhagen, the court would have reached another result had the parties made a prenuptial agreement. Muslims need this information in order to act accordingly. It is therefore important to inform people about their legal rights and obligations when entering a marriage. It would be beneficial if imams who perform the wedding ceremonies in Denmark were familiar with the Danish case law and the Danish legislation. They would then be able to guide future spouses who could then make an informed decision and take necessary precautions.

5. The Danish Minister of Justice reference to the Marriage Act paragraph 56 and 58. Paragraph 56 enables the Courts to give the financially weak party compensation from the other party's separate property. Paragraph 58 enables the Courts to rule against an agreement made by the parties in connection with their separation or divorce.

Bibliography

Andersen, Eigil Lego, (1988) *Gavebegrebet, gavereglerne og deres anvendelsesområder*. Copenhagen: Gad.

Andersen, Paul Krüger *et al*, (2008) *Dansk Privatret en lærebog*. Copenhagen: DJØF.

Danielsen, Svend & Hornslet, Mogens, (1986) *Lov om ægteskabets retsvirkninger*. Copenhagen: DJØF.

Dübeck, Inger, (2003) *Kvinder, familie og formue*. Copenhagen: Museum Tusculanum.

Fournier, Pascale, (2010) "Flirting with God in western secular courts: *Mahr* in the west", *International Journal of Law, Policy and the Family*, 24 (1), (2010), pp.67-94.

Mehdi, Rubya *et al*, (2008) *Law and Religion in Multicultural Societies*. Copenhagen: DJØF.

Mehdi, Rubya, (2007) *Integration & Retsudvikling*. Copenhagen: DJØF.

Mehdi, Rubya, (2003) "Ægteskab, formue og medgift, Ret og sædvane i fire pakistanske landsbyer", in Schaumburg-Müller, Steen & Selmer, Bodil, *Retlig mangfoldighed – en fælles udfordring for retsvidenskab og antropologi*. Copenhagen: DJØF, pp.139-165

Nielsen, Linda, (2006) *Familieretten*. Copenhagen: Gjellerup.

Pearl, David & Menski, Werner, (1998) *Muslim Family Law*. London: Sweet & Maxwell.

Pearl, David, (1979) *A textbook on Muslim Law*. London: Croom Helm.

Petersen, Hanne, (1996) *Home Knitted Law. Norm and Values in Gendered Rule-Making*. Dartmouth: Dartmouth .

Quraishi, Asifa & Vogel, Frank E., (2008) *The Islamic Marriage Contract – Case studies in Islamic Family law*. Cambridge MA: Islamic Legal Studies Program, Harvard Law School Publishing.

Shah-Kazemi, Sonia Nûrîn, (2001) "*Untying the Knot – Muslim Women, Divorce and the Shariah*".

London: The Nuffield Foundation.

Tucker, Judith E., (2008) *Women, Family and Gender in Islamic Law*. New York: Cambridge University Press.

Welchman, Lynn, (2004) *Women's rights & Islamic Family Law – Perspectives on Reform*. New York: Zed Books.

Danish Ministry of Justice, (2003) Besvarelse af spørgsmål nr. 16 af 10. december 2003 fra Folketingets Udvalg for Udlændinge- og Integrationspolitik (Alm. Del – bilag 95). (*Answer of question number 16, on the 10th of December 2003 to the Danish Parliament's Committee of Foreign and Integration politics (Annex 95)*). http://webarkiv.ft.dk/img20031/udvbilag/lib4/20031_7584/20031_7584.pdf

Danish Ministry of Justice, (2004) Notits om undersøgelse af statsamternes og Københavns Overpræsidiums erfaring med anvendelse af udenlandsk ret, herunder især islamisk ret på det familieretlige område af den 19. april 2004 fra Justitsministeriets lovafdeling sags nr. 2003-7702-0021. Dok. LAS20621. (*Note on survey of the regional state administrations experience on how often foreign law, especially Islamic Law, is applied in family matters. The 19th April 2004 from the Ministry of Justice, Law department, case No. 2003-7702-0021. Document LAS20621*). http://webarkiv.ft.dk/?/Samling/20031/udvbilag/UUI/Almdel_bilag312.htm.

Danish Ministry of Justice, (2009) Kommissorium for Retsvirkningslovudvalget den 3. September 2009. Sagsnr.: 2009-793-0052. Dok.: LVM40539. (*Council for the Committee of Law on Legal Effects on Marriage the 3rd of September 2009. Case No.2009-793-0052. Document LVM40539*).
http://www.familiestyrelsen.dk/fileadmin/Filer/PDF/AEgteskab_vielse/Kommissorium_for_Retsvirkningslovsudvalget.pdf.

Judgements and Articles from the Danish UfR, "Ugeskrift for Retsvæsen" (Weekly Journal for Danish Legal System).

U.2005.2314 Ø – Pakistansk "*Mahr*" sidestilles med gave efter retsvirkningslovens § 30, stk. 1. (*Pakistani "Mahr" a gift according to the Law on Legal Effects on Marriage paragraph 30 (1)*).

TFA 2001.159 – den islamiske brudepris *Mahr*'s betydning i dansk ret (*The Islamic bride price Mahr's meaning in Danish Law*) by cand.jur., phd-student Maja H. Nørgaard, Istanbul University.

TFA.1998.36OE.

U.1992B.241 – Kongen som dommer – rettertinget 1537-1660 (The King as a Judge – the Court) by professor, dr.jur. et phil. Ditlev Tamm.

CHAPTER 9

Facing the Unknown/Defacing the Known – *Mahr* in Swedish Courts

Matilda Arvidsson[1]

Two sisters walk up the stairs to their local Swedish district court. They are wearing identical dresses with matching headscarves. Both have come to court – as a last resort – to claim their *Mahr* – their dower.

Law greets them at the entrance. The two sisters present their problem and ask for justice to be made. Law takes a long glance at both of them. He then turns to the older of the two:

"I do not know you. You are foreign and unknown to me. You got married in Cairo. I can see that you have a legal problem. Let me try to decipher that *Mahr*-problem of yours and I will give you a ruling based on my own (mis)reading of it."

After having recognized the older sister, he turns to the younger one:

"I know you. I am sorry but I cannot recognize you at my court. You got married at the mosque in Malmö a few kilometers from these doorsteps."

The two sisters look at each other in astonishment. How can law recognize one of them but not the other? They try to make Law see their identical problems. But Law just shakes his head and asks the older sister to come in, leaving the younger one at the doorsteps. She is free to try voice her concerns at the court. But she is not invited in.

1. I would like to thank Rubya Mehdi and all the participants of the *Mahr* workshop in Copenhagen 2009 for valuable comments and discussions. I would also like to thank Evadne Macedo, Hanna Pettersson, Linnéa Wegerstad, Markus Gunneflo and Paulina Fogel for reading and commenting on the text.

1. Introduction

This text is concerned with *Mahr* in the Swedish legal system. It departs from the two sisters' astonishment: how can law recognize the unknown while it fails to recognize the known? Or put differently: Islamic law is practiced in the everyday life of both Swedish and foreign nationals residing in Sweden. How is it then possible that the Swedish legal system finds it so hard to recognize Islamic law when it does not appear as a case of international character, in other words a private international law case? If *Mahr* is recognized as 'foreign' and 'unknown' which are the legal practices by which *Mahr* becomes 'alienated' or 'othered' by the Swedish legal system?

The primary focus of this text is on judges at Swedish district courts – *tingsrätter* – facing Muslim family law in terms of the Islamic legal institution of *Mahr*. District courts deal with matters of criminal law and civil law, the latter including family law. At the district court – which is the first instance court for matters of criminal and civil law – a selection is made between what can be seen by law and what will remain unseen and unheard[2]. *Mahr* is discussed in this text both in relation to Swedish private international law as it is practiced at the courts and as it appears in court cases where regular Swedish laws have guided the Swedish judge. Published as well as unpublished Swedish court cases from both Swedish district courts and courts of appeals are discussed in the text[3].

In the critical analysis which follows I will argue that Swedish courts 'unknow' *Mahr*. In other words: Swedish courts position *Mahr* as something completely other than Swedish law. This othering is pursued through a number of legal practices at the courts. The othering is also explicitly stated in written decisions and judgments. In most cases, I further argue, Swedish courts do not face the unknown when Muslim family law and legal institutions are brought to court by parties. Rather, they deface – or in other words

2. In most cases permission is needed in order to appeal to the Swedish courts of appeal. Since such permissions are granted generally only in cases of principal legal importance and in cases of judicial mistakes, most cases never reach beyond the district court.
3. The published court cases are RH 1993: 116 and RH 2005: 66 ('RH' stands for *rättsfall från hovrätterna* – cases from the courts of appeals). Unpublished court case from the court of appeals is Svea Hovrätt T 10083-04. Unpublished court cases from district courts are Uppsala tingsrätt T 3289-02, Falu tingsrätt T 3391-05 (conciliation confirmed in a judgement) and Göteborgs tingsrätt T 10691-06 ('T' stands for *tvistemål* – civil suit). In addition there are a number of ongoing cases concerning *Mahr* at Swedish courts.

fail to recognize and discuss – well known Swedish Muslim legal practices. I further criticize Swedish courts for failing to provide proper legal remedies in areas of family law where Swedish and Muslim family law overlap: in particular legal problems in relation to the dissolution of marriage, 'limping marriages' and *Mahr*. I finally stress the need for recalling the voices which remain unheard by law and the importance of further research of the inclusionary/exclusionary functions of law.

While the analysis in this chapter departs from questions on *Mahr* within the Swedish legal system, it arrives at findings which tell us perhaps more about Swedish law, judiciary and legal academia than it does about *Mahr*. In analyzing the techniques and practices by which the Swedish judiciary face and deface *Mahr* something important can be uncovered about law's general functions as well as Swedish law's, judiciary's and legal academia's particular position on *Mahr*.

The text flows from a study of judicial culture at a Swedish district court carried out in 2004-2006 (Arvidsson 2007), a number of interviews with Swedish justices conducted in 2007 concerning their experiences of Islamic law in their capacities as judges (Arvidsson 2010), and my own experiences of professional legal practice as a law clerk and junior judge at a Swedish district court. An additional minor study of *Mahr* cases at Swedish courts and the legal practices concerning *Mahr* among Muslims in Malmö was carried out in 2009.

2. Positioning *Mahr* in a Western Legal Context

Mahr translates into English as 'dower' (e.g. Qaisi 2000/2001: 70). In Swedish *Mahr* has been called *brudpenning* – bride price (e.g. Bogdan 1993; RH 2005: 66).[4] The translations fall short of legal meaning to the term. Many scholars have tried to pinpoint a specific legal meaning arriving at as many different ends as there are different discourses on *Mahr*. *Mahr* is legally construed in a number of slightly different ways varying depending on different legal traditions and national legislations in different parts of the world. This

4. One of the Swedish legal online resources Juridik Idag – published by the leading legal publishing house on the Swedish market Nordsteds Juridik – also refers to *Mahr* as "*brudpenning*": http://www.nj.se/cms/juridikidag/search!open&search=%20T%204594-02, accessed 7 July 2010. For a reference on *saddaq* translated into Swedish as "*brudpenning*" see Lagervall, 2004: 119-143.

diversity makes its meanings complex, something which is reflected in the different chapters in this anthology. In this chapter the Swedish legal interpretation of *Mahr* is traced through the analysis of Swedish court cases and Swedish academic legal literature.

Mahr is one of the central legal institutions in Islamic Law. It is practiced all over the world in Islamic law countries and secular law countries alike. In some countries *Mahr* is part of national legislation (e.g. Sudan, Iran, and Egypt). The only Western country to explicitly incorporate *Mahr* in national legislation – applying only to Muslims – is Greece. In most Western countries (e.g. Sweden) *Mahr* is a prevalent legal practice which falls outside the scope of national legislation.

In very general terms *Mahr* might be described as a fixed value – a sum or goods – which the wife is to receive in part or in whole from the husband on demand or at a specific point of time negotiated and fixed in the marriage contract. The *Mahr* becomes the woman's own property. It is an effect of marriage and it is not considered as a voluntary gift. It is rather an "obligation imposed by law on the husband" (Mehdi 2003: 116). Consequently, close to all Islamic law marriage contracts contain a clause on *Mahr* specifying an amount, objects or both. Islamic law marriage contracts in Sweden follow this pattern (Sayed 2008: 189-190; Svea Hovrätt T 10083-04; Lunds tingsrätt Ä 3939-04; Göteborgs tingsrätt T 10691-06). Many marriage contracts also contain a clause regulating – restricting or nullifying – the right to *Mahr* should the woman initiate a divorce (e.g. Göteborgs tingsrätt T 10691-06).

3. The Unknown and Foreign – How a Swedish Judge Recognizes *Mahr* as Foreign National Law

From the story of the two sisters above we know that a woman married abroad can bring a case concerning her *Mahr* to a Swedish court. This applies if she was married in a country where *Mahr* is part of the national legislation (e.g. Egypt). Thus, a woman's right to her *Mahr* can be recognized and become a legal issue dealt with by a Swedish judge at a Swedish court. As it is a case of international character (Egypt being a foreign country) it becomes a Swedish private international law court case.

The condition for recognizing *Mahr* in these private international law cases is what I refer to as the 'othering' of Islamic law. The Swedish judge is able to recognize *Mahr* and deal with it as a substantial legal issue only because Swedish law can exclude *Mahr* as something which is not Swedish law but rather something foreign and unknown. In what could be described as a series of private international law provisions in conjunction with Swedish judicial practices *Mahr* is qualified, interpreted, and put in perspective of Swedish public order – *ordre public*. In this process of othering the foreign and unknown *Mahr* is presented as the legal issue at hand. However, when studying the process it seems as if more is learned about the character of (Swedish) law than could be learned about the Islamic legal institution of *Mahr*. Little of the judge's time is spent on understanding *Mahr* and more effort is being put into considering the different functions of Swedish law. As will be evident through the analysis below of the Swedish private international law cases on *Mahr* very little is said in the courts' interpretation of *Mahr*. Although – or rather precisely because – foreign law is applied in the two leading Swedish international private law cases on *Mahr* (RH 1996: 166 and RH 2005: 66), it is applied and interpreted in relation to an imagined function within Swedish law. Swedish law, Swedish jurisprudence and Swedish judicial 'know-how' is thus first and foremost what is being presented in the court cases. The reader interested in understanding the Islamic law institution of *Mahr* is thus left short whereas the reader interested in understanding how Swedish judiciary manages to 'un-know' well-known Muslim legal practices will find the court cases analyzed in this chapter very instructive.

3.1 A Private International Law Case is Filed and Accepted at a Swedish Court

Typical cases concerning *Mahr* as a private international law issue at a Swedish court might appear as follows. Two spouses have entered into matrimony abroad in accordance with the law of that land – e.g. in Egypt, Iran or Sudan – and *Mahr* is part of the marriage contract. For some reason one or both spouses file a case for divorce at a Swedish court. A divorce is granted promptly. At the same time the wife petitions for her *Mahr* or such a petition is made at a later stage in conjunction with the divorce case. Or – as in RH 1993: 116 – two spouses have entered into matrimony abroad. They petition for and are granted a divorce abroad, but the divorced wife files a case at a Swedish court concerning her *Mahr*.

When any such a case is filed at the Swedish court, the judge – who is now thinking in terms of Swedish private international law – has to consider if the case falls within the jurisdiction of the court or not – i.e. if the court can accept the case. A Swedish court does (of course) not accept any petition for divorce or *Mahr* sent to it by a spouse who entered into matrimony abroad. The Swedish court might not be the correct legal forum. So, for example two Egyptian nationals without Swedish citizenship and Swedish domicile might not (as a general rule) be granted a divorce at a Swedish court. Neither of them have what the law would call 'sufficient ties' to Sweden. The Swedish legal system – in contrast to the systems of many other Western countries – stipulates in detail in the respective private international laws what qualifies as 'sufficient ties'. There is little room for the judge to open to deliberation. The consequences can sometimes appear as rather odd or even unjust. Whereas one Swedish private international law might consider a petitioner as domiciled and therefore having sufficient ties, another Swedish private international law might have slightly stricter qualifications for domicile and consequently consider the petitioner as not having sufficient ties. It therefore matters greatly how the case is qualified and which Swedish private international law is applied to the case.

A petition for divorce with an additional claim for *Mahr* might be accepted at a Swedish court if the Swedish criteria for divorce in accordance with Brussels II, art 3 (EC 2201/2003). If a divorce case is already opened at a Swedish court, the separate issue of *Mahr* could be brought before the Swedish court and made part of the original divorce case (Lag 1990: 272). If the Swedish court does not have jurisdiction over the issue of divorce or a divorce is already granted by a foreign court, a woman can bring an independent claim of *Mahr* to a Swedish court on one of three grounds: (1) if her husband has economic assets in Sweden, if (2) he has his domicile in Sweden, or (3) if the former spouses agree to Swedish jurisdiction for the issue of *Mahr* or if the spouses agreed to Swedish jurisdiction in the original contract on *Mahr* (Lag 1990: 272: § 2).

3.2 Qualifying the Unknown

In the terminology of Swedish private international law *Mahr* is *okänt*, unknown, or as it is sometimes put: *rättsfrämmande*, alien to law, or *typfrämmande rättsinstitut*, unknown type of legal institution (e.g. RH 1993: 116). It means that *Mahr* is not part of the Swedish legal system and there is no Swedish equivalent institution to it. When the judge finds her – or himself confronted in a court case with such an unknown legal institution she or he must qualify or define it in relation to Swedish law. In other words the judge has to (mis)translate or figure out what *Mahr* is in terms of Swedish law, and what function it fulfils within Swedish law, before entering into material deliberations.

Given that the legal meaning of *Mahr* does not fully translate into Swedish and since *Mahr* has historically and geographically played slightly different roles there seem to be some confusion on the issue of qualifying *Mahr*. Since the qualification is such a crucial step in private international law the issue has gotten some attention and there are a number of suggestions on the different functions of *Mahr* in the Swedish legal academic literature (Sayed 2008: 193-197; Bogdan 1993; Bogdan 2007; and Schiratzki 2001: 55, 73). *Mahr* has been suggested to fulfill a similar function to matrimonial maintenance (RH 1993: 116; Bogdan 2007: 184-185), redistribution of matrimonial property between the spouses (RH 2005: 66; Svea Hovrätt T 10083-04), and – at least hypothetically – as inheritance (Bogdan 2007: 184-185). *Mahr* has further been likened to the old Swedish legal institution of *morgongåva*, a gift of significant value given after consummation of the marriage on the morning after the wedding night (RH 1993: 166; Bogdan, 1993). *Mahr* has also been interpreted in the Swedish context as a kind of gift or *morgongåva* in addition to a conditional liability to pay damages if the husband repudiates his wife (Schiratzki 2001: 55, 73; Schiratzki 2006).

When it comes to *Mahr*, the two leading Swedish court cases RH 1993: 116 and RH 2005: 66 have pointed to two different ways of qualification. However, it is clear from both cases that a Swedish judge should consider the function of *Mahr* in accordance with *lex fori* – the law of the legal forum, i.e. the function *Mahr* would have in Swedish law (Bogdan, 2007: 184). In the first case – RH 1993: 116 – *Mahr* was considered to have similar features to matrimonial maintenance (Bogdan 1993; Bogdan 2007). In the second case – RH 2005: 66 – it was established that *Mahr* should be qualified as an issue belonging to the sphere of economic affairs between spouses (RH 2005: 66; Bogdan 2007).

Although it is not entirely obvious that *Mahr* always should be qualified as an economic issue between spouses this interpretation often seems to be closest to hand.[5]

3.3 Interpreting Foreign National Codes on *Mahr*

When all qualifications are done the judge applies either the foreign national law or the Swedish national law, as pointed out in the respective Swedish private international law. In both RH 1993: 166 and RH 2005: 66 foreign national laws were applied. Once the judge has arrived at foreign law, the judge – or rather the law secretary – sends an official request to *Utrikesdepartementet*, the Swedish Department for Foreign Affairs. Upon a request the Department for Foreign Affairs has to answer the court on the content and if possi-

5. Bogdan however makes a distinction between prompt *Mahr* and the kind of deferred *Mahr* which can only be received upon divorce. Whereas he considers the function of prompt *Mahr* as a redistribution of matrimonial property regime, he argues that the deferred *Mahr* should be considered close to the function of matrimonial maintenance (Bogdan 2007: 184-185).

ble also the interpretation of the foreign law. The answer from the Department for Foreign Affairs includes a photocopy of the foreign code in question, often in an authorized translation to a European language. So, for example, the Iranian code on marriage and divorce comes to Swedish courts in a German translation. A short PM might also be included with references to literature on the foreign law in question.

There is no praxis of hearing (external) legal experts on foreign law or jurisprudence. Legal experts are thus seldom heard at Swedish courts unless the parties bring such expertise to the court as part of their legal argumentation in a particular court case. In some court cases scholars of Islam(ic law) have been heard as expert witnesses. The so called "Radio Islam" case (Stockholms tingsrätt B 8-4-89)[6] where Professor Jan Hjärpe was called as an expert witness is perhaps the most famous case. Written legal opinions, *rättsutlåtande*, have appeared in a few Swedish court cases (e.g. Hjärpe 1989). However, none of the witnesses or expert opinions seems to have been commissioned by the courts.

Faced by the task of interpreting a foreign law on *Mahr* (with the help of the PM from the Department for Foreign Affairs and the occasional written legal opinion) the Swedish judge has to study the Egyptian, Iranian or Sudanese law and apply it to the case as if he or she was an Egyptian, Iranian or Sudanese judge. Swedish judges have – as general rule – no training in Islamic law or jurisprudence. Swedish law schools do not offer Islamic law as part of their mandatory curriculum, though the topic is sometimes touched upon in relation to private international law or comparative law[7]. After having left law school and university education to enter into the professional world, there is very little offered to the Swedish professional jurist in terms of

6. The unpublished court case is available online at Radio Islam's web page http://www.radioislam.org/islam/svenska/fildok/filer/bok/process/dom.htm, accessed 8 July 2010.

7. Lectures on Islamic law have occasionally been offered for example at Örebro University department of legal studies and extra curriculum at the law school at Uppsala University. But lectures which are not mandatory tend to have lesser attendance, and students at Uppsala have reported these lectures not to be *tentarelevant* which translates into English as 'not relevant for the examination of the course'. University courses offered on topics of Islamic law are taught elsewhere, e.g. at Lund University at the Faculty of Theology and at the Center for Middle Eastern Studies. Swedish law students have been reported to travel to Copenhagen University to study Islamic law.

education in Islamic law[8]. So, how does the Swedish judge go about interpreting a Muslim family code?

Swedish judges rarely have the competence to interpret foreign law in accordance with the foreign jurisprudence in question. In this respect Muslim family law is no exception. In interpreting the foreign code on *Mahr* the Swedish judge will have to rely on what he or she learned in law school and what can be learned from fellow judges. Although Swedish judges are likely to be assigned cases involving issues of Islamic law during their careers as judges there seem to be no institutional legal knowledge at the courts on how to approach such cases. The judge will have to deal with the situation as it is generally done at the court, i.e. rely on the general judicial culture and the know-how at his or her court[9].

Judges also rely on what they refer to as 'legal method'. This is a method which is acquired by repetitive adjudication and through peer-learning at the court. Through taking part in the close to ten years long court-internal training in which law clerks become justices the judges develop what they call 'a gut feeling' for how law should be applied and how the problems brought to them by parties should be understood in terms of law (Arvidsson 2007: 23).

As a last resource the judge might consult the scarce literature on Islamic law within the Swedish legal system. For issues concerning *Mahr* that would be a quick read as there is no substantial research published within the field. The interested judge would have to do with short articles (Bogdan 1993; Bogdan 2007; Sayed 2008), brief general references (Hjärpe 2005) or brief references to Iranian legislation on *Mahr* (Schiratzki 2001).

8. *Domstolsakademin*, the national academy for justices, which is run by *Domstolsverket*, the Swedish National Courts Administration, offers occasional seminars where issues of Islamic law are discussed. For example, in 2009 a seminar on Swedish family law focusing partly on Islamic law, family law in a multicultural society and 'honour culture' was offered in Jönköping by *Domstolsverket*, the Swedish National Courts Administration. See *Domstolsakademin Utbildningsprogram*, 2009), p.30. Similarly, *Domstolsverket* has previously offered judges in Southern Sweden to take part in a seminar on honour related issues. In spring 2010 *Lunds Domarakademi*, a local association for judges in Southern Sweden aiming at providing professional further training, offered a seminar on Islamic law with Professor emeritus Jan Hjärpe and Swedish jurist Farzanadeh Dedari.
9. This is a know-how which involves not only the judges but most importantly the backbone of the courts: the law secretaries. In Sweden most law secretaries have been with the same courts for more than 25 years. Although they often lack formal education in law, the law secretaries' experience of practicing law in an everyday setting at the court position them as one of the most reliable sources of legal know-how (Arvidsson 2007).

It remains an open question how Swedish judges go about interpreting foreign national laws which are unfamiliar to them and consequently how misunderstandings can be avoided in areas of jurisprudence where the legal terminology – as well as the legal problems – are unfamiliar to the interpreting judge.

3.4 Ordre Public

Before deciding on the case, the judge must consider if the foreign legal institution is against Swedish public policy, or as it is called in private international law, the principle of *ordre public* (Bogdan 1999: 70). The foreign law must not 'apparently' contradict the foundations of the Swedish legal system. The principle of *ordre public* halts the enforcement of foreign legal institutions (or contracts) concerning issues which would seem to be against public policies or morals. It was established in the RH 1993: 166 that *Mahr* does not contradict Swedish *ordre public*. It was simply stated in the judgment without any explanation. The court cases appearing after 1993 have similarly included no deliberation on the reasons why *Mahr* is not against *ordre public* (e.g. RH 2005: 66; Svea Hovrätt T 10083-4; Göteborgs tingsrätt T 10691-06).

3.5 The Non-Problem of *Mahr* as an Unknown and Foreign Private International Law Question

To sum up the typical Swedish case on *Mahr* and the process a Swedish judge goes through when faced with a claim for *Mahr* one could argue that it is quite unproblematic to define the place of *Mahr* in the Swedish legal system: it is unknown, foreign but not obviously contradicting public policy or the foundations of the Swedish legal system. It is a question so foreign to Swedish law that the court in most cases has to turn to the Department for Foreign Affairs in order to establish its otherness.

There is something quite peculiar about these findings. *Mahr* is understood as a legal institution which becomes relevant to the Swedish judge only as part of foreign national law. Drawing on the analysis above the dichotomy national/foreign law is the key to understanding the place of *Mahr* – as well as Muslim family law in general – in the Swedish legal system. Swedish private international laws acknowledge and respect other national (as well as public international) legal systems but it does not recognize any legal system practiced within a national jurisdiction without being part of the national legal system (or part of public international law). Only by othering *Mahr* in this way can the Swedish judge recognize *Mahr*.

In this respect *Mahr* is not different from any other foreign legal institution. The provisions of Swedish private international law require the judge to qualify, choose between foreign and domestic law, and to consider *ordre public* in all cases of private international law. The inclusionary/exclusionary function of law seems to be quite visibly at work in these court cases concerning private international law. Inclusion (dealing with *Mahr* as a legal issue) is only acceptable when exclusion and othering can be properly carried out (i.e. when *Mahr* is part of a foreign national code so foreign that the services of the Department for Foreign Affairs have to be called upon). Only in excluding the foreign institution of *Mahr* from Swedish law proper is it safe for the judge to include *Mahr* in his or her deliberation on law.

However, the story of *Mahr* in Swedish law does not end with Swedish private international law practices on inclusion/exclusion. Not all Swedish court cases concerning *Mahr* are legal issues of an international character.

4. The Known, Swedish Problem – How the Swedish Legal System Fails to Recognize Islamic Law and Legal Problems within its Own Jurisdiction

The younger sister in our story, the one who got married at her local mosque in Malmö, cannot bring forth her claim for *Mahr* at a Swedish court as a private international law case. She and her former husband are Swedish nationals residing in Sweden. They contracted their marriage in Sweden. There is nothing providing an international character to her case. From her story we know that Swedish law finds it difficult to recognize claims for *Mahr* which cannot be dealt with as private international law cases. In her case Swedish law cannot exclude *Mahr* as 'foreign' or 'other' since she contracted her marriage in relation to Islamic law which is not part of any foreign legislation.

An important question for the younger sister is if it is impossible for Swedish law to include *Mahr* and recognize it as a regular legal claim based on a regular Swedish contract. Such an inclusion would not necessarily mean that Swedish courts would implement Islamic law. It could mean an inclusion of contracts concerning *Mahr* on the same terms as contracts concerning houses, cars or phone bills. In other words it would entail thinking *Mahr* in terms of general contract law. But such an inclusion would necessitate an ability to see beyond what is foreign and other about Islamic law yet not foreign or other enough to exclude as foreign and unknown in relation to Swedish law. In other words, it would mean to see what is simply *law* about Islamic law.[10]

Yet, as will be evident from the analysis below *Mahr* in its known, unforeign and un-other setting is not included by the Swedish judiciary. The inclusionary/exclusionary function of law seems to find no way of including *Mahr* as an all-Swedish legal issue. But it does not seem to be able to explicitly exclude *Mahr* either. Since *Mahr* when practiced by Swedish Muslims in Sweden is not foreign enough to be foreign law, the exclusionary function of law is not able to position *Mahr* as the other. *Mahr* is neither seen as law nor is it regarded as a regular phenomenon or object – something which Swedish law would encompass. Although a long known legal practice among Muslims in Sweden, in non-private international law court cases the meaning of *Mahr* is left entirely to the parties of the case to define. Swedish law and judiciary simply remain silent on the meaning and position of *Mahr*. Voices asking law to hear their claims remain unheard.

4.1 A Non-Foreign Case of *Mahr* Comes to Court

It has been argued elsewhere that a Swedish non-private international law case should meet no legal obstacle if it were brought to court (Bogdan 2007: 176; Sayed 2008: 187)[11]. Yet at the time of writing there are no records of such a court case containing a judicial deliberation on a successful non-private international law claim for *Mahr* at a Swedish court. Whereas this might be partly due to the lack of official court records specifying the material issues at hand, the cases which have been identified lead the analysis in a different direction.

In the one successful non-private international law claim which has been identified, Falu tingsrätt T 3391-05, the parties agreed to a conciliation on what is plainly referred to in the judgement as '*Mahr*': 20 million Lebanese lira – estimated at 100,000 SKr (Falu tingsrätt T 3391-05: 2). It is not possible to establish from the judgement if this was the full contracted *Mahr* or only a part thereof. The conciliation was confirmed in a judgement – *stadfäst för-*

10. I am not taking a legal pluralist stance (i.e. arguing that Sweden ought to recognize parallel and/or coexisting systems of law), as for example Prakash Shah is in the case of the British Muslim Diaspora (Shah, 2010). I am rather suggesting that there is a legal quality to Islamic law which any lawyer would be able to recognize if he or she cared to look for it.

11. This was also suggested in an interview with the person responsible for family law issues at the Islamic Center in Malmö, though the court case allegedly illustrating this seemed to point in the opposite direction (Interview on file with author).

likning. Although the case might be seen as a successful non-private international law case on *Mahr* it does not provide any information on how a court might handle such a claim in a judicial deliberation. The parties' agreement substitutes such a deliberation. The case had initially been filed at the court as *äktenskapskillnad* – a dissolution of marriage case. Such cases rarely contain anything but the judgement on the dissolution as such. A conciliation in a dissolution of marriage case is thus something quite unusual. It is similarly unusual that the court hear the parties in person – as was the case here. The judgement reports the parties to have reached the conciliation at the hearing. Apart from her *Mahr* the applicant (former) wife had initially demanded the court to issue an order to pay a fine – *vitesföreläggande* – of 20,000 SKr unless the (former) husband signed an authorization for her to follow through with a divorce in Lebanon. This claim was not mentioned in the confirmed judgement why it must be assumed that she dropped this part of her claim in the conciliation (Falu tingsrätt T 3391-05: 2).

One of the unsuccessful claims on *Mahr* is Göteborgs tingsrätt T 10691-06. It is a private international law case in which Swedish law was applied. Although a private international law case the Gothenburg case is interesting to comment on in reference to non-private international law cases concerning *Mahr*. Since Swedish law was applied in it the case could serve as a guide to how Swedish non-private international law court cases are dealt with at the courts.

The parties had contracted their marriage in April in Gothenburg with a local imam. Later the same year they entered into marriage at the district court in Gothenburg. At the breakdown of marriage, the same local imam had issued a divorce. The divorce was confirmed by an Iranian court. There was an additional divorce from the district court of Gothenburg.

The three judges sitting on the bench found the evidence in favor of the former husband. He had been successful in showing that the marriage contract and an additional document authorizing the wife to follow through with a divorce contained a clause which nullified the right to *Mahr* should she initiate the divorce (Göteborgs tingsrätt T 10691-06: 9).

4.2 The Unaddressed Objections to *Mahr* at Swedish Courts

In the case from Gothenburg (Göteborgs tingsrätt T 10691-06) the former husband had made a number of objections to why a Swedish court could not address an issue of *Mahr*. Three of these objections are of general interest for court cases concerning *Mahr* where Swedish law is applied (both in Swedish private international law cases and cases not involving private international law at all). Firstly, he argued that the contract on *Mahr* was invalid since it was against Swedish public moral and traditions, and consequently a *pactum turpe* (Göteborgs tingsrätt T 10691-06: 4)[12]. Secondly, he argued that the high amount of the *Mahr* made it practically impossible for him to receive a divorce, something which he argued undermined the Swedish law on marriage and divorce (Göteborgs tingsrätt T 10691-06: 4). In conjunction to his second objection he raised the question of what interests the Swedish law wanted to protect – the question of *skyddsintresse* (Göteborgs tingsrätt T 10691-06: 4). Would Swedish law protect a woman's right to a large sum of money (although she is entitled by law to half of the matrimonial property) rather than a man's right to divorce? A third argument presented was that the amount of the *Mahr* should be subjected to scrutiny by the court (i.e. reduced) due to a number of circumstances specific to the case (Göteborgs tingsrätt T 10691-06: 5).

The court in the Gothenburg case did not find it necessary to address any of the objections after arriving on the right to *Mahr* having been nullified by the clause in the contract. Since the man's objections all concern the position of *Mahr* in Swedish law a deliberation in the judgement of at least some – if not all – of the objections would have been of importance and interest. Unaddressed as they now stand, the objections would most probably be raised again in future court cases on *Mahr*, until properly addressed.

4.3 The Problem of *Mahr* as a Known Swedish Issue

From the two court cases above (Falu tingsrätt T 3391-05 and Göteborgs tingsrätt T 10691-06) we know that is not entirely impossible for Swedish law to recognize *Mahr* as a regular legal claim based on a regular Swedish contract. Yet, at no point do the Swedish judges seem to be able to include *Mahr* in relation to Swedish law. It could be argued that Swedish judges fail to properly address the place and legal status of *Mahr* within the Swedish system, at least when *Mahr* comes to court in its known, un-foreign and un-other form: when *Mahr* refuses to be anything else than a Swedish Muslim legal practice.

Neither of the two judgments mentioned here contain any deliberation on the interpretation of *Mahr* in the context of Swedish law. In the first case from Falu tingsrätt the parties had reached an agreement and no intervention from the judge on the issue of *Mahr* was (or seemed) necessary. The judge simply restated what the parties had agreed to in his judgment. In the second

12. The school book example of *pactum turpe* in Swedish law is a contract on sexual services. A *pactum turpe* can not be enforced by a Swedish court.

case from Gothenburg tingsrätt the judges did not have to comment on *Mahr* either since the court found that the woman – according to the marriage contract – had no right to *Mahr*. In both cases the legal meaning of *Mahr* was left entirely to the parties.

From these cases we can only know that when parties agree on the meaning of *Mahr* Swedish judges have no comments. When the parties do not agree, Swedish judges decides with the one bringing about the strongest evidence in the case and they do so without any independent critical legal analysis of *Mahr*. It is as if the term *Mahr* does not denote anything to Swedish judges but what the parties in the particular case manages to bring into evidence, as if there was no jurisprudence on *Mahr* to consult.[13]

In Swedish court cases concerning houses, cars or phone bills Swedish judges often have an impressive detailed knowledge about the specifics of the objects of legal dispute. The judge considers the evidence brought to a specific case departing from such knowledge. In cases concerning *Mahr* there seems to be no such knowledge. The judge lacking knowledge on *Mahr* might not be a problem in a private international law case concerning *Mahr* since the judge could turn to the Department for Foreign Affairs for expertise. But in a non-private international law court case concerning *Mahr* there is no foreign law to interpret. Should the Swedish judge want to consult the Swedish academic literature concerning *Mahr* it is of little help in this respect, since it mainly discusses *Mahr* as a foreign legal institution in Swedish private international law court cases.[14]

What it takes to succeed in a claim for *Mahr* when Swedish material law is applied is not clear from any of the cases mentioned in this text. But it seems as if it requires a certain kind of voice which the court can hear – a voice which Swedish (female) applicants so far have not been able to raise. Swedish judges also seem reluctant to undertake an independent analysis and position themselves on the status of *Mahr* in the Swedish legal system.

My suggestion is that Swedish judges should make efforts to interpret *Mahr* and position it in relation to Swedish law and that such interpretation should be written in the judgments. Yet counterargument could be that it is not the duty of a Swedish judge to comment on the status of *Mahr*. Swedish

13. An interesting comparison is the unpublished district court case Lunds tingsrätt Ä 3939-04 where the male party to the case not without success introduced a meaning of Islamic law marriages which was translated into Swedish as *förlovning* – engagement – thus carrying no legal significance in Swedish law.
14. The only text which would offer some help to the Swedish judge in non-private international law court cases on *Mahr* would be Sayed, 2008.

judicial culture does not allow the Swedish judge to deliberate *obiter dictum*[15]. In other words he or she should not talk about anything beyond the specific legal issue at hand in the particular court case. Swedish judges are considered as civil servants interpreting the laws handed down by the parliament. Since the Swedish law does not comment on the place of *Mahr* any comments by a Swedish judge risks going beyond the legislative intent. Further, from previous studies on judicial culture in Sweden we know that judges in the court-internal training are taught to write only the absolute necessary minimum in their judgments (Arvidsson, 2010). It is thus in line with general judicial culture for a Swedish judge to avoid any individual analysis or deliberation on the position of *Mahr* in the Swedish legal system in the judgment of a specific court case.

Even if there were cases from the Swedish district courts which addressed the objections mentioned in the Gothenburg case (Göteborgs tingsrätt T 10691-06) and which were to give us clear interpretations on the position of *Mahr* in Swedish law, these cases are not of a binding or even guiding nature. Only certain cases from the courts of appeals and the cases from *Högsta Domstolen* carry a guiding quality. Furthermore, even if there was an instructive case on *Mahr* such a case only becomes practically possible to access for the judge (and the researcher), once it is published – in either *Rättsfall från Hovrätterna* (RH), *Nytt Juridiskt Arkiv* (NJA), or through the juridical news data base *Juridik Idag* – or once it becomes public through general news media.

5 *Mahr* at the Swedish Margins

Many problems and questions surface when reading the court cases above. Or rather, there are many problems arising from reading the relative lack of cases on *Mahr* at Swedish courts. Do Muslims in Sweden not organize their lives in relation to Muslim family law? Are they so few that their legal problems dis-

15. *Obiter dictum* allows the judge some space for strategic manoeuvring in the judicial deliberation. The term suggests argumentation which does not function as precedent for future cases, but which forms extra support for the decision. As Swedish case law is not binding *obiter dictum* in the Swedish setting refers to support for the legal decision which goes beyond the absolute minimum. The Swedish style of writing judgements has a very particular form where arguments are seldom put forward. Consequently it is often impossible to figure out what led the judge to his conclusion in the particular case.

appear at court records as insignificant? Do Swedish Muslims not experience legal problems? Do they not bring their legal problems to Swedish courts? If Swedish Muslims come to court, are their voices not properly heard? Are Swedish judges at all aware of the legal problems experienced by Swedish Muslims?

There are no official statistics of how many Muslims live in Sweden. Suggestions vary as much as between 150,000 and 400,000 persons, largely depending on the definition of who counts as a Muslim (Ouis 2003: 75).[16] For the purpose of the argument in this chapter, the exact number of Muslims living in Sweden is of less importance. It is enough to know that it is a significant number and that some – though certainly not all – of these Muslims practice their faith by organizing their lives in reference to Muslim family law[17].

Some Swedish Muslims enter into matrimony at Swedish mosques[18]. A number of these ceremonies are ministered by imams who are authorized by Swedish law to perform marriages in relation to Swedish law.[19] Some marriages are contracted only in reference to Islamic law[20]. Others are contracted simultaneously in reference to Islamic and Swedish law. All marriages officiated in reference to Swedish law by persons authorized to do so – e.g. imams, Catholic priests or Jewish rabbis – should be registered at *folkbokföringen*, the Swedish Population Registration at the Swedish Tax Authorities.[21] How-

16. According to Ayoub Chibli, responsible for family law issues at the Islamic Center in Malmö, an estimated 70 000 Muslims live in Malmö (Interview on file with the author).
17. This can be established from the court cases appearing at Swedish courts, from the study in relation to the practices of *Mahr* in Malmö which this text in part flows from, and studies carried out on the practices of Islamic law in Sweden by other researchers. See for example Sayed, 2008: 189-190.
18. See for example the unpublished court cases Lunds tingsrätt Ä 3939-04 and Göteborgs tingsrätt T 10691-06. See also interview with Ayoub Chibli on file with the author.
19. Sweden has a tradition of authorizing ministers of different "*trossamfund*", religious communities, to perform marriages in accordance with Swedish law. See Lag (1993: 305) om rätt att förrätta vigsel inom andra trossamfund än Svenska kyrkan.
20. There are many reasons why Swedish couples would prefer to have a marriage in reference only to Islamic law. Marriages where the husband is entering into a second matrimony (without divorcing the fist wife) can only be contracted in reference to Islamic law since polygamy is not allowed in Sweden.
21. Such a registration with the Swedish Population Registration has no legal effect. A marriage made in reference to Swedish law is thus not invalid if it is performed correctly but not registered. However, in practice all Swedish authorities – including

ever, there is no enforcement of the obligation to register all marriages. At times, the wedding officiate (the imam, priest or rabbi) leaves the act of registration to the newly wed.[22] The newly wed might choose to have their marriage registered with the Swedish authorities. They might also prefer not to register it. Some marriages officiated in reference to Swedish law are consequently never registered with the Swedish authorities.[23]

There are no official statistics concerning the number of marriages contracted in these ways. Neither is there any official statistics concerning how many Swedish Muslims have contracted marriages in accordance to Muslim family law abroad. Occasionally records are at kept at mosques and Muslim congregations of marriages officiated there.[24] The individual Swedish wedding officiates are required to keep copies of all weddings they have performed. Through these records we know that at least some Swedish Muslims enter into matrimony in reference to Islamic law and that *Mahr* usually is part of the marriage contract (Sayed 2008: 189).

As marriage and divorce – with the accompanying issues of *Mahr* and distribution of marital property – is something which both Islamic and Swedish laws cover, it is not hard to imagine that disputes concerning Muslim family law should habitually be brought to Swedish courts. But the surveys concerning court cases on *Mahr* from which this text in part flows, seem to point in the opposite direction. There seem to be very few cases concerning *Mahr* brought to Swedish courts. We know that a number of disputes concerning

Swedish courts – rely on the information found in the Population Registry. All information on civil status is assumed to be included in the registry, and the information found there is assumed to be correct.

22. This is done by handing over the signed marriage document to the parties who are then to mail it (or hand it over in person) to the Swedish Population Registration.

23. The question if a marriage was contracted in reference to Islamic law only, or in reference to both Islamic and Swedish law was one of the key questions in the unpublished court cases from Lunds tingsrätt: T 43-02; T 329-02; Ä 3939-04; Ä 4029-04; T 912-05; T 4777-05 and T 3352-06. The registration at the Swedish Population Registration was left by the imam to the married couple. The woman of the couple registered the marriage with the Swedish authorities only several years after the ceremony took place. At this point the man denied ever having intended the marriage to be registered in reference to Swedish law.

24. Such records are kept for example at the mosque in Uppsala where a number of the Imams are certified to perform marriages in accordance to Swedish law, see Sayed 2008: 189, note 3. See also Göteborgs tingsrätt T 10691: 9, where the wedding officiate – in this case a man authorized by Iranian authorities to perform marriages in Sweden in reference to Iranian Muslim family law – kept a "book" over all marriages he had officiated.

Muslim family law and *Mahr* surface every year at Swedish Muslim congregations. The Islamic Centre in Malmö receives 350-400 cases a year concerning such disputes, an estimated third of these concerning issues related to the dissolution of marriage and *Mahr*.[25] Out of these, only one is known to have become a court case concerning *Mahr* at a Swedish district court.[26]

When checking the number of court cases against the estimated number of practitioners of Muslim family law in Sweden, something seems to be slightly wrong. How come issues of *Mahr* remain unheard of at Swedish courts, when they seem to surface elsewhere in the world at national courts? (e.g. Zaman 2008; Rogalin 2007; Fournier 2006; Jones-Pauly 2008; Mehdi 2003).

5.1 Marginalizing Judicial Culture

It has been indicated above that Swedish judges, as a general rule, lack basic training or orientation on issues of Islamic law. Even so, it is not unlikely that a Swedish judge has to deal with issues of Islamic law during his or her career as a judge. As is evident from this text Islamic law might appear in a Swedish private international law case or in a regular Swedish court case. Even so, *Mahr* is evidently not at the focus of attention at Swedish courts.

In part this can be explained by the inclusionary/exclusionary function of law. That which is included by exclusion (*Mahr* in private international law cases) at Swedish courts is not necessary to discuss since it is foreign and not part of Swedish law. And that which is neither included nor excluded (*Mahr* in non-private international law cases) cannot be discussed as there is no language for such un-issues.

In a number of interviews with judges at a district court conducted in 2007, the judges claimed to have little but sufficient knowledge of Muslim family law, i.e. not more or less knowledge than they had of any other foreign legal system (Arvidsson 2010). Indian and Iranian Muslim family laws were mentioned as legislation which they had come across in their work as judges in matters of marriage and divorce, though none of them could recall having dealt with matters concerning *Mahr*. When introduced to it, they all understood *Mahr* as an issue of Swedish private international law, thus only of their concern if a foreign national law on *Mahr* were to be applied in one of their court cases. None of the interviewed justices considered issues of Muslim family law as legal problems in their everyday work. And, since *Mahr* is

25. See interview on file with the author.
26. At the time of writing the case is still pending at the district court in Malmö.

not part of the Swedish legal system, they did not consider problems concerning *Mahr* to be problems of law unless there was a foreign national law involved. "It might be a problem", as one justice put it, "but it is not a problem of ours". Even so, justices seem to be aware of the difficult situation in which many Swedish Muslim women find themselves when caught between the Islamic and the Swedish legal system: a place they are put partly as a consequence of Swedish justices being unable to recognize their legal distress.

Through the interviews general Swedish judicial culture surfaced as an explanation of the relative disinterest in Islamic law at Swedish courts. Issues like *Mahr* which are difficult to position in law's inclusionary/exclusionary dichotomy become marginalized in such cultures. In addition, Swedish juridical language is quite conservative and does not invite new legal institutions to emerge.

There is a circulation of juridical language within the Swedish judicial culture where laws are drafted and commented on by the very same persons who later appear as judges applying and interpreting laws in courts.[27] A particular legal discourse is established and maintained through this circulation. The laws, the legal handbooks and the law school textbooks recycle and reinforce this discourse. Voicing a word such as *Mahr* in this linguistic field is not an easy enterprise, at least not if you want to be heard.[28] Before a new word – e.g. *Mahr* – can become part of the discourse, it must be accepted by authorities on Swedish law and properly circulated in Swedish laws, in law handbooks, in law school textbooks, and in Swedish judgments.

This marginalizing judicial culture is not a response to Islamic law in particular, but rather a specific part of the techniques of exclusion which can be found in the Swedish legal system.

5.2 *Mahr* at the Margins of Swedish Court Cases

In my experience as a law clerk and junior judge at a Swedish district court, I have found that issues of *Mahr* often appear in the margins of other court cases concerning family law. These cases are not filed as cases concerning *Mahr*. Instead they might be filed as dissolution of marriage, custody of children, or maintenance. If the women in these cases had access to the Swedish juridical language and thus managed to properly formulate their claims for *Mahr* in the correct Swedish legal terminology, these cases too would have

27. The circulation of juridical language could be seen as part of the establishment of a symbolic capital (Bourdieu, 1986: 46-58).
28. Swedish juridical language is here seen as a separate linguistic field (Bourdieu, 1986).

become cases concerning *Mahr*. But because they lack the necessary legal knowledge, or because they lack access to Swedish legal language, or because they do not receive proper legal representation, or because they prefer not to, or for any other reason, they do not (manage to) make their claims heard at Swedish courts.

These marginal appearances of *Mahr* are rarely noticed at Swedish courts. Sometimes the references to *Mahr* are obscure. At times they are so obscure that you have to be schooled in Muslim family law in order to see it in the legal documents. In court cases without hearings – e.g. dissolution of marriage cases – it is particularly hard to hear what is being argued in the margins. Consequently, women lacking voices which the courts are able to hear fall short of successfully pursuing their claims for *Mahr*. They remain caught in the margins. Sometimes objections to the dissolution of a marriage seem to refer to an underlying problem of receiving or keeping the *Mahr*. In other cases it appears as if the *Mahr* has been set up as items or assets which the woman cannot access after a Swedish law divorce. In these latter cases the woman's permanent residency in Sweden often depends on the continuation of the marriage (Lunds tingsrätt T 3487-04; Fredriksson, 2007: 44-45).

In cases concerning custody of children and child maintenance, issues of *Mahr* are often related to the legal conflicts. During preparatory hearings preceding the main hearing of a case underlying issues and conflicts are often unearthed by the judge (and subsequently addressed in order to conciliate the parties). However, when it comes to *Mahr* Swedish judges seem unaware of the impact that such an unsolved issue can have on the legal concern at hand in the particular case. Further, the judge is obliged to *ex officio* try to conciliate the parties in a custody or child maintenance case. But in order to do so, the judge often has to get a full picture of the conflicts between the parties. Unless the parties explicitly mention *Mahr* the judge would fail to examine that part of the conflict.

5.3 Intersections between Muslim Family Law and Swedish Law – 'Limping' Marriages and *Mahr*

From a number of Swedish court cases in which Islamic and Swedish law intersect we know that the dividing line between Swedish law and Islamic law is not as obvious as one would like to imagine (Arvidsson 2010). Although Swedish law and Islamic law are two entirely separable legal systems, in practice it is at times hard – or even impossible – to differentiate between a legally binding act performed in order to provide a legal consequence in accordance with Swedish law and an identical act performed in order to provide a legal consequence in accordance with Islamic law. Especially so when one and the same speech act (Serle, 1969) or performative act (Butler 1997) provides legal consequences in regards to both spheres of law. In both Swedish law and Islamic law (Siddiqi 2010: 19-20) marriage (and marriage contracts) comes into effect through the verbal agreement – the "performative utterance" (Austin 1975: 6-7).

The Swedish legal system of marriage and divorce, *äktenskapsbalken*, seems to cause a certain amount of confusion on this point. Marriages performed at mosques in Malmö, Uppsala or Gothenburg might be valid according to Swedish law, although to the observer it is a performance according to Islamic law and ritual and nothing more.[29] Not everyone entering into matrimony in the mosque is fully aware of the fact that *certain* parts of the legal bond which the matrimony institutes between them *but not other* parts become valid according to Swedish law and are enforceable in Swedish courts. Figuring out which parts of the legal bond are enforceable in Swedish courts – or how to make certain parts of the legal bond enforceable – is not an entirely easy business. When the spouses utter the phrase "I do" (or any equivalent phrase) in front of the imam, it is not entirely obvious what that act of speech refers to. Are they announcing their legal bond in relation to Swedish national law, Islamic law, or both?

We have what might be called a 'singular form' where marriages are performed in reference to both Swedish national and Islamic law in the same ritual. But, the form for divorce is entirely separate and thus 'dual': one form for Swedish law (at the district court) and one form for Islamic law (often performed by the imam).

The problems which Muslims in Sweden experience due to this dual form of divorce are known not only to researchers and the members and leaders of Swedish Muslim communities, but also to Swedish judges (Arvidsson 2010; Roald 2003: 133-188; Sayed 2008: 199). However, Swedish judges do not think of these problems as problems of Swedish law. In the words of Swedish district court justice Björn Serrander, interviewed on the problems of the dual divorce processes: "It is what it is" (Serrander 2009).

In the dual divorce process, women often get caught in between. The situation is referred to as 'limping marriages'. A divorce is granted from a Swedish court, but the (former) husband refuses a divorce in reference to Islamic law. The woman who is caught between the two legal systems finds it impossible to claim her *Mahr*. Needless to say, the dissolution of marriage in

29. This is the case if the marriage officiate – e.g. the imam – has been granted permission by the Swedish authorities to officiate marriages in accordance to Swedish law and does so in a way which is also in accordance with Islamic law.

reference to Swedish law has no effect in Islamic law. Most Islamic legal traditions do not recognize a woman's right to divorce, and only few Swedish imams are willing to grant a woman a divorce (Roald 2003: 164)[30]. It is in this intersection between Swedish and Islamic law that problems concerning *Mahr* are understood as gender related.[31]

When the Muslim woman is granted a divorce by a Swedish court, she might have to trade her right to *Mahr* for an Islamic divorce, thus buying her way out of the marriage (e.g. Göteborgs tingsrätt T 10691-06). In such a situation the 'limping' wife might turn to her local mosque for help in negotiating for at least some part of her *Mahr*.[32] The practice of trading *Mahr* (in part or in whole) for a divorce is widely known and discussed throughout the Islamic world. It is also noted to be prevalent among certain groups of Swedish Muslims (Darvishpour 2003; Göteborgs tingsrätt T 10691-06).

5.4 Marginal Precautions to Ensure the Right to *Mahr* in Sweden

How then could a woman who got married in a mosque in Malmö, Uppsala or Gothenburg make sure she receives her contracted *Mahr*? One suggestion is to make Swedish district courts divorces enforceable in reference to Islamic law, leading automatically to an Islamic divorce (Roald 2003: 156). Before that can become a reality, changes in the Swedish law on divorce has to be made, e.g. in relation to *Mahr*. The Swedish law would have to ensure the woman's right to *Mahr* in a way which would be acceptable in terms of Islamic law.

Another suggestion is to make marriages entered into in relation to Islamic law an impediment to Swedish law marriage regardless of the national or non-national character of the Islamic law in question. The Islamic Center in Malmö has been actively reaching out to politicians in the Swedish parliament in order to promote such a change in the Swedish legislation. To this date, there have been no legislative initiatives pursue by the Swedish parliament in this direction.

30. The enforceability of these Swedish Islamic divorces relies entirely on the husband accepting such a divorce. See also interview with Ayoub Chibli on file with the author.
31. This gender imbalance is suggested to be a problem among the Muslim community in Malmö by the Swedish imam Adly Aby Hajal ("Sverige den bästa islamiska staten", 2009) as well as by Ayoub Chibli, the wedding officiate and responsible for family issues at the Islamic Center in Malmö, see interview on file with author.
32. At the Islamic Center in Malmö Ayoub Chibli takes part in organizing negotiations between spouses with limping marriages. See also "Sverige den bästa islamiska staten", 2009; and the conciliation in Falu tingsrätt T 3391-05.

Yet another suggestion in order to bring issues of *Mahr* from the margins to the centre of Swedish court cases would be to instruct judges to habitually raise the question of *Mahr* in court cases concerning *Mahr*-related conflicts. That would require Swedish judges to know something about Muslim family law. Calling parties to a preceding hearing in cases of dissolution of marriage where there are objections to the divorce would be another suggestion on how to bring issues of *Mahr* to the attention in Swedish court cases.

Departing from the current situation and legislation, there are measures which can be taken in order to ensure a woman's right to *Mahr*. If the woman is not successful in enforcing her claim for *Mahr* through other means, she might turn to the Swedish legal system for relief – phrasing her petition as something that might be easily recognized by Swedish judges. In doing so, she would have to rely on the current Swedish judicial language. Her success depends on whether she took precautions before entering into matrimony or not. As noted by Swedish lawyers and scholars of law alike, some Swedish Muslim women have taken measures to ensure the enforceability of their rights to *Mahr* at Swedish courts by making their husbands sign prenuptial agreements equivalent to the *Mahr*, or by making them sign a contract of matrimonial property during marriage (Dedari 2006).

Such contracts – if made in accordance with Swedish national law – are enforceable at Swedish courts and in case of a divorce the woman will find little or no problem receiving a title to the agreed-upon property or asset. Similar legal strategies are advocated by Swedish Muslim feminists (e.g. *Islamisk Feministisk Front*, no 5).

However, a prenuptial agreement requires the woman to take legal measures ensuring her future rights to *Mahr* before any problems of enforceability have occurred. She might need legal assistance or professional legal advice in order to formulate her rights to *Mahr* in Swedish juridical language, to ensure that her rights are fully protected according to Swedish law. While it might come across as a good idea to anyone entering into matrimony to take such precautions, many Muslims consider a stipulation of *Mahr* in the marriage contract as precaution enough. Yet, following the Swedish court cases on *Mahr* there is no legal certainty on the position of *Mahr* in relation to Swedish law. It has not been made clear by Swedish courts under which circumstances contracts on *Mahr* are enforceable in Swedish courts. A stipulation of the *Mahr* in the marriage contract is thus not enough.

6 The End: Facing/Defacing *Mahr* at Swedish Courts

It could be successfully argued that much of what is being presented and argued in this chapter is old news. *Mahr* as other and foreign to Swedish law is not new. It has long been known that the Swedish legal system recognizes issues of *Mahr* as matters of Swedish private international law; i.e. as foreign national law. The details of Swedish private international law in relation to *Mahr* have been set by the Swedish court cases RH 1993: 166 and 2005: 66. The private international law aspects of those court cases have been duly discussed in the Swedish legal academic debate. Further, the practical details of how a Swedish justice goes about his job recognizing *Mahr* as an issue of private international law is little else than the writing down of the know-how of any jurist who has been working at a Swedish district court. It is equally well known that Swedish Muslim(a)s who enter into matrimony in Sweden and thus fall outside the scope of Swedish private international law, face substantial problems in enforcing their rights to *Mahr*. Finally, the part which Swedish judicial culture plays in this must have come as no surprise to anyone familiar with Swedish law and judicial practices.

Departing from the story of the two sisters seeking out Law, the main findings in this text resides in the two sisters' astonishment when they call out: How can law recognize one of us but not the other? How can law recognize the unknown while law fails to recognize the known? How can law face the unknown while it defaces the known? The re-callings of those questions have gradually been pursued above. Through the analysis of *Mahr* in the Swedish legal system it has become apparent that Law can only face you if you are so foreign and other that there is no risk of you becoming included as a proper part of Law. When you become too familiar, too close and too much like Law, there are a number of techniques and practices by which you are defaced and unheard by Law. In Swedish court cases *Mahr* remain paradoxically as both known and unknown. It is recognized yet unrecognizable. Though appearing to be one and the same thing, *Mahr* is seen as different things depending on who is voicing a legal concern at the court, and from which position such a voice is coming.

The techniques and practices of unknowing *Mahr* in Swedish private international law cases have been unpacked throughout the analysis above. *Mahr* has through this analysis become an example of law's ability to include that which is excludable through a process of alienation and othering. The dichotomy foreign/national is central to this othering of *Mahr*. When *Mahr* can be faced as foreign national law Swedish law can include it as a foreign element in a singular particular court case. In this way the Swedish law, its courts and its judges can recognize and face *Mahr* as a legal issue which can be dealt with by ways of general judicial know-how and legal method. These are cases which are so foreign that the Department for Foreign Affairs has to be called in to guide the Swedish judge on the foreign law and legal institution. *Mahr* is in these instances included because it is excludable. The Swedish courts can face *Mahr* because it is unknown. This is the situation in which we find the older sister of our story.

But although Swedish law, its courts and its judges seem to be able to recognize *Mahr* as a legal problem in Swedish private international law cases, there remains a problem in seeing what *Mahr* is. There seems to be a certain degree of misreading when Swedish judges embark on interpreting foreign national codes on *Mahr*. In this respect basic training in Islamic law would be of some help, as well as a better response from Swedish legal academia on issues concerning Islamic law within the Swedish legal system. But discursive interventions from the legal academia usually have little effect on the general Swedish judicial culture and only part of the problem has to do with knowledge concerning *Mahr*.

Further, not all issues concerning *Mahr* can be dealt with at Swedish courts by the othering techniques of Swedish private international law. It is more difficult to 'unknow' *Mahr* when it is an all-Swedish tradition and part of a marriage contracted by Swedes in Sweden. *Mahr* also becomes harder to face for the Swedish law, its courts and its judges in this non-private international law setting. This is the situation in which we find the younger sister of our story. The techniques of othering which are known from Swedish private international law cases cannot be applied as the dichotomy foreign/national no longer applies. *Mahr* in these non-private international law cases is neither foreign nor is it national law. In terms of Swedish juridical language it becomes unspeakable.

When women come to Swedish courts – as the younger sister of our story did – presenting their all-Swedish problems concerning the enforcement of *Mahr*, the responses which greet them are several but similar. Sometimes these women's voices seem to be unhearable, too marginal, or too obscure for the Swedish judge to hear. The judge's ear is not trained to hear Islamic law, nor is the judge's ear trained to hear that which cannot be defined within the foreign/national law dichotomy. *Mahr* is in these cases not seen as law or part of a particular legal system with its own jurisprudence. Had Swedish judges seen *Mahr* as part of law, the study of Islamic jurisprudence had become a natural means in understanding its' particular legal features. *Mahr* is not understood as a regular contractual issue either. Had Swedish judges understood contracts on *Mahr* as equivalent to contracts on houses, cars or phone bills they would perhaps have an extensive cultural knowledge about it as well as an independent analysis on its position in relation to Swedish law.

In court cases where *Mahr* is a non-private international law issue, Swedish judges fall short of finding a place from where they can position themselves in relation to *Mahr*. *Mahr* is treated as an object which they know nothing about but which is known enough not to be foreign. The judges (most often) have no cultural knowledge of it. Swedish judicial culture does not encourage the judge to undertake an independent analysis of the nature of *Mahr* and its position in relation to Swedish law. Instead, the interpretation of *Mahr* is left to the stronger of the parties with the better resources for being heard at the court.

All these responses by which Swedish law, its judiciary and its legal academia (de)face *Mahr* are guided by silence. The problems which arise in the intersection between Islamic and Swedish law fall outside of what is, and perhaps can be, properly addressed in discourses from behind the Swedish bench. *Mahr* is only one example of such a crossroad issue. In some of these cases Swedish law and judiciary fall short of providing legal remedies to problems which by all means are issues of law. These are cases where law seems to provide promises it doesn't fulfill. Yet, other issues appearing at the crossroads of Islamic and Swedish law fall outside the field of vision of law. Those are the issues which are too un-foreign, too known, too un-other to answer to law's inclusionary/exclusionary function. Swedish judges are trained not to see and not to hear that which can neither be excluded nor be included. Consequently, certain issues remain unaddressed and become none of law's concern.

Perhaps there are very good reasons for women not to seek out Law in the way the two sisters of our story did. Through this text it has become apparent that *Mahr* is rarely taken to Swedish courts – at least relative to the yearly number of Swedish disputes on *Mahr* which surface elsewhere in dispute resolution forums. Perhaps *Mahr* is something which Swedish law, judiciary and legal academia can never come to proper terms with and perhaps rightly so. There are instances of incompatibility where Islamic law cannot embrace Swedish law and Swedish law is unable to embrace Islamic law. Further, law surely does not have an answer to all problems, and *Mahr* is not a legal institution which would gain – in terms of sophistication of jurisprudence – from an inclusion into Swedish law.

Sisters might find themselves stranded on the doorsteps to Law also in the future when they approach Law with problems which appear in the intersection between Islamic and Swedish law. This intersection can be seen as a place of legal distress with no proper resolutions in sight. But it can also be understood as a unique place where the nature of law can be re-searched. At crossroads like these, law's functions – like the inclusionary/exclusionary function studied in this chapter – as well as our own expectations of law seem to surface.

Bibliography

Arvidsson, Matilda, (2007) "The Presence of Absence of Personal Identity: Everyday Conditions of Practicing Law", in Arvidsson, Matilda and E. Önnerfors (eds.), *Jag sträcker mig in i framtiden*, Lund: Corpus Iuris, pp.3-30.

Arvidsson, Matilda, (2010) "Shari'a from behind the bench: court culture, judicial culture and a judge-made discourse on Shari'a at a Swedish district court", in Nielsen, Jørgen S., and L. Christoffersen, (eds.) *Shari'a as Discourse: Legal Traditions and the Encounter with Europe*, Aldershot/Burlington: Ashgate, pp.97-115.

Austin, J. L., (1975) *How to Do Things with Words*, Oxford: Clarendon Press.

Bogdan, Michael, (1993) "Islamisk brudpenning (*Mahr*) inför svensk domstol", *Svensk Juridisk Tidskrift*, vol.78, no.7, pp.597-600.

Bogdan, Michael, (1999) *Svensk internationell privat- och processrätt*, 5th edition, Stockholm: Nordsteds Juridik.

Bogdan, Michael, (2007) "Något om den kollisionsrättsliga bedömningen av islamisk morgongåva (*MAHR*)", in Franzen, Torstein, J. Giertzen, and G. Cordero Moss (eds.) *Rett och toleranse. Festskrift til Helge Johan Thue*, Oslo: Gyldendal Akademisk, pp.175-185.

Bourdieu, Pierre, (1986) "The Forms of Capital", in Richardson, John G. (ed.) *Handbook of Theory of Research for the Sociology of Education*, New York: Greenwood Press, pp.46-58.

Butler, Judith, (1997) *Excitable Speech: A Politics of the Performative*, London: Routledge.

Darvishpour, Mehrdad, (2003) *Invandrarkvinnor som bryter mönstret. Hur maktförskjutningen inom iranska familjer i Sverige påverkar relationen*, Stockholm: Almqvist & Wiksell International.

Dedari, Farzaneh, (2006) Interview in the radio show *Människor och tro* 12 June 2006 on Muslim women in Sweden between Swedish law and Muslim family law, available online at http://podradio.nu/feed/rss/219/, accessed 30 December 2009.

Domstolsakademin Utbildningsprogram, (2009) Stockholm: Domstolsverket.

Fournier, Pascale, (2006) "In the (Canadian) Shadow of Islamic Law: Translating *Mahr* as a Bargaining Endowment", *Osgoode Hall Law Journal*, Winter, Vol. 44, No. 4, pp.649-677.

Fredriksson, Katja J., (2007) "Sharia in Norwegian Courtrooms?", *ISIM Review*, no.20, pp.44-45.

Hjärpe, Jan, (1989) http://www.radioislam.org/islam/svenska/fildok/filer/bok/process/pro13.htm, accessed 8 July 2010.

Hjärpe, Jan, (2005) *Shari'a – Gudomlig lag i en värld i förändring*, Stockholm: Nordstedts.

Islamisk Feministisk Front, no 5, http://www.geocities.com/islam5front/index.html, accessed 2 April 2009.

Jones-Pauly, Christina, (2008) "Marriage Contrats of Muslims in the Diaspora: Problems in the Recognition of *Mahr* Contracts in German Law", in Quraishi, Asifa and F. E. Vogel (eds.), *The Islamic Marriage Contract*, Cambridge: Harvard University Press, pp.303-321.

Juridik Idag http://www.nj.se/cms/juridikidag/search!open&search=%20T%204594-02, accessed 8 July 2010.

Lagervall, Rickard, (2004) "Att bryta tystnaden: Hustrumisshandel och den samtida debatten om en reform av familjelagen i Marocco", in Österberg, Eva and M. Lindstedt Cronberg (eds.), *Våldets mening: Makt, minne, myt*, Lund: Nordic Academic Press, pp.119-143.

Mehdi, Rubya, (2003) "Danish Law and the Practice of *Mahr* among Muslim Pakistanis in Denmark", *The International Journal of Sociology of Law*, vol. 31, pp.115-129.

Ouis, Pernilla, (2003) "Att leva som muslim i Sverige", in Ouis, Pernilla, and A. Roald, (eds.) *Muslim i Sverige*, Stockholm: Wahlström & Widstrand, pp.73-99.

Qaisi, Ghada G., (2000/2001) "Religious Marriage Contracts: Judicial Enforcement of '*Mahr*' Agreements in American Courts", *Journal of Law and Religion*, vol.15, no.1/2, pp.67-81.

Radio Islam http://www.radioislam.org/islam/svenska/fildok/filer/bok/process/dom.htm, accessed 8 July 2010.

Roald, Annsofie, (2003) "Är islam en kvinnofientlig religion?" in Ouis, and A. Roald (eds.), *Muslim i Sverige*, Stockholm: Wahlström & Widstrand, pp.133-188.

Rogalin Siddiqui, Tracie, (2007) "Interpretation of Islamic Marriage Contracts by American Courts", *Family Law Quarterly*, Fall, Vol. 41, Iss. 3, pp.639-659.

Sayed, Mosa, (2008) "The Muslim Dower (*Mahr*) in Europe – With Special Reference to Sweden", pp. 187-208, in Boele-Woelki, Katarina and T. Sverdrup (eds.), *European challenges in contemporary family law*, Antwerpen: Intersentia.

Schiratzki, Johanna, (2001) *Muslimsk familjerätt – i svenskt perspektiv*, 2nd edition, Stockholm: Nordstedts Juridik.

Schiratzki, Johanna, (2006) Interview in the radio show *Människor och tro* 12 June 2006 on Muslim women in Sweden between Swedish law and Muslim family law, available online at http://podradio.nu/feed/rss/219/, accessed 30 December 2009.

Serle, John, (1969) *Speech Acts*, Cambridge: Cambridge University Press.

Serrander, Björn, (2009) Interview with justice Serrander in "Sverige den bästa islamiska staten", 5 March in Skånskan.se (Skånska Dagbladet) http://www.skanskan.se/text/20090304/NYHETER/50908892/1056/*/*/MALMO/-sverige-den-basta-islamiska-staten, accessed 30 December 2009.

Shah, Prakash (2010) "Between God and the Sultana? Legal Pluralism in the British Diaspora", in Nielsen, Jørgen S., and L. Christoffersen, (eds.) *Shari'a as Discourse: Legal Traditions and the Encounter with Europe*, Aldershot/Burlington: Ashgate, pp.117-139.

Siddiqi, Mona, (2010) "Clarity or Confusion – Classical *Fiqh* and the Issue of Logic", in Nielsen, Jørgen S., and L. Christoffersen, (eds.) *Shari'a as Discourse: Legal Traditions and the Encounter with Europe*, Aldershot/Burlington: Ashgate, pp.17-27.

"Sverige den bästa islamiska staten", 5 March in Skånskan.se (Skånska Dagbladet) http://www.skanskan.se/text/20090304/NYHETER/50908892/1056/*/*/MALMO/sverige-den-basta-islamiska-staten, accessed 30 December 2009.

Zaman, Saminaz (2008) "Amrikan Shari'a: The Reconstruction of Islamic Family Law in the United States", *South Asia Research*, Vol. 28(2), pp.185-202.

Legislation

Lag (1904: 26) om vissa internationella rättsförhållanden rörande äktenskap och förmynderskap.

Lag (1993: 305) om rätt att förrätta vigsel inom andra trossamfund än Svenska kyrkan.

Court Cases:

Published Court Cases

RH 1993: 116
RH 2005: 66

Unpublished Court Cases

Svea Hovrätt T 10083-04
Falu tingsrätt T 3391-05
Göteborgs tingsrätt T 10691-06
Lunds tingsrätt Ä 3939-04
Lunds tingsrätt Ä 4029-04
Lunds tingsrätt T 43-02
Lunds tingsrätt T 329-02
Lunds tingsrätt T 912-05
Lunds tingsrätt T 4777-05
Lunds tingsrätt T 3352-06
Lunds tingsrätt T 3487-04
Stockholms tingsrätt B 8-4-89
Uppsala tingsrätt T 3289-02

CHAPTER 10

Muslim Marriage and *Mahr*: The Experience of British Muslim Women

Samia Bano

Introduction

There are many social, cultural and religious reasons why British Muslim women choose to participate in traditional religious marriage ceremonies. In the popular imagination Muslim marriages are often associated as being *arranged* or *forced* which in turn subscribes to the idea that the experience of marriage for all Muslim women is one based upon oppressive and archaic religious traditions. In this chapter I begin by drawing upon interview data with a group of young British Pakistani Muslim women to explore the meanings attached to one aspect of the Muslim marriage process, the *nikah* in order to evaluate its importance from the standpoint of the women. I then analyse existing English caselaw to better understand the validity of Muslim marriages in English law with a particular reference to *Mahr* and contract law. In the final part of the chapter I discuss, the introduction of the new Muslim marriage contract to consider its validity and significance in relation to the recognition of *Mahr* in English Law and question whether such developments contribute to enhancing the rights of Muslim women in Britain.

Family Life and Muslim Communities in Britain

The experience of migrant family life in Britain has been extensively analysed and discussed by sociologists, anthropologists and more recently family law scholars. (Eekelaar 2002: 9-17, 23-26; Beck-Gernsheim 2001; Maclean 2004) The migration patterns of Muslim communities to Britain have been extensively documented in anthropological and sociological research (Ballard, R. 1994). The largest groups of South Asian Muslim migrants emerged from Pakistan in the 1950's and 60's from rural farming areas of the Mirpur district and some parts of Punjab,[1] to satisfy the acute shortage of labour following the post-war boom in Britain. According to Ballard, the notion of '*desh pardesh'* encapsulates how South Asian Muslims reconstruct a 'home away from home' to maintain cultural and religious links with original homelands and to keep 'customs and culture alive in Britain (Ballerd 1996: 4). In her study Shaw (Shaw1994: 37) outlines the continuation of cultural traditions such as '*biraderi*' membership, kinship migration and informal networks such as the tradition of '*lena-dena*' within the Pakistani Muslim community in Oxford. It becomes clear that one of the early aims of South Asian communities migrating to Britain was to sustain a cultural identity and, "as a culturally enclaved minority in the West, many are having to come to terms with an experienced, everyday loss of autonomy and cultural control which permanent settlement in Britain entails" (Werbner 1994: 226). The anthropologist Roger Ballard[2] describes South Asian Muslim families as part of the 'corporate' family structure. According to Ballard corporate families exist in many ethnic communities but are particularly associated in the UK with families of South Asian origin. There are differences and distinctions within all families yet certain core characteristics are identifiable. In European kinship, the critical relationship is between nuclear family members whereas a wide network of inter- and intra-generational ties and obligations binds members of corporate families. Women's personal conduct is connected to notions of 'honour' or 'shame', which affect the entire family. Ballard argues that these characteristics have assisted transnational families to negotiate a globalised

1. Most Pakistani's are drawn from just a few areas in Pakistan: mainly from Faisalabad and Jhelum Districts in Punjab, Mirpur District in Azad Kashmir, and the Attock District in the North Western frontier Province. See Shaw (1994) and Werbner (1988).
2. According to Ballard corporate families originate from "the swath of territory which runs from North Africa through the Eastern Mediterranean and the Middle East to South Asia". See R Ballard 'Inside and Outside: Contrasting Perspectives on the Dynamics of Kinship and Marriage in Contemporary South Asian Transnational Networks' in R Grillo (ed) *The Family in Question: Immigrants and Minorities in Multicultural Europe* (Amsterdam: University of Amsterdam Press, 2008) 37 – 70. South Asia remains the largest source of marriage migration (although not of child migration) to the UK; *Control of Immigration Statistics UK 2007* (Home Office 10/08, 2008) p 28.

world in which they face structural disadvantages of immigration control, discrimination and poverty.

Today there is growing literature, which seeks to understand identities as multiple, fluid, dynamic and partial and which can only be understood in interaction with other identities, ethnicities and social structures (Ali, Kalra and Sayyid 2006). More recently discussion has focused on the complex, shifting and fragmented identities within the South Asian diaspora. This understanding of identity, as fluid and changing[3] has led many commentators to conclude that at specific times, a particular aspect of the group identity will emerge as more important than at other times (Modood 2000). In Britain empirical research suggests the emergence of a '*renewed*' Muslim religious identity within South Asian Muslim communities (Afshar 1992; Anwar 1998; Burlet & Reid 1998; Dwyer 2000; Modood 2000; Werbner 2000). In this way the Pakistani diaspora has been transformed as part of the 'Muslim diaspora' or Muslim Umma (Castells 1997).

Muslim Family Law in Britain

In Britain there have been some demands for Muslim personal laws to be recognized in English law under the context of multiculturalism and the 'rights' discourse. However, these demands are both sketchy and do not necessarily reflect the viewpoints of many British Muslims. In English law, religious laws and practices are defined as ethnic customs (Poulter 1992, 1998) which are recognized, as long as they are not deemed 'unreasonable' nor clash with the principles of English law (this also includes violation of any international treaties to which Britain maybe signatory).[4] Menski notes that

3. And recognizing a distinction in group identity between a 'mode of oppression' and 'mode of being' (see Modood 1990: 56)
4. Legislation to protect specific cultural and religious practices include: The Race Relations Act 1976 which aimed to promote equal opportunities and to eliminate discrimination in employment, housing, education and the provision of goods and services. The legal system has over time recognised certain other demands of ethnic minority groups. The Shop Act 1950 exempted Jews from Sunday trading laws. The Slaughterhouses Act 1979 allows the slaughter of animals for the purpose of obtaining kosher and halal meat for the Jewish and Muslim communities; and since 1976, a Sikh with a turban may ride a motorcycle in Britain without wearing a crash helmet under the Motorcycle Crash Helmet (Religious Exemption) Act, which is otherwise compulsory. In addition, voluntary-aided religious and denominational schools are funded by the state, as are army chaplains and university theology faculties.

the framing of these claims drive from western human rights approach and asks "who determines the criteria for what is acceptable and what is not? Should the official law restrict itself to controlling the limited space that it recognises, knowingly ignoring the rest of the social field, or should it attempt to control the entire field while being prepared to make concessions to diversity?" (Menski 1998: 68). This point has more recently been addressed by the Archbishop of Canterbury, Dr Rowan Williams, in his speech on cultural and religious diversity to the Royal Courts of Justice in February 2007. In what can now be largely referred to as the *Sharia debate* (following the considerable media and public policy attention) Dr Williams argued that the minimum universal liberal values of justice, equality and fairness must – in response to moral and cultural diversity – be applied in a manner whereupon all members of society are able to express their identity and loyalty to both a religious identity and the state. The case made for the positive accommodation of some unspecified form of Islamic law in Britain under English law. However the use of British Muslims as an example to consider the possible accommodation of religious systems of law into English law proved extremely contentious (Bano 2008).

In Britain existing literature presents the socio-legal reality of Muslims in Britain as a complex scenario whereby official and customary laws interact to produce a new set of hybrid laws.[5] In attempting to develop a conceptual framework, which both adopts a 'postmodern approach' to the study of law and recognises pluralism and diversity in social life, Menski (Menski 1993; Pearl and Menski 1998) employs the analytical framework by the jurist Masaji Chiba (Chiba 1986) and constructs a legal model he defines as '*Angrezi Sharia*'. According to Menski, Asian Muslims in Britain have not simply given up Islamic law but combine Islamic law and English law to form '*Angrezi Sharia*'. He describes a three-fold process generated by internal conflicts within Asian communities and leading, as mentioned, to the creation of 'British Asian Laws in Britain. The first stage occurred at the time of migration. At this stage ignorance of the legal system meant that customary practices continued to be observed. For example, up until 1970 many Asians did not register marriages and this later resulted in huge matrimonial disputes. Subsequently, however, Asians learnt to adapt to English law but rather than abandon their customary traditions, they built the requirements of English law into them. The result has been that new British Muslim, Hindu and Sikh law, unique to Britain, has emerged, differing in some important aspects from the

5. For an overview see Yilmaz, I. (2002: 28: 2, 343-354).

Indian, Pakistani or Bangladeshi laws and customs. This was the second phase, which created the corpus of precedent law Menski labels '*Angrezi*' law. The third stage in this process might involve abandoning ethnic customs and religious personal laws altogether, and practising only state law, but this has not happened. Thus English law remains the official law while *angrezi sharia* is the unofficial law. As part of this complex process, redefined Muslim laws in Britain have become 'hybrid' and thus "all ethnic minorities in Britain marry twice, divorce twice and do many other things several times in order to satisfy the demands of concurrent legal systems" (Pearl and Menski 1998). This analysis contributes to a better understanding of the development of a British legal discourse which comprises of a complex interplay of cultural, social values, Islamic legal practices with state law norms and values. In doing so it demonstrates how law evolves and develops over time emphasizing both the commonalities and differences between and within the different legal orders.

Civil Registration of *Nikah*-Marriage

The requisites of a valid *nikah* contract include 'legal capacity' (individual to be of sound mind and has reached puberty), consent, acceptance and the dower or *Mahr*.

The interview-data highlights the importance many women attached to Islamic interpretations of marriage and the Muslim marriage process.

The research also explored the number of marriages which complied with the Marriage Acts 1949-94 and were registered according to civil law in comparison to those whose marriages comprised the religious marriage only, the *nikah*. The data in this study found that less than half the sample who had married with a partner domiciled in England had registered their marriages, meaning that the largest group of women in this sample were those who in effect were deemed unmarried according to English family law. This raises the obvious question of why the majority of women had not registered their marriages according to the formalities of civil law which affords women greater legal protection should the marriage end in divorce. It may also reinforce the argument pursued by some legal scholars who argue that in order to accommodate the needs of British Muslims who intentionally choose to avoid using state law increases the need to introduce some kind of parallel legal system in matters of family law. At first glance, this absence of formal registration of marriage seems to legitimize this argument but as data in this study illustrates on closer inspection we see that the picture maybe a little more complex. What becomes clear is that in the majority of cases in this study, the women had in fact expected their religious marriages to be registered in accordance with the Marriage Acts 1949-94 but upon completion of the religious ceremony and once consummation of the marriage had taken place some husbands had simply refused to register the marriage according to civil law.

The essence of these arguments are predicated on the need to raise public awareness to the fact that Muslim women are deliberately failing to register their religious marriages according to the formalities of civil law raising the need therefore to introduce a formal process that is able to accommodate the needs of all Muslims in Britain. At first glance, the absence of formal registration of marriage seems to legitimize such arguments but on closer inspection the picture is a little more complex than at first envisaged. What becomes clear is that such outcomes of non registration must be understood in relation to power relations and the situated positioning of women in family and marriage relationships (Anthias 2002). For example it is difficult to ignore the relations of power and the gendered cultural norms and values that underpin the decisions made by husbands and male members of the new found family, many of whom choose not to formalize the marriage according to civil law. These women had experienced a loss of decision-making and autonomy in the marriage process, they had relied upon a level of trust and reciprocity from their husbands that the marriage would be registered and this trust had been violated.

All these outcomes led some women to call for the introduction of a parallel legal system as a means of redressing their situations. The extracts below from interview data reveal some of the underlying reasons of why marriages were not registered according to civil law:

Well to tell you the truth I honestly thought that the Muslim marriage certificate would be recognised I was quite shocked when I found out that it wasn't. I thought hold on a minute we got married didn't we? I had a massive wedding I've got the wedding photos to prove it, the wedding cassette to prove it. I have all this to prove it so how can they turn round and say to me that sorry no it's not recognised. The only difference is...the only thing that we didn't do is swap some vows in the registry office I mean that's the only difference (Mina, London).

I said to him we need to get registered and he said oh no we don't cause the Muslim certificate is recognised now and I was so naïve I believed him so I thought oh well it must be. He said yeah well I thought it wasn't as well and last time I got registered it was just a big hassle to be divorced and I believed him (Sadia, Birmingham).

It is noteworthy that these extracts reveal the precarious situation in which many of the women found themselves. For example of the sample only two women had been unaware of the validity of the *nikah* according to English law and believed they were legally married. A further two women had agreed with their husbands to forego civil registration for financial reasons. But the largest groups of women involved in non registration of marriages were those women who were aware of the need to register their marriage according to civil law and had fully expected their marriages to be formalised. Hence the consequences for the women of being intentionally misled led them to facing a multitude of social and legal problems.

Those women who had believed that their *nikah* had been a legally recognised form of marriage also speculated on the lack of available information for their misunderstanding. Blame had been directed towards Imams and community leaders.

I find it shocking that Pakistanis have been in this country for decades and decades and still no-one seems to know if the *nikah* in England is recognised or not? Solicitors and the community need to be trained, especially the Imams we go to them for advice so its really important they know at least what's going on (Shazia, London).

Hence these women clearly lacked power and position within their newfound family to successfully negotiate the formal registration of marriage and they remained dependant on the willingness/ unwillingness of their husbands to comply. Disempowered many women described their bitterness on having relied upon the trust of their husbands trust only to be let down. As one interviewee explained,

I think a lot of people are naïve they just trust their husbands in that they will get a registered marriage. Its not that they don't know about registry or that they don't want it, they are just naïve in believing their husbands. I tell all my friends now that you must have a legal marriage first because if you have an Islamic marriage first then they will not agree to do a civil marriage. I mean you can do it on the same day there's nothing stopping you doing that. Because I really think that guys would begin to take marriages more seriously (Salma, London).

The extracts below from interview data reveal some of the underlying reasons why religious marriages were not registered according to civil law:

> Well I understand that Islamically it says that you have to have a *nikah* in order for your marriage to be recognised but I would have been happy if it had been registered straight away then I would have felt that I am on the safe side at the end of the day. I'm not happy with what

> happened to my marriage at all, my marriage was planned and the breakdown of my marriage was planned (Shazia, London).

It is noteworthy that these extracts reveal the precarious situation that many of the women found themselves in. For example, of the sample only two women had been aware that religious marriages did require formalization but had believed that the *nikah* contract was evidence that the marriage had complied with formal registration of marriage. A further two women had agreed with their husbands to forego civil registration for financial reasons but no further explanations as to why this was so were given. But the largest groups of women were those who were aware of the need to register their marriage according to civil law and had expected their marriages to be formalised. Interestingly, this group of women had believed that their *nikah* certificate was a legally recognised document and directly blamed the lack of available information for their confusion. In particular blame was directed towards Imams and religious leaders who were performing such marriages.

In a context where women may engage in a plural set of social and legal 'practices' the ambiguity surrounding the legitimacy of the *nikah* contract in Britain can therefore leave some women facing adverse consequences. In this context such outcomes of non-formalisation must be understood in relation to the situated position of many women in their family and marriage relationships (Anthias 2002). Equally it is difficult to ignore the relations of power and the gendered cultural norms and values that may underpin the reasons for why the husband is so unwilling to formalize the marriage.

Locating the 'Self' in the *Nikah* Process

Muslim marriage, as with all sites of cultural and religious practice is mediated by complex relations of power. This space is experienced differentially by its participants and its boundaries shift and adapt over time. In this section the personal experiences of *nikah* are analysed with the women in this study. Of particular interest is the ways in which the women challenged, resisted, accepted, redefined or displaced the 'boundaries' of the *nikah* process and the meanings and negotiations they attached to it. For example, how did they perceive the religious, symbolic and functional aspects of such a process? What procedures did they rely upon and what were the outcomes of their participation?

Of the sample, 22 women described in personal terms the 'importance' they attached to the *nikah*. Being married 'under the eyes of God' was a commonly used phrase and the experience of Muslim marriage represented not only an important symbolic marker as part of their personal religious identity but the practice legitimized their marriage in the form of a public ceremony which allowed them to publicly display their membership to the Muslim '*Umma*' (Muslim community):

> I've never questioned it, its all part of being a Muslim. If you're a Muslim you would have one... it doesn't even have to be that you're really religious. Getting married in God's eyes is more important than getting married for English law (Raheela, London).
>
> The registry marriage was a formality; it was the *nikah* that was important. It's the '*nikah*' that's binding in the Islamic setting and its at that point whether you have the registry marriage or not that you're considered to be married by people in the family, the community you know people who know you, know your family, we're all Muslims and we know what's important to us (Sameena, Birmingham).

The data reveals that for many interviewees participating in the *nikah* ceremony forms an integral part of their future lives as married Muslim women, a form of belonging to the Muslim *umma* and an integral part of their Muslim identities. For others the ceremony itself fulfilled a functional role and was viewed simply as one part of the marriage process.

The *nikah* ceremony as been described as "One matrimonial party expresses '*ijab*' willing consent to enter into marriage and the other party expresses '*qubul*' acceptance of the responsibility in the assembly of marriage ceremony. The contract is written and signed by the bride and groom and their two respective witnesses. This written marriage ('*Aqd-Nikah*) is then announced publicly" (Hussanii 2010: 13). The assembly of *nikah* is addressed with a marriage sermon (*khutba-tun-nikah*) by the Muslim officiating the marriage. In marriage societies, customarily, a state appointed Muslim judge (*Qadi*) officiates the *nikah* ceremony and keeps the record of the marriage contract. However any 'trustworthy practicing Muslim' can conduct the *nikah* ceremony, as Islam does not advocate priesthood.

The documents of marriage contract/certificate are filed with the mosque (*masjid*) and a copy given to the parties. The sermon invites the bride and the groom, as well as the participating guests in the assembly to a life of piety, mutual love, kindness, and social responsibility. Marriage (*nikah*) is considered as an act of worship (*ibadah*). It is virtuous to conduct it in a Mosque keeping the ceremony simple. The marriage ceremony is a social as well as a religious activity. There are 3 primary requirements: (1) mutual agreement

(*Ijab-O-Qubul*) by the bride and groom; (2) Two adult and sane witnesses and (3) *Mahr* (marriage-gift) to be paid by the groom to the bride either immediately (*muajjal*) or deferred (*muakhkhar*), or a combination of both

The process of the *nikah* therefore embodies a wide range of experiences for Pakistani Muslim women that include social strategies, practical compromises and for some dealing with issues of coercion and parental pressure to marry. Most interestingly this dynamic lived experience of the *nikah* process also brings to the fore issues of consent in Muslim marriage. The experience of religious marriage in real-life situations leads to interesting data on how the women understood the meaning and limits of consent means in Muslim marriage.

This idea of consent as one of empowerment was discussed amongst the women with terms such as "being empowered" "permitted" and "my rights" being frequently used. The idea that Islam promotes equality between the sexes emerged significantly as some women spoke with enthusiasm of Islam as spiritual journey, drawing upon Islamic thought to better understand their duties, rights and autonomy as Muslim wives. No discernable differences emerged between those women of a Punjabi or Azad Kashmiri background, and the discussions primarily focused on the need to develop a fuller understanding of marriage in Islam actually means.

> When my parents starting talking about getting married I started reading around what marriage in Islam actually means. What I read made sense to me. As a Muslim woman I have the choice to marry whoever I want as long as he's a Muslim. My parents wanted me to have an arranged marriage because that's what Pakistanis do and I did understand that was important to them. I'm not saying that culture isn't important to me, cause I love speaking Punjabi and everything else but I wanted to choose who I could marry and Islam gave me that (Sadia, Birmingham).
>
> I've read quite a bit around Islam and Muslim women and rights in marriage and all that…I understand its very important to make sure a woman gives her consent. But I think most parents still want to give their consent to who you marry, even if they're a Muslim, they still think that's the most important thing. So I had to sit my parents down and talk to them, you know, explain that it's my consent that matters! (Shabana, London).

An understanding of the rights of Muslim women in marriage enabled many of the women to interrogate and challenge the power relations in the family on matters of choice of marriage partner and issues of consent. Using Islamic rules as a base upon which to interrogate cultural practices that may have denied them the space to voice their opposition to the marriage these women were able, therefore to negotiate and in some cases to see through solution.

In this study the *nikah* ceremony was performed in the family home, the wedding premises (often described as the 'wedding hall') and the local mosque. It is useful to note that Islamic literature imposes little restrictions on where the marriage can take place. Interestingly no marriages performed in a licensed mosque according to the Places of Worship Registration Act (1855) and only one interviewee had checked prior to the religious marriage taking place as to whether the mosque had been registered as a licensed building. Unable to clarify this issue she had nevertheless gone ahead with the *nikah,* on the understanding that her religious marriage was due to be registered under civil law, shortly afterwards.

Eade (1996) points out that the location for the *nikah* ceremony largely depends upon family expectations and cultural traditions and is created "purely by ritual and sanctioned practice and is not dependent upon the creation of any juridically claimed territory or formally consecrated space, or indeed, the production of architecturally specific place" (Eade 1996: 231). This was confirmed by findings in this study.

> My mum made it pretty clear that the *nikah* was going to happen in our house. Apparently that's the way it's always been done in our family and yes I was ok with that. She discussed it with me and I was ok with it (Nighat, London).
>
> We had the *nikah* first. My parents did that. We had it in the wedding hall and the Imam came from his aunt. I think traditionally the Imam who conducts the ceremony is meant to come from the groom's side they're meant to provide you with the Imam. So the Imam came from the aunt and he was known to the family for about 30- 40 years. He had done their aunts marriage and all her brothers and sisters marriage in Pakistan (Fauzia, London).

In terms of the length of the ceremony and the participation of the women it was described as quick which involved their minimal participation.

> It was really quick, over in like 2 minutes. He asked me (the Imam) whether I gave my consent and I said yes, I mean he only asked me once, which I don't think is right. Then he said something in Arabic

> and that was it really. All over in 2 minutes in my parent's front room (Sameena, Birmingham)
>
> I don't remember much about it cause it happened so quickly but then I think its meant to be like that in Islam, you know marriage is just a contract, somebody asks you, you say yes and then that's it (Zareena Bradford).

Interestingly, the presence of witnesses at the *nikah* ceremony generated interesting discussion. Under Hanafi law, a contract can only be fulfilled in the presence of witnesses, which can be either two males or one male and two females (see Nasir 1990). The presence of witnesses also acts as a symbolic public representation that the marriage is taking place. As Mirza, points out "the presence of the witnesses is essential for the valid solemnization of a marriage as their attendance ensures publicity, this being the decisive symbol that demarcates the line between lawful wedlock and fornication or *zina*" (Mirza 2000: 14).

In this study, the witnesses to the *nikah* ceremony comprised primarily of male members of the family, including fathers, uncles and brothers. By contrast, female witnesses were involved in only two cases and in each case involved family friends. The *nikah* ceremony acquired specific meanings and significance for the women as described below.

> There's 2 witnesses from his side, 1 witness from my side. My witness was my uncle and his witnesses were his 2 uncles. My part of it was that before they come and do the *nikah* bit in the mosque they come and ask me whether I agree to the marriage. I was at home and they came over, they asked me, well they basically said you are getting married to such and such person and do you agree to it and you have to say *geehaa* (yes) three times and that was that, done. Then they go to him I'm not sure what happens in the mosque but basically they ask him the same question. I think they do a lot of prayers (Salma, London).
>
> Women aren't allowed in the mosque so it was upstairs in my mum's house and it was just us ladies in the room. Then they went to the mosque where he was and they said to the *maulvi* the girl has said yes three times and she signed this paper and that was the marriage certificate. Then he went through more or less the procedure but its just a bit longer because what they do before is give a bit of a lecture before the *nikah* itself you know they just tell him about how they should look after a wife etc. after they ask him what they asked me and I think the men have to say yes twice, I think so I'm not quite sure and then basi-

> cally then everyone congratulated him and then he came to the hall where the reception took place. And that is it…basically everyone eats (Shabana, London).
>
> Initially the Imam didn't ask me 3 times so my mum had to ask him to do what he hadn't. He asked me just once and my mum had to go and get him to do it properly and then he came and asked me 3 times (Fauzia, London).

On the one hand, these experiences illustrate some of the ambivalences the women experienced with the *nikah* as the process is neither straightforward nor uncontested. In fact the site of the *nikah* marks both the physical presence of the different parties involved including the marriage partners, male witnesses, the Imam, parents and wider family members. For some women, therefore this process was difficult, protracted and complex. Some women complained that they had been sidelined in the process as a whole, as their participation was minimal in what was in actual fact supposed to be a shared public space. For others, both the meaning of *nikah* and their presence as participants was symbolic, on a deeply personal level and part of their understanding of what it means to be a Muslim woman. Yet all the women in this study interacted, engaged and closely identified with the *nikah* ceremony. Significantly for those women who had been forced into marriage the *nikah* ceremony certainly did not mark the end of their attempt to challenge the validity of the marriage but for these women it was also closely associated as a marker of discipline and control and understandably these women disengaged with the process. However for many women the *nikah* represented the most distinctive part of the Muslim marriage process which fulfilled specific duties and provided social and moral legitimacy of their marriages within the Muslim community and under the 'eyes of God'..

> It sort of marked a different status in the eyes of people. It was from then on that I had the status of coming into the family. I mean lots of doors opened then, I mean socially and community wise that I wouldn't have had otherwise (Anisa, Bradford).

The discursive framework of the *nikah*, therefore is undoubtedly based upon specific gender relations that underpin the marriage process. The formal aspect of this process, the *nikah* contract creates an interesting space for many women who are able to challenge the unequal cultural norms embedded in marriage practices for women belonging to Pakistani Muslim communities.

Mahr in the Nikah Contract

A final element of the *nikah* contract involves the *Mahr* or dower, described as "a sum of money or other property which the wife is entitled to receive from the husband in consideration of the marriage" (Mulla 1995 at 387 quoted in Ali 2001, p.158). Hussaini (2010) describes *Mahr* as "a token commitment of the husbands responsibility and may be paid in cash, property or movable objects to the bride herself. The amount of *Mahr* is not legally specified, however moderation according to existing social norm is recommended. The *Mahr* may be paid immediately to the bride at the time of marriage, or deferred to a later date, or a combination of both. The deferred *Mahr,* however, falls due in case of death or divorce". The Qu'ranic verse 4: 4 states "And give the women (on marriage) their *Mahr* as a (*nikha*) free gift". Yet precisely what constitutes as the *Mahr* is open to some dispute in Islamic literature and as Ali points out, that rather than being perceived as a form of consideration in the contract it is largely understood as a debt to be repaid to the wife by the husband in event of death (Ali 2001: 158). Pearl and Menski (1998: 80) point out that the wife may lose the whole *Mahr* in two situations: First, if the marriage is dissolved by the husband before consummation, in various situations akin to annulment (see also Nasir (Nasir 1990: 54) and secondly, if the marriage is dissolved by an action of the wife before consummation, the most common example being probably her exercise of the 'option of puberty', she is not entitled to any dower (see Nasir 1990: 54-55). In this way the *Mahr* is an effect of the marriage contract and not an exchange for the marriage.

The amount of *Mahr* is expressly stipulated in the *nikah* contract[6] and therefore is a mandatory requirement that can either be paid immediately or be partly deferred. As Khadija Ali explains, "If there is a written record of the marriage contract then details of the *Mahr* would normally be included within it as it is an essential element of the marriage contract; although an Islamic marriage is still valid without a *Mahr* being declared, when the wife is then entitled to call for a *Mahr*, the value of which is to be determined by an Islamic judge based upon certain conditions. If a dispute then arises as to the *Mahr* it may be possible to apply contractual principles under English law to enforce the agreement in the civil courts"[7] (Ali, Khadija 2010: 3). The con-

6. According to Islamic legal principles this payment can be paid promptly at the point of marriage or deferred and to be paid after the breakdown of marriage. See Engineer 1992.
7. See Shanaz v Rizwan (1964) 2 All ER 993

tractual use of *Mahr* in Muslim marriages among Muslims living in Europe has led to questions of "whether it is reconcilable with the gender equality principle" (Rutten: 46).[8] In her work Fournier (Fournier 2010) discusses how Muslim marriage and *Mahr* travels from Islamic legal orders to European legal orders and describes these 'legal transplants' as complex, contradictory and at times in flux. Subsequently as Fredriksen points out, the process of translation reveals that "*Mahr* can be treated in different ways: *Mahr* as an integral and essential part of the Islamic marriage contract; *Mahr* as a substitute for post divorce maintenance; *Mahr* as the division of the surplus of marital profits, as *Mahr al-mithl* and *Mahr* as a gift" (Fredriksen 2010: 93).

There is a notable absence of cases regarding *Mahr* in English case law. In Shahnaz v Rizwan [1964] 3 WLR 1506 the parties had contracted their marriage in India with a clause that stipulated deferred *Mahr* in the contract. In 1959 the husband instigated divorce proceedings against his wife and she in turn brought an action in English law in the hope of recovering £1,400, equivalent to the deferred *Mahr*. The case revolved around the central issue on whether or not the claim for *Mahr* could be heard within the jurisdiction of English law? The matter therefore rested on whether there was a contractual issue to consider.

The husband argued that due to the nature of marriage being polygamous or potentially polygamous English courts had no jurisdiction to consider the claim. Winns J concluded it was a contractual rather than a matrimonial issue "while it can in the nature of things only arise in connection with a marriage by Mohammedan law (which is ex hypothesi polygamous), it is not a matrimonial right. It is not a right from the marriage but it is a right in persona, enforceable by the wife or widow against the husband or his heirs". The force of this case was largely removed by the Matrimonial Causes Act 1973, which essentially gives the English court a broad discretion in financial provision. This case illustrates that the force of contract law can be used in cases of recognizing *Mahr* in Muslim marriage contracts. In this case the Muslim marriage itself is deemed a consideration of the contract—in essence Muslim marriage was viewed as a prenuptial agreement.

The second case Qureshi v Qureshi (1972) involved the case of a couple, the wife, an Indian citizen and the husband a Pakistani citizen. They married in Britain at the Kensington Register Office in 1966. Upon breakdown of marriage a few months later that was followed by a religious divorce issued by the husband the principal issue of this case surrounded the argument made

8. *Mahr* and Gender Equality in Private International Law

by the wife that the marriage subsists and the husband continues maintenance. If however the marriage has dissolved then she wished to claim the dower as stipulated in the religious marriage contract plus some maintenance. The question before the courts therefore was where the couple was domiciled to consider the validity of the marriage. The courts concluded that the marriage was valid.

On the question of *Mahr* Rutten sums up the key difference between the two cases as she explains, "A significant difference between the Shahnaz and the Qureshi judgments is that, in Shanaz, the wife was excluded from seeking ancillary relief on the basis that the marriage was considered potentially polygamous, while in the case of Qureshi the marriage was considered monogamous so the wife could seek ancillary relief. As the husband was planning to return to Pakistan, the only realistic way for the wife to get any money after the divorce, as the court saw it, was through *Mahr*, as this would be easier to enforce by English courts than any ancillary relief."

In a more recent case Uddin v Choudhury & Ors (2009) the issue of *nikah* as a valid marriage, the process of religious divorce and the use of an expert from a British Shariah Council were raised. The case centered on the breakdown of marriage that had been agreed by both families. A religious ceremony had taken place but the marriage had not been registered according to civil law. The dispute centered on the amount of *mehr* (*Mahr*) the bride retained due to the breakdown of marriage. The issue of *nikah* as a valid marriage, the process of religious divorce and the use of an expert from a British Shariah Council were raised. The case centered on the breakdown of marriage that had been agreed by both families. A religious ceremony had taken place but the marriage had not been registered according to civil law. The dispute centered on the amount of *mehr* (*Mahr*) the bride retained due to the breakdown of marriage. The ruling stipulated that the gifts made were not returnable even if the marriage had failed as they were not conditional upon the marriage and were not part of the dowry or *Mahr* but simply gifts.

The contractual nature of Muslim marriage has also led to interesting discussion on the extent to which the nikah allows women "some legal autonomy in order to bargain over her own destiny" (Haeri 1990: 57). Muslim feminist literature points to the underlying assumptions of ownership and purchase within the contract and its legitimacy of a patriarchal understanding of the male-female relationship. For Muslim feminist scholars concerns are raised over how female bodies become obvious sites for sacrifice, discipline and control (see El-Nimr 1996, Abu-Odeh 1996). Coulson describes that the *nikah* contract constitutes a sale due to the 'transfer of an absolute propriety" (Coulson 1964: 111). This is accepted by Haeri (1990) who argues that the *nikah* embodies an inherent determinism of male-female relations that act as a justification for the existing sexual inequalities and explains, "Because marriage is a contract from an Islamic point of view, the phenomenon of intercourse, *vatye*, is inevitably intertwined with monetary exchanges. The underlying assumption here is two-fold. First, as 'purchasers' in a contract of marriage, men are 'in charge' of their wives because they pay for them and, naturally they ought to be able to control their wives' activities. Secondly, women are required to submit that for which they have been paid, or promised to be paid. It follows therefore that women ought to be obedient to their husbands" (Hareri 1990: 58). The ideological representation of women as wives, daughters and mothers remain central to the role of *Mahr* in the *nikah* contract.

In this study, three key issues emerge, firstly the confusion the women expressed between the *Mahr* and dowry, secondly the failure by the women to negotiate a 'reasonable' amount of *Mahr* as part of the *nikah* contract and, finally the limited use of the *nikah* contract to retrieve the *Mahr* upon breakdown of marriage and divorce. Only thirteen women upon completion of the *nikah* had obtained a copy of the *nikah* contract. The contract included personal details such as name, age, address, date of birth, the date and place of marriage and the signature of witnesses. However the women reported the contract stipulated only a nominal sum for the *Mahr,* ranging from between £100-£200. For most women, therefore the *nikah* contract was simply a part of the *nikah* ceremony rather than a contractual agreement stipulating the rights and responsibilities of both parties and if necessary to be invoked upon breakdown of marriage.

However for women whose marriages had not been formalized and registered according to civil law, the *nikah* contract represented an opportunity to claim back the *Mahr*. Therefore in cases where the religious marriage is not formally registered, the *nikah* contract is rooted in the idea of 'justice' where the women may actively engage in strategies to claim back the *Mahr*. The significance of the *nikah* contract from a general document to one used to enforce the rights of Muslim women can therefore be dependent upon registration of marriage. But the *nikah* contract can serve as a useful mechanism, upon which the marriage breakdown and the divorce can for some be managed, negotiated and possibly settled.

In this study the women described the *Mahr* as *Mahr*, '*haq mehr*', '*jahez*', 'dower' and 'dowry' and to some extent this conflation of terms complicates the ways in which the *Mahr* is understood as part of the *nikah* contract. The extracts below highlight some of the narrative found in these discussions.

Haq mehr is the property or the sum of money or whatever you want it to be which the woman can ask for from her husband at any time during the marriage but at the divorce it has to be passed over. I know from other peoples wedding that you know things can stop there for hours and hours you know because there's a problem with the '*haq mehr*', you know like the guys side is saying you know we thought we'd get something else, and the girl's side think something else has been arranged. Or sometimes it's so enormous the sum the girl couldn't get out of the marriage because the guy's side wouldn't be able to pay that. There's a lot of politics around the amount that you put forward. But Islamic law says it should be something like for 3 months or something like that (Shabana, London).

The whole idea of the *mehr* is that you show the value of that particular individual. It has to be a reasonable amount of money as well that's the other thing that I was aware of as well, it can't just be something that's a throwaway sum of money that's not going to cause any hardship to the man if there is a divorce. It's got to be something that means something to him not that's something that's just done for the sake of doing it. For me it's a form of protection and I was quite definite on that (Fauzia, London).

The Imam was in the room with my father and some men and he talked to my father about whether he was happy giving me away and what the *haq mehr* should be. You know we hadn't even discussed it before. I didn't know what it meant and I don't know what they decided (Rubina, Birmingham).

The problem that arose at the time of the *nikah* like when we were talking about what was going to happen and all the procedures. But they hadn't mentioned anything about the *mehr* or clothes, you know exchanging of gifts and we were beginning to think this was a bit strange. My mum was getting a little worried because it had come up to 2 weeks before the wedding and still nothing had been mentioned. In our family it's important for the girl to be given clothes before she gets married. My mother told my future mother in law and the response was well as far as the *mehr* is concerned we're going to set it at the same amount as we set our other son's and I can't allow her to have a higher *mehr* than my other daughter in law. As far as I'm concerned they're equal (Sameena, London).

Nothing, I have nothing to show that's it's an Islamic marriage. I don't even have a certificate. I think he did make a certificate and he said come next week but I never went back. At that point I didn't think

> it was important so I don't know what the dower was for my marriage but I think they gave us some clothes (Nasima, London).

This confusion between *Mahr* and dowry does not itself challenge the value the women placed upon the *nikah* contract and the centrality of the *Mahr* to the *nikah* contract. Instead what becomes evident is the complex interwoven religious marriage process with cultural norms and practice all interacting within a cultural setting that then shapes the temporal and spatial boundaries of the *nikah* ceremony itself (Bhabba 1994). In this way some women sought to distinguish the religious and cultural practices that underpin the *nikah* ceremony. Yet many women were also placed at the margins of the decision-making and negotiation processes that underpinned the terms upon which the *Mahr* was included as part of the *nikah* contract. Interestingly these women also called into question their personal lack of knowledge and ignorance of Islamic principles relating to marriage.

> For me to get the *nikah* right was really important. But I didn't know I was really stupid at the time I really didn't know everything. I knew some of what I was entitled to but I really didn't know the level of my rights. For instance I didn't know I could stipulate terms of divorce at the time of the *nikah*. I didn't know I could ask for the rights to divorce at that time or I didn't know I could stipulate various other things at the time of the contract. I just went as far as saying that look if you're going to give a *mehr* it has to be a reasonable amount and it has to be an agreement between me and him not your parents or not your aunts or anyone else (Fauzia, London).
>
> I did not know much about it actually I think I learnt more about the *nikah* after I got divorced. Like for example that in Islam you can have a pre-nuptial arrangements, you don't have to change your name when you get married in fact its better to keep your own name, you don't have to agree to agree to live with the guy's parents. Its up to him to look after his family but he's got no right to impose it on you, things like that. So I found out things like that and I was surprised really. I could have said that before I married him but I didn't because I don't think it's the right way of starting a relationship by splitting him from his family if he doesn't want to do that I didn't want to come between them but I didn't make that as a condition. I now know a lot of girls do that these days (Salma, London).
>
> When the *Imam* was conducting the ceremony. Although he had written the correct amount of the *mehr* on the certificate that he had, af-

> ter I said yes 3 times and I was seated officially next to my husband and when they got me to sign the thing I noticed on the certificate next to the *mehr* amount they had written deferred and I didn't know what that meant. And I saw it and I thought well I didn't agree to this but I there was about 100 people there and I couldn't say anything. I just noted it and I thought well it shouldn't really mean anything so I just signed my name to it but no-one had consulted me as to whether this *mehr* was deferred or not because the understanding behind the *haq mehr* is that its supposed to be paid to the wife preferably before the marriage is consummated. There wasn't any mention of it being paid. I mean it doesn't have to be paid but at least I could have been spoken to about why a deferred term was included in the contact (Naheed, London).

What becomes clear is that for this group of women the gendered nature of Muslim marriage can sideline the position and participation of Muslim women meaning that some are simply unable to engage with this process and actively negotiate the terms of the *nikah* contract. This is not, however, to lose sight of the fact that the women stressed the importance of the *nikah* ceremony and the *nikah* contract as a significant part of the marriage process and as part of their Muslim identity.

Reforming Religious Marriage for Muslims in Britain

Such concern over the non formalization of religious marriage and the limited use of the *nikah* contract has led to some attempts by religious scholars in Britain to strengthen the *nikah* contract by producing a standard *nikah* contract for all Muslims in Britain. This document was launched in August 2008 by the Muslim Institute to address issues of gender inequalities upon breakdown of marriage.

Marital agreements (including pre-nuptial, post-nuptial and separation agreements) are not binding in England and Wales – even those entered into in jurisdictions where such agreements are fully binding. These issues have been addressed in recent cases, notably *MacLeod v MacLeod* [2008] UKPC 64 and *NG v KR (Pre-Nuptial Contract)* [2008] EWHC 1532 (Fam) (application to appeal allowed: *Radmacher v Granatino* [2008] EWCA Civ 1304) Marital agreements are however being given increasing weight in ancillary relief proceedings (see for example *K v K (Ancillary Relief: Prenuptial Agreement)* [2003] 1 FLR 120). Many have called for a review of this area of law, notably Sir Mark Potter P. in *Charman* v *Charman* [2007] EWCA Civ 503 at [124]-[126].[9] The Law Commission for England and Wales has now included Marital Property Agreements in its 10th Programme of Law Reform; the Commission's project will commence in September 2009 and a report and draft Bill are expected in September 2012[10]. In many jurisdictions, marital agreements can be binding and this has led to discussions on how such issues can be addressed by the English legal system.

The legal developments have raised the question of the extent to which *nikah* contracts mirror the increasing use of pre-marital contracts in English law. As previously discussed marriage in Islamic law is underpinned by a strong contractual relationship and one key element of this contract is an "agreement between future spouses on the financial consequences of the dissolution of the marriage" (Franck 2009: 236). So what is the relationship between prenuptial agreements in England and the religious marriage contracts such as the *nikah* contract? As Franck explains further, "The debate on the enforceability of premarital contracts is embedded in a long-standing dispute on the nature of marriage. Should marriage be regarded as a contract, and therefore the mere result of a bargain by autonomous self-interested parties?" (Franck 2009: 237).

In Britain mosques are often not registered as religious buildings in order to perform marriages that conform to English law and hence religious marriages are not formalised according to civil law procedure. This new marriage contract, drafted by the Muslim Institute was launched to provide women with written proof of their marriage under Islamic law[11] and the reforms of the contract include:

- removing the requirement for a 'marriage guardian' (*wali*) for the bride, who, as an adult, can make up her own mind about whom to marry.
- enabling the wife to initiate divorce and retain all her financial rights agreed in the marriage contract.
- forbidding polygamy whether formally or informally in the UK or abroad
- encouraging mosques to register to perform marriages

9. See Resolution in "A more certain future" www.resolution.org.uk/site_content_files/files/a_more_certain_future___resolution.pdf
10. (www.lawcom.gov.uk/marital_property.htm).
11. The contract is the work of Dr Ghayasuddin Siddiqui, Founder Director of the south London-based Muslim Institute The UK's model contract has been downloaded some 17,000 times since its launch two years ago – or nearly 50 copies a day

Dr Siddiqui claims that the contract will bring Muslim marriages in Britain into line with positive developments in Muslim family law 'across the Muslim world.' Activist and researcher Cassandra Balchin points to the usefulness of such contracts in promoting the rights of Muslim women based on the principles of equality, justice and fairness. She explains,"there have recently been major initiatives around model marriage contracts with a firm commitment to advancing equality within the family. Despite the great diversity of laws and practices across the Muslim world, the conditions women insert into the contract when they get the chance are remarkably similar. They want greater financial autonomy and security, a fairer division of property reflecting their contribution to the family's finances, freedom of mobility and equality in decision-making, a monogamous relationship, and, should mutual understanding break down, then equal access to divorce. In other words, the presumed standard model of Muslim marriage, which regards the male as head of household, just isn't working in women's eyes. This model is an edifice built entirely on the concept of *qiwamah* (translated variously as superiority, guardianship, being in charge of, responsibility) which is derived from one of the most contested Qur'anic verses regarding gender relations (*Surah al-Nisa*: 34)" (Guardian On-line March 2010). Such contracts can therefore be viewed as part of the process in reforming Muslim marriage practices. However critics point to the creation of parallel legal systems. Neil Addison[12] argues that it continues "the unfortunate trend of separating Muslims from the general community in Britain. The Contract will still permit Imams to perform Muslim Marriage ceremonies when the couple are not married in accordance with British Law; indeed the existence of such a 'model' contract endorsed, as this is, by lawyers and MPs gives the seal of approval for the continuation of marriage ceremonies which have no legal legitimacy under British law. It is in fact an encouragement to illegality."

The use of religious marriage contracts also raises questions on the extent to which common contract norms are based on gendered assumptions. Traditional feminist scholarship on the position of women in the law of contracts points to the voices of women being sidelined and marginalized and the law of contract being inherently marginalized and phallocentric (Pateman 1988). However, as Linda Mulcahy points out, more recently, "a considerable amount of work has focused on contract as an alternative to marriage and the use of contract in intimate relationships more generally. It has been argued, for instance, that contract has the potential to foster a non-exploitative con-

12. Discrimination lawyer author of Religious Discrimination and Hatred Law

ception of 'private' relationships, although feminists have also argued that using contracts in this sphere could merely entrench existing bargaining inequalities" (Mulcahy 2005: 5) Thus for feminist scholars the key question is the extent to which contract law can be used to develop models of contract relationships based on pluralism and diversity. New ways of using and understanding contract law are based on "context sensitive model of contract relationships" (Mulcahy 2005: 19) which offer multiple perspectives and outcomes.

Conclusion

Marriage embodies a wide range of experiences for Pakistani Muslim women, based upon practical compromises to social strategies and for some, coercion and compulsion to marry. It is within this dynamic lived experience, closely related to their identities as British Pakistani Muslim women that we can explore what *Mahr* in Muslim marriage means to them and how it is interpreted.

In this study it became apparent that for various reasons most women had not attached much importance to the *Mahr*. However upon breakdown of marriage for some women this situation had radically changed. It prompted a number of the women to concentrate their efforts in retrieving the *Mahr* for two reasons. Firstly for women whose marriages had not been registered according to civil law, the importance of *Mahr* lay in the belief that they were entitled to some kind of financial redress upon breakdown of marriage. Secondly where the *nikah* contract had been a focal point of negotiations prior to marriage, the women concentrated their efforts on keeping any financial monies or goods received upon marriage while also seeking to obtain a Muslim divorce.

However given the fact that the terms dower and dowry were used interchangeably it often meant that such demands were reframed within the context of culture rather than the application of religious legal principles. To remedy this situation we now have the introduction of *a* new marriage contract agreed prior to the marriage and which clearly stipulates the terms of both marriage and divorce. In theory this development not only ensures women are given 'legal protection' but in doing so they gain greater control over matters concerning divorce and separation. As one interviewee explained,

> I wasn't aware that I could demand my rights when I got married. I didn't even know that if the marriage broke down and it wasn't my fault I could demand maintenance under Islamic law. I don't understand that has Muslim women we're not taught this, why not? We didn't register the marriage and when he walked away I was left with nothing (Salma, London).

Bibliography

Abu-Odeh, Lama, (1996) 'Crimes of Honour and the Construction of Gender in Arab. Society,'pp.141-194 in Mai Yamani (ed.), Feminism and Islam, London.

Afshar, Haleh, (2005) 'Behind the Veil' in Women and Islam: Critical Concepts in Sociology (ed) Haideh Moghissie. London: Routledge Muslim Women and Feminisms: Illustrations from Iran, *Social Compass* 54 (3)

Afshar, H., (1994) 'Muslim Women in West Yorkshire: Growing up with Real and Imaginary Values amidst Conflicting Views of Self and Society' in Afshar, H. and Maynard, M. *The Dynamics of 'Race' and 'Gender'*, Taylor and Francis, London.

Ali, Nasreen, Vrinder S Kalra and Salman Sayyid, (eds.) (2006) *A Postcolonial People: South Asians in Britain* , Hurst & Co.

Ali, N., (2006) Imperial Implosions: Postcoloniality and the Orbits of Migration, in (eds) Ali, Nasreen, Vrinder S Kalra and Salman Sayyid *A Postcolonial People: South Asians in Britain,* Hurst & Co

Anthias, F., (2002) 'Beyond Feminism and Multiculturalism: Locating difference and the politics of location', *Women's Studies International Forum*, 25: 3, 275-286.

Anwar, M., (1998) *Between Cultures: Community and Change in the lives of Young Asiana*, Routledge.

Badawi, Z., (1995) 'Muslim Justice in a Secular State', in M. King (ed.), *God's Law versus State Law*, London, Grey Seal.

Ballard, R., (2008) 'Inside and Outside: Contrasting Perspectives on the Dynamics of Kinship and Marriage in Contemporary South Asian Transnational Networks', in R Grillo (ed) *The Family in Question: Immigrants and Minorities in Multicultural Europe,* Amsterdam: University of Amsterdam Press.

Ballard, R., (1994) 'The Emergence of Desh Pardesh', in Ballard, R. et al (ed) *Desh Pardesh: The South Asian Presence in Britain*, London, C.Hurst & Co.Ltd.

Bano, Samia, (2008) Muslim Family Justice and Human Rights: The Experience of British Muslim Women, JCL 2: 2, 1-29

Bano, Samia, (2008) "In Pursuit of Religious and Legal Diversity: A Response to the Archbishop of Canterbury and the 'Sharia debate' in Britain", *Ecclesiastical Law Journal*, Vol 10, No 2

Bhabba, H., (1994) *The Location of Culture*, Routledge

Beck, U and E Beck-Gernsheim, (2001) *Individualization,* London: Sage.

Bhimji, Fazila, (2009) 'Identities and agencies in religious spheres', *Gender, Place and Culture*, vol 16, Issue 4, Aug 2009, p365-380

Bhopal, Kalwant, (1999) South Asian women and arranged marriages in East London. In *Ethnicity, gender, and social change,* ed. Rohit Baror, Harriet Bradley and Steve Fenton, 117-134. Basingstoke: Macmillan.

Bredal, Anja, (2005) Arranged marriages as a multicultural battle field. In *Youth, otherness, and the plural city: Modes of belonging and social life,* ed. Mette Andersson, Yngve Lithman & Ove Sernhede. Gothenburg: Daidalos.

Bunt, G., (1998) 'Decision-Making concerns in British Islamic Environments', in *Islam and Christian-Muslim Relations*, 19: 1, 103-113.

Burlet, S and Reid, H., (1998) 'A Gendered Uprising: Political Representation and Minority Ethnic Communities', *Ethnic and Racial Studies* 21, pp 271-287.

Castells, M., (1997) *The Rise of the Network Society*, Oxford: Basil Blackwell.

Chiba, M., (1986) *Asian Indigenous Law and its Interaction with Received Law*, (Kegan Paul International, London and New York).

Coulson, Noel J., (1964) *A History of Islamic Law*, (1964 Edinburgh, U.P., Edinburg; Repr 1978).

Dwyer, C., (2000) Negotiating Diasporic Identities: Young British South Asian Muslim Women', *Women Studies International Forum* 23, pp 475-486.

Eade, J., (1996) 'Nationalism, Community and the Islamization of Space in London', in Metcalf, D.B. (ed), *Making Muslim Space in North America and Europe*, Berkeley, University of California Press.

Eekelaar, J., (2002) *Family Law and Personal Life* (Oxford: Oxford University Press, 2002), pp 9-17, 23-26.

Eekelaar, J. and M. Maclean, (2004) 'Marriage and the Moral Bases of Personal Relationships', *Journal of Law and Society* 31(4) 510-38.

El Nimr, R., (1996) Women in Islamic Law, in Feminism and Islam edited by M. Yamani (1996) in Mai Yamani (ed.), Feminism and Islam, London pp 87-102.

Fournier, Pascale, (2010) "Flirting with God in western secular courts: *Mahr* in the west", *International Journal of Law, Policy and the Family*, 24 (1), pp.67-94.

Franck, Jens-Uwe, (2009) "So hedge therefore, who join forever: understanding the interrelation of no-fault divorce and premarital contracts", *International Journal of Law, Policy and the Family*, pp 235-264.

Haeri, S., (1990) Law of Desire: Temporary Marriage in Islam, London I.B Tauris.

Hussaini, M.M., (2010) An-Nikah, The Marriage. A copy of this article can be obtained at www.sailahmuslim.com

Khadija Ali, (2010) Islam and English Law: Marriage, Divorce & Children, (unpublished paper).

Menski, W., (1993) 'Asians in Britain and the question of adaptation to a new legal order: Asian laws in Britain?', in Israel, Milton, Wagle, N. (ed*) Ethnicity, identity, migration: The South Asian context*, University of Toronto Press.

Mirza, Q., (2000) 'Islam, Hybridity and the Laws of Marriage', *Australian Feminist Law Journal*, 14 1-22.

Mulcahy, L., (2005) The Limitations of Law and Altruism – Feminist Perspectives on Contract Law pp1-19 in (eds) L. Mulcahy and S. Wheeler, *Feminist Perspectives on Contract Law*, Glasshouse Press.

Modood, T., (2000) 'The Place of Muslims in British Secular Multiculturalism' in: Alsayyad, N. Castells, M. and Michalak, L. (eds.) *Islam and the changing identity of Europe*, University Press of America, Lexington Books.

Nasir, JJ., (1990) *The Islamic Law of Personal Status*, Graham and Trotman.

Neil, Addison, (2010) Sharia is not the problem here, The Guardian, 8 July 2010 http://www.guardian.co.uk/religion-sharia-marriage-registration-islam

Neil, Addison, N., (2007) Religious Discrimination and Hatred Law, Routledge Cavendish.

Pateman, C., (1988) The Sexual Contract, Oxford: Polity.

Pearl D and Menski, W., (1998) *Muslim Family Law* Sweet & Maxwell.

Poulter, Sebastian M., (1992) 'The Limits of Legal, Culture and Religious Pluralism', in *Discrimination: The Limits of Law*, Hepple, Bob and Erika M.Szyszczak eds, Mansell, London

Poulter, Sebastian M., (1992b) The Muslim Community and English Law', *Islam and Christian-Muslim Relations* 259-273.

Poulter, Sebastian M., (1998) *Ethnicity, Law and Human Rights*, Clarendon Press, Oxford.

Rohe, Mathias, (2006) 'The migration and settlement of Muslims: The challenges for European legal systems'. In: Prakash Shah and Werner F. Menski (eds.) [2006]: *Migration, diasporas and legal systems in Europe*. London: Routledge-Cavendish, pp. 57-72.

Shaw, A., (1994) The Pakistani Community in Oxford, Ballard, R., in Ballard, R. et al (ed) *Desh Pardesh: The South Asian Presence in Britain*, London, C.Hurst & Co.Ltd.

Werbner, P., (2002) 'The place which is diaspora: citizenship, religion and gender in the making of chaordic transnationalism', *Journal of Ethnic and Migration Studies*, 28: 1, 119-133.

Wilson, Amrit, (2006) *Dreams, questions, struggles: South Asian women in Britain*. London: Pluto Press.

Yilmaz, I., (2002) 'Challenge of post-modern legality and Muslim legal pluralism in England', *Journal of Ethnic and Migration Studies*, 28: 2, 343-354.

Index

Q

R

S